DATE DUE

GAYLORD   PRINTED IN U.S.A.

CLASSIC CONNECTIONS

❖❖❖ ❖❖❖ ❖❖❖

Turning Teens on to Great Literature

Holly Koelling

Libraries Unlimited Professional Guides for Young Adult Librarians Series
C. Allen Nichols and Mary Anne Nichols

A Member of the Greenwood Publishing Group

Westport, Connecticut · London

Library of Congress Cataloging-in-Publication Data

Koelling, Holly.
    Classic connections : turning teens on to great literature / Holly Koelling.
      p.   cm. — (Libraries Unlimited professional guides for young adult librarians,
    ISSN 1532–5571)
    Includes bibliographical references and index.
    ISBN 1–59158–072–2 (pbk. : alk. paper)
    1. Teenagers—Books and reading—United States.   2. Young adults—Books and
reading—United States.   3. Libraries and teenagers—United States.   4. School
libraries—Collection development—United States.   5. High school libraries—Collection
development—United States.   6. School libraries—Activity programs—United
States.   7. Best books.   I. Title.   II. Series.
    Z1037.A1K64   2004
    027.62'6—dc22   2004048644

British Library Cataloguing in Publication Data is available.

Library of Congress Catalog Card Number: 2004048644
ISBN: 1–59158–072–2
ISSN: 1532–5571

First published in 2004

Libraries Unlimited, 88 Post Road West, Westport, CT 06881
A Member of the Greenwood Publishing Group, Inc.
www.lu.com

Printed in the United States of America

The paper used in this book complies with the
Permanent Paper Standard issued by the National
Information Standards Organization (Z39.48–1984).

10 9 8 7 6 5 4 3 2 1

For Kim Lafferty

You have not been, nor shall you ever be, forgotten.

CONTENTS

SERIES FOREWORD

We firmly believe in young adult library services and advocate for teens whenever we can. We are proud of our association with Libraries Unlimited and Greenwood Publishing Group and grateful for their acknowledgment of the need for additional resources for teen-serving librarians. We intend for this series to fill those needs, providing useful and practical handbooks for library staff. Readers will find some theory and philosophical musings, but for the most part, this series will focus on real-life library issues with answers and suggestions for front-line librarians.

Our passion for young adult librarian services continues to reach new peaks. As we travel to present workshops on the various facets of working with teens in public libraries, we are encouraged by the desire of librarians everywhere to learn what they can do in their libraries to make teens welcome. This is a positive sign since too often libraries choose to ignore this underserved group of patrons. We hope you find this series to be a useful tool in fostering your own enthusiasm for teens.

Mary Anne Nichols
C. Allen Nichols
Series Editors

PREFACE

Stuff your eyes with wonder.

—Ray Bradbury, *Fahrenheit 451*

Ray Bradbury's well-known classic work, *Fahrenheit 451*, has long been a favorite of mine. It's among only a small handful of books that I've read, reread, and read again over the years. Through what seems at first reading like a sparse, simple story of a bleak futuristic society, Bradbury delves deep into the fundamental issue of freedom of thought and action from censorship and control.

The following passage is one that continues to move me at each and every reading. It also, I think, describes well the act of reading a great book—stuffing one's eyes with wonder. To set the scene, erstwhile firefighter Guy Montag has just narrowly escaped from the city and society in which books are burned, in which no independent thought, self-realization, or growth is possible. Both overwhelmed and elated by his harrowing journey, he finds himself in the company of a small collective of people who live outside the confines of the city. These people value the great minds of the ages above all else and have memorized their now forbidden written works so that they can never be lost.

Granger, a member of this collective, helps Montag in his journey toward personal freedom. As the city begins to collapse and burn in the distance, Granger shares with Montag advice his grandfather gave him:

> " 'Stuff your eyes with wonder,' he said, 'live as if you'd drop dead in ten seconds. See the world. It's more fantastic than any dream made or paid for in factories. Ask no guarantees, ask for no security, there never was such an animal. And if there were, it would be related to the great sloth which hangs upside down in a tree all day every day, sleeping its life away. To hell with that,' he said, 'shake the tree and knock the great sloth down on his ass.' "
> "Look!" cried Montag.
> And the war began and ended in that instant.
>   (Bradbury 1991, 157–158)

Classics are not just the musty, old, irrelevant tomes that teachers of yore, and some teachers today, have required teens to read in the classroom because they're "good" for them. Classics are the cream of the literary crop, works of magnificence and meaning, lovingly crafted by men and women who possessed the drive and talent to express with depth and beauty both the real and imagined stories of tantamount importance to us all, teens included. By connecting teens with the classics that will move them and provide them with food for thought and growth, you can help these young people on their journeys toward personal freedom, help them see the fantastic world out there for them, and encourage them to stuff their eyes with wonder.

WORKS CITED

Bradbury, Ray. 1991. *Fahrenheit 451*. New York: Ballantine Books. (Orig. pub. 1954.)

ACKNOWLEDGMENTS

First and foremost, acknowledgment goes to Christopher for creating with me an environment in which to think, learn, and go forth. Why try to deny it—I dig his stuff.

Next, my thanks go to Di Herald, who had a hunch about me despite a neck-and-neck run against another candidate, and gave me my first professional job as a Popular Materials/Young Adult Librarian at the Mesa County Public Library in Grand Junction, Colorado. I may never have professionally connected with teens without having witnessed Di's gentle, quirky, fearless ways with them, and her genuine appreciation for, admiration of, and attention to them as young human beings who might benefit from a love of books and libraries. The real affection they returned to her was enviable, and the books they read due to her influence, awe-inspiring. As if a job weren't enough, Di, her husband, Rick, and both their children, Nate and Chani, took me into their home, fed me, entertained me, and loved me in a time of great personal turbulence.

A great deal of appreciation goes to YALSA for being such an active and interesting division of the ALA, and for giving me the opportunity early in my career to serve on Best Books for Young Adults with professional greats like Karlan Sick, Sally Estes, and Mike Printz, and to interact with other dedicated professionals connected to the library world who serve youth, including author and publisher, Marc Aronson, and Kathleen Doherty of TOR Books. Thanks in specific to Hazel Rochman, whose *Tales of Love and Terror: Booktalking the Classics, Old and New* (1987) was the first of its kind and the inspiration for this updated book on the subject.

Thanks to Chapple Langemack for oh, so many things, but specifically here for believing I might possess enough knowledge and experience to contribute content to her *Booktalker's Bible*, which led to an offer to write this book. And thanks to Kirsten Edwards, that veritable walking encyclopedia and teen services librarian without equal, for brainstorming with me over Chapter 8.

And, without question, acknowledgment goes out to the many, many teens over the past ten years who have fascinated me, made me think, blown my mind, cracked me up, made me mad, broken my heart, given me hope, and generally transformed me into much more than I'd ever be without them. Right on.

INTRODUCTION

Wouldn't most teens rather read—if they read at all—a Sweet Valley University Super Thriller, *Fearless #8*, a Lurlene McDaniel tearjerker, the sixth *Tom Clancy's Net Force*, Christopher Pike's Last Vampire series, or whatever else is big at the time, than pick up a literary classic? For that matter, wouldn't most adults rather read a John Grisham, Sue Grafton, or Catherine Coulter than dig into Ralph Ellison's *Invisible Man* or Ayn Rand's *Atlas Shrugged*? Probably. At any age, would a classic take some effort, be a bit of a challenge, something of an investment in time and thought? Certainly. Is it worth the investment? Definitely!

Can teens be as fascinated, horrified, thrilled, shocked, *moved* by classics as they are by their popular reading choices? Can their tears be jerked? Yes, and at times infinitely more so, but they likely don't know it. Classics have played an essential role in the American secondary curriculum for generations. Any self-respecting teen is likely to distrust their value based on this fact alone! If having to study and take tests on classics in the classroom weren't enough to sour the stomach of even the most literature-friendly teen, the traditional manner in which those classics have been taught may be enough to do the trick.

Although there have been, and will continue to be, many fine educators who care about teens and about how they are introduced to the wonders of reading classic literature, there are as many or more who have simply assigned standard curricular classics to meet educational goals, have taught them chapter by verse, line by line, often to test teens on a right-or-wrong textbook interpretation. The classics selected to play this less than desirable role have often been the less than desirable classics, at least to a teenage person. When groans of disinterest and plaintive questions regarding relevance have arisen in the classroom, teens have been presented with the "they're good for you" defense. Death knell! Although the primary point of introduction between teens and classics, classroom assignments have not inspired life-long literary friendships.

More recently, an educational trend has emerged that asserts classics are inappropriate reading for teens, and many educators are not including them in the secondary curriculum at all. Discarding the value of classics for teen readers is as unfortunate as teaching them poorly. The exemplary works of times past and present, the defining works of the human condition—the classics—can be of great worth and enjoyment to teens, and as the classics are far more often introduced to youth by adults than discovered by them on their own, this educational moratorium is a real tragedy.

TEENS NEED YOU: BE THEIR LITERARY CONNECTION

What's to be done? How can a history of poor classics connections with teens be repaired? How can a current trend of no classics connections with teens be averted? How can you, a librarian or educator, both in the library and classroom, foster a meaningful relationship between teens and classics, bring great works of literature to young people that can be a true pleasure for them as readers? It's not so hard as you might think! By cultivating a relationship with the classics yourself and by sharing what you learn with teens, you can play a pivotal role in helping teens find the right classics for them, in connecting them with literary kindred spirits. You— yes, you!—can help make classics meaningful for teens rather than mandatory, can make the right kinds of classics visible and accessible.

It's a professional privilege as adults, as library professionals, and as educators, to help teens make these literary connections. In addition to connecting teens to the pleasures of popular reading, you have the opportunity to guide them toward the expansion of knowledge, understanding, and experience that the classics can so exceptionally engender, toward the sheer pleasure reading them can provide. Teens need you, need your guidance, whether they know it or not! What happens to young people when isolated and left strictly to their own devices? Just ask Piggy in William Golding's *Lord of the Flies*!

WHAT'S THIS BOOK ALL ABOUT AND WHAT WILL YOU FIND HERE?

With the exception of Hazel Rochman's book, *Tales of Love and Terror: Booktalking the Classics, Old and New* (1987), and excluding educational resources that provide tips and techniques for using classics in formal classroom instruction, there just isn't anything out there to help both teen-serving librarians and educators bring meaningful, enriching, and just plain enjoyable classics reading experiences into young lives. A book that provides practical ideas for how to best connect teens to classic literature outside the formal instructional context is clearly needed. So, here it is! This book is written for librarians and educators, and can be helpful to just about anyone who works with teens and wants to turn them on to great literature. So, if you're a teacher, parent, youth leader, or school administrator who works with teens and literature, don't be deterred by the book's series title!

Plain and simple, this book is about successfully connecting teens with the classics. It explores why you—public librarians, school librarians, and educators who work with teens at the secondary level—should strive to make these classics connections with teens, and is a practical step-by-step guide that will help you through the process of selecting, understanding, promoting, presenting, and otherwise meaningfully connecting teens aged 12 to 18 from all walks of life and levels of experience to a wide range of classic literature, in the public library, in the schools, and in alternative educational environments. From a big-picture look at the classics to what teens can gain from reading them, from how to form a solid and enjoyable relationship with the classics yourself to how to promote them with teens in your libraries and classrooms, this book provides both the inspiration and the practical tools you'll need.

Part One lays the groundwork. The chapters in this section explore just what classics are and what teens can find in them, discuss how to cultivate a strong relationship with the classics yourself, help you develop an understanding of teens both as growing people and as readers, and take a look at the kinds of classics and classics combinations out there that can appeal to teen readers.

Part Two helps you make it all happen—successfully connecting teens with classics, that is! The chapters in this section look at how to provide great readers' advisory services for teens, both one-on-one and through readers' advisory tools. They suggest ideas for how to connect teens to classics through additional programs and activities, such as classics book groups, theater activities, and reading incentives. They take an in-depth look at techniques for meaningfully and dynamically booktalking the classics. Part Two includes a chapter on how to develop, maintain, and display classics collections in libraries for both public and school librarians, and a chapter on how to connect with and promote classics in schools and the teen community for public librarians.

Throughout the book you will find the thoughts and perspectives of public and school librarians, educators, authors, publishers, parents, and teens, and in the booktalking chapter you'll find a selection of sample booktalks. Some chapters conclude with resource lists to help you select and more thoroughly understand both the classics and teens, and in turn more successfully connect the former to the latter. Appendices provide additional resources toward the same goal. In addition to a selection of short starter classics booklists found within the text, an appendix provides expanded starter classics booklists in fiction and nonfiction subjects.

What you won't find in this book is any in-depth, critical discussion of popular young adult literature. The merits of young adult literature fill numerous books and untold articles—so it doesn't fill this book! That said, using young adult literature in tandem with classic titles to bring greater pleasure and connectedness to teen readers is briefly explored, and mention is made of the teaching debate pitting young adult literature against the classics in the classroom as a heads-up on a current issue of concern in secondary education. Although this book does not for even a moment suggest that classics are the only literary connections to be created and fostered with teens, it is specifically about connecting teens with classics.

HOW TO USE THIS BOOK

The chapters in this book are arranged in a step-by-step order, that is, the book begins where you might best begin, and each consecutive chapter naturally follows and builds on the previous one. If you are a fledgling librarian or educator, or are simply new to the idea that teens can enjoy the classics, you might read the book cover to cover to get the most out of it.

Each chapter treats a particular aspect of the total process in making great classics connections with teens. If you are a little further along in your teen-serving career, you might start with the chapters you feel you need the most assistance from. You may be an educator who has a strong background in teen stages of development and the characteristics of teens as readers but needs help developing classics booktalking skills. You may be a librarian who already has a strong understanding of collection development and display but needs help understanding the types of classics that might appeal to teens in various stages of development. You may need to learn a little more about how to start a teen classics book discussion group or implement a classics reading incentive program. Whatever the case may be, you can dip in and out by chapter as best suits your needs.

Fledgling professional or grizzled field veteran, there's loads of great information for you in this book, written to educate and entertain, and ultimately to do a bang-up job bringing teens and classics together, so I encourage you to read it all!

Part One

Laying the Groundwork

1

WHAT ARE THE CLASSICS AND WHAT'S IN THEM FOR TEENS?

Just what are the classics? That's a good question, and one that lends itself to lively debate! Lots of different folks from lots of different times and places have had much to say regarding this question—including today's academics, authors, educators, librarians, and yes, teens themselves. It's a good idea to take a look at what people from the distant past and the present think the classics *are*, and an even better idea to define classics for the purpose of this book—so we're all on the same page, so to speak! We'll do all that in this chapter. From there, we'll take a look at just what's in the classics for teens, why young people might both enjoy and benefit from the classics, and why as librarians and educators, you should help those young people make the most meaningful classics connections.

WHAT ARE THE CLASSICS AND JUST WHO SAYS SO?

It's okay to admit it. Although you probably have some idea, you might be asking yourself right about now, "Okay, what exactly *are* the classics?" And, as a librarian or educator who does enjoy a verifiable authority, you are probably also asking yourself, "And just who says so?"

Let's see. . . . Are you thinking classics are those works from the aptly named classical periods of Greece and Rome? You know, writings by folks like Aeschylus, Socrates, Euripides, Archimedes, Thucydides, Aristotle, and that mostly unpronounceable lot? Homer? Ovid? Plato? Or is that Pluto, as one of my teen library patrons asserted when looking for "That Pluto guy's book about the Atlantis place"? He was, I'm sure, referring to Plato's *Critias* and *Timaeus*. I'm certain he got the reference, albeit a bit twisted, from host Ted Danson's then-airing A&E presentation, *The Search for Atlantis*, which is a wonderful example of a different medium's ability to attract teens to classic works, and which will be covered later. How about Marcus Aurelius and Julius Caesar, Virgil and Livy? Sure. These and many more are considered classic authors of classic works by a large enough number of experts to make it so.

Maybe you're thinking of the literary classics as defined by the academic canon. Yes, those "dead white guys," the Anglo-European males with a few Anglo-European women thrown in for good measure, a.k.a. the Western Canon. It's a good time for a brief mention here about classics and the canon. It seems like "canon" is a word used predominantly at the collegiate level, but another "c" word is important at the secondary level: curriculum! Curriculum is at the heart of the secondary school "canon." You shouldn't forget that, and we'll take a look at curriculum in Chapter 5 with "must-know" classics, and again in Chapter 10 when making classics connections in schools and your community.

But then again, you might be thinking about literary classics accepted as such beyond the academic canon, great works of literature that encompass a larger world of ethnic, gender, and cultural experience and lifeways. You might be thinking about authors who've won the Nobel Prize in Literature, or the Pulitzer Prize for Letters, the National Book Award, the Booker Prize, and so on. Or you could be thinking about nonfiction classics beyond the "greats" of Greece and Rome. How about biography and memoir? Philosophy? Political thought and treatises? Social history? Poetry and drama? No doubt, there is at least one work accepted as a classic by someone who should know, in just about every imaginable subject and across the entire written record.

What Do Classics Have in Common? The People Speak!

Just for a little mental fun, let's gather together purported classics experts and classics authors in an imaginary yet finely appointed dining room. Let's wine and dine them. After all, "*In vino veritas*," says Pliny

(1957, 45). Invite a reputedly conservative supporter of the Western Canon, say, Harold Bloom. Invite the staff of *Feminista!*, a noted online feminist journal whose team compiled a list of "100 Great 20th Century English-language Works of Fiction by Women" in response to the lack of women writers on Modern Library's "100 Best" novels list (since 1900). Bring in a couple of Nobel Prize winners from around the globe. Japanese novelist, Kenzeburo Oe, and Mexican poet/essayist, Octavio Paz, might be good choices. Add in highly lauded contemporary women authors of color, say, Toni Morrison, Isabel Allende, and Amy Tan. Throw in renowned scientist and classic science fiction author, Arthur C. Clarke (you've got to entice him from Sri Lanka), and N. Scott Momaday, Kiowa author of the Pulitzer Prize–winning *House Made of Dawn*. Don't forget South African novelist, Nadine Gordimer, and Canadian novelist, Margaret Atwood. Ask them to talk about what makes a classic a classic.

Apart from soup, nuts, and all the courses in between, who knows, really, what might happen at an imaginary dinner party with literary leaders of this magnitude? But it would come as no surprise if, during the fiery debate that ensues sometime between the fish and the fowl, common definitions of classics—accepted by all our guests—were revealed.

Leaving the mucky-mucks at their dinner party, what might folks more like us have to say about the classics? I bet we'll share some common definitions. Elizabeth O'Boyle, 8th grade literature teacher at Canyon Park Junior High School in Bothell, Washington, says, "How do I define classics? Simply put I would say that a 'classic' is a timeless piece of literature that kids (or people) can relate to at any time in history because the issues the characters encounter don't change even though the times do" (2002).

Library employee and parent of an 8th grade teen, Rochelle Coons, defines a classic this way:

> There are so many layers and tangents to the word "classic" that is it difficult to simply limit it to a one-sentence definition. But in its purest form, I think it would be a work that has stood the test of time. What makes a classic a classic would be how it has resonated throughout all time. A work can be centuries old and even though society and politics have changed, there are aspects of the human condition that are timeless. The astute reader will find a common philosophical thread or condition that speaks to, moves and touches the soul. (2003)

Educational Services Coordinator for the King County Library System (KCLS) in Washington State, JoAnn Vanderkooi, describes a classic as "a work judged to be of literary quality and whose themes have sustained importance and relevance over time—involving commonalities of the human condition" (2002).

Jackie Lockerby, Minnesota high school senior and teen reader extraordinaire, has this to say:

> Classics are a lot of different things. A lot of times, it's just a book that has stood the test of time, one that people still like after it's been outdated. Other times, it is a book that was extremely original, or just plain awesome. (For instance, in my opinion, the Harry Potter books are classics, although they haven't stood up to a test of time yet, as there hasn't been one.) (2002)

Here are a few statements from a group of Bothell (Washington) High School seniors, who remain anonymous and will for the remainder of this book, because they forgot to put their names on the surveys they completed!

- A classic is "something that can help define the human experience, and that applies to any time in history."
- "When I think of a classic, I think of some piece of literature that makes people think and apply knowledge to their own mind. A classic is something that is never forgotten, and every generation can relate to it in some way."
- A classic is "a book that is influential and well-known through the years."

And, my personal favorite:

- "A classic is a book that was written by one of the great writers in the 16th, 17th, 18th, 19th and 20th century. They are really old. And written in English that is a little old."

What've we got so far? In the style of Homer, let's make an epic list of similar words and terms. From folks like us: timeless, resonant, original, of literary quality, relevant, common to the human condition, awesome, defining of the human condition, thought-provoking, unforgettable, influential, well-known, and, lest we forget, really old.

That's a whole lot of opinion, albeit mostly educated. Let's go to both the electronic and traditional reference collections and look in a few standard reference resources for some learned and widely accepted definitions. The *Oxford English Dictionary* (*OED*) online defines "classic" with words and phrases like these: first class, of the highest rank or importance, of acknowledged excellence, model, standard, leading, of literary note, historically famous.

The same dictionary also refers quite a bit to the Greek and Roman writers and their literature. Understandable, though, when we go to E. Cobham Brewer's *Dictionary of Phrase and Fable* (the crusty old 1898 edition neatly formatted online through Bartleby.com) and learn just where the word "classics" comes from. It turns out the Romans were divided into six classes of society. If being in the highest class weren't reward enough, those folks also received the laudatory label, *class'icus*, to further differentiate them from the *infra classem*, namely, everyone else, a.k.a., the rabble! Over time, and with cultures that strongly valued the literary arts, the *class'icus* label ended up applying to the best authors as well. Over more time, the label traveled outside of the classical world and became a standard descriptive term for not only the best authors, but the best literary works.

The *American Heritage Dictionary of the English Language*, 4th ed. (2000) fleshes the *OED* out a bit. In addition to the same sorts of definitions to be found in the *OED*, we have words and phrases that include: having lasting significance or worth, enduring, refined, harmonious, elegant, definitive, a superior or unusual example of its kind.

And *Roget's II: The New Thesaurus* 3rd ed. (1995) caps it off with words and phrases like: archetypical, quintessential, representative, and "characterized by enduring excellence, appeal, and importance." Then it refers the motivated synonym seeker to the word "good"!

Let's add from our reference resources to our epic list: first class, of the highest rank, important, model, standard, leading, of literary note, historically famous, of acknowledged excellence, the best authors, the best literary works, of lasting significance or worth, enduring, definitive, refined, superior, unusual, archetypical, quintessential, representative, appealing, harmonious, elegant, and just plain good.

Time to move on to some of the great quotes about classics. It wouldn't hurt, after burying our noses in reference resources, to let a humorist have his say. Mark Twain on the classics: "'Classic.' A book which people praise and don't read" (1989, 241) and, "A classic—something that everybody wants to have read and nobody wants to read" (1996). Twain knows a classic to be of value and praiseworthy, and tongue-in-cheek though it may be, it also states something that most of us sometimes mistakenly believe to be true, especially with teens—no one wants to read the classics. We'll explore this later on in Chapter 4 when we talk about teens as readers.

On the more serious side, we've got quotes about the classics from a selection of noted authors and literary critics. Charles Augustin Sainte-Beuve (if you think his name is long, try reading some of his essays), nineteenth-century French literary historian and critic, informs us in his essay, *What Is a Classic?*, that "the idea of a classic implies something that has continuance and consistence, and which produces unity and tradition, fashions and transmits itself, endures" (1909–1914).

Ezra Pound, in his *ABC of Reading*, wrote, "A classic is not a classic because it conforms to certain structural rules, or fits certain definitions (of which its author had quite probably never heard). It is classic because of a certain eternal and irrepressible freshness" (1996).

Carl Van Doren, as quoted by James Thurber in November of 1950, said, "A classic is a book that doesn't have to be written again" (1950).

One of Italo Calvino's many definitions of a classic, published in a *New York Review of Books* article and later (with a different translator) in a posthumous collection of thirty-six literary essays entitled, *Why Read the Classics?*, reads, "A classic is a book that has never finished saying what it has to say" (1986, 19).

Then, added to our epic list from these folks are: praiseworthy, eternal, and fresh. I think Van Doren might be describing classics as definitive, and Sainte-Beuve and Calvino are surely describing their enduring quality. We've already got those on our list.

If given the time and opportunity, and if so inclined, I'm sure we could come up with an endless supply of people who've uttered—or will do so at a moment's notice—any number of remarks, both passionate and cavalier, concerning classics. Not being so inclined myself, let's suffice with what we have here already! Call them what you like—classics, great books, great works, best books—from dictionary definition to critical essay, from junior high/middle school literature teacher to school librarian, from humorist to public librarian, to teens themselves, some core concepts seem to hold true for the majority.

To close this exploration, let's return to the many-named Sainte-Beuve. Considered by many in his field to be the first and best-ever literary critic, consider his statement—one of exceptional beauty and breadth—about those luminaries (often defined as classics themselves) who pen the world's great works:

> A true classic, as I should like to have it defined, is an author who has enriched the human mind, increased its treasure, and caused it to advance a step; who has discovered some moral and not equivocal truth, or revealed some eternal passion in that heart where all seemed known and discovered; who has expressed his thought, observation, or invention, in no matter what form, only provided it be broad and great, refined and sensible, sane and

beautiful in itself; who has spoken to all in his own peculiar style, a style which is found to be also that of the whole world, a style new without neologism, new and old, easily contemporary with all time. (1909–1914, 3)

Classics Defined for This Book

Given all these venerable opinions, let's say, for the purpose of this book, that a classic is:

> Any work of literature (fiction and nonfiction, prose and verse) from times long past to the recent past that is acknowledged with some consensus— through the test of time, through literary and/or social review, or through the award-winning status of the work or its author—to be of exemplary merit for its form or style, its original or unique expression of enduring or universal concepts, or its unique reflection of the conditions of its people and times.

So, where does this lead you? To a very inclusive list of classics, I should think, which can give you lots of choices when working with teens. Don't agree with me? Sort of agree, but not completely? That's okay. This book is still going to work for you! I can compile and pass on some of the commonly held opinions about what makes a classic a classic, and from that I can set a definition for this book. In the end, though, any given definition hinges on opinion. When working with teen readers, though, just make sure *your* definition is first, defensible, and second, meaningful and useful to the teens, parents, and other colleagues in your environment (more later on this, too!). Beyond this book, you can seek out the many resources available to you, a number of which are included in this book, to help you define classics to your greatest satisfaction and make appropriate classics choices to promote to teens.

WHAT'S IN THE CLASSICS FOR TEENS?

Sure, there are teens out there proactively seeking the classics. Not loads, but some. If a public librarian, you might find a number of homeschooled teens in individualized reading programs are actively using your library to study the world's great works, to meet both educational and personal goals. Librarian or educator, you will find educationally motivated teens who are proactively seeking out classics in the schools— those in advanced placement classes, honors societies, and some of the more language arts–inclined college-bound types. Educational advancement and intellectual enhancement is considered a reward by a certain segment of the teen population. Some of you may find there are just those certain teens who love to read, love to explore new reading experiences, and are open to and in fact attracted to the classics. All these teens have at least some understanding of the value of classic literature in their lives, have some idea what's in the classics for them to find and enjoy, but alas, they are a minority. Any and all teens, regardless of any immediate understanding of what they might find in the classics and regardless of all other factors that make them just who they are in life, can enjoy and benefit from reading the classics.

Are meaningful reading experiences for teens only to be found in classics? No way. Classics are not *uniquely* qualified for this role, but they are *exceptionally* qualified. Let's first list a few benefits found in classics for teens, benefits that come to them purely through reading and enjoying these books, and then we'll follow with a closer look at each one. These aren't the only benefits teens might experience in reading the classics—all reading experiences are ultimately personal and the magic created between each reader and a book will be of a unique mixture—but they are some of the more notable ones.

So, what's in them for teens?

- A good read
- An appreciation for quality
- An expansion of thought and experience
- An introduction to life's possibilities
- An ethical guidepost
- A trip through history
- A cultural initiation
- A common point of reference
- A change of pace
- An intellectual challenge
- An educational foundation

A Good Read

Simply, classics are superb literature. Many of them tell engrossing stories peopled with both alluring and repellent characters. Loads of them are chock full of fascinating, absorbing, seminal information containing our human history of thought and movement. Classics present ideas of consequence with depth, complexity, originality, and imagination.

Just like everyone else, teens deserve the opportunity to explore and relish these outstanding books. As Michael Clay Thompson, long-time literature teacher and author of *Classics in the Classroom* so eloquently says, "To be ignorant of humanity's most wonderful stories, metaphors, and ideas is more than a pity, it is a deprivation of joy and enlightenment, a loss of brightness in life" (1990, 3). Or, as Max Brown, my 17-year-old friend, said when reading Robert Penn Warren's *All the King's Men*, "Man, this book is *sweet*."

An Appreciation for Quality

Classic literature exposes teens to works of quality, to many of the best expressions humanity has to offer. Those engrossing stories and all the literary elements that make them so, the fascinating information, those consequential ideas offered in rich language through myriad styles from subtle to defiant, have long impacted readers because they are of greater quality than other books, and express ideas of greater consequence than other books. As the American poet W. H. Auden says, "Some books are undeservedly forgotten; none are undeservedly remembered" (1989, 10).

In reading classics, teens can begin to develop an appreciation for what defines that quality, and to develop powers of discrimination and discernment that can be put to use in their lives ahead. And reading quality literature can contribute to an all-around sense of aesthetics and can assist teens in creating a highly satisfying relationship to other things of beauty.

An Expansion of Thought and Experience

Classics can provide teens with information and experiences they would never otherwise have, with people they would never meet, in times and places they could never go. They provide opportunities for young people to stand alone, apart from family, off the block, beyond neighborhood and school, to bear witness to far more than they have personally experienced in lives more closely prescribed than they will be in adulthood.

Fiction and nonfiction alike, classics allow teens to experience people not like themselves in times and places foreign to their own, whose circumstances they often have yet to consider as remote possibilities, let alone face. Classics allow teens to look into the course of human history, its philosophies, events, accomplishments. Teens are given entry into what has happened, is happening, and can happen.

Such reading experiences are expansive—they help to dissolve the self-centeredness of childhood, they engage the intellect, stretch the imagination, and help teens to use that intellect and imagination to begin the process of adult experience and self-definition.

An Introduction to Life's Possibilities

For the majority of teens who are still operating within that prescribed world of childhood, and for those who face challenging life circumstances, the world of possibilities is more than likely not obvious. How do these young people begin to understand what's out there, what compels them in what's out there, and how they might begin to make the choices that will direct their future lives? How do they confirm that it is a right and within their power to explore it at all? One very good way is through reading the classics.

Classics can open up entirely new and heretofore unimaginable worlds to teens. Through reading about both real and fabricated people, places, times, events, and even other planets populated with alien lives, teens are given the opportunity to broaden their understanding of what a life might be. Through an introduction to other forms of conduct and conviction, teens can learn about individual and societal norms and deviances—physical, behavioral, philosophical, spiritual—different from their own.

Exposure to those differences can lead to the expansive, liberating knowledge that there is more than one way of living a life. These views into lifeways and different value systems may help keep teens from cementing too narrow a view of what's normal, a view that might prevent growth or may even cause them harm.

In a sense, classic literature is a four-star menu for life's possibilities, a complex list of savory, delectable dishes, with some of the gross stuff, like boiled tongue and rutabagas, mixed in. Without a menu, how do teens know the full range of possibilities available so they can steer clear of the less than desirable of life's dishes and select those that make their mouths water?

An Ethical Guidepost

Classics are full of personal and societal conflicts and issues, are rife with ethical dilemmas. When teens read them they are exposed to both fictitious and real people, throughout time and in every imaginable circumstance, who have dealt out and dealt with those life challenges. Through reading, teens experience both the positive and adverse consequences of human ethics and actions (or lack thereof) from varying viewpoints. High school teacher, Tim Gillespie, in his article, "Why Literature Matters," explains that:

> Literature portrays lives that have complicated problems and tough choices, and invites us to engage with them, to imagine living out life's vexing dilemmas along with the characters we meet. By its truthful portrayal of life's complex moral choices, literature draws us in, submerges us into a story, and summons our imaginative power to identify with characters. Literature thus might be one antidote to the disease of disconnection that afflicts us. (1994, 18)

Classics allow teens to vicariously experience the world of human challenge and choice in ways that will personally move them, allow them to examine conflicts and issues they have not personally seen or faced, and to empathize with or reject the behaviors and actions of the people they are reading about. Through their responses, teens can begin to form and strengthen their own moral convictions.

Teens are given an opportunity to role play through classics, to imagine how they might act if placed in a similar conflict or ethical predicament, without requiring them to acquire immediate, practical knowledge beforehand. In this way, great literature can partner with family and society in helping teens define their own personal moral code, their own personal sense of honor—safely, privately, and hopefully before they are called upon to respond to difficult ethical situations in their own adolescent and adult lives.

Those who *have* at a young age experienced difficult ethical situations may find content in the pages of great books that makes the events of their own lives more understandable. Diane Rosolowsky, former college professor and current librarian, believes that "one of the conditions of adolescence is a sense of isolation, singularity" which teens are certain "belongs to them alone." She feels "the classics teach that teens are not singular or alone, that in fact what they experience is not just *their* condition, but the *human* condition" (2002). In reading, teens may find good company with those facing dilemmas within a book's pages, and this may both comfort them and contribute to more successful ethical decision making in their own futures.

The exposure through reading good and important books is significant to the ethical development and choice-making skills of both children and teens. Jim Trelease, well-known educator and author of (among many other books) *The Read-Aloud Handbook*, believes that:

> Common sense should tell us that reading is the ultimate weapon—destroying ignorance, poverty and despair before they can destroy us. A nation that doesn't read much doesn't know much. And a nation that doesn't know much is more likely to make poor choices in the home, the marketplace, the jury box and the voting booth. . . . The challenge therefore is to convince future generations of children that carrying a book is more rewarding than carrying guns. (1995, xxvi)

A Trip through History

Classics can provide a meaningful historical context for teens so they can better understand where they came from, who they are, whose company they keep, who they can be, and how they might go on without being fated to repeat the same old mistakes.

Marcus Tullius Cicero, the great Roman orator of the Golden Age—not long before B.C. became A.D.—believed that without an understanding of history, a human being, and humanity at large, could not grow up. For you Latin buffs, Cicero actually expressed in section 120 of *Orator*, "Nescire autem quid ante quam natus sis acciderit, id est semper esse puerum," which in a modern-day living language means, "To be ignorant of what occurred before you were born is to remain always a child" (Cicero 1939).

The University of Colorado's Norlin Library in Boulder has an inscription in the lintel above the west entrance by late University President George Norlin that is based on Cicero's words. It reads: "Who Knows Only His Own Generation Remains Always a Child." On the east entrance to the library is the inscription, "Enter Here the Timeless Fellowship of the Human Spirit." What striking messages to read when entering a library, a storehouse of the records of human thought and experience! And, to carry Cicero and Norlin a step further, there's the well-known statement by philosopher George Santayana, found in the first volume of *The Life of Reason*, which asserts, "Those who cannot remember the past are condemned to repeat it" (1905–1906).

Fiction and nonfiction, poetry and prose—all the great written works—are a part of teens' birthrights as human beings. They are the lasting thoughts and expressions of all those who came before them, the reflections of events and times and peoples. Teens belong to this human time-line. Classics mirror, have influenced, and in some instances may even have defined, who we are as unique civilizations and as an entire species today.

By introducing teens to great works that bring them a meaningful look at their world through time, you are inviting them into a larger realm than the one they've inhabited as children, one they will soon be a part of themselves. And this invitation can lead teens to a larger perspective, a greater understanding of the struggles and victories of the human condition, and, I believe, an edge up on growing into compassionate, civilized, productive members of families, communities, countries, and ultimately, the world. When asked what he would like his teen daughter to experience from reading the classics, Scott Driscoll, University of Washington literary writing instructor, responded with, "a sense of awe and a much larger awareness of the world and how it came to be the way it is" (2002).

In tandem with true historical classic works, teens can discover the past in classic fiction, and may in fact conclude that these stories offer a more immediate and visceral way to explore the course of human history. In Sigrid Undset's *Kristin Lavransdatter* trilogy, teens can experience the life of a young woman in fourteenth-century Norway who, regardless of the love of her family, is controlled by men from beginning to end, and whose life is filled with hard labor and the bearing of many children. They can step back in time to the French Revolution and witness the swift changes in society and the perils for the privileged classes, in Charles Dickens's *A Tale of Two Cities* and Baroness Orczy's *The Scarlet Pimpernel*. They can travel with Rutherford Calhoun, a newly freed slave in 1830s New Orleans who, to his horror, realizes the ship he's jumped to escape marriage is a slave clipper bound for Africa in Charles Johnson's *Middle Passage*. They can experience the gut-wrenching working environments of Chicago's meatpacking plants in the early 1900s, and the filthy conditions under which meat was processed for human consumption, in Upton Sinclair's *The Jungle*.

A *Seattle Times* article from August 30, 2000, shared a story both horrifying and inspiring. Titled "Vandals Sentenced to History Lesson," the article describes nine teenagers who in February of the same year vandalized the Golden Triangle Veterans Park in Port Arthur, Texas. The teens, all between 17 and 19 years of age, did extensive damage. A series of concrete benches were pulled up and turned over, the glass windows in a fighter jet cockpit and in a helicopter were broken, the helicopter's

door was pulled off and taken away, and numerous plaques commemo-
rating veterans from five wars were torn down.

Instead of receiving a maximum sentence of 180 days in jail, the judge,
with the involvement of Herb Stafford, a Veterans of Foreign Wars Post
Commander, sentenced the teens to learning about American soldiers and
the sacrifices they've made for the free democracy enjoyed by these youth.
Among other things, the teens were ordered to watch *Saving Private Ryan*,
a contemporary World War II film on its way to becoming a classic in its
own right, and to read Tom Brokaw's *The Greatest Generation*, a highly-
lauded contemporary nonfiction work about the ordinary, everyday people from all walks of life in our society whose sacrifices during World War
II brought about America as we know it today.

Both the judge and commander believed that a sense of history brought
home to teens through works of great impact might have a civilizing effect on them, even if those teens were raised in a world not especially civilized itself. Had literature teacher Michael Clay Thompson presided on
this case, he may have sentenced in a similar fashion. He firmly believes
that "classics can help to inoculate children against stupidity and cruelty,
and inspire them with the love of thought" (1990, 5). And he asks, "Can
you imagine a young adult who had been educated in the classics . . . can
you imagine this young adult delighting in the violence, misogyny, big-
otry and simple-mindedness which pervades certain aspects of society? I
can not" (1990, 4).

A Cultural Initiation

Individually and in groups, teens are naturally, and to some extent necessarily, self-absorbed. They tend in the early teen years to create closed
societies within which they rigidly define themselves and others according to some teen cultural sense of what is right and good, and fault or ignore everything else. This sort of self-orientation and disinterest in the
larger cultural reality should (hopefully and with a few nudges from the
rest of us) give way as teens mature from the early to later adolescent
years and take a greater interest in their own immediate cultural world,
their cultural heritage, and human cultural history at large.

Reading classic literature can help to develop that larger cultural
knowledge for teens, and can play a role in meaningfully initiating teens
into their own culture and its heritage and into a richer understanding of
other cultural traditions, both past and present. It will also help them understand the origins of literary references from the past that have influ-

enced or even created present thought, and are commonly used in the today's language. Or, as Carol Jago, a middle/high school English teacher in California for almost thirty years and author of *With Rigor for All: Teaching the Classics to Contemporary Students* wryly remarks, so that teens can understand New Yorker cartoons! (2000, 76).

You've likely seen those lists that highlight the differences between the common knowledge of generations. You know, facts like a person born in 1987 has never lived in a world without personal computers, has never known a world without AIDS, has never seen a record album or used a turntable, may never have seen a nun in a habit, believes all games are programs played through an electronic box, and that sort of thing. Time does not stand still and each generation comes to young adulthood with a different cultural reality than the one before it. And what came before that cultural reality was another one, and another one, and so on. The preceding cultural reality has in part built the current one, which will in part build the next. No culture occurs in a vacuum; it is heavily influenced by and comprised of the past. Teens need the opportunity to gain an understanding of this very important fact.

Born in 1963 and as a teen in the mid- to late 1970s, I had no real sense of history and its impact on my culture—not the turbulent current state of affairs at that time, not the cultural history both immediate and important to my parents' generation, and definitely not deep history. But that history contributed greatly to the culture in which I existed as a young person. A perfect example would be that, unlike my mother, and due in large part to a series of women's rights advocates over the past two or so centuries and up through the feminist movement of 1960s and 1970s in America, I had not been taught from childhood that while still in high school I should start looking for a husband with whom to have babies as my single and only acceptable contribution as a woman.

Did I truly understand this? No. Did I even know about the generations of women in my cultural tradition, many of whom lived deeply restricted and unfulfilled lives before me? Not to any great degree. Was I appreciative of the freedom from limitation I'd been granted due to the actions of strong and persevering women? Not really. How could the value of my comparatively unrestricted cultural experience as a young woman in America in the 1970s have been made meaningful to me?

One way might have been through reading any number of the great books that treat the condition of being female in the Western cultural tradition. Mary Wollstonecraft's *A Vindication of the Rights of Woman* (1792) is not beyond a high school reader. Nor are Virginia Woolf's *A Room of*

One's Own (1929), Simone de Beauvoir's *The Second Sex* (translated to English in 1953), or Betty Friedan's *The Feminine Mystique* (1963). Fiction works like Kate Chopin's *The Awakening* and Charlotte Perkins Gilman's *The Yellow Wallpaper*, both written in 1899, can give teen readers a sense of the Western cultural conditions for women at the turn of the last century. Alice Walker's *The Color Purple* (1982) and Amy Tan's *The Joy Luck Club* (1989) can bring teen readers a sense of the cultural conditions faced by American women of color, women who carry the burdens of being female in more than one cultural tradition.

Had I been exposed to any of these works, and a great many more, in my high school years I might have understood how unique in Western history it was to have been told with conviction by my mother, "You can be anyone you want to be." I might have given thanks as a beneficiary of centuries of strong women rubbing against the grain, many of whom suffered social censure at the very least for their actions. I might have taken pride in being in the historical company of a sisterhood of women who cared about who they were and who they could be. I might have started earlier in life to act in ways that contributed to an even greater freedom for women in the future, within my own cultural tradition and beyond. I might have been less awkward, less ashamed in my adolescent femaleness.

Classic literature can give teens entry into the horrors and wonders of their own culture so they can first understand it and their place in it, and second, use that knowledge to support that culture or to effect change within it as they grow into adulthood.

A Common Point of Reference

Classics can create a common point of reference for teens. Books of exceptional beauty and impact, books that reflect the universal human experience, are not just read in one town, one nation, or even on one continent. These books affect readers who have access to them worldwide. If a teen has read a great book and had some strong feelings about it, it would not be the least bit surprising—especially in this time of technological connectedness—to find another teen in the next town over, across the country, in Canada, Portugal, Sweden, or Japan who has read the same book and felt as strongly about it.

Classics generally have universal themes, archetypal characters, issues that cross social and political boundaries—that's a big part of what makes them classics. They depict historical events and present human philosophies that carry weight beyond their time and place. To read and share in those events and philosophies with other human beings from all walks of life brings diverse teens together at the same table in a conversation common and relevant to them all.

A young woman in France, although not poor, uneducated, nor black in early 1900s America, will not find Alice Walker's *The Color Purple* alien to her understanding of the plight of women who are not protected by racial and economic privilege. In fact, by reading Walker's book, this young French woman has the opportunity to become more in tune with an existence shared by many women in many cultures around the world. Youth in both Canada and Japan can relate to the terror Josef K. feels in Franz Kafka's *The Trial* when he is accused of an unknown crime and processed through a strangely vague and menacing justice system with no voice, until he doubts himself and comes to passively accept his very death. Being voiceless, being incapable of defending one's innocence in a world that has no ears to hear it, is a common fear, one that often starts in the teen years. Josef K. may be in an unknown society in a deliberately ill-defined place, but his case will not be lost on teen readers from any number of different cultures.

At 10:54 AM on February 28, 2001, the city of Seattle experienced an earthquake with a magnitude of 6.8. That's quite a respectable magnitude, but fortunately, the earthquake occurred at a depth of fifty-two kilometers below the earth's surface and caused minimal damage to people and property. It was a real shaker nonetheless, and caused a great deal of fear and insecurity for the residents of the Pacific Northwest (especially those who were standing in the shower at the time!).

Some days after the event a friend of mine commented, "Well, at least all of Seattle experienced it together." The remark seemed strange to me at first, but the more I thought about it, the more I liked it. He was expressing the idea that despite the disruption the earthquake caused, it also produced a common experience for people who otherwise had little in common, and that common experience was a positive thing. The earthquake, something clearly of significance for everyone who felt it, allowed people to share a common point of reference and communicate about it across age ranges, ethnicities, and lifeways. It was months before I stopped asking and answering the question, "Where were you when the earthquake hit?" with people who otherwise would have remained complete strangers.

Earthquakes and other colossal forces of nature are not the only things that provide common points of reference for people. Music, the universal language, does so. Films do so. And, of course, books do so. Great books do so all the more. The Seattle Public Library, Washington Center for the Book, and librarian Nancy Pearl began a community-wide reading program in 1998 called, "If All of Seattle Read the Same Book," a program still running today. The idea behind the project is to encourage a communal reading experience of exceptional literature that will lead to shared exploration of ideas and issues. What is this but creating a common point of reference? The program was of such appeal that it has since spread to numerous other states and Canada. Wouldn't it be incredible if a special teen version of this program got started somewhere and spread like wildfire?

A Change of Pace

Do you ever have trouble sitting still and allowing yourself to be drawn into a rich reading experience? I wish I could say no, that I'm always ready to stop and read a book, but I can't. There are many times when I just won't slow down enough to engage in reading, or when I'm too distracted by my life's schedule of events or the people in it to provide myself a chunk of time in which to read. Perhaps you, like me, become accustomed to the rapid pace at which your life moves and resignedly let go of whatever reins you have in your hands to let it run at breakneck speed. Does it at times seem like too great a challenge to bring that charging beast to a halt, climb out of the saddle, and lay in the grass for a sunny afternoon with a wonderful book?

There are many teens who would understand. Busy teens—many of them with lives actively scheduled from dawn to dusk—are even less likely than adults to know when to slow down and experience a beneficial change of pace, to sit peacefully in solitude and open the literary door to another world. Many teens need to be encouraged to take personal time, and when not simply hanging out in an unstructured way (which my partner calls "power lounging" and which I believe is critical for teens to do), they need to be encouraged to indulge in solitary pursuits that are long and leisurely, full of thought and wonder. Like reading!

This reminds me of a scene from a recent film, *Kate and Leopold*, which despite being a cheesy time-travel romance, has an interesting scene in which Leopold (the gentlemanly and not unattractive third Duke of Albany who, for your viewing pleasure, has been ported through time from 1876 to the present) is invited to Kate's apartment for dinner. She serves him a less than savory plate of food, and stands agog when he sets it aside and requests the next course. From there, a befuddled Leopold expresses his dismay at how modern people don't take advantage of multiple-course meals to slow down, sit still, ruminate, and connect to thoughts, feelings, and dreams.

Despite the fact that Leopold is an aristocrat and of a small and privileged percentage of a larger population that was probably subsisting on boiled meat, boiled greens, boiled pudding, and whiskey, it is still an important point! Without the multiple-course meal option, reading—and reading the great works in specific—is one of the best ways for teens to slow down, sit still, ponder, muse over, contemplate, meditate on, speculate, deliberate upon, digest, and generally connect to themselves and the people within the pages of books in an otherwise fast-paced, action-oriented time and place.

Conversely, there are those teens who are completely at loose ends, restless and numb with boredom. These teens need to be encouraged to join in the pleasures that great books can provide them; and they deserve to be introduced to books that can fill the long, empty, dry times with imaginative stories and glimpses into the real world of human life and experience. The thoughts, feelings, and questions those books engender will be enriching and may inspire teens to reject the habit of being bored and to pursue the many experiences life can hold, and the many possibilities it can offer them.

An Intellectual Challenge

Okay, this is certainly not something you'd be likely to advertise to teens themselves because it smacks of the "they're good for you" litany, certain to send teens with even the most remote senses of self-respect and self-preservation screaming in the opposite direction. Classics can and most likely will provide teen readers with both intellectual and practical challenges that will stretch their minds, encourage new patterns of thought, response, and reasoning, and develop increased language skills—including verbal and written communication skills. An expanded capacity for thought and greater facility with language through regular exposure to unfamiliar ideas, and regular reading of more complex plots with more complex sentence structures and diverse vocabulary, can bring a great deal to teens' present and future lives.

Dr. Jay Giedd at the National Institute of Mental Health in Bethesda, Maryland, in association with McGill University in Montreal, conducted a long-term study of the child and adolescent brain and determined that the brain experiences significant synaptic growth as well as regular loss of unused gray matter (believe it or not, the brain reshapes itself!) in preadolescence and throughout adolescence. Before this study, it was a commonly held belief that 95 percent of the brain's formation was completed by age 5 or 6.

Dr. Giedd believes his results indicate that what teens do and don't do at these stages of adolescent brain development will contribute in great degree to the final physical form of their brains, which is synonymous with capacity and which will ultimately determine the course of their lives. According to *FRONTLINE* producer Sarah Spinks's online article on teen brain research called, "Adolescent Brains Are Works in Progress," Dr. Giedd explains his "use it or lose it principle" like this: "If a teen is doing music or sports or academics, those are the cells and connections that will be hardwired. If they're lying on the couch or playing video games or MTV, those are the cells and connections that are going to survive." If this research holds true, the reading of great works is not just figuratively, but literally, stretching teen minds to last a lifetime.

If you'd like to read Spinks's article, you'll find it at http://www.pbs. org/wgbh/pages/frontline/shows/teenbrain/work/adolescent.html. The article is within *FRONTLINE*'s companion Web site to *Inside the Teenage Brain*, a television program which aired in 2002 and which is now available on video. Just leave off the work/adolescent.html part from the above Web address, and you'll find yourself at the main Web site. You'll also find similar information about adolescent brain development at CNN fyi.com's *Your Brain* section at http://www.cnn.com/fyi/interactive/news/brain/newsroom.html.

An Educational Foundation

Whether or not you believe college entrance exams like the SAT and ACT are useful gauges of high school achievement and reliable predictors of college achievement, they are the primary method colleges and universities use to select or reject student applicants.

Michael Cardman of the *Education Daily* reports that The College Board, owner of the SAT, has determined that rising math scores compared with constant or slightly declining verbal scores over the past ten years, indicate a de-emphasis of English composition and grammar in high school curricula (Cardman 2002, 1). Because colleges require students to be accomplished readers and writers who can first demonstrate a mechanical mastery of reading and writing, and second, comprehend, evaluate, interpret, and communicate about what they've read, The College Board is adding an essay writing section to the SAT to first appear in the exam beginning March 2005. Criteria used in grading this new portion of the exam will include "basic grammar, sentence structure, paragraph formulation and evidence of thinking" (Cardman 2002, 2). Evidence of thinking . . . imagine that! Gaston Caperton, College Board president, hopes this change to the exam will motivate high schools to put the same energy into reading and writing as is put into math and science (Cardman 2002, 1).

On the basis of entrance exam scores, many colleges and universities simply cull out prospective students who don't meet the requirements for reading and comprehension. For colleges with open door policies, students are required to take assessment tests, and those who can't demonstrate basic reading and writing skills are required to enroll in basic skills courses and pass them before enrolling in core courses. Either way, students who somehow made it through high school without developing sufficient reading skills are at a distinct disadvantage in continuing their education.

Do a quick and dirty search on the Internet using key phrases like "reading requirements" or "basic skills" combined with "college" or "college entry," or any other phrases that might describe the same concepts. You'll see quite a long list of links to colleges and universities that require entering students to take mandatory assessment tests in basic skills. It is unfortunate, indeed, to see such a strong need for assessment of *basic* skills at this level of education.

Teens bound for college can gain a great deal academically from reading classics, for all of the reasons we've just explored in this section and many we probably haven't! In addition to their introduction to children's classics as very young people, teens should be exposed to classics in the middle grades and in high school. Great literature provides them with compelling reasons to think critically and will be a strong contributor in laying a foundation for their continuing education.

And, through reading classic literature, teens may also discover what they'd like to study in college to set the course for their adult lives. It's possible that by reading Stephen W. Hawking's *A Brief History of Time*, a high school teen might become fascinated with the theory that a human body would be stretched into a spaghetti-like strand before breaking apart into tiny particles within a black hole, and may go on to become and an astrophysicist and fold space!

For teens who don't think about going to college in the middle grades or early in high school, but who do read classic literature, the skills gained just in reading and thinking about these sorts of books will leave a door open to successfully pursue additional education later on, either in a formal academic environment or as self-motivated lifelong learners, if they so choose. You want them to have that choice.

SUMMING IT UP

Although defined in many ways by many people throughout history, almost all definitions of the classics share fundamental core concepts that you can use to determine your own definition, and then use as a foundation to make the best classics connections with teens in your library or school. Why make classics connections with teens at all? In addition to their fundamental values as defined, classics can provide teens with quality reading experiences; the means to broaden their thinking and understanding; a link to history, culture, and the world around them; a reason to change the direction and pace of their lives for a time; intellectual and educational expansion; and, perhaps most importantly, a plain, old good read!

WORKS CITED

American Heritage Dictionary of the English Language. 2000. 4th ed. Boston: Houghton Mifflin.

Auden, W. H. 1989. *The Dyer's Hand and Other Essays.* New York: Random House: Vintage International. (Orig. pub. 1948.)

Bothell High School Seniors. 2002. Written responses to questionnaires. Bothell, WA: 2 October.

Brewer, E. Cobham. 1898. S.v. "Classics." In *Dictionary of Phrase and Fable.* Philadelphia: Henry Altemus. Also available online at: http://www.bartleby.com/81/ (accessed 28 October 2002).

Brown, Max. 2002. Conversation with the author. Kenmore, WA: 29 November.

Calvino, Italo. 1986. "Why Read the Classics?" *New York Review of Books* 9 October: 19–20.

———. 1999. *Why Read the Classics?* Translated from the Italian by Martin McLaughlin. New York: Pantheon Books.

Cardman, Michael. 2002. "SAT Math Gains, Verbal Drops Reflect High School Curricula." *Education Daily.* 28 August. Available online from: Infotrac Onefile, a Gale Group Database, Farmington Hills (MI) (accessed 9 March 2003).

Cicero, Marcus Tullius. 1989. "Orator," Chapter 34, Section 120. From *Cicero: Brutus, Orator,* translated by H. M. Hubbell (1939). In *Respectfully Quoted: A Dictionary of Quotations Requested from the Congressional Research Service.* Washington DC: Library of Congress. Also available online at: http://www.bartleby.com/73/ (accessed 3 November 2003).

Coons, Rochelle. 2003. Written response to questionnaire. Bothell, WA: 10 January.

Driscoll, Scott. 2002. Written response to questionnaire. Seattle, WA: 22 October.

Gillespie, Tim. 1994. "Why Literature Matters." *English Journal* 83 (8): 16–21.

Jago, Carol. 2000. *With Rigor for All: Teaching the Classics to Contemporary Students.* Foreword by James Strickland. Portland, ME: Calendar Islands Publishers.

Lockerby, Jackie. 2002. Written response to questionnaire. Faribault, MN: 22 October.

O'Boyle, Elizabeth. 2002. Written response to questionnaire. Bothell, WA: 18 June.

The *Oxford English Dictionary*. Oxford, UK: Oxford University Press. Available online at: http://dictionary.oed.com (accessed 29 October 2002).

Pliny. 1957. *Pliny's Natural History: An Account by a Roman of What Romans Knew and Did and Valued.* Compacted from the many volumes of Historia Naturalis by Loyd Haberly, Fairleigh Dickinson University. New York: Frederick Ungar Publishing Co.

Pound, Ezra. *ABC of Reading.* In *The Columbia World of Quotations.* New York: Columbia University Press, 1996. Also available online at: http://www.bartleby.com/66/18/45218.html (accessed 10 October 2003).

Roget's II: The New Thesaurus. 1995. 3rd ed. Boston: Houghton Mifflin.

Rosolowsky, Diane. 2002. Conversation with the author. Kenmore, WA: 28 August.

Saint-Beuve, Charles Augustin. "What Is a Classic?" In *Literary and Philosophical Essays*. Vol. XXXII. The Harvard Classics. New York: P. F. Collier & Son, 1909–1914. Also available online at: http://www.bartleby.com/32/202.html (accessed 20 November 2002).

Santayana, George. 1996. "Reason in Common Sense," Chapter 12 of *Life of Reason* (1905–1906). In *The Columbia World of Quotations.* New York: Columbia University Press. Also available online at: http://www.bartleby.com/66/29/48129.html (accessed 3 November 2003).

Spinks, Sarah. 2002. "Adolescent Brains Are Works in Progress." Alexandria, VA: PBS and WGBH Boston/FRONTLINE. Article published in association with *Inside the Teenage Brain* television program 31 January 2002. Available online at: http://www.pbs.org/wgbh/pages/frontline/shows/teenbrain/work/adolescent.html (accessed 3 April 2003).

Thompson, Michael Clay. 1990. *Classics in the Classroom.* Monroe, NY: Trillium Press.

Trelease, Jim. 1995. *The Read-Aloud Handbook.* 3rd rev. ed. New York: Penguin Books.

Twain, Mark. 1989. "Chapter XXV." *Following the Equator: A Journey around the World*. New York: Dover Publications. (Orig. pub. 1897.)

———. 1900. Speech given at the Nineteenth Century Club in New York City on 20 November. In *The Columbia World of Quotations.* New York: Columbia University Press, 1996. Also available online at: http://www.bartleby.com/66/47/62047.html (accessed 10 October 2003).

Van Doren, Carl. Quotation attributed to Van Doren and quoted by James Thurber in the *Bermudian*, November 1950. In *The Columbia World of Quotations.* New

York: Columbia University Press, 1996. Also available online at: http://www.bartleby.com/66/11/62711.html (accessed 10 October 2003).

"Vandals Sentenced to History Lesson." 2000. *Seattle Times*, 30 August, final edition.

Vanderkooi, JoAnn. 2002. Written response to questionnaire. Issaquah, WA: 29 October.

2

GET TO KNOW THE
CLASSICS—READ!

What can you do behind the scenes to prepare for your role in connecting teens with classics? A lovely image it may be, but I doubt that you've had the opportunity to set aside an hour or two in each workday to lean back in a comfy chair at a nicely appointed desk in your softly-lit office to become absorbed in a study of the great works of the ages—so you can talk about them with teens!

Although it is likely that a lot of you librarian and educator types have one sort of degree or another in literature or related subjects, and have read many a classic work beyond the usual required texts, you just can't keep up with the world's literary sorts—college professors, literary critics, disaffected Berkeley and Cambridge bookstore clerks—well, unless you're a middle grades or high school literature teacher. But even then, you may have focused on just a small handful of curriculum titles once you finished your own education and started educating others, and just aren't up to that high literary mark.

Those of you who, like myself, found your way to your teen-serving careers without that ubiquitous literature degree may be particularly behind in exposure to and understanding of classic literature. Having spent many of my undergraduate years engaged in nonacademic pursuits—swirling paint around a canvas while drinking student union mochas and going retro with Cat Stevens's *Tea for the Tillerman* on my Walkman so I could feel angst-ridden and soulful—I found myself as a librarian inexperienced in a body of literature that I valued and wanted to share with teens, but just hadn't read as widely as I'd have liked.

What can you do, given all the other responsibilities you have as a librarian or educator, to increase your exposure to and knowledge of classic literature, to gain an expertise, an ease with these books, that you can put to use with teens? To begin, you can and must read classic literature. This chapter will explore why you should do so and how to get started.

Okay, a few words of encouragement before reading any further! This is the first chapter of several that will help you with the behind-the-scenes or groundwork-laying parts of connecting teens with classics. But this doesn't have to happen all at once (there's no conceivable way it can!), and it doesn't have to happen before any meaningful interaction with teens can take place. Preparing to connect teens with classics is an ongoing process: it will be successful after the first book you read and share with a teen, and will add up to even greater success over time.

That said, to know classic literature is to read it. It's obvious and inescapable. This is a tall order, I know, but you must ultimately find the time to do so! English teacher and author, Carol Jago, discusses in *With Rigor for All: Teaching the Classics to Contemporary Students*, how critical it is to "take better care of ourselves as readers" when working with teens and asserts, "keeping my own love for books and for talking about books active and alive helps me be a better literature teacher. The more honestly I model the habits of mind of a lifelong reader, the more likely students are to follow my lead. Teenagers spot a phony a mile away" (2000, 141).

"If adults model love of ideas and words, and read enthusiastically, children will model that;" writes literature teacher Michael Clay Thompson in his book, *Classics in the Classroom*, however, "if adults model bibliophobia and anti-intellectualism, children will imitate that, too." Thompson, like Jago, believes "the love of books can not be simulated. You must be the reader you wish a child to be" (Thompson 1990, 7).

This all translates readily to you and me. Whether you work in a library, classroom, or alternative group educational environment and call them library patrons, students, or just plain teens, you've got to be a reader to create readers. And you need to have more than a passing sense of the classics you're promoting. This may not hold true all of the time, but it will hold true almost all of the time. Jago is right—teens usually know when you don't know what you're talking about, and this is not only not good for them, it's not good for your continuing credibility with them.

Why read the classics? There are probably as many reasons to read the classics as there are readers, but here are a few that might apply to you.

READ FOR PERSONAL PLEASURE, PROFESSIONAL BENEFIT

On the personal side, reading classics is both a challenge and a pleasure, and can be of immense value to you as a reader for most, if not all, of the same reasons we've explored regarding teens. And, hey, life's short. Get the good stuff in while you can! In his *A Week on the Concord and Merrimack Rivers*, Thoreau said, "Read the best books first, or you may not have a chance to read them at all" (1849, 114).

On the professional front, in addition to your work with teens, having read a wide selection of classics will also benefit you while acting as a readers' advisor to adults in your professional environment, be they faculty and staff in your school or the adults who come to your public library.

READ TO CONNECT WITH TEEN READERS

The most important reason you should read the classics is to make strong classics connections with teen readers. You can't just look smart, you have to be smart, and that means knowing what you're promoting. You can't fake it—teens will find out, which is bad for you and bad for them. And, if you don't read those classics, how will you be able to share a personal reading response with teens, which may be the single deciding factor in whether or not they try a classic?

Make Informed Recommendations

Despite those core elements that bind them in common, classics are highly diverse in content. They treat a wide range of both simple and complex themes. They are written in as many unique styles as they have authors. Some are brief, lyrical, and deceptively simple pieces, others are disjointed streams-of-consciousness, and others yet are lengthy, densely worded epics with straight narratives. Characters represent varied and disparate points of view, from the alienated to the childlike to the absurd to the malevolent. Settings cover all times, places, and conditions. Some classics can be fully understood on their own, others require some knowledge of their time or subject to fully appreciate. Length does not equal intellectual challenge. Descriptive blurbs are designed to attract a reader and sell the book, yet are misleading in fully describing its contents. Suffice it to say, you've got to know what is in one to match it to an individual teen.

Let's say you did manage to "sell" a classic to a teen without having read it yourself. With a modicum of knowledge about the book and the right sort of words, you've interested that young reader. Okay, that might work from time to time. There are, in fact, tried and true readers' advisory techniques to do just this, legitimate techniques, as there is no way any one person can read the wealth of the world's classics and speak from personal knowledge about every one out there (we'll talk about readers' advisory techniques in Chapter 7). It can, though, be a less than desirable technique when connecting teens to classics. Classic literature just isn't the sort that lends itself well to this sort of readers' advisory.

Say a teen has strolled into your library or classroom and has expressed a miraculous desire to read, oh, a creepy classic, something like *Dracula* or *Frankenstein*. That teen is looking to you to make a smart suggestion. You haven't read any creepy classics yourself, but you suspect as an 8th grader with a self-admittedly average reading level, she's not going to have a successful reading experience with those particular two books just yet. What've you got that she can lay her hands on right away? There's Irving's *The Legend of the Sleepy Hollow*. That might do. It is, after all, short, and Disney animated it. There's Stevenson's *Dr. Jekyll and Mr. Hyde*. That one's supposed to be super creepy, it's not too long, and it has that obvious good-versus-evil theme that teens find so compelling. Don't we all? Then there's H. G. Wells's *The Invisible Man*. That one is definitely a longer book than the other two, and from having read the blurb on the back, it seems to you like one with a more complex and serious theme.

What will you recommend of the available choices? If I hadn't read these books, I'd probably go with *The Legend of Sleepy Hollow*. Short book, with gangly schoolteacher and sturdy-yet-handsome local—both wooing beautiful farmer's daughter. Short, crisp autumn days, big party with feasting and dancing, headless horseman. Sounds like good stuff.

Fortunately, I have read this book and it is good stuff. But having done so, I'm certain it's not going to be the most successful choice for an average reader in the 8th grade. Sure, it's short, but it takes a long time to read. The language is antiquated and quite a challenge to settle in to even as an experienced reader. What average 8th grade reader is going to be sucked in to a book in which the opening sentence—with the sole purpose of informing the reader that the story takes place in "Tarry Town"—is seventy-nine words long, and in which that gangly schoolteacher is referred to as an "affrighted pedagogue"? So, having read it is to know it, and I'm not likely to recommend it to this reader at this time.

Dr. Jekyll and Mr. Hyde is out for now, too. It's creepy all right, and the good versus evil theme is strong and especially fascinating due to its focus on the potential for good and evil inside a single individual. But having read it, I know the language in this work is also challenging in its way, and that Mr. Utterson, Dr. Jekyll's lawyer, tells the story. In fact, not only does Mr. Utterson tell the story, but the book begins with Mr. Utterson relating to the reader something someone *else* told him about a Mr. Hyde. There's not a thing wrong with this. Stevenson used distance and point of view in a specific way to create his story just as he wanted it, and I was both fascinated with and strongly affected by this book. But it employs a method of storytelling that I think an average 8th grade reader might have trouble entering on his/her own.

That leaves us with Wells's *The Invisible Man*. I've read this one, too! It may be longer than the others, and it may seem particularly complex in story and theme, but among the three, it is in my opinion the most accessible to an average teen reader in the 8th grade. The language is the closest to contemporary of the three. It starts off with a bang and keeps a fair pace throughout. It follows a linear narrative. It is about an invisible man who does not at all enjoy being invisible. In fact, he is violently, insanely, opposed to it. Huh? Who wouldn't enjoy being invisible? Intriguing. And, it's good and creepy. I think my 8th grade reader could not only have a successful reading experience, even if she didn't pick up on all its complexities, but would actually find this one compelling.

No One Likes a Phony, Just Ask Holden Caulfield

Recommending classics you haven't read can be a problem in a larger setting as well. Maybe you're a librarian, and you've brought a group of classics to a classroom on short notice, quickly introducing each one through a few salient features to the class. What if you didn't admit up front that you hadn't read them, and a teen asked you a probing question about one or the other of them? This is not all that uncommon in my experience.

You'd have to: a) lie like a rug, or b) admit your lack of knowledge about the book. One hopes the first is not an option for you, even if you are a silver-tongued devil! The admission is your only choice and it comes at a bad time, that is, after the fact. Credibility issue. Worse, what if you've misrepresented a book, interested a teen in it, and contributed to a disappointing reading experience when that teen gets home and into a book that's not at all like you described it? You've got egg on your face—a hard condition to overcome with teens—and that teen is out a good read.

If you are an educator in charge of your own classroom, you can control this. Don't give yourself short notice, and read first what you intend to recommend! If you are a school or public librarian, though, you may be called upon to promote classics in the classroom without reasonable time to prepare. In a perfect world, this would never happen. You need time to select titles, read them, digest them, mark passages you might like to read out loud, think about how you might introduce each particular book to a group of teens. You might decide to make a list of points you don't want to miss for more informal discussion of these books with a class. You may want to write, memorize, and practice more formal booktalks. You may need to read background information about an author, his or her work, the time in which it is set, or an issue it addresses. You may want to tie the classics in with contemporary young adult titles. You may choose to track down images to show with the books. Whatever the case may be, you need time. Sometimes—when in that perfect world—you will have a reasonable amount of it. Sometimes you won't.

When circumstances force you to talk about classics you haven't read, undesirable as this is, you need to let your teens know this. It's just plain respectful. Although I prefer an expert be available at the giant electronics retailer to talk to me about which video camcorder to buy, I know it's not likely. Given the probability that the guy I need to help me lay my hands on a particular camcorder doesn't know much about them, I'd sure prefer it if he tells me so, instead of trying to fake his way through a lack of expertise—even if he's doing so with the best of intentions. Why? Because it's dishonest, and I'm too smart for that. I'm going to catch it right away, and it's going to bug me, and that guy and his place of business are going to lose credibility with me.

You can apply this to your relationship with teens. Be honest with them about what you do and do not know, what you have and have not read, what you can and cannot personally recommend. Just like Holden Caulfield in *The Catcher in the Rye*, teens can't stand a phony. Just like everyone else, they deserve this honesty and are too smart for the alternative.

How'd It Make You Feel? Teens Can Relate

Last but certainly not least, you should read the classics because when your reading experiences profoundly move you, it will show. When you fall in love with a character who dies and you mourn his or her passing, it will touch your teen audience. When you loathe a despicable sort, or feel the power and force of a true hero, teens will recoil from or cheer those characters with you. When you are sucked into the sooty streets of Dickens's London and can barely conceive the conditions under which people—*children*—scraped by, teens will share your stunned disbelief. When you describe the feelings of invisibility Ralph Ellison's black man experiences in the white culture, and your horror at the reading of it, your teen audience will also partake in the sorrow and rage of such a societal dismissal, and will identify with it.

Classics are packed full of the most powerful expressions and reflections of the human condition, a condition with which teens can and will relate, at least to some degree, even if they haven't yet experienced its many facets. Teens understand well enough, and sometimes deeply, grief, hatred, heroic salvation, poverty, disease, and loss of identity in a cruel world. If you haven't read the books, you can't bring these powerful responses as a reader into play when working with teens, and you've lost the strongest connection you can make, one human being to another, one reader to another.

HOW TO FIND GREAT CLASSICS TO READ

How do you get started? The usual way—pick something and read it. Then do it again! Sounds simple, and usually it is, but I've found that I need as much help at times as the next reader in making selections. You may especially feel the need for guidance when you're reading from such a large body of literature, one with which you may have minimal familiarity and feel the need to narrow down and focus in on classics you can recommend to teens after you've read them. There are a number of resources that can help you.

First, if you are a public librarian, honor the seasoned readers' advisors on your own library staff; if you are a school librarian or educator, seek their assistance at your public library. If they are not particularly savvy to teen readers you may have to turn down a few offerings, but give them the chance. They are themselves incredible resources and are knowledgeable about a wide variety of print and electronic readers' advisory tools as well. Their expertise is hard come by, and their work is, in my opinion, amongst the most challenging in the library profession.

Seek assistance from other colleagues in your work environment. In my experience, most public library employees are avid readers, and you will find any number of them both learned and passionate about one sort of reading or another, including the classics. The same holds true for a large number of educators and school personnel. Put the word out that you are looking for meaningful, riveting, soul-searching, laugh-out-loud, and what-else-have-you classics that might be great reading for teens, and you'll be surprised at the number of recommendations you'll get.

If you are an educator, you probably have a broad range of professional and personal resources to help you find classics to read that might be successful choices to share with teens. If you are a librarian, you might consider asking the participants on a library-related listserv, electronic mailing list, or online discussion group that focuses on teens, on literature, or on both. YALSA-BK, PUBYAC, and Fiction_L are all good places to start.

YALSA-BK

From the Young Adult Library Services Association, including current subscription instructions http://www.ala.org/Content/Navigation-Menu/YALSA/Electronic_Resources/Websites_and_Mailing_Lists.htm:

Purpose: An open list for book discussion. Subscribers are invited to discuss specific titles, as well as other issues concerning young adult reading and young adult literature. It is also an opportunity for subscribers to learn what has been nominated for Best Books for Young Adults, Popular Paperbacks for Young Adults and Quick Picks for Reluctant Young Adult Readers and to discuss those books. Cumulative lists of nominations for the lists will be posted by each of the committees. Subscribers will have the same opportunity as observers who attend ALA conferences and meetings to voice their opinions about nominated books. From time to time nominations for other YALSA lists may also be posted. Young adults are especially welcome to subscribe and to discuss books they are reading, especially those who belong to book discussion groups.

Uses: Discuss books for young adults
Discuss titles nominated for the YALSA lists
Discuss issues concerning young adult reading
Discuss issue concerning young adult literature

PUBYAC

Mission statement quoted from PUBYAC's homepage http://www. pallasinc.com/pubyac/:

> PUBYAC is an Internet discussion list concerned with the practical aspects of Children and Young Adult Services in Public Libraries, focusing on programming ideas, outreach and literacy programs for children and caregivers, censorship and policy issues, collection development, administrative considerations, puppetry, job openings, professional development and other pertinent services and issues. The name PUBYAC amalgamates the most important aspects of the discussion: PUBlic libraries, Young Adults, and Children. PUBYAC was initiated at the School of Library and Information Science, Pittsburgh, PA on June 1, 1993.

Fiction_L

The Morton Grove (Illinois) Public Library's electronic mailing list on readers' advisory issues, providing links to subscription and posting information, booklists, and archives. From the Fiction_L homepage http://www.webrary.org/rs/flmenu.html:

> Fiction_L is an electronic mailing list devoted to reader's advisory topics such as book discussions, booktalks, collection development issues, booklists and bibliographies, and a wide variety of other topics of interest to librarians, book discussion leaders, and others with an interest in reader's advisory. Fiction_L was developed for and by librarians dealing with fiction collections and requests; however fiction lovers worldwide are welcome to join the discussion. Among the topics discussed have been: genre study, bibliographies, workshops, audio books, reading clubs, and print and electronic resources. The discussion is not limited to fiction, but rather covers all aspects of reader's advisory for children, young adults and adults, including non-fiction materials.

If you have the opportunity, talk to parents who read, and ask them which classics they'd like to see their teens read. This can be quite illuminating.

Ask teens! You may have to ask quite a few to get to one who reads the classics, and this ratio is at its most extreme in the middle/junior high school grades, but once you've got a teen or two who pursue classic literature on their own and can talk to you about it, you have a view into a perspective of immense value. No particular "type" of teen reads clas-

sics; there are teen classics readers out there of every ilk. Find them and
draw out their recommendations. I cannot imagine much I'd enjoy more
than to read a classic on the suggestion of a teen.

In addition to seeking out great classics reading recommendations from
the people around you, there are many excellent books and Web sites to
help you select classics from a wide variety of time periods, cultures, and
genres. At the end of this chapter, you'll find lists of both print and online resources to help you select classic literature to read. At the end of
Chapter 5 you'll find lists of selected anthologies of poetry and short story
classics, and at the end of Chapter 7 you'll find a list of genre guides,
many of which focus specifically on genre classics. In upcoming chapters
you'll find short starter lists of classics by genre and topic to appeal to
teens—and appeal to you—and hey, you might just check out Appendix
C, which provides even more lists of classics in a variety of subject areas
of special interest to teens—and might I say again, to you, too! Appendix
A provides a selection of online sites currently offering free full-text classics you can read on your computer or download to a handheld data de-
vice.

I haven't been able to find any magazines or journals to point you to
that regularly review new releases of classics, but you might note as you
read through book reviewing resources when you find mention of a classic with a favorably reviewed and potentially teen-friendly new translation, new forward, in-text notes, or afterword.

SET A READING SCHEDULE, MAKE A
READING PLAN

Once you have a sense of one or more titles you intend to read, you
might consider setting a schedule for reading them. Are you given time
to do some reading on the job? If yes, don't ever leave that position! If
no, you will have to do your reading outside regularly scheduled work
hours. The good or bad of this is a discussion for another time and place,
but the bottom line is that whatever time you do have for the pursuit of
classics reading, you might want to formalize it.

How might you do that? I'd recommend a schedule. Without a reading schedule in addition to all the other tasks and goals I schedule, I
would not have read nearly so many classics as I have. As with all sched-
ules, this sort will work best if designed with a keen grasp of reality in
mind! Set your schedule with realistic reading goals so you can succeed
in meeting them. To master the obvious, this will encourage you and keep

you going! Depending on other responsibilities I have both personally and professionally at any given time, I set a reading schedule that I'm fairly certain I can meet. Right now, I schedule by the book, meaning I set a span of time in which I will be capable of reading a particular title from cover to cover. I allow time for research or follow-up reading and booktalk writing before scheduling another book to read. I keep in mind that I have many other things to do, including other reading projects. I have also, at other times, scheduled my reading by the chapter. Do what will work best for you.

A schedule can also serve as a sort of long-range plan, allowing you to plan out the scope of your reading over a period of time. Do you need to read broadly, sampling classics from around the world and across time? If you are not well acquainted with classic literature, this is probably the way to go. Or do you have a specific goal in mind—filling a gap in your knowledge, pursuing a passion, or finding titles with themes that you know your teens are interested in? Do you want to focus on classics by women, classics set in specific time periods—the French Revolution, Bolshevik Russia, the 1960s in America? Do you want to read classics describing the African American experience? How about genre classics—science fiction, mystery, romance? Classics with themes that appeal to teens—coming-of-age, alienation, oppression?

In what time frame would you like to accomplish your reading in any particular area? Is it best for you to dig in and read huge chunks of a classic in a few sittings, or are you the sort of reader who would prefer to dip in for short passages on a regular, longer-term basis? If you're the latter, you might consider an online service like *Classic Novels in 5 Minutes a Day!*, a free Web site at http://www.classic-novels.com that will send you daily installments of classic books of your choice that amount to about five minutes of reading each.

Whatever the case may be, you can use a schedule to be your very own classics project manager, or personal reading trainer, if you will.

THE MORE, THE MERRIER! JOIN A BOOK DISCUSSION GROUP

Have you ever thought about joining an adult book discussion group? It's all the rage. Even the American Library Association is engaged—they provided multiple book discussion sessions at the annual conference in 2003 for, what do you know, a classic! The program, "One Conference, One Book," allowed members to discuss Margaret Atwood's *The Hand-*

maid's Tale, and went so far as to bring in the author to read from her work.

Many book discussion groups read and discuss classics, especially contemporary classics. Group members often research various aspects of the current reading selection, including background information on the book's content and the author's life and writing intent. This could be a good way to engage in a schedule of reading, and practice thinking about and discussing the meaningful aspects of what you've read. Just a quick note here: you can make good use of book group discussion guides from the Internet. Publishers, private organizations, and book groups that meet online provide them. A quick search on the Internet using a phrase like "book discussion guides" will pull up numbers of them. These are designed to give group members more background and direction so that they can structure more successful discussions.

You might find local book discussion groups through your library or school, community bookstore, or local newspapers. Or you can join online discussion groups, that is, if you don't mind that no one will be showing up once a month with homemade snacks! A good place to start in the online community is the Great Books Foundation at http://www.great books.org. You may already be familiar with the Junior Great Books program, but the Foundation promotes adult reading programs as well. From their Web site:

> The Great Books Foundation is an independent, nonprofit educational organization whose mission is to provide people of all ages with the opportunity to read, discuss, and learn from outstanding works of literature. Founded in 1947 by Robert Maynard Hutchins, then president of the University of Chicago, and philosopher and scholar Mortimer Adler, the Foundation was established to encourage lifelong learning for all citizens. As part of a grass-roots movement to promote continuing education beyond the classroom, the Foundation aimed to provide opportunities for all Americans to participate in a "Great Conversation" of some of the world's best writing.

Although membership in the Great Books Foundation requires an annual fee, a great deal of information is available to nonmembers free of charge through the Web site. Of note, the Foundation provides a database of over 700 local Great Books discussion groups with over 15,000 members, searchable by state. You may not know it, but a Great Books discussion group could be meeting in your local library, school cafeteria, or at your neighbor's house! If you can't find any Great Books discussion groups in your area, the Web site provides tips on how to start your own.

(So do many other Web sites and books, just surf the Web and check your library catalog for a wealth of information on starting and conducting successful book groups.)

Many individual online book discussion groups feature or include classics. You might consider joining one of these instead of searching for a book discussion group in your community, or starting your own. Online book discussion groups have a flexibility that traditional book groups can't offer—you can write in when you have something to say and read remarks from others at any time, day or night. Here are a few possible starting points:

Constantreader.com: The Website for Discerning Readers
http://www.constantreader.com/
The Classics Corner within the larger site offers a monthly reading selection of a classic work. A brief synopsis of the work is followed by a link to free online audio version if available. A link to Amazon.com is provided for purchasing options. The site is free, but registration is required to participate, or Web users can simply read postings anonymously without registering.

The New York Times Books Forums
http://www.nytimes.com/books/forums/index.html
The *New York Times* offers a hosted reading group that discusses a work each month, including a wide range of classics titles in addition to contemporary fiction and nonfiction. All selections are determined by forum member votes. Additional literary forums are provided in various subject areas, such as African American Literature, Science Fiction, Asian Literature and Culture, and numerous forums on specific authors. An archive of book discussions accessible by author is also available.

The Reader's Place
http://www.thereadersplace.com/
Described as "an online community for all booklovers who are looking for intelligent, informative, insightful and thought-provoking discussions," this site provides access to numerous book forums, including classics and pre-nineteenth century literature, nineteenth-century literature and twentieth-century literature.

The Washington Post Book Club
http://www.washingtonpost.com/wp-dyn/style/books/bookclub/
The *Washington Post* offers an online book club with a monthly reading selection, featuring an opening article. An archive provides information about previous selections, transcripts of past book discussions, and the schedule for upcoming months' book club titles. "Books & Reading Talk" is a public forum for book club members to discuss current and past reading selections.

GIVE YOURSELF A JUMP START AND LEARN HOW TO SKIM

All right, all this said, what if you just don't have time to read and achieve maximum comprehension of a healthy selection of the classics in your collection before teens call on you for your expert opinion? While no substitute for reading a book word for word, cover to cover, you can skim classics to get at least a general sense of their content and reading level. I would urge you never to do this for a prearranged classroom talk or program, but given the pace of your professional and personal worlds, you may have to jump-start your familiarity with your collection through rapid reading or skimming, and then follow up with thorough reading over time.

There are many books that help with skimming for content, rapid reading, remembering, and so forth. You might consider starting with Mortimer J. Adler's *How to Read a Book* (1972). Adler, not coincidentally, was the pioneer of the Great Books program, which we've already talked about. Classics book notes and study guides (we'll talk about them in Chapter 3) can provide an immediate entry into a classic work, and in tandem with skimming, can give you the jump start you might need.

DON'T LIKE IT? TRY THE RULE OF FIFTY

In the next chapter we'll talk about how to better understand a classic you are reading but with which you may be struggling. Before we get to that, it's time to mention the difference between not *getting* it and not *liking* it. You might be intrigued by a work, but it's firing up the old synapses in ways that feel a little funny and leave you a bit confused. You could fall in love with one part of a book and feel completely befuddled by another. You could find the style and tone of the writing absorbing, but not make sense of the plot or theme of a book. You could more or less understand and enjoy what you're reading, but you might have a sneaking suspicion you're not quite with it, not quite going all the way down the road the author intended you to travel. These sorts of reading experiences are bound to leave you a bit unsure, but gaining some sort of understanding of and confidence in these books is a worthy goal.

Or . . . you could truly dislike the book. Good for you! This is *your* reading experience, *your* taste, *your* sensibility, and *your* time. If what's challenging you turns out to be your complete and utter disregard for a particular work, stop reading it. Who needs that kind of unpleasantry? Not you! And, since you never want to promote a book to teens that you absolutely loathed yourself, it's wasted time on that front as well. It doesn't mean the book isn't one of the greatest ever. It very well may be. But any book is in a relationship with its reader. If you're the reader and you don't care for the relationship being created, there's nothing wrong with putting down that book.

I use something called the "Rule of Fifty." This is by no means original, many people have made it their mantra, but it's quite useful, and gives you permission as a reader (if you haven't already given yourself permission, which I hadn't for a considerable length of my reading life) to cease and desist when reading something that makes you miserable. The Rule of Fifty is simple: if you are fifty pages into a book and it has left you cold, unmoved, bored out of your ever-loving wits, sick with longing for any other sort of activity including paying the bills and scooping up after Rover, who has taken care of a great deal of personal business in the yard, you can PUT IT DOWN.

Fifty pages makes good sense to me—it's far enough along to be through the setup and into the heart of the book. At fifty pages, the book is not likely to drastically change in plot, tone, characterization, pace, content, and that sort of thing. I got through fifty pages of Evelyn Waugh's *Brideshead Revisited* recently and thought my time might be better spent getting out the Swiffer® and attracting dust balls from under the bed with it. The horror! Waugh is considered one of the greatest men of letters ever to come out of Britain. He was offered a Commander of the British Empire award, no less. Jeremy Irons and Anthony Andrews starred in the BBC production of this very book.

Okay. I can't deny the value of author or book and wouldn't want to. I certainly would never deny the appeal of Anthony Andrews! I just found no way to create a positive relationship with this book myself, what with upper-crusty privileged Oxford men calling each other "dear" on every page and drinking to excess on a daily basis, not to mention one of them toting around a large teddy bear named Aloysius to whom he ascribes emotional content. However, this is a beloved book to a relative of mine, who has read it time and time again. We are most certainly all different! But, as it steered me toward dry mopping, it had to go. I've now moved on to another, more meaningful choice for me as a reader, and hope to take the enjoyment I get from that book and pass it on to teens.

You might devise your own reading rule of more or less pages, as long as it grants you permission to move on from books that don't work for *you*, no matter how lauded they may be. And, once you've given yourself this permission, you can transmit the same general idea to teens that it's okay to not like a book, personal opinion counts, and there's no need to waste time when there are plenty of other great books out there to choose from. Just don't reinforce this in a classroom with an assigned text!

DON'T FORGET THAT READING CLASSICS IS FUN!

One last and critically important thing: reading classics isn't going to add up overnight. *Don't put too much pressure on yourself*. Reading takes time, and even when challenging, it should always remain a pleasure. Read classics to learn, to enjoy, to be inspired, educated, enlightened, horrified, thrilled, amazed, amused, and made aware of more than you believed was out there—and in you. Read to share the power of that experience with young people.

SUMMING IT UP

You must read the classics yourself to make the best classics connections with teens. Not only will you benefit personally, you can pass on both your enjoyment and knowledge of what you read to teens in your library or classroom. You will not only be better able to help teens make successful classics choices for their reading levels, stages of development, and interests, you will increase your credibility and connection with them by sharing what you know about a classic work and how it made you feel. There is much you can do to maximize your time as a classics reader, from finding the best classics to read to developing a personal reading plan, from joining a book discussion group to learning the fine art of skimming and practicing the "Rule of Fifty." Most importantly, remember that all your efforts are worth it—you are reading to share the power of those classics with teens!

WORKS CITED

Adler, Mortimer Jerome, and Charles van Doren. 1972. *How to Read a Book*. Revised and updated ed. New York: Simon and Schuster.

Classic Novels in 5 Minutes a Day! Wichita, KS: Classic-Novels.com. Available online at: http://www.classic-novels.com (accessed 9 October 2003).

Fiction_L. Morton Grove, IL: Morton Grove Public Library. Available online at: http://www.webrary.org/rs/flmenu.html (accessed 1 March 2003).

The Great Books Foundation. Chicago: The Great Books Foundation. Available online at: http://www.greatbooks.org/home.shtml (accessed 28 June 2003).

Jago, Carol. 2000. *With Rigor for All: Teaching the Classics to Contemporary Students*. Foreword by James Strickland. Portland, ME: Calendar Islands Publishers.

PUBYAC. Pittsburgh: School of Library and Information Science. Available online at: http://www.pallasinc.com/pubyac/ (accessed 28 June 2003).

The Reader's Place. Available online at: http://www.thereadersplace.com/ (accessed 10 October 2003).

Thompson, Michael Clay. 1990. *Classics in the Classroom*. Monroe, NY: Trillium Press.

Thoreau, Henry David. 1987. "Sunday." *A Week on the Concord and Merrimack Rivers*. Orleans, MA: Parnassus Imprints, Inc. (Orig. pub. 1849.)

YALSA—Electronic Resources—Websites and Mailing Lists. Chicago: Young Adult Library Services Association. Available online at: http://www.ala.org/Content/NavigationMenu/YALSA/Electronic_Resources/Websites_and_Mailing_Lists.htm (accessed 28 June 2003).

RESOURCES TO HELP YOU CHOOSE CLASSICS TO READ

The resources listed here are by no means comprehensive, but are a pretty big sampling of the many available to help you choose classics of all kinds to read. Additional resources that may be helpful for selecting titles to read can be found within Chapter 3, and in the expanded list at the end of that chapter: "More Classics Resources with a Broad Scope." You might also take a look at "An Annotated List of Resources about Classics and the Canon" in Appendix B for additional classics selection ideas.

General

Anderson, Stevens W., ed. 1992–. *The Great American Bathroom Book (GABB)*. Salt Lake City, UT: Compact Classics.

Bauermeister, Erica, Jesse Larsen, and Holly Smith. 1994. *500 Great Books by Women: A Reader's Guide*. New York: Penguin Books.

Bratman, Fred. 1994. *The Readers' Companion: A Book Lover's Guide to the Most Important Books in Every Field of Knowledge, as Chosen by the Experts*. New York: Hyperion.

Burt, Daniel S. 2001. *The Literary 100: A Ranking of the Most Influential Novelists, Playwrights, and Poets of All Time*. New York: Checkmark Books.

Campbell, W. John, ed. 2001. *The Book of Great Books: A Guide to 100 World Classics*. London: Metro Books.

Conway, J. North. 1993. *American Literacy: Fifty Books That Define Our Culture and Ourselves*. New York: W. Morrow.

Dear Author: Students Write about the Books That Changed Their Lives. 1995. Collected by *Weekly Reader's Read*. Introduction by Lois Lowry. Berkeley, CA: Conari Press.

Estell, Doug, Michele L. Satchwell, and Patricia S. Wright. 2000. *Reading Lists for College-bound Students*. 3rd ed. New York: ARCO; Distributed by Prentice Hall Trade Sales.

Givens, Archie, ed. 1997. *Spirited Minds: African American Books for Our Sons and Our Brothers*. New York: W. W. Norton.

Kanigel, Robert. 1998. *Vintage Reading: From Plato to Bradbury; A Personal Tour of Some of the World's Best Books*. Baltimore, MD: Bancroft Press.

Lewis, Marjorie, ed. 1996. *Outstanding Books for the College Bound: Choices for a Generation*. Chicago: American Library Association.

Major, David C., and John S. Major. 2001. *100 One-Night Reads: A Book Lover's Guide*. New York: Ballantine Books.

McGrath, Charles, ed. 1998. *Books of the Century: A Hundred Years of Authors, Ideas and Literature: From the* New York Times. New York: Times Books.

Nagan, Greg. 2000. *The Five-Minute* Iliad *and Other Instant Classics: Great Books for the Short Attention Span.* Illustrated by Tony Millionaire. New York: Simon and Schuster.

New York Public Library. 2001. *The New York Public Library Literature Companion.* Edited by Anne Skillion. New York: Free Press.

Recommended Reading: 500 Classics Reviewed. 1995. Pasadena, CA: The Press.

Rexroth, Kenneth. 1986. *Classics Revisited.* New York: New Directions.

———. 1989. *More Classics Revisited.* New York: New Directions.

Rodriguez, Max, Angeli R. Rasbury, and Carol Taylor, comps. and eds. 1999. *Sacred Fire: The QBR 100 Essential Black Books.* Foreword by Charles Johnson. New York: John Wiley.

Rubel, David, ed. 1998. *The Reading List: Contemporary Fiction; A Critical Guide to the Complete Works of 110 Authors.* New York: H. Holt.

Seymour-Smith, Martin. 1998. *The 100 Most Influential Books Ever Written: The History of Thought from Ancient Times to Today.* Secaucus, NJ: Carol Publishing Group.

Strouf, Judie L. H. 1997. *The Literature Teacher's Book of Lists.* West Nyack, NY: Center for Applied Research in Education.

Award Winners and "Bests"

Carter, Betty. 2000. *Best Books for Young Adults.* Chicago: American Library Association Editions.

The Europa Directory of Literary Awards and Prizes: A Complete Guide to the Major Awards and Prizes of the Literary World. 2002. London: Taylor & Francis.

The National Book Awards: Winners and Finalists 1950–2001. 2002. New York: National Book Foundation.

The Newbery and Caldecott Awards: A Complete Listing of Medal and Honor Books. 2002. Chicago: Association for Library Service to Children.

The Newbery and Caldecott Medal Books, 1986–2000: A Comprehensive Guide to the Winners. 2001. Chicago: American Library Association.

Smith, Henrietta, ed. 1999. *The Coretta Scott King Awards Book, 1970–1999.* Chicago: American Library Association.

AN ANNOTATED LIST OF ONLINE "BESTS"

Booklists abound on the Web, and following is a selection of "bests" booklists you can use to help make strong classics reading selections.

The African American Literature Book Club
http://aalbc.com
Based upon 3,861 votes cast through an online form or send in a vote via e-mail to the AALBC.

Top 50 Authors of the 20th Century
http://aalbc.com/books/thebestauthors.htm

Top 100 Books
http://aalbc.com/books/thebesttitles.htm

Best of the Century: The Best Books
http://www.amazon.com/exec/obidos/subst/features/c/century/books
-best-of-century.html/102-3621410-7398508
Arranged by decade, this is Amazon.com's editors list of their 100 finest fiction
and nonfiction titles of the century. Links to Amazon.com's Best of the Century
in children's and genre fiction categories are provided.

The Chronicle Western 100
http://www.sfgate.com/cgibin/article.cgi?file=/chronicle/archive/1999/11/11
/DD16098.DTL&type=books
The San Francisco Chronicle's list of the best fiction by Western states authors,
from a poll with 600 respondents.

Classics of Science Fiction
http://classics.jameswallaceharris.com/
Created by James Wallace Harris and Anthony Bernardo, this site features essays, reference tools, and lists of classic science fiction (both compiled by Bernardo
and collected from the Web).

The 50 Best Books of the Century
http://www.isi.org/publications/ir/50best.html
An annotated list of the Intercollegiate Studies Institute's five best and forty-
five almost-as-good nonfiction works of the past century.

The Hungry Mind Review's 100 Best 20th Century Books
http://www.bookspot.com/listhungry100.htm
A combination of fiction and nonfiction works selected by the Hungry Mind
Institute as the past century's best books.

The Modern Library 100 Best
http://www.randomhouse.com/modernlibrary/100best.html
The aim of the "100 Best" list project simply was to start people talking about
great books, according to Modern Library's Web site. The Modern Library editorial board (comprised of authors, historians, critics, and more) produced both a
fiction and nonfiction list, then conducted a reader's poll for each.

Modern Library 100 Best Novels (The Board's List and the Reader's List)
http://www.randomhouse.com/modernlibrary/100bestnovels.html

Modern Library 100 Best Nonfiction (The Board's List and the Reader's List)
http://www.randomhouse.com/modernlibrary/100bestnonfiction.
html

Modern Library 100 Best Novels: The Radcliffe List
http://www.randomhouse.com/modernlibrary/100rivallist.html

The Nobel Prize in Literature
http://www.nobel.se/literature/index.html
The Nobel Prize in Literature is awarded to those who "shall have conferred the greatest benefit on mankind" in the preceding year and that one part be given to the person who "shall have produced in the field of literature the most outstanding work in an ideal direction." This section of the Nobel Web site features laureates and their works, articles by the laureates and other authors, and an educational section to listen to Nobel Literature Radio or play a literature game.

The Northport, NY Selections for the 60 Best Books of the Century
http://www.georgehart.com/sculpture/bookball-titles.html
The staff at the Northport Public Library set up voting booths for two months in the Summer of 1999 for patrons to cast their votes for the Best Books of the Century. The above list is the result of tabulating the community's many votes.

The 100 Best Non-fiction Books of the Century
http://www.nationalreview.com/100best/100_books.html
Under the leadership of *National Review* reporter John J. Miller and a panel of authors, journalists, and historians, comes this nonfiction list in reaction to Random House's then-impending release of its Modern Library 100 Best Nonfiction list.

100 Great 20th Century Works of Fiction by Women
http://www.literarycritic.com/feminista.htm
From *Feminista!* magazine in response to the Modern Library lists. To create the list, women's online forums and lists were queried. List displayed by Literarycritic.com.

Our Readable Century: From Mencken to Mailer, Woolf to Wolfe; A Compendium of Memorable Books from the Last 100 Years
http://www.januarymagazine.com/features/20thintro.html
From January Magazine and edited by J. Kingston Pierce, this site features the responses of well-known contemporary authors to a questionnaire designed to "determine which volumes had struck personal chords or somehow influenced the behavior of these ardent readers."

The Pulitzer Prizes
http://www.pulitzer.org/index.html
The Pulitzer Prizes homepage with links to resources, archive (searchable database of winners and nominated finalists), history (Joseph Pulitzer and The Pulitzer Prizes), and forms. Prizes include Biography or Autobiography (1917–), Drama (1917–), Fiction (1948–), General Non-fiction (1962–), History (1917–), Novel (1917–), and Poetry (1922–).

Ruminator Review's 100 Best 20th Century American Books of Fiction and Nonfiction
http://www.ruminator.com/hmr/100.html

From the *Ruminator Review*, a theme-based quarterly book review magazine, now in its fourteenth year and published in St. Paul, Minnesota. The books were chosen by five writers: Mary Moore Easter, Heid E. Erdrich, Bill Holm, David Mura, and George Rabasa, under the direction of Bart Schneider, editor of the *Ruminator Review* and J. Otis Powell of The Loft Literary Center in Minneapolis.

The Top 100 Books of All Time
http://books.guardian.co.uk/news/articles/0,6109,711520,00.html

Quoted from the *Guardian* newspaper's online site: "Full list of the 100 best works of fiction, alphabetically by author, as determined from a vote by 100 noted writers from 54 countries as released by the Norwegian Book Clubs. Don Quixote was named as the top book in history but otherwise no ranking was provided."

3

UNDERSTAND THE CLASSICS
WITHOUT A PH.D.

Public librarian, school librarian, new educator, or even veteran educator, you may be a little insecure in your own knowledge of the classics and in your ability to make strong classics connections with teens. Not to fear! You can easily increase your understanding of classic literature without going back to school for another degree. This chapter will help you get started, and may save you from coughing up tuition and sitting in an ice-cold classroom in one of those uncomfortable, molded plastic seats with the tiny attached mini-deskette on the right. Really, who are they kidding, anyway, and what about the left-handers?

You may not want to admit it (I never do!), but you could find yourself having trouble "getting" the book you're reading. We'll talk a bit about that in this chapter and why you shouldn't let it bother you, because there's help at hand. You can take a clue from teens themselves and use classics study tools to help you learn a little something more about literature at large, literary movements and time periods, a particular classic work, or an author. This chapter provides representative examples of many of these tools, both traditional and electronic, including resources with a broad scope, resources to better understand a particular classic and its author, resources to develop a sense of the time and setting of a classic, and resources in media formats.

The literary canon and the controversies surrounding it impact curriculum in secondary education and in turn affect the classic works selected for teens in middle/junior and high school. If you are a public librarian with little knowledge of the educational world, or if you want to refresh your knowledge as a school librarian or educator, a look at the canon and its issues could be useful to you. Although this book doesn't delve into this topic, a wide variety of books, articles, and essays on classics, the canon, and the opinions held about them exist, and a selection is noted in Appendix B for your personal edification. These resources are often more collegiate in focus, but they can provide a broad framework on which to hang your understanding of the history and politics of classic literature in education, if you are so inclined. From there, you can make your own applications to service to teens.

UNDERSTANDING THE CLASSICS (EXCEPT FOR JAMES JOYCE'S *ULYSSES* . . .)

You've probably heard any number of teens shrug and mutter, when referring to a classic they were assigned in school, "It was okay, I guess," or, "I didn't really like it," or "It was boring." In fact, some of the time they truly are *guessing* it was okay, because they didn't read it! Other times they just aren't interested in or capable of expressing their experience of a book. It's also possible they really didn't like what they read. It happens. We all read lots of stuff we don't like. And, let's face it, there are books of all sorts that are not particularly exciting and the reader becomes bored, bored, bored.

On the other hand, some of the time teens just can't allow themselves to appreciate anything assigned in class and their reluctant five-word responses represent a form of quiet rebellion. It's possible, though, that all of these responses (and a few more) are really a teen's way of admitting, "I just didn't get it." There are lots of reasons why teens may not "get it" with classic literature, whether they are reluctant or willing readers, and we will explore this in upcoming chapters.

Do You, Like, Get It?

How about you? How do you respond to classics you've read? You are certainly capable of expressing your responses with a considerably larger vocabulary than the average teen. It's unlikely at your stage of life that anyone is assigning them to you, so you're probably not locked in a state of educational rebellion! You may legitimately dislike or feel you can't personally resonate with what you've read, and can willingly admit it and describe the reasons the work did not engage you. But how willing are you to admit you don't "get it?"

It's not hard for me to admit that I don't readily get Thomas Pynchon's *The Crying of Lot 49* or *Gravity's Rainbow*. It's even easier for me to admit I don't at all get James Joyce's *Ulysses*. I mean, really, who does? There's no disgrace, no public censure in these admissions—at least not outside the learned halls of the Ivy League's literature departments. There may be a bit of concern, however, were you to openly proclaim to your colleagues that after having read them, you struggled with the issues of social class and convention in Jane Austen's *Pride and Prejudice*, or you lack an understanding of the importance of H. G. Wells's *War of the Worlds* as a seminal classic of science fiction. You may especially feel so as a teen services librarian or educator. Aren't you, as an adult and professional who works with our nation's youth, supposed to get this stuff? How are you supposed to connect teens to classics that you, yourself, have not grasped?

Unless you are a veteran literature teacher and are confident you are making great connections between teens and the classics in your classroom and in your one-on-one interactions with them (in which case you are at least one leg up on the rest of us and probably aren't reading this book!), your role as a librarian or educator is not to serve as literary expert to your teen population. It's okay not to be a crack literary critic. In fact, not "getting it" at first reading, and admitting to the teens that you didn't, may encourage them to relate to you more openly. A Bothell High School senior told me her best experience with a classic is "when it clicks . . . like, I got it!" Just like teens, it's normal not to read every classic you pick up with ultimate understanding. Like teens, it's okay to need to be guided, to study a bit to enrich your understanding. And, like teens, your greatest satisfaction will come when you, like, get it!

Challenge: A Turnoff?

Jago, who is a veteran literature teacher, writes about the difficulties of teaching literature to teens, who in her experience want everything to be easy and fun: "I wish that learning were as natural as breathing. It isn't. Reading a classic, like learning a language, takes applied effort" (2000, 26). This is true for teens, and it's true for you! Reading classic literature not only takes time, it will at times require effort beyond your experiences as a reader of contemporary popular literature—although those efforts don't have to be intensely time-consuming and are usually quite enjoyable. Keep in mind, both in the reading of each classic work and in its study, you will be learning fascinating stuff, and what you learn can be passed on to teen readers. There's nothing better than that!

This may beg the question: why should you read and promote books to teens that might be hard "to get"? Well, we can go back to Jago's statement that it's a matter of fact that learning is a stretch, and learning to read and understand classics is no exception. We can hark back to Chapter 1 and the discussion of what can be found in classics for teens. Getting to what's in those classics can take effort, especially for a young person who is still developing his or her reading and comprehension skills, critical and evaluative skills, compassion and empathy skills, big-picture life-viewing skills, and so on.

It can also take effort for you, even with a greater piece of life behind you and a greater mantle of maturity on your shoulders. Is this effort a turnoff? I hope not! I haven't experienced that it is for most teens. A boring book is a turnoff for teens and adults alike, and a book may be a real drag to teens who can't connect with it due to themes and meanings either too immature or too mature for them, or settings and cultural depictions still too alien to them, although not always. (We'll talk a little bit more about teens and reading challenges in Chapters 4 and 7.)

USING CLASSICS STUDY TOOLS (LIKE TEENS DO!)

Here's the cool part: once you've found intriguing reading you believe also has a good chance of being meaningful to teens, but feel you might need a little boost to understand it more thoroughly before promoting it to them there are lots of resources out there to help you. Teens know a few of them and in my experience aren't the least bit embarrassed to make use of them when needed. Follow their lead and take advantage of the resources listed below and found at the end of this chapter.

Broad Scope Reference Resources

There are almost as many reference resources on renowned authors and their works as there are stars in the sky, or grains of sand on the beach, or maybe even angels who can dance on the head of a pin. From multivolume sets of vast scope to single volume works of particular focus, you've got numerous choices to pursue your personal classics education.

These types of resources are particularly useful for the broad view of an author's life and work. Do you need to know what Langston Hughes looked like, brief facts of his life history and how it contributed to his status as one of the most highly lauded writers of the Harlem Renaissance? And what about the Harlem Renaissance, why's that so important to our literary tradition? Are you interested in a list of his complete works? How about some basic facts about those works—characters, form, imagery, plot, theme? Need help interpreting one of his poems or short stories? Would you like to know what the critics think of him? Who were his contemporaries? These questions, and many more, about Langston Hughes and just about any other author you can imagine, will be answered in brief in single-volume resources that provide short factual synopses, and at length in multivolume sets that provide longer articles or essays.

You shouldn't have any trouble laying your hands on at least a small selection of reference resources on acclaimed authors and their works. Many are also available through subscription-based online databases, and I'll note the ones that can be found online. If your school or public library doesn't have access to these resources either in print or electronic form, they are likely to be found in a larger public or academic library system.

Following are examples of well-known resources, with emphasis on the literature of the Western world. For more classics resources with a broad scope, including resources that focus on unique geographical regions, ethnic experiences, and women writers, see the list at the end of this chapter.

The World

They're all here—the literary luminaries and their significant works from the earliest writings to the present. These are examples of broad scope resources especially good at introducing you, and in turn helping you introduce teens, to the literary world across time and its many cultures.

Contemporary Authors: A Bio-bibliographical Guide to Current Writers in Fiction, General Nonfiction, Poetry, Journalism, Drama, Motion Pictures, Television and Other Fields. 1981–. Detroit: Gale Research Company.

In my opinion, this is the be-all, end-all broad scope author resource. Multiple series add up to hundreds of volumes of information on approximately 100,000 writers from English and non-English speaking countries. In addition to a scope that includes writers of virtually every literary form, *Contemporary Authors* includes "literary greats of the early twentieth century whose works are popular in today's high school and college curriculums and continue to elicit critical attention" (vii, v. 112, New Revision Series). Available online through *Literature Resource Center* (Gale), and *Biography Resource Center* (Infotrac/Gale).

Reference Guide to World Literature. 1995. 2 vols. Edited by Lesley Henderson, Sarah M. Hall, Associate Editor. New York: St. James Press.

From ancient Greece to the present, this two-volume work includes entries for 490 writers and essays for over 500 individual literary works. Some contemporary writers are included, but the focus is on the historical. Entries on writers include a biographical sketch, a bibliography of the writer's works, a bibliography for further study, and a signed article on the writer by a literary expert. This resource is an expanded, revised edition of *Great Foreign Language Writers.*

America

Louisa May Alcott, Kate Chopin, Ralph Waldo Emerson, William Faulkner, Ernest Hemingway, Ken Kesey, Harper Lee, Edgar Allen Poe, Henry David Thoreau, and Mark Twain are among the many, many American "literary greats" whose works teens are, or are likely to become, exposed to in their middle and high school years, and whose creative efforts are unique and exceptional reflections of this nation's literary landscape. You won't have any trouble finding information on these canonized, popular authors.

You should include the literary masters of African America, Asian America, Hispanic America, the First Nations, and feminine America in your reading plan to gain some understanding of their unique roles in America's literary history. The American literary world cannot be measured without the significant body of exceptional and evocative literature coming from American ethnic writers and women; no balanced appreciation of our past and present as a nation can be gained without them. The wealth of our literary tradition includes the great works of writers like Maya Angelou, James Baldwin, Shirley Jackson, Carson McCullers, Maxine Hong Kinston, Frank Chin, Bharati Mukherjee, Sandra Cisneros, Sherman Alexie, N. Scott Momaday, Louise Erdrich, and so many more.

Many of the general American writers resources now include the ethnic and gender experience in literature, and a wide range of sources are dedicated specifically to introducing you these works. Listed here are examples of outstanding resources, broad in scope, on American writers in general, from all times, ethnic experiences, and walks of life. The list at the end of this chapter provides additional general resources, as well as resources that specifically treat writers of diverse ethnicities and gender views in America.

Benet's Reader's Encyclopedia of American Literature. 1991. Edited by George Perkins, Barbara Perkins, and Phillip Leininger. New York: HarperCollins Publishers.

This single-volume resource is comprised of dictionary-style entries, from brief to detailed, on the literature of the United States (with some entries for Canada and Latin America) from exploration through the early 1990s. Available online through *General Reference Center* (Infotrac/Gale).

Masterpieces of American Literature. 1993. Edited by Frank N. Magill. New York: HarperCollins Publishers.

This resource contains detailed information on almost two hundred fiction and nonfiction literary masterpieces of the American culture, from colonial times to the present. Brief facts about each author and fiction work are followed by a lengthy essay including character lists, descriptions and relationships, an overview of the narrative, and critical response. Nonfiction works include an essay-style discussion of the work's major concepts and content.

Classics and Their Authors

The resources listed above and at the end of this chapter, as well as the resources listed at the end of Chapters 2 and 7, and in Appendix B, can go a long way toward helping you understand authors and classic literature. There may be times, though, when the broad scope is just, well, too broad. You may need to narrow your search (sound familiar?) to find more detailed information, or just *more* information, on a particular author or classic.

Are you interested in Louisa May Alcott's family life and if she borrowed from it to pen *Little Women*? Having read Tim O'Brien's *The Things They Carried*, do you wonder if the author was himself a Vietnam veteran, and if so, how those experiences merged with his artistry as a writer to create one of the most moving literary works that exists on men at war? Magazine and newspaper articles, as well as other sources of information often found in online article databases, are regular sources of detailed information on authors and works. Autobiographies, biographies, resources that focus on unique author facts, and literary biography resources will also provide far more detail on an author's life, times, and writings than you'll get from those broad scope resources.

Need help figuring out what certain characters in a classic novel are up to, what they are meant to convey? How about getting a basic diagram of a complicated story arc and plot, or a solid introduction to how the theme is introduced and maintained throughout the novel? Want to be sure you get the meaning of a book's title? How many of you are certain you know precisely why Harper Lee called her great book on coming-of-age, racism, and the courage and integrity to stand for what's right, *To Kill a Mockingbird*? Why did Ken Kesey call one of his greatest works about individuality versus conformity *One Flew Over the Cuckoo's Nest*? Don't furl your brow at those book notes and study guides! Barron's, Bloom's, Cliffs, SparkNotes, and more, not to mention a wide array of study guides on classic authors and their books are here to save the day! Need help while you're reading, with in-text notes that explain and enhance the text? Look to annotated or enhanced editions of classics works published for just this purpose.

Want to know how a book published within the last one hundred years or so, now considered or in the process of being considered a classic, was originally received by critics and general reviewers? Although broad scope resources provide some critical context, you'll get far more detail from book review resources and articles. Literary criticism resources will give you even more detail yet, and for the great books of all ages.

Articles

It's always fruitful to do an article search when you are interested in knowing more about an author or a specific work. Both older classic authors and certainly contemporary classic authors and their works are regularly "in the news." Historical and current magazine and newspaper articles are full of intriguing writing on literary people, works, and topics. It's not uncommon to find other sorts of information when searching online article databases, including television and radio transcripts and interviews.

You may also find articles you'd never have thought were out there with unique takes on your author or book. I found an article on how Wishbone, the TV terrier, has been a significant force in connecting children to the greats works of Austen, Irving, Poe, Twain, and others, when searching for articles on Charles Dickens. When searching for articles on comedic classics, I found an article that rather persuasively compared the sitcom, *Friends*, to Shakespeare's *Much Ado About Nothing*, and suggested those similarities could bridge a gap from teens' easy understanding of the same situations and forms in popular culture to those found in greater complexity in the Bard's work. Lots of food for thought!

There are any number of newspapers and magazines that deal with literary themes, and it would be far beyond the scope of this book to list them all. The old standbys—*The Atlantic Monthly, Harper's, The New Republic, The New York Review of Books, The New York Times Book Review, The New Yorker*—are definitely worth browsing. A quick search on the Internet will bring up list upon list of literary periodicals you might consider looking at, but you can do quite well with articles found in more general resources.

Your best bet might be searching general online magazine and newspapers databases like *Bigchalk eLibrary* (formerly *Electric Library*), Infotrac's *General Reference Center* and *Expanded Academic ASAP, Proquest,* H. W. Wilson's *Essay and General Literature Index* and *Readers Guide to Periodical Literature,* among many others, for articles on your author or work. In additional to general, popular interest periodicals, some of these databases will index most or all of the literary periodical standbys and a surprisingly large number of the more esoteric periodicals as well. If none of these online databases are available at your school or public library, one or more will be available at a larger public or academic library.

Author Information

If you want in-depth information about an author, an autobiography or biography will do the trick. Seems obvious, but it's always worth a mention. You might, despite your certainly advanced skills as a reader, consider biographies about literary figures written for and marketed to teens. They're designed to attract readers with shorter attention spans who need a good, basic life overview that features interesting facts to hold their interest. Unless I really want to dig in to an author biography solely for my own purposes, I head straight for the teen stuff. In addition to the single titles put out by just about any publishing house you can imagine, you might look for teen biography series by youth-friendly publishing houses, or may have access to biography databases at your library.

Biographies are also good for those unique facts of an author's childhood, adolescence, and adulthood which, when passed on to teens, make a stronger connection to that author as a real flesh and blood person than without them, even if that author wore a toga and quaffed wine mixed with water and honey from his very infancy, or wore whalebone stays and a stomacher laced tightly around her torso and rarely, if ever, bathed!

In addition to the in-depth information found in autobiographies and biographies, you might try a resource like this one for fast and interesting author facts:

Glossbrenner, Alfred, and Emily Glossbrenner. 2000. *About the Author: The Passionate Reader's Guide to the Authors You Love, Including Things You Never Knew,*

Juicy Bits You'll Want to Know, and Hundreds of Ideas for What to Read Next. San Diego: Harcourt.

    This single-volume resource includes fiction writers only. All one hundred and twenty-five writers are high-interest (with Web sites, fan clubs, biographies, etc.) and must have significantly impacted culture or are known as leaders in particular genres. All major types and styles of writing are represented, and many major authors who did not make the final list are referred to in "If You Like . . ." reading lists.

Or you might look into reference sets like these two for greater detail than a fast facts resource, but with a little less detail than a full auto/biography:

American Writers: A Collection of Literary Biographies. 1974–2002. 4 vols., 10 supp. Leonard Unger, Editor in Chief. New York: Scribner.

    The first four volumes provide in-depth essays introducing the lives and works of ninety-seven well-known American writers, originally published in pamphlet form by the University of Minnesota between 1959 and 1972. Arranged alphabetically by author, essays include a biographical profile, a bibliography of the author's books, and a detailed look at his or her work. Supplements continue to add an additional fifteen to twenty authors per volume to the set.

Dictionary of Literary Biography. 1978–1980. 6 vols. Detroit: Gale Research Company.

    Each of the six volumes in this set treats authors in historical context, with emphasis on the professional life of the author. Volumes include: "The American Renaissance in New England"; "American Novelists Since World War II"; "Antebellum Writers in New York and the South"; "American Writers in Paris, 1920–1939"; "American Poets since World War II" (2 vols.); and "American Novelists since World War II" (Second Series). Available online through *Literature Resource Center* (Gale).

Book Notes, Study Guides, and Enhanced Works

From the basic facts found in book notes, to the more detailed literary discussions provided by study guides series, to in-text critical guidance found in enhanced works, there are numerous tools published specifically to assist you, the reader, in making a more successful and meaningful connection to the author, text, and their larger literary context.

Book Notes

Yes, it's true, from Barron's to Bloom's to Cliffs, I'm sure you're aware of, or are a part of, the disapproving if not menacing shadow hanging over book notes! There are enough teens out there with an unfortunate tendency to use them in place of actually reading a classic to raise a hue and cry in the educational world. But surely, these are cases of decent resources being used in an inappropriate way! Don't fault the book notes, which are designed as quick reference resources to make classics more accessible and more meaningful to a reader, not to be read in their place.

Book notes are pamphletlike series containing basic information on classics commonly taught in secondary and college entry-level literature courses. That basic information tends to mirror what educators most often require students to understand after having read (allegedly!) the book. Whether this sort of educational requirement creates a good or bad relationship between young people and classics is a worthy debate that we will not take up in this book, but you will find a near-monumental number of books, articles, and essays addressing just this in the educational literature, if you are inclined to pursue it. Common book note series include Barron's Book Notes, Barron's Literature Made Easy series, *Bloom's Notes*, *Cliffs Notes*, and *SparkNotes*. These can be found in any combination of print and electronic versions. Independent online sources like *Book Rags* at http://www.bookrags.com, *Pinkmonkey.com* at http://www.pinkmonkey.com (surprise), and *Novelguide.com* at http://novelguide.com (another surprise!) provide a similar style of information.

Book notes can be a real aid to you when trying to make more sense of any particular classic, and they are invaluable for helping you recall the salient points in a classic you haven't recently read and just don't have time to read again before promoting it to teens. Common elements in book notes include an introduction to the life of the author, an overview of the work as a whole, descriptions of major characters, chapter summaries, rudimentary critical analysis of the work, review or study questions, and bibliographies. Many also provide extras: a brief overview of the time and setting of the book; the elements of writing such as plot and structure, symbolism, and style; and bibliographies of additional materials related to the book's theme. For example, *Cliffs Notes* includes a bibliography of intellectual freedom and censorship resources in its 1996 book notes for Bradbury's *Fahrenheit 451*.

Many books provide basic information on classics in a format similar to book notes, just bound in a single volume or in a set. You might consider Magill's *Masterplots: 1,801 Plot Stories and Critical Evaluations of the World's Finest Literature* as a comprehensive, twelve-volume bound set of book notes, and make similar use of them. The content, although condensed at three to five pages per classic, is similar to the individual pamphletlike book notes, with major characters, plot synopses, critical remarks, setting notes, and so on. You'll find loads of literary resources with Mr. Frank Northern Magill's name on them. Of note is the Masterplots II series, which includes African American Literature, American Fiction, British Fiction, Drama, European Fiction, Poetry, Nonfiction, Short Story, Women's Literature, and World Fiction sets, many with supplemental volumes to bring them up to date.

For a touch of the irreverent, you might take a look at Plotbytes at http://www.schoolbytes.com/plotbytes/index.html, part of the schoolbytes.com Web site. A plotbyte is "like a Cliff Note, except it's not written by a 67 year old professor who doesn't own a TV and thinks the world revolves around Shakespeare and his plays. Plotbytes are written mainly by grad students from some of the top schools in the USA. They are really smart, but also have a decent sense of humor and actually go out on weekends" (http://www.schoolbytes.com/plotbytes/about.php). Each plotbyte contains background information, facts about main characters, a synopsis of the plot, chapter summaries, and "things to make you look smart," which includes those extras like themes and analysis. At this time, there are over one hundred plotbytes at the Web site, all written with tongue-in-cheek.

Study Guides

So, what's the difference between book notes and study guides? There are a lot of similarities and a considerable amount of duplication between them. Although study guides, like book notes, are also published to provide information on those classics commonly taught, they tend to be more comprehensive, more narrative, and offer a greater depth of information into a classic, its themes, its relationship to and reflection of its times, significant literary characters, critical reviews, the life and additional works of the author, and more. Study guides also explore larger themes in literature beyond single classic works, like literary movements and genres. Many are written for the secondary level and will provide you with relatively quick and interesting reading material on the book, author, or literary topic you'd like to know more about.

There seems almost no end to these sorts of resources, and you can thank editor Harold Bloom and Chelsea House Publishers for the lion's share of them. Look for *Bloom's Major Dramatists*, *Bloom's Major Novelists*, *Bloom's Major Poets*, *Bloom's Major Short Story Writers*, *Bloom's ReViews: Comprehensive Research and Study Guides*, *Major Literary Characters*, *Modern Critical Interpretations*, and *Modern Critical Views*, to name a few. No kidding. Other well-known study guide series include Greenwood Press's Literature in Context series, Greenhaven Press's Literary Companion Series and Literary Movements and Genres, Lucent's Understanding Great Literature, and Twayne's Masterwork Studies (a Gale publication).

Speaking of Gale, this incredible publishing company is not lagging far behind Magill and Bloom. There's Gale's brand-new *Gale Study Guides to Great Literature: Literary Masterpieces*, *Gale Study Guides to Great Literature: Literary Masters*, and *Gale Study Guides to Great Literature: Literary Topics*. Gale also publishes a literary series for students, designed to provide basic information for understanding works most commonly studied by young people in classrooms, including *Drama for Students*, *Epics for Students*, *Literary Movements for Students*, *Nonfiction Classics for Students*, *Poetry for Students*, *Shakespeare for Students*, and *Short Stories for Students*. All of the "for Students" series titles are available for purchase (currently around four dollars each) through online booksellers as digital e-books in PDF format, for both Windows and Mac platforms.

Enhanced Works

If you really feel like going for the gusto, you might be interested in reading enhanced works. A couple of well-known publishers of enhanced literary masterpieces are W. W. Norton with the *Norton Critical Editions* and Viking-Penguin with the *Viking Critical Library*. These editions provide in-text footnotes, commentary, critical evaluation, historical information, images and passages from related works, and much more, in a single volume incorporated with the classic work itself.

I can't say I've ever made it through one of these—they tend to be scholastically rigorous and intellectually weighty (Norton describes its critical editions with phrases like "comprehensive pedagogical apparatus") and they detract from, rather than enhance, the work for me. I also find little information here that has any real application in interactions with teens. You'll do much better, I think, with the resources already mentioned. Nonetheless, they're out there and I'd be remiss not to mention them.

An exception to this may be Barron's Classic Novels series. New in 1999 with six unabridged titles in the series, each book contains additional information written specifically to help secondary students reach a greater understanding of that classic work. An introduction provides context for the work, and in-text and bottom-of-the-page commentary explains unusual words/phrases and summarizes narrative action. An additional "Fast Forward" and "Rewind" feature guides the reader who wishes to skim past lengthy or difficult content without losing the storyline, and a study guide arranged by chapter concludes each enhanced classic.

Book Reviews

Reading the original reviews of a classic before it achieved its status as such is an excellent way to get a sense of how readers first experienced a book before its canonization and before academic interpretation and dissection have begun. Those first reviewers didn't have any preconceived notions of the value of that classic-to-be (with, perhaps, the exception of new works by authors already well-known and well-received), nor was it suggested by their literary society that they feel about it in any particular way. Apart from your own experience with a classic, and the opinions of friends, colleagues, and book group members, these first reviews are the next best place to find genuine, immediate reader-to-book responses from other adult readers. For original reviews you are, of course, predominantly limited to those published in the last one hundred years or so, unless you like to put on those little white gloves and rifle through cardboard boxes at historical archives, or dig deep into the subscription-based Internet.

You might also keep your eyes peeled for reviews of new editions of the time-tested classics that evaluate new forwards or introductions by famous persons or the merits of new translations. Added front matter can be both interesting and illuminating, casting a new light on older works, but the quality of a translation is critically important to a reader's experience of a book. A translation can turn a lyrical, subtle French work into a lyrical, subtle French work in English, or it can reduce it to a choppy, disconnected, plodding work in English.

Even an excellent translation done fifty or one hundred years ago can be of lesser appeal than a translation done five years ago, or last year. Translation is not just a matter of language, it's a matter of the language style and usage particular to a time. Just compare two highly reputable versions of the Bible—the King James and the New International versions—to see what I mean! "Thee" becomes "you," and "verily" becomes "in truth" or "truthfully," and so on. You should look for those recent editions of time-tested classics that have been favorably reviewed, as they will be both more accessible and more enjoyable to you and your teen readers.

The following examples of book review resources that are likely to include the classics are well known and easy to find, either through the Internet, or in both print and electronic formats at larger public and academic libraries. You can also search any online general magazine or newspaper article database you have access to for book reviews in a wide variety of magazines and newspapers for the full range of years indexed in each database.

The Book Review Digest. 1905–. Annual cumulation. New York: The H. W. Wilson Company.

This resource indexes 109 "leading" magazine reviews of fiction and non-fiction books, for children and adults, published or distributed in the United States and Canada. An abstract is provided for each book. Citations for all available reviews are listed, and three to four book review excerpts are usually featured. Available in print and on CD-ROM. An expanded version is offered as an online database by subscription (*The Book Review Digest Plus*).

The Book Review Index. 1977–. Bimonthly, with annual cumulations. Detroit: Gale Research Company.

Over six hundred publications are indexed to provide citations to reviews of books and other media, including magazines, audio books, and electronic media. Citations of reviews are included for both new and older materials.

Books in Print with Book Reviews. New Providence, NJ: R. R. Bowker. Available through subscription online at http://www.bowker.com/bowkerweb/catalog 2001/prod00001.htm.

This online resource contains full bibliographic information on 3.5 million titles, including their current publication status. Over half a million full-text reviews for titles are provided from sources such as *Boston Book Reviews, Horn Book, Kirkus, Library Journal, Publishers Weekly,* and *School Library Journal.* Other version of BIP are available in print and on disc.

New York Times Book Review. 1923–. Weekly. New York: The New York Times Company.

Available each week in the Sunday paper, *The New York Times Book Review* takes an in-depth look at the world of literature, with essays and articles about books, authors, literary history, and literary themes; book reviews; and both bestseller and themed lists. Also available online at http://www.nytimes.com/pages/books/review/ to registered users (registration is free).

New York Review of Books. 1963–. Biweekly with intermittent monthly issues. New York: A. W. Ellsworth, et al.

The biweekly Review began in 1963 and was designed to publish the thoughts and opinions of America's greatest writers on books, music, theater, dance, film, and cultural and political issues. Both print and electronic versions are available by subscription, and some content is available free on the Web site at http://www.nybooks.com.

Literary Criticism

As a teen services librarian or educator, you many not find the majority of literary criticism especially helpful as a specific field of thought and genre of writing, either for your own use or for teen readers. Although the *Concise Oxford Dictionary of Literary Terms* defines literary criticism as "the reasoned discussion of literary works" (1990, 48), most single works in this genre are entirely too academic and abstruse to be of any use to you or to the teens with whom you work. Only aficionados of the "pedagogical apparatus" would find them reasoned!

The genre still bears mentioning here for a couple of reasons: 1) The subject term "criticism" is a common one in many library catalogs, and when combined with authors' names or specific classic works, often points to basic resources in addition to the dense, ivory tower brain cloggers. 2) Many outstanding reference sets use the word "criticism" in their titles to define a more accessible brand of literary thought, and you can turn to these to discover how others in the world of literature think or have thought about an author or title.

If you are certain the Web site you are using has a reasonable authority, the Internet is not a bad place to find accessible literary criticism resources. You might start at the Internet Public Library's *Literary Criticism Collection* at http://www.ipl.org/div/litcrit/, which provides links to "critical and biographical websites about authors and their works that can be browsed by author, by title, or by nationality and literary period." As for print resources, following is one of the most commonly used reference sets providing a basic understanding of literary works from all genres in their critical context.

Contemporary Literary Criticism: Criticism of the Works of Today's Novelists, Poets, Playwrights, Short Story Writers, Scriptwriters, and Other Creative Writers. 1988–. Annual. Janet Witalec, Project Editor. Detroit: Gale Group Inc.

In addition to introductory information on authors and their works, CLC provides passages of published critical opinion on the works of more than 2,000 creative writers now living or who died after December 31, 1959. The set has a series of cumulative, nationality, topic, and title indexes. Available online through *Literature Resource Center* (Gale), Select edition only.

Many additional literary criticism reference sets with specific focuses are published and can be found in larger libraries. The Gale Group publishes numerous ethnic, genre, and historical literary criticism series, including *Black Literature Criticism, Hispanic Literature Criticism, Drama Criticism, Poetry Criticism, Shakespearean Criticism, Short Story Criticism,*

World Literature Criticism, *Classical and Medieval Literature Criticism*, and *Nineteenth-Century Literature Criticism*. Many of these sets are available online in part through the *Literature Resource Center* (Gale).

Times and Settings of Classics

Think back again to Chapter 1 and the section on how classics can help teens take a meaningful trip through history. They can, of course, do the same for you. The classic work itself may have everything incorporated that you need to gain the utmost, real sense of its time and place, but then again, it may not. Or, it may just be far more tantalizing as a story or as a real piece of recorded history if you only had a few extra pieces of historical fact to color in your picture of its time and place.

I'll bet the kinds of things you now find compelling in history are considerably different from the facts you were taught in the classroom when you were a teen and young college student. You no longer need the dates and details of military campaigns or the geopolitical patterns of human movement and migration (did you ever?), as much as you need a basic overview of the time in which your book took place, a rudimentary understanding of the force and effect of the large-scale events of that time and place, and a hearty portion of the more gritty historical details thrown in to make it all come alive.

Even better, learning about the way the people of that time lived—how they were brought up, how they spoke, what they wore, what they ate, how they cleaned themselves, if they cleaned themselves, how they celebrated, what they understood to be fact and myth, what they believed to be good manners and bad, what frightened them, what made them happy, what they worshipped, how they were governed, what it was like to be male or female, how they courted and married, how they raised their children, what they died from, how they made sense of the world around them—may seem mundane but is really quite fascinating, and to my mind is the most genuine reflection of the human condition. Brought to bear, these facts can make your reading experience much more vivid and penetrating.

Not only will it be compelling for you as a classics reader to know more, it will be knowledge you can pass on to teens when connecting them to classics with historical settings. Teens are often a highly visceral lot who can be attracted through some of the grislier, juicier details that make other times in history more real to them (there will be more on this in upcoming chapters).

You can, certainly, cull many of the engrossing details of a time and place from the history books and audiovisual media on your library's shelves. There are reference resources as well that place literature within its historical context, resources that describe eras and decades in general, and resources that describe the fascinating, and sometimes thoroughly repelling to our modern sensibilities, facts of daily life through history you can use to further your understanding of the time in which your classic work takes place, and of the people of that time.

Provided below are a few reference resources that place a classic work in the context of its time and location, describe major events referred to but not detailed in the work, and give unique details about the customs and beliefs of the characters in your classic.

The first two resources are annotated as they are uniquely relevant to classic literature. I've included two short lists of popular resources on decades and eras and on daily life in history for you to dip in to when you need them, or when you'd like to introduce teens to resources with fascinating historical facts related to a classic work. Whatever you might like to know about a time or setting of a classic can be found in these and other resources like them, which will go far toward enhancing your reading experience and toward engaging teen readers.

Literature in Historical Context

Literature and Its Times. 1997. 5 vols., 1 suppl. Edited by Joyce Moss and George Wilson. Detroit: Gale Research.

This unique five-volume resource was created with students in mind and provides a detailed examination of three hundred important literary works in their historical context. Selected for their frequent use in educational environments, works include novels and stories, nonfiction of various sorts, plays, and poetry. Volumes are arranged chronologically by time period. A supplement provides information on an additional one hundred titles. Available online through *Literature Resource Center* (Gale). Selections only.

World Literature and Its Times: Profiles of Notable Literary Works and the Historical Events That Influenced Them. 1999–. 12 vols. (in progress). Edited by Jane Moss. Detroit: Gale Group Inc.

Each volume in this set focuses on the literature of a country or region, and places each literary work in its historical context. Each entry includes an overview that links the literary work to its genre, its time, and its place, and is followed by a report describing significant historical events related to the work. Lists of additional information for further exploration are provided. Volumes currently available cover Latin American, African, British and Irish, Spanish and Portuguese, and Middle Eastern literatures. Additional volumes will cover Asian, French, German, Indian, Italian, Jewish and Russian literatures.

Eras and Decades

American Decades. 1994–2001. 10 vols. Edited by Vincent Tompkins. Detroit: Gale Research.

American Eras. 1997–1999. 8 vols. Detroit: Gale Research.

American History by Era. 2003. 9 vols. San Diego, CA: Greenhaven Press.

America's Decades. 2000. 10 vols. San Diego, CA: Greenhaven Press.

Our American Century. 1997–1999. 17 vols. Alexandria, VA: Time Life Books.

U.X.L American Decades. 2002. 10 vols. Edited by Tom Pendergast, Sara Pendergast, and Rob Nagel. Detroit: Gale Group.

World History by Era. 2002. 10 vols. San Diego, CA: Greenhaven Press.

Facts of Daily Life

The Greenwood Press "Daily Life through History" Series. 1995–. 25 vols. Westport, CT: Greenwood Press.

Writer's Guide to Everyday Life. 1993–. Multivolume series with periodic changes to series title. Cincinnati, OH: Writer's Digest Books.

Classics in Educational Media

From literary video series about authors and works, to cable programs, to televised book clubs—any of which may have companion Web sites—these forms of educational media can be powerful tools to help you get a handle on and perhaps inspire you to develop a passion for a particular classic work or author. And once you start looking for literary educational media through your library catalog and on the Internet, you'll be amazed at just how much is out there.

Don't equate educational media with those old classroom filmstrips, you know, the ones from the 1960s and 1970s where you heard a "bong" and turned a little metal wheel on the side of a massive, green cast-metal projector to advance the filmstrip one frame, or the ones from the 1980s where the film all ran off the back of the second reel and thwapped repeatedly as it spun until someone called in the A/V Specialist from down the hall to feed it through again!

Today's educational media is slick, compelling, absorbing stuff. It's produced for a much wider audience than the classroom, for anyone interested in the wonders of the topic being examined. It's come a long way in narrative and visual style. And it commonly integrates the topic into its broader social, historical, and political contexts, connects the dots, so to speak, rather than separating the topic out and examining it alone as much educational media have done in the past.

A one-hour cable broadcast on H. G. Wells's *War of the Worlds* can explore the author's life history and career, his personal drives and obsessions, and the challenges, fears, and fascinations of the work's time in history. It can feature images of the author throughout his life, of life in general around the turn of the last century, and perhaps even include audio clips of music of the time. It might show you the original book cover and subsequent covers as published over the past one hundred-plus years. The broadcast might include a piece on Orson Welles's "War of the Worlds" radio program which caused public hysteria and total pandemonium among America's listeners, and might discuss why such hysteria could mount so easily over such a far-fetched tale—or is it so far-fetched? In fact, the Learning Channel/Discovery Channels's *Great Books* series, annotated below, includes a program on *War of the Worlds* that does just this.

Just as an interesting aside, *War of the Worlds* actually takes place in Victorian England. Orson Welles had the story adapted to modern New England to make the radio program more appealing to Americans. Little did he know how great the impact would be. In any case, this style of integration can be critical in bringing far greater meaning to your experience of a classic and to your understanding of its original value and value through time. Plain and simple, these sorts of media are great stuff, and there's no lack of them out there on literary topics.

It's also a good idea to have some knowledge of these media resources to steer teens toward when they need or just want information about a classic book or author in a nonprint format that's not the made-for-TV movie or film version! We'll talk about making specific connections between teens and classics through other media formats such as films and audio books in several upcoming chapters.

Here are a few representative examples to give you the idea:

C-SPAN American Writers: A Journey through History
http://www.americanwriters.org/index_short_list.asp

C-SPAN American Writers II: The 20th Century
http://www.americanwriters.org

C-SPAN, the National Cable Satellite Corporation, keeps permanent archives on its companion Web site for two television programs on American writers that originally aired in 2001 and 2002. The first set of programs looks "at the lives and works of selected American writers who have chronicled, reflected upon, or influenced the course of our nation." The second set "brings together writers, scholars, historians and actors to examine the lives and works of selected Twentieth

Century American Writers who have influenced our nation's history." All television programs are available in high-quality video to watch online through cable-modem and broadband technology.

ExxonMobil Masterpiece Theater Book Club
http://www.pbs.org/wgbh/masterpiece/bookclub/index.html
    The Masterpiece Theatre Book Club provides materials for viewers of Masterpiece Theatre's screen adaptations of classic literature to also read and discuss the original books. Three screen adaptations air on PBS stations each spring and fall, and the Web site provides a brief description of each original work followed by a series of discussion questions.

Great Books. 1993–1996. Videocassettes. 10 vols. Produced by Dale Minor. A presentation of Discovery Productions in association with Cronkite Ward. Narrated by Donald Sutherland. Bethesda, MD: Discovery Communications. (Originally televised on the Discovery Channel.)
    The Learning Channel/Discovery Channel's *Great Books* series still airs from time to time on Discovery cable channels and is available for purchase or through your public or academic library on videocassette. Each program takes an in-depth look at a literary masterpiece believed at its publication to have changed the way people look at the world, and which still retains its impact today.

Oprah's Book Club
http://www.oprah.com/books/classics/books_classics_news.jhtml
    Oprah's Book Club is back and features literary classics. Three to five books will be examined each year. The Web site will provide study guides for interested readers.

SUMMING IT UP

You do not have to go back to school for another degree to find out what you need to know about classic literature! As a reader yourself and in your work with teens it is not necessary to be a literary expert or critic, but you still may have to reach a little for meaning and understanding. That's just in the nature of some classics. Don't let that turn you off! There are times when teens have to reach, too, and it can be well worth the effort for you both. There are many resources available to help you educate yourself about the classics, from broad scope reference resources to materials specific to classics works and their authors, from resources that place classic works and their authors in their historical context to educational media. By pursuing a greater understanding, you can enhance your own classics reading experiences, and pass those experiences on to teens.

WORKS CITED

Baldick, Chris. 1990. *The Concise Oxford Dictionary of Literary Terms*. Oxford: Oxford University Press.

Bothell High School Seniors. 2002. Written responses to questionnaires. Bothell, WA: 2 October.

C-SPAN American Writers: A Journey through History. Washington, DC: C-SPAN, National Cable Satellite Corporation. Available online at: http://www.americanwriters.org/index_short_list.asp (accessed 27 March 2003).

C-SPAN American Writers II: The 20th Century. Washington, DC: C-SPAN, National Cable Satellite Corporation. Available online at: http://www.american writers.org/ (accessed 27 March 2003).

Green, Ranny. 1995. "For Some Classic Viewing, Don't Miss Wishbone." *Seattle Times*, 22 October: final edition, H6.

Internet Public Library: Literary Criticism Collection. Ann Arbor, MI: University of Michigan School of Information. Available online at: http://www.ipl.org/div/litcrit/ (accessed 14 April 2003).

Jago, Carol. 2000. *With Rigor for All: Teaching the Classics to Contemporary Students*. Foreword by James Strickland. Portland, ME: Calendar Islands Publishers.

Plotbytes. Available online at: http://www.schoolbytes.com/plotbytes/index.html (accessed 26 March 2003).

Simon, Richard Keller. 2000. "Much Ado about 'Friends': What Pop Culture Offers to Literature." *The Chronicle of Higher Education* 46 (41): B4–B6.

MORE CLASSICS RESOURCES WITH A BROAD SCOPE

In addition to the resources already mentioned in this chapter, the following resources can provide you with a broad perspective or overview on authors and their classics works.

The World

General

Major 20th-Century Writers: A Selection of Sketches from Contemporary Authors. 1999. 4 vols. Edited by Bryan Ryan. Detroit: Gale Research.

Masterpieces of Women's Literature. 1996. Edited by Frank N. Magill. New York: HarperCollins.

Western Europe

British Writers. 1979–1984. 8 vols. Edited under the auspices of the British Council and Ian Scott-Kilvert, General Editor. New York: Scribner.

European Writers. 1983–1990. 14 vols. Edited by William T. H. Jackson; George Stade, Editor in Chief. New York: Scribner.

America and the Americas

General

American Ethnic Writers. 2000. 2 vols. Edited by David R. Peck; Tracy Irons-Georges, Project Editor. Pasadena, CA: Salem Press.

Hart, James David. 1995. *The Oxford Companion to American Literature.* 6th ed. With revisions and additions by Phillip W. Leininger. New York: Oxford University Press.

African America

African American Writers. 1991. Valerie Smith, Consulting Editor; Lea Baechler, A. Walton Litz, General Editors. New York: C. Scribner's Sons; Toronto: Collier Macmillan Canada; New York: Maxwell Macmillan International Group.

Masterpieces of African-American Literature. 1992. Edited by Frank N. Magill. New York: HarperCollins.

American Women

American Women Writers: A Critical Reference Guide from Colonial Times to the Present. 1979–. 4 vols. Edited by Lina Mainiero; Langdon Lynne Faust, Associate Editor. New York: Continuum Publishing Company, a division of Frederick Ungar Publishing Company.

Modern American Women Writers. 1991. Elaine Showalter, Consulting Editor; Lea Baechler, A. Walton Litz, General Editors. New York: Scribner; Toronto: Collier Macmillan Canada; New York: Maxwell Macmillan International.

The Oxford Companion to Women's Writing in the United States. 1995. Cathy N. Davidson, Linda Wagner-Martin, Editors in Chief. Elizabeth Ammons, et al., Editors. New York: Oxford University Press.

Asian America

Asian American Literature: Reviews and Criticism of Works by American Writers of Asian Descent. 1999. Edited by Lawrence J. Trudeau. With advisors, David Henry Hwang, Ravindra N. Sharma, and Kenneth Yamashita. Detroit: Gale.

Asian American Novelists: A Bio-bibliographical Critical Sourcebook. 2000. Edited by Emmanuel S. Nelson. Westport, CT: Greenwood Press.

Latin America

(Includes writers from Central and South America as well as North America.)

Latin American Writers. 1989, 2002. 3 vols., 1 supp. Carlos A. Sole, Editor in Chief. New York: Scribner.

Masterpieces of Latino Literature. 1994. Edited by Frank N. Magill. New York: HarperCollins.

Shirey, Lynn. 1997. Latin American Writers. New York: Facts on File.

Smith, Verity, ed. 2000. Concise Encyclopedia of Latin American Literature. London; Chicago: Fitzroy Dearborn.

Native America

Whitson, Kathy J. 1999. Native American Literatures: An Encyclopedia of Works, Characters, Authors, and Themes. Santa Barbara, CA: ABC-CLIO.

4

MAKE SENSE OF TEENS AS GROWING PEOPLE AND AS READERS

The teen years are a period of rapid growth and change. A 12-year-old suburban boy probably still thinks girls are gross and experiences a perfect life in a good dirt bike and a few steep hills in the neighborhood. When that boy turns 18, that bike may be a car or motorcycle, one he's been driving legally for a couple of years. That high-pitched squeal of excitement as he's racing down a hill has become a deep baritone he's making good use of to bawl out another driver who just cut him off on the highway. The same hormonal changes that deepened his voice an octave or two are driving him toward romantic involvement rather than away from it. He's old enough to vote and to die for his country; a bike and a hill no longer define his world.

Also no longer a part of his world are the books which captivated him in his childhood and early teen years. His growth and change are not just physical—they're emotional, psychological, intellectual. The same goes for girls. Although the physical changes may not be quite as dramatic on the outside, they are indeed underway. Girls are developing into young women during the teen years, and as their bodies and minds change, so do their interests in reading.

Your job is to understand and acknowledge each teen as a developing being—one whose interests and abilities are in a process of vast change between the ages of 12 and 18—before you can identify his or her interests and abilities as a reader, and before you can make meaningful classics connections.

This chapter is here to help! It begins with a look at teens as growing people, including summaries of expert opinion that lend insight into teenage developmental stages. At the end of the chapter you'll find a short list of online resources on adolescent development you can use for further study. It then looks at teens as readers in a general sense, through the results of teen reading surveys and the current professional literature regarding teens as readers, including primary sources of adolescent literacy data and literacy support. It also provides a few brief lists describing the characteristics of teen readers, based on commonly held views in the current literature. It then explores the relationship between teen readers and the classics in particular, and takes a look at the classics' reputation with teens, teen readers' positive experiences with classics, common barriers to teen classics connections, and whether teens are up to the literary reading challenges they may find in classics. If you'd like to find out how your local teens think about the classics, you'll find out how to create and disseminate your own homegrown local survey.

UNDERSTANDING TEENS AS GROWING PEOPLE

Okay, so everyone's an individual, and teens are among the first to let you know that they don't like to be labeled. They're unique, just like everyone else! Fair enough. When I hit 30 years of age, I didn't want anyone telling me that I was leaving my carefree youth for a stage of life in which I'd naturally develop an interest in settling in somewhere to grow roots. No one could have convinced me that I was beginning a broader stage of development that tended toward a less narcissistic and more outward focus on family, work, and community.

So, here I am ten years later in the Pacific Northwest, after moving around the West every couple of years since I was a teen. It's a place I call home and don't think about leaving. I'm in a job I've kept for a number of years and have strong professional and personal ties to my community. I own a home with my significant other, and I like to stay there on Halloween and give out bite-sized Snickers to toddlers in pea pod costumes. I also like to make stews and bread puddings in my pressure cooker to feed to people. Huh. How did that happen? I'm not completely sure, but I believe I must have grown into a new stage on life's continuum! As much as I'd like to be singular in all ways (and in any number of ways, I am, as are you), I do believe a wide swath of other late 30- and early 40-somethings in America may be doing their own version of the same sort of thing, and comparisons could be drawn.

When you reach a certain age, your stages of development are determined by decades. You are, allegedly, not doing a whole lot of changing in short order. Not true for children, and especially not true for teens! The teenage years are a time of drastic upheaval and growth in just about every area. In seven years or so, teens go from the just postchild stage to full-on young adulthood. The gap between childhood and adulthood is vast—physically, emotionally, psychologically, spiritually—and it's the teens' task to bridge it. In this, I truly believe teens are our life continuum warrior class. That we made it through, and that teens today make it through to adulthood in an even more complex and consequence-laden world, never ceases to amaze.

Of course, each individual develops at his or her own pace, and that development is dependent on many factors—genetics, cultural values, upbringing, socioeconomic status, and individual personality, to name a few—but that development takes place within a larger construct. Teens share a common workload in their growing-up process.

According to Professor Robert Havighurst of the University of Chicago, teens have eleven developmental "tasks" they must complete to make it to adulthood. They must:

1. Adjust to a new body
2. Adjust to a new intellect
3. Deal with an increased academic expectation to demonstrate critical and formal thought
4. Develop the ability to verbally express themselves with meaning
5. Develop identity, a personal sense of the unique self
6. Begin to consider how they will occupy themselves as adults and which vocation or profession they will pursue
7. Establish independence from their parents, beginning with emotional and psychological separation
8. Create healthy and useful relationships with peers
9. Take control of their sexual selves, which must be successfully merged with personal values
10. Embrace a personal value system
11. Learn to control their impulses and demonstrate mature behavior, as accepted in the adult world

Eleven is a pretty big number in this context!

See How They Grow, Understand How They Read

Understanding the immense changes in maturation and focus that occur during the adolescent years can give you a real edge in connecting teens to classics—or any literature, for that matter. Of course, your first goal should always be to draw out the individual and find good literary matches for that unique teen, but you can benefit considerably from knowing the larger developmental stages of the age of the teen with whom you're working. This is not to say that teens will only read in areas they personally understand and identify with at the time. Far from it. Like other readers, teens like to explore the unfamiliar, they like to learn, they like to escape. Many teens like to challenge themselves to "read ahead" of their level—both technically and experientially. That is, they like all the same things from their reading experiences that you do. But when you're talking about classics and trying to make a connection to a sort of literature that is often going to challenge a teen reader, you have a good tool for making that connection by familiarizing yourself with developmental stages so you can attract teens to books that tap into topics or themes of value to them, and for which they are receptive.

A broad sense of adolescent developmental stages can provide you with additional information which teens themselves may not be able to give you when you're trying to put the right book in hand. For instance, I've never heard a teen say, "You know, I'm only 12, so I'm not really into coming-of-age books that explore the upper-teenage quest for independence and separation from parents and other adults." I *have* heard a younger teen say, when I've tried to connect him to a classic with a theme that just doesn't compel him yet, "Uh, do you have anything else?" Older teens have readily informed me and usually with a bit of a curling upper lip, that a classic is too "babyish" when handed one below their level of experience and interest, or that they read *that* one in 7th grade. Appalling. I've also had teens say nothing at all, just give me that baleful, disappointed look. Horrible!

You shouldn't mind pulling out lots and lots of books for teens who want "something else" besides what you've just recommended. Your ego must be tucked far, far away! In fact, it's an excellent, no-pressure way of getting teens to take out classics from the library and try them on for size. But you should attempt to minimize the occurrence of that baleful look, try not to disappoint, and you should most definitely avoid wasting a teen's time.

Teen Development by Age and Grade

Following are developmental facts compiled by age and grade, cobbled together and paraphrased from Parent Soup's online Development Tracker, the American Academy of Child and Adolescent Psychiatry, and the Columbia University College of Physicians and Surgeons *Complete Home Medical Guide* online, which provide basic descriptions of the normal physical, emotional, social, and intellectual stages of teen development. These might give you useful insight into the teen psyche, and might help you make more successful classics matches with teens in the library or classroom.

Just a reminder: there are always exceptions to any rule. Although these stages are a highly useful resource when working with teens, your powers of observation and your skill in drawing out each teen to understand his or her individual reading interests and requirements is of far superior value!

Before you delve into the following breakdown by age and grade, keep in mind that in general, the middle school/junior high years revolve around:

• Physical and emotional changes and comparison of those changes with peers
• Social conformity
• The beginning stages of authority rejection
• Increasing academic challenge

The high school years revolve around:

• Personal emancipation, including the move away from family and toward meaningful peer relationships (including dating)
• Risk taking
• Interest in the future (especially in choosing an individual role in life)
• High academic challenge

Ages 12 to 13, 7th Grade

This age brings the onset of puberty. Hormonal changes contribute to dramatic mood swings, and physical changes often make these young teens uncomfortable in their own bodies, estranged from them. Despite this discomfort, teens in this age range are often fascinated by their bodies (even though it doesn't seem to lead to a heightened sense of hygiene for boys!), and girls in particular are focused on how their bodies fit or fall short of societal standards of beauty. Moodiness and swift changes in physical attributes may throw identities into a state of flux, which can lead to lowered self-esteem and unpredictable behavior.

Teens in the 7th grade are in the process of forming close personal friendships, but they are not yet developing social groups. These friendships revolve around competitive comparisons in all areas of their lives, including their families. Popular culture (e.g., movies, television shows, rock stars) matters a great deal at this time. Teens in the 7th grade are developing increased language skills, and can often read adult-level magazines and newspapers for information that interests them.

Ages 13 to 14, 8th Grade

Growth spurts are predominantly over for girls and begin to slow for boys in the 8th grade. Personal, and especially physical, privacy becomes increasingly important. Teens at this age alternately desire freedom from family and to be coddled by family, but strictly on their own terms. They are asserting independence, developing personal beliefs of right and wrong, and will challenge others' beliefs. They are openly rebellious with adults and often believe their parents are interfering in their well-being. Teens in the 8th grade desire to be part of a larger mixed-sex peer group, and will willingly conform to its standards. This is an egocentric and self-obsessed stage, and teens often think they are being examined in detail by those around them.

Intellectually, teens in the 8th grade are for the first time able to link what they read to their own personal experiences. They are interested in books that tie in with their life stage. Their vocabulary is rapidly increasing, they have a basic understanding of literary techniques and can use them in their own writing, and they can differentiate between fact and opinion. They are sensitive to their academic standing and may form a self-defeating identity around it.

Ages 14 to 15, 9th Grade

These teens are experiencing a greater sense of self and are more at peace within. They are not without their insecurities, though, and continue to worry about physical appearance. Boys are especially active in physical development at this age, with the growth of facial and body hair and the deepening of voice. Teens in the 9th grade are at the height of rebellion with adults, especially parents. Being considered a distinct individual is critical to them at this time, and they may force the issue. They exhibit a wider range of interests and a greater awareness in and attraction to the outside world. They are developing deductive reasoning and are interested in reasons in general.

Socially, teens in the 9th grade are less self-obsessed, and although they care deeply about their own opinions, this lessening of egocentricity allows them to explore other views and either persuade others of their own views or compromise on them. They are able to consider the human condition at large, separate from their own personal lives. They will begin to develop their own sense of values and moral code.

They will seek additional friendships based on shared interests and worldview, which will be more intimate than ever before. They will continue to be involved in mixed-sex peer groups and are interested in dating. Some may be having sex. Their educational world is much more complex and high expectations can produce significant stress.

Ages 15 to 16, 10th Grade

Individual personality becomes even stronger in the 10th grade. Teens feel the need to dabble in a variety of self-images and will continually test their boundaries—and others' boundaries as well. Teens often places themselves in the hero's role and fantasize about it, which can produce an idealism that leads to positive action in life or an idealism that mistakenly produces a sense of strength and immunity to the consequences of life. Teens at this age do not yet have a sense of their own mortality. When unsure, teens may be emotionally wrapped up in themselves while processing information. They can be emotionally mercurial, rapidly changing from a mature calm to juvenile display. Intellectual skills will become focused more specifically on particular interests.

Teens are developing taste and discernment and are becoming more discriminating in their choices, including reading. They seek out and appreciate intellectual challenge and want to talk about all sorts of issues, including spirituality and religion; social issues that affect people their age, such as abortion, AIDS, date rape, school violence, and teen pregnancy; and larger social issues, such as the death penalty, euthanasia, hate crimes, homelessness, and disarmament. There is increased involvement in school activities.

Teens in the 10th grade become physical risk takers, especially boys, and physical injury is common. They seek adventure and a wide range of experiences. Peer pressure is strong to engage in mind-altering substances like drugs and alcohol. An exaggerated sense of freedom comes with the ability to drive and with jobs that provide personal income. Girls are physically mature, are more accepting of their unique biology; boys are still growing (until the early twenties). Statistically, about half of all boys and a quarter of all girls have had sex by age sixteen.

Ages 16 to 17, 11th Grade

Teens in the 11th grade are experiencing an end to the wild physical changes of their early adolescent years. They may be more willing to experience unique friendships and different social environments they wouldn't have dared before. Academic standards are particularly high in the 11th grade, especially for the college bound. With high expectations at school comes stress, and teens at this age may need to be reminded to play. Writing and speaking skills are increasingly strong. A unique sense of humor is in evidence. Teens in this stage of development can apply abstract thought, reasoning, and logic to real life situations. They are intellectually able to perceive shades of gray. They are no longer solely guessing at outcomes: decision making is based on experience. They are not as shocked as younger teens at the painful realities of life and of events and conditions in the world.

There is a strong focus on relationships, especially romantic, and teens will spend a great deal of time navigating this territory. The need for personal space continues to grow and these teens don't just want personal freedom, they expect it. They have by now developed a sense of individual direction. Sex is quite common in this stage of development, for both boys and girls.

Ages 17 to 18, 12th Grade

Teens in 12th grade are approaching adulthood with more confidence and trust in their own adult abilities. They have critical thinking skills in place to solve problems and have a solid mastery of complex issues. Although they are not spending much time with family, they are becoming more open to the opinions of parents and other adults, and are more likely to communicate with them about their lives and social situations when present. They may even feel they can give good advice to the adults in their lives regarding those adults' problems and issues.

This is a time of intense academic stress for the college bound, and connections with and respect for teachers may dramatically increase. Social groups begin to take second place to intimate relationships with the same or opposite sex. These relationships may be brief, but they are intense and often involve excruciating and lengthy breakups. Teens in the 12th grade often begin to try on adult roles to determine who they might become in the future.

There are loads of books that deal with all aspects of adolescence for the interested reading public, for parents and for teens themselves. If you'd like additional insight into the growing up of teens, check for books on the subject at your local library, or link to the Web sites on adolescent development provided at the end of this chapter.

UNDERSTANDING TEENS AS READERS

What do teens have to say about their reading habits and interests? Why do they read? Why don't they read? If they read, what sorts of books or other reading materials attract them? If they don't read, what might attract them to the pleasures of reading? How do teens feel about the classics in specific? What's their reputation with teens, and what are teens' responses to classics they've read? What are the common barriers to making meaningful classics connections with teens? How do teens feel about the reading challenges they find in classics? By seeking answers to these sorts of questions, both from teens themselves and from the professionals who study them, you will have many more tools to help you build stronger classics connection with teens.

A Little Skepticism Is Healthy!

I'll put my neck on the block right here (is that my head in the basket?) and state that apart from bona fide literacy research, which we'll look at below, I take the surveys of teens and the general literature discussing how teens do and don't read with many a grain of salt. In the years I've worked with teens, and in my personal relationships with them, I haven't detected many broad-scale patterns that have remained constant enough to lay claim to, with a couple of exceptions. Your experience may be different, but since I just mentioned mine, I ought to tell you what those are!

First, it does seem to be true that on the whole teen boys are not attracted to books with female protagonists, and it does seem to be true that on the whole teen girls are not nearly so gender-concerned when selecting books to read. Second, no matter how thrilling the literary joy ride, teens often associate books assigned in the classroom with work, not pleasure, especially in the middle grades.

I urge you to consider the source and apply a certain amount of healthy skepticism when familiarizing yourself with the literature. Even national or international surveys are still small samples of teen society that are not likely to be fully representative of the overall diversity in age, gender, ethnic experience, socioeconomic condition, educational background, and more, of the world of teens. Any measurement tool (such as a survey) has its own built-in biases, regardless of rigorous attempts on the parts of its creators to remain objective. Once collected, data can be interpreted in a number of ways. Many of the books and articles out there come from educators who may experience teen readers in the classroom only, an environment that cannot truly describe or define teens as readers in general. And, data that represent a national or international trend just may not hold true at the local level, which is where you are!

Whether you do or don't put stock in surveys, literature, and compiled teen opinion, you should put stock in teens themselves. The best way to understand the teens in your community is to start with one reader or prospective reader, ask questions, and listen to the answers. Engage in a conversation with a teen about favorite books and magazines, best and worst reading experiences, reading challenges, beloved childhood authors. Find out why a teen doesn't read, or doesn't enjoy reading.

Don't be afraid to talk to groups of teens, off-the-cuff or in arranged (but casual) meetings. My experience with teens in groups has always been great—they feed off of and build on each other's ideas, and you get lots of thoughts and opinions that wouldn't have come out otherwise.

Observe teens in your library or classroom. If in groups, listen to what they are saying to each other, try to determine the sorts of things that interest and matter to them. Be discreet, though. No hovering! As my mother always said, "If you remain quiet and watchful, people will rapidly reveal themselves." And, it goes without saying—but I will anyway—don't intrude in or eavesdrop on any private conversations. Between interacting with them and observing them, you'll learn most of what you really need to know about teens and their relationships to both reading in general and to the classics in specific.

Teen Readers and the Surveys

There have been several surveys over the past few years that either address or include teens as readers, and you may be surprised to discover the results reflect that teens are highly interested in reading, both to support practical goals and simply for pleasure. The National Education Association (NEA) conducted a poll on the reading habits of adolescents, dated February 2001, but it has been removed from the NEA Web site and I defy you to try to find it elsewhere (free of charge, anyway!). Of note, The American Library Association's Young Adult Library Services Association (YALSA) reports this hard-to-locate survey found that teens between the ages of 12 and 18 rated reading as the first most important skill required to succeed in life.

In 1999, Teenage Research Unlimited (TRU), a marketing group that researches teen needs and wants, conducted a survey of 2,000 teens, ages 12 to 19, and found that 61 percent of them read for pleasure. You can read additional details about this survey in the July-August 1999 issue of the now-defunct *Book* magazine. (You could also go to TRU's Web site at http://www.teenresearch.com, but you have to become a paying subscriber to view their reports.) *Book* magazine conducted its own small reading survey of 425 high school teens in six states that same year, half of whom reported they read two or more books each month, and some of whom said they wished they had more time to read. *Book* also reported on older teens' interest in reading materials other than books, which is quite high—71 percent read magazines and 70 percent read newspapers (Kloberdanz 1999, 35).

Then there's the SmartGirl survey. For Teen Read Week in October 2002, the American Library Association and SmartGirl surveyed teens about reading. The results are posted online at http://www.smartgirl.org/reports/1493716.html. Results reflect the responses of 6,458 teens, a considerable number more than the 2,809 teens who responded to the first survey in 2000. Sixty-three percent of the respondents were girls, 37 percent were boys. Although respondents in the 2000 survey were identified by gender (which for a few of the results made a considerable difference, like the part where 41 percent of the girls most often read for pleasure compared to only 23 percent of the boys), the 2002 survey does not provide results by gender. In any case, on the following page is a distillation of survey results for all respondents.

Of note, top ten results from respondents are also included for kinds of books, types of characters, best book read for fun, and best books ever, and these results are fun to look at. Interestingly enough, in the category of "Top Ten Best Books Ever 2002," eight of the ten books selected by surveyed teens are broadly considered classics.

Results of 2002 SmartGirl Survey

- Almost 74% of the respondents who said they like reading a lot are themselves advanced readers. Only 22% of the people who don't like reading are advanced readers.
- 58% of the respondents "always read things that they are passionate about."
- 54% of the respondents read constantly for their own personal satisfaction, 26% read only what they are required to read for school, and 21% don't read much at all.
- Almost 3,200 respondents agreed or strongly agreed that they wish they had more time for pleasure reading.
- The reasons the respondents read are: just for the fun of it (55%), to learn new things (54%), for school (42%), because they're bored and there's nothing else to do (30%).
- The reasons the respondents don't read are: because it's boring (19%), no time (19%), and it isn't cool (7%).
- 21% of the respondents have friends who like to read and discuss books.
- Considerably over half of the respondents read 0 to 3 books per month. Approximately 25% read 3 to 10 books per month. Approximately 13% read more than 10 books per month. (Based on examination of a pie chart with no percentages provided.)
- Favorite reading materials for respondents are books for pleasure (by a long shot), followed by fashion, music, and sports magazines. Manuals are respondents' least favorite reading material. Class books (not precisely defined) are pretty low down on the list, too.
- Respondents visited public libraries an average of once every three months, and school libraries once a week.
- Over half of the respondents were read to a lot as children, 34% were read to some of the time as children, 10% were rarely read to as children, and 5% were never read to as children.
- Respondents primarily get their books at school libraries, followed by public libraries, bookstores, as gifts, from parents, from friends, and from teachers.

Teen Readers in the Professional Literature

Just what is the professional literature? It's a huge and weighty beast comprised predominantly of a broad range of statistical reports based on long-term research, educated opinion, not so educated opinion, essays, articles, books, and so forth by folks of all sorts—government agencies, independent advocacy and research organizations, publishers, editors, educators, marketing firms, librarians, and that ilk—who care about teens, how and if they read, and what that means for their lives, for society at large, and for the future. Long sentence, big-picture stuff!

It's a good thing to familiarize yourself with the larger trends and issues in, shall we use the official term just this once, "adolescent literacy." It's a useful framework on which you can hang the teen reading trends and issues you observe in your local community. Even if you find that some of the larger trends don't show in your community, it's good to know what's going on outside your community. Some of this information is sobering, some of it hopeful. All of it will go a long way toward convincing you how much you really do matter in the reading lives of teens and how great an impact you can make by successfully introducing them to great books that will matter to them.

But wait, you couldn't possibly wade through all of the available literature about teens and reading and still get started on your classics reading plan! Lots of literacy research and current discussion about teens and reading deals more specifically with how educators can work with teens in the classroom environment to increase literacy skills, promote a positive relationship with reading, and help teens thoroughly comprehend what they read. If you are an educator, hey, that's great! If you are a librarian, this is not so much your bailiwick. To help you out, you'll find a few (and hopefully relevant) entry points into the literature below, including well-known sources of teen literacy data, organizations and programs that lead in teen literacy support, and some of the myths and truths of teen readers as expressed in current books, articles, and essays.

YALSA has in the past maintained an outstanding set of Web pages providing a lengthy list of current Web sites, surveys, and publications about teens and reading. With the recent redesign of the ALA Web site, you may have to do some investigative work to get to it. If you can't find it, drop them a line and let them know you want this information made readily available.

Teen Literacy Data

Unlike small-sample surveys of teens and general opinion about teens as readers, this is the stuff you might not need to take with so many grains of salt. The data provided through the U.S. Department of Education are based on long-term, detailed research and assessment. The RAND Corporation is a fifty-year-old research and analysis organization of the highest repute. These are two of the most well-known providers of current data on teen literacy, and you can use the information they provide to identify trends in and the current state of adolescent reading at large. Although we won't explore it here, you might also check out the National Reading Conference, a literacy research and discussion organization at http://www.nrconline.org.

The Nation's Report Card
http://nces.ed.gov/nationsreportcard/

Under the guidance of the Commissioner of Education Statistics at the National Center for Education Statistics (NCES) in the U.S. Department of Education, the National Assessment of Educational Progress (NAEP) conducts annual assessments of a broad sample of American students at the 4th, 8th, and 12th grade levels in the arts, civics, geography, math, reading, science, and U.S. history.

The reading assessment, conducted since 1971, looks at how youth are reading across the nation during different stages of academic development. How does the assessment work?

- Students read complete texts from typical grade-appropriate sources.
- Students read three types of texts representing different contexts for reading:
  - reading for literary experience
  - reading for information
  - reading to perform a task (grades 8 and 12 only)
- Students answer a combination of multiple-choice and constructed-response questions.
  (from the NAEP Web site http://nces.ed.gov/nationsreportcard/reading/results2002/)

The 2002 reading assessment was conducted with about 270,000 young people, including 8th grade teens in 4,706 schools and 12th grade teens in 725 schools across the nation. The 2003 assessment has been completed and results will be available at the above Web site in fall 2004. The NAEP also provides average scores by gender, ethnicity, and state.

So, what did they find out this year, and how does it compare with the numbers in the past? The bottom line is that 4th grade reading scores improved slightly in recent years but matched 1992 scores, 8th grade reading scores remained relatively unchanged since 1998, and 12th grade reading scores declined since 1998. Teen readers on the whole demonstrated basic proficiency at reading, but did not demonstrate advanced skills in reading comprehension and ability to communicate about what they've read. The actual numbers and how they fall into the NAEP's reading achievement levels (base, proficient, and advanced) are provided through the Web site.

What does this mean? Most folks believe it means teens are getting a short shrift in school when it comes to reading. After the 8th grade, teens aren't being cultivated as readers and aren't advancing beyond the basic levels of reading they achieved in the 8th grade. They can read the words, but they don't know what the words mean.

In 2002, the NAEP began a new trial assessment in reading and writing in five urban school districts in Atlanta, Chicago, Houston, Los Angeles, and New York City (which only participated at the 4th grade level). If you are a public or school youth services librarian or educator in one of these areas, it might be useful to you to explore this in detail. You can find a full report at http://nces.ed.gov/nationsreportcard/reading/results2002/districtresults.asp.

The RAND Reading Study Group
http://www.rand.org/multi/achievementforall/reading/

Under contract with the U.S. Department of Education's Office of Educational Research and Improvement (OERI), fourteen experts in reading and reading-related studies were brought together as the RAND Reading Study Group to research and report on the state of reading at the secondary level. The report lays out a ten- to fifteen-year research plan to study and address urgent issues in reading, including reading comprehension, instruction that promotes that comprehension, how to test reading comprehension, and how to produce positive reading outcomes in youth so they can increase understanding through reading.

The RAND report, *Reading for Understanding: Toward a R&D Program in Reading Comprehension* (2002) includes a great deal of statistical and general information about teen reading and comprehension and can be downloaded in full or viewed by chapter at the Study Group's Web site.

Teen Literacy Support

With an increasing understanding of the literacy needs of America's teens, some dedicated organizations in recent years have taken on the task of providing public support for teen literacy improvement and for just plain encouraging teens to read for fun. Of note are YALSA, which initiated the nationwide Teen Read Week program to encourage teens to read for pleasure, and the International Reading Association (IRA), an extraordinary organization dedicated to improved literacy for all, with a specific focus on adolescent literacy.

ALA/YALSA and Teen Read Week
http://www.ala.org/ala/yalsa/teenreading/teenreading.htm
(the 2004 URL)

YALSA initiated Teen Read Week several years ago to support library promotion of reading for fun with teens. Teen Read Week occurs each October, and youth services librarians around the country are encouraged to join this national campaign at their local level. A committee chooses a different reading theme each year, and support materials and graphics are available for purchase from the association.

During this week, YALSA encourages school and public librarians to visibly celebrate reading for fun with teens in their libraries, schools, and communities and offers ideas to do so, including reading-related programs, colorful displays, bookmarks, booklists, promotions, surveys (the official Teen Read Week survey is also the SmartGirl survey), book reviewing contests, raffles, and prizes.

The International Reading Association
http://www.reading.org

The IRA is comprised of members in ninety-nine countries from a wide range of literacy-related professions, including educators at all levels of instruction, reading specialists, librarians, researchers, and many more. The organization's primary goal is to encourage and support high-level literacy by providing tools for improved reading instruction, distributing reading-related research and information, and by motivating a love of life-long reading.

In 1999, the IRA's Commission on Adolescent Literacy published *Adolescent Literacy: A Position Statement* (available in print or as a PDF download from the IRA Web site at http://www.reading.org/pdf/1036.pdf), which begins by unequivocally stating that adolescents *deserve* the same attention to literacy development that is given to children in the early years. Why? According to the position statement, adolescents on the brink of adulthood in the twenty-first century will need advanced reading and writing skills more than at any other time—simply to engage in the tasks of adult daily life and to successfully synthesize the volume of information they will be confronted with in an ever-increasingly complex society and world. And more, a high level of literacy will improve their imaginative capabilities so they might contribute to a better society and world, perhaps even participate in its design—for their own futures and beyond.

The position statement also details seven principles for supporting teen literacy growth, all starting with the words, "Adolescents deserve. . . ." Pages four through nine of the PDF document provide a detailed look at these principles. It turns out that your efforts connecting teen readers with the classics fit right into these principles—from representing the value and importance of literacy in adolescents' communities, to providing access to reading materials that appeal to a broad range of young readers at varying levels of interest and skill! The position statement also includes an extensive list of articles and other publications that address each principle.

The IRA also produced a joint position paper with the National Middle School Association, available at the IRA Web site. This paper, "Supporting Young Adolescents' Literacy Learning: A Joint Position Paper of the International Reading Association and National Middle School Association," includes a basic list of educational services middle schools should provide teen readers. It also provides bulleted "call to action" lists for educators, a wide variety of administrators, educational support staff, and family and community members to help middle school teens improve their literacy skills. If all of this weren't enough, visit the IRA Web site's section on adolescent literacy for an extensive list of related publications and links.

Characteristics of Teen Readers

The professional literature includes articles, essays, and books that express many viewpoints on and ideas about teens as readers, some written by people who work directly with teens, others written by people who work in various professions related to or reliant on teens. Some of these viewpoints and ideas are based in fact; others are passionate opinion. Some are contradictory, but many are similar. One way or the other, it's all fascinating stuff!

If you want to explore the teen reader topic in the literature, you can browse the literature-rich Web sites of the organizations listed above, dig into periodical and special topic databases, or start with the short list of current resources at the end of this section. I've also provided a short list of periodicals that regularly include articles on teen readers you might pursue for further information. Again, if you are a librarian, keep in mind that the majority of these resources are based in the educational world, and you may from time to time have to pick and choose the content that's most relevant to youth services librarianship and to making classics connections.

If you aren't inclined, or just don't have time to read up on this topic, and so that you can bundle up on the couch with a cup of steamy coffee, a chocolate croissant, and that next classic you've chosen to become engrossed in, I've pulled together for you a few short-but-sweet lists of the commonly held views about teens as readers found in the current literature.

Commonly Held Views About Teens as Readers

Why teens don't read:

- Peers discourage reading as a positive activity
- Reading is not valued in the home
- They have not been nurtured as readers in the classroom
- They are not introduced to reading materials that attract their interest
- They have economic and cultural barriers to reading and learning, including difficulties with the English language, and a lack of opportunity due to poverty
- Poor readers associate reading with failure

Why teens do read:

- They enjoy it
- To find out what they need to know
- To get better grades in school
- To continue their education past high school
- They know they need to read well to succeed in life

(continued)

(continued)

What teen readers want:

- To have lots of reading choices
- To make their own pleasure reading choices
- Guidance on what they might read without pressure to make a particular choice
- To make their own reading choices for school assignments (not to be limited to one title)
- Time to read for pleasure
- Their cultural identity and experience represented in reading choices
- To talk about what they read in a respectful environment, with peers and with adults

What male teen readers want:

- Reading choices with protagonists they can model
- Reading choices with action
- Alternatives to traditional fiction, such as magazines, graphic novels, and nonfiction books
- Social acceptance of reading
- Adult male modeling of reading

In addition to the surveys, literacy data, and information from support organizations listed above, this information on teen readers was compiled with the help of these resources:

Abrahamson, Maria. 2001. "Why Boys Don't Read." *Book* January/February: 86–88.

Aronson, Marc. 2000. "The Myths of Teenage Readers." *Publishing Research Quarterly* 16 (3): 4–9.

Baker, Marianne I. 2002. "Reading Resistance in Middle School: What Can Be Done?" *Journal of Adolescent and Adult Literacy* 45 (5): 364–366.

Clinton, Patrick. 2002. "Literacy in America: The Crisis You Don't Know about, and What We Can Do about It." *Book* September/October: Available online at: http://www.bookmagazine.com/issue24/literacy.shtml (accessed 29 August 2003).

Jones, Patrick, ed. 2002. *New Directions for Library Services to Young Adults*. Chicago: American Library Association.

Here's a short list of a few magazines and journals that regularly explore teen literacy issues:

Education Week. 1981–. Irregular weekly. Bethesda, MD: Editorial Projects in Education, Inc.

English Journal. 1998–. Bimonthly. Urbana, IL: National Council of Teachers of English.

Journal of Adolescent and Adult Literacy. 1995–. Monthly. Newark, DE: The International Reading Association.

Reading Today. 1985–. Bimonthly. Newark, DE: The International Reading Association.

Teen Readers and the Classics

Teen responses to reading in general can be consciousness-raising for you as a librarian or educator and can translate to the classics to some degree, but you should also explore teens specifically as classics readers (or not!) to get a more thorough understanding of their relationships (or not!) to this sort of literature. By doing so, you give yourself a greater understanding of both the hurdles and rewards in making successful classics connections with teens.

How Teens Think about the Classics

What reputation do the classics have with teens? For those who haven't yet read any classics on their own or have only tried one or two that weren't good matches, or for those who have only experienced classics as required canonical reading in the classroom, the reputation is generally not so great. I'll bet if you asked the teens, parents, and educational colleagues in your area, you'd get responses similar to the ones I'll share with you here. Remember that reputation and reading response are different things—reputation is an ascribed response without lots of direct knowledge or relationship to something, and reading response is a specific reaction based on first-hand experience.

Let's start with a few written responses from those anonymous Bothell (Washington) High School seniors when asked if classics have a good or bad reputation with teens.

A few of them say it all depends:

- "Some good, some bad . . . depends on size, and content of the book."
- "I think classics have both reputations. It all depends on what you read."

A few more say classics have a distinctly bad reputation with teens:

- "Bad, because most teens think they will be boring."
- "Bad, because a classic to some teens means something that is boring and uninteresting."
- "They have a bad rep. because many teens see them as VERY long books that are hard to understand."

And here are a couple with smacks for peers and compliments for the classics!

- "I think sometimes bad because a lot of teens are too simple minded and don't want to take the time to read something beautiful."
- "Depends, bad only because the majority of teens don't read. Good because they have ideas in them that a teen needs to understand to make them feel more whole."

Jackie Lockerby, the passionate teen reader from Minnesota you first met in Chapter 1, goes with the bad reputation, too:

> Bad! "Classic" is very, very often synonymous with "boring." Until one is used to the different writing styles, classics are difficult to read and truly understand, and not a lot of people take the time to learn to understand those styles. To use Shakespeare as an example [once again], most teenagers think he is incredibly boring. And yet, his stories are full of everything that our modern bestsellers are: everything from murder and impossible love to dirty jokes and insulting humor. He covers nearly every topic under the sun, from the obviously unsuccessful lovers of *Romeo and Juliet* to the laughter-filled and ironic courtship of Benedick and Beatrice in *Much Ado About Nothing* (Awesome book, [smiley face]). (2002)

University of Washington writing instructor and parent of a teen, Scott Driscoll, says, "Bad. Teens think they are universally boring" (2002), and KCLS Educational Services Coordinator, JoAnn Vanderkooi, agrees. "I think they have a bad reputation with teens. The impression of teens is that the classics are very long, boring and arduous to read, with lengthy sentence structure and dated and difficult vocabulary. Why?—because sometimes that is true" (2002).

These remarks come from a small group of respondents, so again, take any larger application with a grain of salt. It wouldn't be a surprise, though, if the larger application holds true. Feeling dismayed? Understandable! But that's part of what this book is all about, getting around the negative stuff and making meaningful classics connections with teens. By doing so, you will contribute to a real classics reputation tide-turning!

Positive Teen Experiences of the Classics

If you're feeling discouraged, don't forget that two of the Bothell High School seniors above wrote that although the reputation of classics was bad with teens, their personal beliefs about classics include that they are "beautiful" and full of ideas "to make them feel more whole." Right on! That's not to say there aren't teens who've read classics and had rotten reading experiences. I'm sure with a larger sample of teens, we could list any number of negative remarks about the classics. It could be that a teen picked up a classic on his or her own that was too mature, too long, too dark, too experimental, too dry, what have you. It could be that a teen was strongly encouraged to read a classic that was not personally resonant or relevant. It could be any of the myriad reasons bad matches are made between readers and books. And teens, in my experience, can be especially prone to sweeping generalities—if one classic is a dud, it follows that all classics are duds. You've got to do your best to stop that line of reasoning!

In the next section we'll look at some of the common reasons why teens are turned off to the classics, and throughout the remainder of the book we'll explore practical ways to help them make more successful classics connections. Since this section is sandwiched between our look at the mostly-bad reputation classics have with teens and the following section on classics turnoffs for teens, let's bolster your possibly sagging spirits now with a few remarks that reflect positive classics reading responses.

The Bothell High School seniors, when asked what their classics readings experiences were like, expressed:

- "GOOD! I loved [this expressed with a heart symbol] 98% of them!" (This teen, whom I feel I can safely assume is a young woman, put two extra colored-in hearts around Jean Jacques Rousseau, though she didn't note what she read of his. Amazing!)
- "*Catcher in the Rye* was fun to read and gave me another view on life."
- "*Little Women* taught me a lot about life and dreams."
- "I like the classics that I have read. I think it was a great experience, but at times it had its downside." (Alas, this teen did not expound on the downside.)
- "*Little Women*. I love that book and it has a lot of great messages in it. Life lessons."
- "*Frankenstein* because I thought it was really well put together and very interesting."

And this, from a master of redundancy:

• "Depends on the book, but always meaningful and thought provoking, depending on the book."

From Jackie Lockerby:

Earth-shattering would probably describe my response to *Anne of Green Gables* and *Chronicles of Narnia*. For one, those books were the first books I ever read that weren't part of some very clichéd series like the *Baby-sitters Club*. They were also the end of my reading any of those series, and the beginning of my reading everything I could get my hands onto. (2002)

And Rochelle Coons, parent of a 14-year-old teen who loves to read classics, shares:

The classics have a good reputation with my teen because she sees that they can have the double benefit of pleasure and learning. She also realized these stories have a strength within them that will linger throughout a lifetime. That's not to say she will like every classic she ever reads, but she recognizes and does have a respect for them and will be able to even find value in things which may not be to her personal taste. (2003)

Common Barriers to Teen Classic Connections

Reputations are often formed and passed on with minimal (or no) real understanding or experience, so let's go a bit beyond reputation and look more specifically at what, in the world of real and direct reading experience, can turn teens off to the classics. From teen, parent, educator, and librarian responses, I compiled this list of common classics turnoffs.

Common Classics Turnoffs

It's a turnoff when a classic is:

- Boring and dry
- Too difficult for a teen's reading level
- Beyond a teen's intellectual capability
- Too mature for a teen's social understanding

(continued)

(continued)

- Too long for a teen's attention or patience spans
- Not relevant or resonant to a teen's internal or external worlds
- Written in an unfamiliar style with unfamiliar language
- Required reading at home or in school regardless of personal interest or response

It's a turnoff when a classic doesn't:

- Encourage a personal or emotional response
- Have enough action or forward movement
- Have an attractive cover

It's a turnoff when adults:

- Tell teens to read specific classics without being able to tell them why they are important
- Don't help teens find meaning in classics through themes or other elements with which they can relate
- Don't provide any historical or thematic context for understanding a classic
- Tell teens, "It's good for you"

The following chapters in this book will help you avoid the turnoffs and emphasize what turns teens *on* in books to help them make the best possible classics connections.

Are Teens up to a Literary Challenge?

We've just listed common turnoffs to classics connections with teens, significant among them being language and content beyond a teen's intellectual and other developmental levels. I think it's important here to differentiate between a classic that is out of reach and a classic that is a challenge. As stated above, a book that is too difficult for a teen's reading level, beyond a teen's intellectual capability, or too mature for a teen's social understanding is out of reach. A book that is not "too" anything, but may be a reading challenge, is not inherently a bad thing and can in fact be attractive to a teen reader.

Sure, there are plenty of teens who don't read much, if at all, let alone read a book that might take some effort. There are a fair number of teens who do read, but, often having never read one, believe classics are just as horrifying an experience as being forced to eat boiled tongue and rutabagas. On the other hand, you will meet plenty of teens in your career as a librarian or educator who don't read much because they are discouraged and can't seem to connect with books that challenge them enough. You will encounter teens who want great books that mean something to them and move them and are willing to accept any challenge involved in finding that meaningful reading experience.

A large number of reading teens, as well teens who strive to lead a book-free existence, will admit to you that they loved it when their teacher or parent read Barrie's *Peter Pan* to them in elementary school, or when they read Grahame's *Wind in the Willows* for the first time on their own. I've had even the most reluctant, arms-crossed-over-chest, slouched-in-their-seats teens admit to a fondness for the classics of their childhood. Scan a few pages of those classic children's books sometime and note the enormous number of quite sophisticated vocabulary words within. When a book is magical and meaningful, complexity doesn't stop young readers for an instant. Michael Clay Thompson has a truly fascinating section in his book that lists, in alphabetical order, samples of vocabulary words from these two books and other classics for young people (1990, 8–13). You might pick other childhood and crossover classics off your library's shelves and note the complexity of structure and language.

Teens are no less, and are arguably far more, capable of meeting literary challenges than are children. In my experience with teen readers, a challenging classic—one that is not simply too difficult for a teen reader—is not a turnoff or stopping point for teens, not nearly so often as common stereotypes of teen readers might suggest. Like adults, a challenge is something many teens anticipate as readers, something to be relished. A Bothell High School senior, who, when asked how he responded to the classics he's read, said, "I liked them because they were interesting and hard to read." Another senior at the same school, in response to the same question, said the classics she'd read were, "very meaningful, sometimes challenging to understand but worth the challenge." In a 2001 *Book* magazine article, John Sexton, a teen services librarian in Ashland, Oregon, spoke about his son, a reluctant reader, who picked up a work of classic fiction and enjoyed reading it. "He's never had too many emotional responses to fiction, but he had one to this book. It's a classic book. It's a hard book. And he liked it—it made him angry" (Abrahamson 2001, 86).

Yes, you may say, but those quotes are from or about older teens. What about the early middle grades readers? My experience has shown me that younger teens also like a good challenge and, like all people of all ages, are innately curious about and interested in what is presently beyond them. What you select to promote to teens in middle/junior high school will necessarily be different, but I believe they are no more likely to reject a book that takes a little time and effort than one that doesn't—if it is within reach and does not set up a younger reader for frustration and failure.

Your Very Own Homegrown Classics Survey

Why not conduct your own local survey specific to teens as classics readers? Although I've said I take surveys with several grains of salt, I do think you could gain some interesting insight into your local teen population with a survey that allows teens in your school or community to tell you how they feel about the classics. And not only would you collect information that could help you connect teens to classics, you are giving them the opportunity to tell an adult in their environment what they think about something, which is an invaluable opportunity to a group of young people who do not generally feel they are heard or understood. Good stuff all around.

You might start by thinking about what you'd like to know. What do the teens in your local population think classics are? What reputation do classics have with them? Do you want to know whether they've ever read any, and if so, what their reading experiences were, best and worst? Who introduced them to classics? What are their best and worst experiences with other librarians and educators regarding the classics? Do you want to have an idea of the most popular sorts of themes or characters that currently resonate with teens? There are loads of interesting questions you could ask that would allow you to gain additional insight to build better classics collections, read more successfully yourself from the wide range of classic literature out there, and better promote classics to teens in your library or educational environment.

If you do design a classics survey for teens, you'll want to make it attractive, keep it simple, and think about how to get it to teens. You might consider some sort of incentive to complete the form, like a one-time removal of fines in the library, an extra credit point, or a free book for filling out the survey.

You can follow all the usual media channels available to you, like having it printed in school newspapers and PTA bulletins. You could ask to have it loaded on your school library Web site, or if you're a public librarian, on all your service area school Web sites and on your public library's Web site. It would be great if you could manage to have your technical folks design a survey that could be filled out online. You could ask to have an advertisement for your survey read with daily school announcements or on the student video news network for a period of time. Or you could go the old-fashioned route and have a bunch of those attractive surveys you designed laying around on tables in your school library, classroom, school cafeteria, public library teen area, and other highly visible places teens may go. If you are a librarian, you might even ask to visit classrooms yourself to explain why it's important to you to learn what teens think about classics and hand out copies of your survey.

In the end, you've got to make it easy for them to get their responses back to you. Have drop-off boxes every place you've got surveys, and a few other places as well. Make it clear on the survey the many locations where teens can turn them in. Collecting these will likely involve some legwork on your part, but will be worth the effort.

SUMMING IT UP

To understand teens as a broad range of young people in rapid stages of growth will better equip you to understand and assist them as readers in general, and as readers of the classics in particular. This understanding, coupled with the theories about and characteristics of teen readers, will go a long way toward helping you remove reading barriers and encourage strong classics connections for teens of all ages and stages of development. Remember that not all teens go through these stages of development at the same time in the same way, so always make classics connections with each individual in mind. For the thoughts and opinions of teens in your community, both as readers in general and as readers of the classics, just ask them!

WORKS CITED

Abrahamson, Maria. 2001. "Why Boys Don't Read." *Book* January/Feburary: 86–88.

The Adolescent Years. New York: The Columbia University College of Physicians and Surgeons. Available online at: http://cpmcnet.columbia.edu/texts/guide/toc/toc08.html (accessed 4 January 2003).

Aronson, Marc. 2000. "The Myths of Teenage Readers." *Publishing Research Quarterly* 16 (3): 4–9.

Baker, Marianne I. 2002. "Reading Resistance in Middle School: What Can Be Done?" *Journal of Adolescent and Adult Literacy* 45 (5): 364–366.

Bothell High School Seniors. 2002. Written responses to questionnaires. Bothell, WA: 2 October.

Clinton, Patrick. 2002. "Literacy in America: The Crisis You Don't Know about, and What We Can Do about It." *Book* September/October: Available online at: http://www.bookmagazine.com/issue24/literacy.shtml (accessed 29 August 2003).

Coons, Rochelle. 2003. Written response to questionnaire. Bothell, WA: 10 January.

Driscoll, Scott. 2002. Written response to questionnaire. Seattle, WA: 22 October.

Havighurst, Robert. *Developmental Tasks of Normal Adolescence*. Bloomington, IN: School of Education, Center for Adolescent and Family Studies. Adapted from Gary M. Ingersoll's book, *Normal Adolescence*, forthcoming. Available online at: http://education.indiana.edu/cas/devtask.html (accessed 4 January 2003).

The International Reading Association. Newark, DE: The International Reading Association. Available online at: http://www.reading.org/ (accessed 29 August 2003).

Jones, Patrick, ed. 2002. *New Directions for Library Services to Young Adults*. Chicago: American Library Association.

Kloberdanz, Kristin. 1999. "So You Don't Think Kids Read Anymore? Think Again. Turns Out They're Booksmart." *Book* July/August: 34–38.

Latest Survey Results: Teen Read Week 2002. Ann Arbor, MI: Smartgirl.org. Available online at: http://www.smartgirl.org/reports/1493716.html (accessed 16 March 2003).

Lockerby, Jackie. 2002. Written response to questionnaire. Faribault, MN: 22 October.

Moore, David W., et al. 1999. *Adolescent Literacy: A Position Statement*. Newark, DE: The International Reading Association.

Normal Adolescent Development: Late High School Years and Beyond. Washington, DC: American Academy of Child and Adolescent Psychiatry. Available online at: http://www.aacap.org/publications/factsfam/develop2.htm (accessed 4 January 2003).

Normal Adolescent Development: Middle School and Early High School Years. Washington, DC: American Academy of Child and Adolescent Psychiatry. Available online at: http://www.aacap.org/publications/factsfam/develop. htm (accessed 4 January 2003).

The Parent Soup Development Tracker. New York: iVillage.com: The Women's Network. Available online at: http://www.parentsoup.com/tracker (accessed 4 January 2003).

RAND Reading Study Group. Santa Monica, CA: RAND Corporation. Available online at: http://www.rand.org/multi/achievementforall/reading/ (accessed 29 August 2003).

Reading 2002 Major Results. Washington, DC: United States Department of Education, Institute of Education Sciences, National Center for Education Statistics, National Assessment of Educational Progress. Available online at: http://nces.ed.gov/nationsreoprtcard/reading/results2002/ (accessed 29 August 2003).

Teen Reading: Teen Read Week. Chicago: American Library Association, Young Adult Library Services Association. Available online at: http://www.ala. org/ala/yalsa/teenreading/teenreading.htm (accessed 29 August 2003).

Thompson, Michael Clay. 1990. *Classics in the Classroom*. Monroe, NY: Trillium Press.

Vanderkooi, JoAnn. 2002. Written response to questionnaire. Issaquah, WA: 29 October.

ONLINE RESOURCES ON ADOLESCENT DEVELOPMENT

The Adolescent Years
http://cpmcnet.columbia.edu/texts/guide/toc/toc08.html
   The Columbia University College of Physicians and Surgeons *Complete Home Medical Guide* online provides a chapter on all aspects of adolescent development, including physical and psychosocial/social development.

The Child Development Institute
   These links on Erickson's and Piaget's developmental stages are from the Child Development Institute, founded by Robert Myers, Ph.D., a Clinical Child Psychologist with twenty years of experience working with children, adolescents, and their families.

   Stages of Social-Emotional Development in Children and Teenagers
   http://www.childdevelopmentinfo.com/development/erickson.shtml

   Stages of Intellectual Development in Children and Teenagers
   http://www.childdevelopmentinfo.com/development/piaget.shtml

Development Tracker
http://www.parentsoup.com/tracker/
   From Parent Soup's online Development Tracker: "This year-by-year guide helps you follow your child's development from the toddler years through 12th grade. You'll find a range of skills for each age and grade level, from academic abilities to social development and growth spurts."

Developmental Tasks of Normal Adolescence
http://education.indiana.edu/cas/devtask.html
   This link from the Indiana University Center for Adolescent Studies provides a list of eleven developmental tasks that adolescents will normally accomplish in making the transition to adulthood, as originally described by Professor Robert Havighurst of the University of Chicago. Adapted from Gary M. Ingersoll's book, *Normal Adolescence* (Bloomington, IN: Center for Adolescent Studies, forthcoming).

   Normal Adolescent Development: Middle School and Early High School Years
   http://www.aacap.org/publications/factsfam/develop.htm

Normal Adolescent Development: Late High School Years and Beyond
http://www.aacap.org/publications/factsfam/develop2.htm.

From the American Academy of Child and Adolescent Psychiatry, these fact sheets for families describe the normal phases of adolescent development for both the early and late teen years.

5

FIND AND COMBINE CLASSICS
TO ATTRACT TEEN READERS

As a librarian or educator, the primary methods available to you for connecting teen readers to great classic reading, listening, or viewing selections are through teen-friendly classics collections in your library or school, merchandizing and display, direct and "passive" readers' advisory, programs and activities, and booktalking. The remainder of this book will look at each of these methods in detail. But before you can use any of those methods to connect teens to the classics, you need to know the best classics out there to connect them to!

This chapter—the last of the behind-the-scenes, groundwork-laying chapters—takes a look at the many types of classics you can use in your work with teens, including the shorter formats, and a few categories of "must-know" classics. It then explores some simple techniques to capture teen interest and many of the combinations you can make between the classics, and between classics and just about everything else, to attract teen readers and bring compelling and meaningful reading experiences into their lives.

By knowing what kinds of classics are available to you and to teens, and by thinking about how you might combine them, you will be far better equipped to make the most meaningful classics connections for individual teens, to develop outstanding displays in your classroom or library, to provide appealing readers' advisory tools for teens and colleagues, to explore interesting ideas for classics book discussion groups and other programming activities, and, last but not least, to dynamically booktalk the classics to classrooms and other teen groups.

CLASSICS OF ALL KINDS FOR TEENS OF ALL KINDS

Most folks equate classic literature with the sorts of full-length titles Penguin, Bantam, or Signet publish. You know, the ones with the painterly portraits and landscapes on the covers. That tends to amount to a handful of Russians, a large portion of Brits, and a number of Americans from the turn of the last century. Not only are there far, far more classics than are dreamt of in a single publisher's line, there are far, far more formats of classic writing than the novel or full-length nonfiction book.

When connecting teens to literary classics, think outside of the box—or outside of the book. Include classics of all kinds. Why? Because there are teen readers of all kinds! Don't forget classic short stories, plays, poems, fairy tales, myths, legends, and maybe even essays and speeches. Some of these are among the most powerful, most emotionally and spiritually rousing writings you'll find, and most of them are not as lengthy as a book and can interest and engage teens who at the present time can't or won't invest in anything longer.

Short Stories

Short stories vary from really short shorts, which aren't generally longer than one or two typeset pages, to near-novellas. Just like books, they come in all flavors—from lighthearted, silly fluff to heavy-duty depth, from mainstream fiction to genres of all sorts. Just like books, there are great classics among them. Stories have all the elements of great fiction—from rich characterization to compelling story arc, from plot complication to climax and resolution—they just do it in considerably fewer pages. They can pack a real intellectual, emotional, and psychological punch and are great choices with teens of all kinds, and perhaps especially with reluctant and struggling readers.

Short story classics are found in many places: in collections by individual authors, in anthologies, on the Internet, you name it. You won't have any trouble finding them to share with teens. In addition to the short story lists that follow, there's a list of "Selected Anthologies of Classic and 'Best' Short Stories" at the end of this chapter.

Short Story Classics

- "A & P," John Updike (1962)
- "The Gift of the Magi," O. Henry (1906)
- "The Lottery," Shirley Jackson (1948)
- "The Necklace," Guy de Maupassant (1884)
- "The Notorious Jumping Frog of Calaveras County," Mark Twain (1867)
- "An Occurrence at Owl Creek Bridge," Ambrose Bierce (1891)
- "The Shawl," Cynthia Ozick (1981)
- "The Sky is Gray," Ernest J. Gaines (1968)
- "Where Are You Going, Where Have You Been?" Joyce Carol Oates (1967)
- "Yentl the Yeshiva Boy," Isaac Bashevis Singer (1962)

Genre Short Story Classics

- "The Cold Equations," Tom Godwin (1954) Science Fiction
- "Comanche Woman," Fred Grove (1963) Western
- "The Guns of William Longley," by Donald Hamilton (1967) Western
- "Haircut," Ring Lardner (1926) Mystery
- "A Jury of Her Peers," Susan Glaspell (1917) Mystery
- "The Monkey's Paw," W. W. Jacobs (1902) Horror
- "The Nine Billion Names of God," Arthur C. Clarke (1967) Science Fiction
- "Quitters, Inc.," Stephen King (1978) Horror
- "Sandkings," George R. R. Martin (1979) Science Fiction
- "The Tell-Tale Heart," Edgar Allen Poe (1843) Horror

Plays

The middle and high school years are a time when teens are increasingly exposed to dramatic works in literature classes, drama classes, and in school drama productions. A fair number of teens are involved in theater arts of some sort in their schools, be they smaller classroom-produced skits or larger-scale theatrical productions. Even those teens who aren't participants in the dramatic side of the middle and high school grades are often easy to interest in plays. Don't forget to connect interested teens to the richness and meaning to be found in classic dramatic works.

There are many plays that have themes that will be appealing to teens, from classical antiquity to the present. There are reference resources galore just waiting on the shelves of your local libraries that can help you select and understand plays. There are often film and television versions and various sorts of spoken word versions that you can use to bridge to classic plays for teens in your library or classroom, or incorporate into booktalks.

This all leads me to Shakespeare. The Bard is a challenge to most teen readers, and to most adult readers, for that matter. The hurdles of unfamiliar language and structure are there, to be sure. If you are an educator who connects teens to the Bard in a meaningful way in your classroom, well, good for you! If you are a librarian, it might be hard to sell teens on Shakespeare's works in your library, or as a booktalker without an assignment tie-in, or without working in tandem with an educator who can carry the instructional end.

You can be of great value in connecting teens to those comedies, histories, and tragedies, though, as a booktalker who does have an assignment tie-in. You might consider including modern versions of the same stories, or include tales based on Shakespeare like Charles and Mary Lamb's *Tales from Shakespeare*, in your booktalks. You might also bring along a few book notes or study guides about Shakespeare (they are legion) so teens can be reassured that lots of folks need a little extra help with those two gentlemen of Verona, the merry wives of Windsor, and all those bloody Henrys. You probably needed some help in preparing those booktalks! We'll talk more in the following section about classics combinations, but you can also tie Shakespeare's works in to media performances. Or, you might booktalk one of Shakespeare's plays with a handful of contemporary teen fiction titles that are set in the Elizabethan age or include Shakespeare as a character.

All in all, despite the difficulty of the subject matter for most teens, Shakespeare is, well, Shakespeare, and if as a librarian you already have or can develop the confidence to promote the Bard—especially if you have any opportunity to work in partnership with an educator so teens have a strong support system while delving in—do it!

Here are a couple of starter lists to whet your whistle for classic drama, the Bard, and beyond.

Drama Classics

- *The Cherry Orchard*, Anton Chekhov (1904)
- *Cyrano de Bergerac*, Edmond Rostand (1897)

(continued)

(continued)

- *A Doll's House*, Henrik Ibsen (1879)
- *Henry V*, Shakespeare (1600)
- *The Importance of Being Earnest*, Oscar Wilde (1895)
- *Lysistrata*, Aristophanes (411 B.C.)
- *Major Barbara*, George Bernard Shaw (1905)
- *The Misanthrope*, Molière (1666)
- *Oedipus the King*, Sophocles (429 B.C.)
- *Romeo and Juliet*, Shakespeare (c. 1595)

Modern Drama Classics

- *The Crucible*, Arthur Miller (1953)
- *Fences*, August Wilson (1985)
- *A Man for All Seasons*, Robert Bolt (1954)
- *The Miracle Worker*, William Gibson (1957)
- *The Odd Couple*, Neil Simon (1965)
- *Our Town*, Thornton Wilder (1938)
- *Pygmalion*, George Bernard Shaw (1913)
- *A Raisin in the Sun*, Lorraine Hansberry (1959)
- *Rosencrantz and Guildenstern Are Dead*, Tom Stoppard (1967)
- *A Streetcar Named Desire*, Tennessee Williams (1947)

Poems

A surprising number of teens enjoy poetry. Many of them write it. There's something about this literary form that packs an emotional and psychological punch that is meaningful to teens. I've always had great success connecting teens of all ages to poetry, from contemporary street poetry, to Japanese haiku, to longer forms of poetry like narratives and ballads.

A year or so ago a rather large whale washed up dead on a beach in Oregon. Being of such a size, residents were incapable of doing anything but holding vigil over the carcass while it began to decompose. It was all over the local news, and while everyone waited for what seemed like weeks for some governmental agency to do something about it, people became attached to this dead beast. We all developed some sort of sad fondness and protectiveness, a sorrowful recognition of this animal's majesty even in death, stench, and decay.

As I watched the continuing news stories about the whale, I thought off and on about a classic poem I'd once read in an anthology called, "The Wellfleet Whale." I dug it up again to see if it was as good as I'd remembered it. It was. This poem, by Stanley Kunitz, who served as the United States Poet Laureate in 2000 at the age of 85, is considered one of the greatest nature poems of the twentieth century. The poet wrote it some time after coming across a sixty-three-foot finback whale stranded on a Cape Cod beach, still alive and making horrific noises. Kunitz relates that when he touched the whale, it opened its eye, looked directly into his, and died in a shudder. In that look, said the poet, was a clear recognition (Kunitz, 1988).

I decided to give this poem a try one April when I was promoting poetry with 8th graders for National Poetry Month. It was a slightly longer and definitely more verbally challenging poem than the rest I'd brought, and the only classic (albeit contemporary) poem I included. I brought a picture of the Oregon whale I'd pulled off the Internet, and passed it around. I recapped the story behind the image and shared how it had made me feel. I then told them another such whale had so moved a famous poet that he wrote an incredible tribute to the animal after touching it and looking into its eye before it died. I then read the poem.

The response was incredible. I think we all talked together for another ten or fifteen minutes about sick, injured, and dead animals we'd run across and how that made us feel, about our own love for our animal friends and what it's like when we lose them, and about how great it is that we can use words in a beautiful way to explore and express our feelings. It was awesome. Did these 8th graders get every word in the poem? I don't think so. Did they get the meaning of the poem? I believe most of them did. And they had a rich and moving response through exposure to the power and meaning of an extraordinary classic work. That's a hopeful thing, indeed, for their future lives as readers.

Don't assume teens can't handle or appreciate the longer epic poems. Just listen to what my 17-year-old friend Max Brown had to say about *Beowulf*:

> At first I was intimidated by the rough English that the translation of Beowulf provided . . . but once I got into it, I realized that it's not a poem in the traditional sense. I mean, Beowulf is a badass. Really, think about it: To slay the demon, Grendel, that has been plaguing the land, Beowulf doesn't use a sword or shield or armor or anything. He casts aside all his tools of war and goes hand to hand with the thing. I mean, dude. He rips off the beast's arm and breaks its claws backward with his bare fists! Are you jok-

ing me? How cool is that? Even though it's been centuries since Beowulf was written, I can still appreciate a kick-ass battle scene. I realized later that Beowulf's casting aside of his sword and armor and everything was symbolic of his not needing to rely on any other influences than himself to defeat Grendel . . . but at the time the whole dismemberment thing was just straight wicked. And they say teens can't appreciate literature . . . (2003)

For the younger set, you might connect them with quality adaptations of epics and longer narrative poems to give them a familiarity with outstanding classic works that they can draw on later in high school or college. There are many of them that, although marketed to smaller children, are more appropriate for the upper elementary and lower middle grades. For example, I pulled a beautiful adaptation of Geoffrey Chaucer's *The Canterbury Tales* off the shelf the other day with sophisticated but appealing illustrations and a thoughtful, intelligent retelling of a number of the tales. This adaptation by Barbara Cohen and illustrated by Trina Schart Hyman could be a great way to introduce teens in the 7th and even 8th grades to an age-old classic in verse that would presently be beyond them in its original form.

There are loads and loads of classic poems, from short, witty limericks to the great epics. You have choices beyond choices! Here's a short list of classic poems from modern times to get you going. At the end of the chapter you'll find a list of selected classics poetry anthologies, and in Appendix C, you'll find short lists of classic narrative/epic poems and other classic poems from days of yore.

Classic Poems from Modern Times

- "The Cremation of Sam McGee," Robert W. Service (1907)
- "Daystar," Rita Dove (1986)
- "Do Not Go Gentle into That Good Night," Dylan Thomas (1952)
- "El Gato," Jimmy Santiago Baca (unknown)
- "The Negro Speaks of Rivers," Langston Hughes (1921)
- "The Red Wheel Barrow," William Carlos Williams (1923)
- "The Road Not Taken," Robert Frost (1915)
- "Snake," David Herbert Lawrence (1923)
- "Traveling through the Dark," William Stafford (1960)
- "The Wellfleet Whale," Stanley Kunitz (1983)

Fairy Tales, Myths, and Legends

I included Max's response to *Beowulf* in the poems section, but I just as well could have put it here. Teens, being in an extreme state of growth, are a ripe audience for extreme stories with extreme archetypal characters, and extremity is what makes up a whole lot of our world's fairy tales, myths, and legends.

Hansel and Gretel get tempted by a candy house and captured by a nasty old biddy with a chip on her shoulder and a gnawing hole in her belly, and the mean old broad ends up getting shoved in an oven and cooked for her efforts. What's not extreme about that? The great Athenian, Theseus, dared to seek out the half bull, half human Minotaur in his labyrinthine lair, just so he could bash the monster to death with his bare fists (not having brought a more durable instrument of destruction with him). The monster was sleeping at the time, which some might consider gave Theseus an unfair advantage, but overall, job well done. That's not mild stuff. We've got Beowulf and Grendel with their "kick-ass" confrontation, broken claws and all! And we've got any number of other fairy tales, myths, and legends with all the wild, gnarly, gory, extremes of the human condition, plus its conflicts, choices, and consequences. They're easy to find in your libraries, and they're virtually all classics! What's not to like? We'll talk more about fairy tales, myths, and legends later in this chapter in Classics Combo #4.

Essays and Speeches

Essays and speeches will not be among the more common shorter classic works you're likely to promote, but let's include a few remarks about them anyway. Which essays you promote, and how you present them to teens can be either a positive starting point for intellectual exploration or a confirmation of dullness and irrelevance. Don't forget some essays are classics because of their long-time ability to engage readers and expand their thinking about a subject, and you can be a major player in communicating that to teens.

You may find that famous or classic speeches can make a time period more immediate and real to teens. Speeches can be particularly effective as part of a booktalking presentation. They are most often written either to convince an audience of an agenda or in response to a significant event. They are created to be spoken aloud, but are often incredible pieces of writing in themselves that are merely enhanced by outstanding delivery.

You might share a few remarks about a speech, the time in which it was originally delivered, the person who delivered it, its affect on its audience. You might also play audio or video recordings of the original speech as a part of your booktalking presentation for greater impact.

A great example of a theme in which classic speeches can be promoted is civil rights issues in 1960s America. You could create an outstanding display of images, books, and audio and video recordings of speeches from the era. You could create a list on the theme to share with teens. You could bring a little bit of everything to a booktalking presentation. You've got a broad range of teen fiction titles to choose from, you've got loads of high-interest nonfiction and biography works to choose from, you've certainly got literary classics. How about adding in Martin Luther King Jr.'s "I Have a Dream" speech? There is no doubt that Dr. King's speech is a classic, and there's no doubt it will be meaningful to and will move teens.

Or, your theme might be World War II, and you might have decided on a chronological display, booklist, or booktalk starting with Pearl Harbor and moving forward. Following a book that focuses on the bombing of Pearl Harbor, you might promote Roosevelt's December 8, 1941 address to Congress asking for a declaration of war—you know the one, the "date which will live in infamy" speech.

Although promoting these classic works may be infrequent, they do have their time and place if you're open to them, and they can mean a great deal to teens who may otherwise not be introduced to the formal written thoughts of great thinkers that shifted common perception and set trends, or to the words which moved history along or stopped it dead in its tracks. Keep essays and speeches in mind.

MUST-KNOW CLASSICS

Once you start talking with teens in your classrooms and libraries, you'll find that some classics just stand out for one reason or another. From time to time you're likely to hear remarks like, "we already read that in class," or, "our teacher assigned that last year," or, "my friend had to read that in her honors English class." That's because some classics are commonly used in the curriculum.

When working with a classroom group as a school or public librarian, your educational hosts might regularly request you bring award-winning titles to booktalk. Many classics are award winners—how could they not be? Educators often require that teens in their classrooms read award winners, simply because they are outstanding books and also to raise the reading bar, if you will, for teens who might otherwise have difficulty advancing beyond certain reading ruts. No value judgment here, but I can't tell you how many times an exasperated middle school educator has asked me to help get one of his or her teens off R. L. Stine's *Goosebumps* books! By familiarizing yourself with the literary and genre awards and their winners, you'll have a leg up on both a commonly requested book-talking theme and on making a broader range of classics connections with teens in general.

In your career as a librarian or educator working in school libraries and classroom environments, you will certainly need more than a passing familiarity with challenged and banned books and the issues and sensitivities surrounding them. You'll find a majority of the books challenged and banned by concerned citizens in America are lauded as classics by others, and you'll find this conflict present in educational environments and in your community.

Knowing about these three categories of classics will benefit you when making classics connections with teens.

Curriculum Classics

Just as colleges have a literary canon, middle/junior high and high schools have literature or language arts curriculums which are based on learning standards, requirements, frameworks, or expectations (all kinds of words are used to describe this) determined at both the state and local levels. Educators select individual literary works to be studied based on these standards and their relationships to other educational units. They usually plan the details of each year's literary curriculum in advance, and often prepare new or add to existing literary booklists for students to select from for additional assigned reading.

If you are an educator, you already know all this! If you are a school librarian, you are aware of your school's curriculum and are aware of which literary works will be studied in which grades, and of what sorts of lists teens are given to choose classics from for additional assigned reading. If you are a public librarian, you are probably not in "the know," so it's a good idea to find out. Ask your educational colleagues about their literature or language arts curriculums so you can better understand what is taught and expected from teens in each grade. Ask for that year's list of classic titles to be studied in the classroom, and ask for any reading lists that a teacher may have pulled together for teens to use for additional assigned reading. Here are a few reasons why this is good idea:

- You learn about the literature-related goals educators have for their students in each grade, which will help you to better support your colleagues, to select classics to house and promote in your library, and to booktalk in classrooms.

- You are better prepared to assist teens in selecting the best titles for their reading interests, given the lists from which they will have to pick additional assigned reading.

- You can suggest books to teens in your library and suggest booktalk themes to your educational colleagues to tie in to an upcoming literature-related assignment.

- You can create companion displays in your library to coincide with the study of particular classics.

- You know which books to exclude from any booktalks you might be planning that year (you don't want to talk titles already studied or about to be studied, unless suggested by yourself or requested by an educator).

- You have lists of teacher-approved classics titles from which to build supporting collections in your library (or, if you are a small library with a restricted budget, you know which titles you can refrain from purchasing as they'll be available in the schools).

- You know the classics teens may have the "do I *really* have to read this?" response to, and you can better prepare to break through their barriers regarding the merits of those particular titles, or steer them toward other titles that won't elicit that response and will be meaningful reading experiences for them.

Many classics are used in middle grades and high school reading lists, and which titles are used more frequently than others depend on the language arts curriculum and preferences of educators. That said, here's a couple of short lists of classic titles that seem to be used in the curriculum more often than not:

Frequently Assigned Middle Grades Curriculum Classics

- *The Adventures of Tom Sawyer*, Mark Twain (1876)
- *The Call of the Wild*, Jack London (1903)

(continued)

(continued)

- *The Diary of a Young Girl*, Anne Frank (1947)
- *Johnny Tremain*, Esther Forbes (1943)
- *The Outsiders*, S. E. Hinton (1967)
- *The Pearl*, John Steinbeck (1947)
- *Roll of Thunder, Hear My Cry*, Mildred Taylor (1976)
- *Shane*, Jack Schaefer (1949)
- *To Kill a Mockingbird*, Harper Lee (1960)
- *Treasure Island*, Robert Louis Stevenson (1883)

Frequently Assigned High School Curriculum Classics

- *Animal Farm*, George Orwell (1945)
- *Beowulf*, Anonymous (9th century)
- *The Crucible*, Arthur Miller (1953)
- *The Great Gatsby*, F. Scott Fitzgerald (1925)
- *The Hound of the Baskervilles*, Sir Arthur Conan Doyle (1902)
- *Lord of the Flies*, William Golding (1954)
- *Our Town*, Thorton Wilder (1938)
- *The Red Badge of Courage*, Stephen Crane (1895)
- *Romeo and Juliet*, Shakespeare (c. 1595)
- *The Scarlet Letter*, Nathaniel Hawthorne (1850)

Award Winners

A great number of award-winning books truly are classics, or are classics in the making. Some award winners are older books that are standing the test of time, others are contemporary classics highly lauded. All are original, remarkable, notable, important works. It's a good idea to familiarize yourself with major literary awards, both for teens and adults, and know their award categories, as you will find a significant number of great books with award-winning status that you can meaningfully share with teens. Look in the lists at the end of Chapter 2 for books and Web sites that describe a multitude of award winners and "bests."

Surely, none of you would scoff at books written by the authors who have won the Noble Prize in Literature, nor would you curl a lip at the books that have won the Pulitzer Prize or the National Book Award in their many categories—including a young adult category in the latter. You might easily be convinced that the highest literary award given in Britain and the Commonwealth, the Booker Prize, contains a long list of classic titles. I'm sure none of you would question that many of the titles that have won the Newbery Award, the Coretta Scott King Award, and the new Michael L. Printz Award are classics of children's and teen literature. I wonder, though, how likely many of you would be to accept that the books that have won the Golden Spur Award for great Western writing, or the Edgar Award for mystery writing, or the Hugo and Nebula Awards for science fiction and fantasy, are truly classics?

Genre fiction always gets a short shrift in the world of High Literature. This is highly unfortunate, as genre fiction can be some of the most original, daring, provocative, far-reaching, *interesting* writing to be found. It is also some of the writing most appealing to teen audiences. It's my firm belief that had the Nebula or Hugo been awarded in 1817, 1897, and 1898, there could be no doubt that Shelley's *Frankenstein*, Stoker's *Dracula* and Wells's *War of the Worlds* would have been in the running at the very least, and most likely award winners. Regardless of the time of their inception, you should have a familiarity with these sorts of genre awards and their winners, and draw from them in equal measure with literary fiction award winners when making classics connections with teens. Several of the booklists provided in Chapter 7 feature or include genre classics, and that same chapter concludes with a list of genre guides. Both can help you get started with your own reading plan and in making classics connections with teens.

Not only should you know about award winners to broaden the literary choices you can draw from for your own reading plan, and to promote to teens through displays, booklists, and one-on-one interactions, you should know about award winners so that when scheduling a classroom visit to talk about classics or when working with educational colleagues on reading assignment support, you can encourage the inclusion of these outstanding works.

Because there are so many award organizations that select an annual award winner, and because there are so many award winners that are also considered classics, the sheer volume of choices can be overwhelming. When promoting award winners to teens, you might narrow the field a bit. You could pick a particular award, genre, or award year to highlight.

Why not pick a year or range of years in which teens in a particular grade might have been born, and do a display or booklist or booktalking presentation based on the works that won awards during that time? Most teens, especially those in the middle grades, are fascinated by the year they were born. It's not uncommon for them to have assignments in late elementary and early middle school, often as Boy Scouts or Girl Scouts, to find significant events or look at newspaper headlines from the year they were born. This can be a great way to tie in to that, and to help teens cement an understanding of the point in time at which their personal histories began! Of course, the younger the teens, the more contemporary the award winners and the classics you are promoting. You could do a great display like "1988: A Great Year for All You 16-year-olds and a Great Year for the Classics!" or something like that. If promoting such contemporary classics won't work for you, you might pick a significant year in history, maybe one that matches an educational unit being studied, and promote classics that won prominent literary and genre awards that year. You might, for example, pick 1941—the year Pearl Harbor was bombed, or 1963—the year John F. Kennedy was assassinated.

Challenged and Banned Classics

A significant number of the classics have been challenged or banned in one or more community. Given all that we've explored regarding the nature of classic literature, this should not come as a surprise! As a librarian or educator, you may be most familiar with challenges and bannings through the annual ALA-sponsored Banned Books Week campaign, but the campaign's title is really more of a promotional phrase than it is an accurate description. Not all books that are challenged end up being banned. It's a good idea to know the difference between the two. According to the Office for Intellectual Freedom (OIF):

> A challenge is an attempt to remove or restrict materials, based upon the objections of a person or group. A banning is the removal of those materials. (ALA Web site)

Why might something be challenged or banned? The OIF reports the top reasons for the one hundred most frequently challenged books of the past decade (1990–2000):

- Sexually explicit content
- Offensive language
- Content unsuited to age group

- Occult theme or promoting the occult or Satanism
- Violence
- Homosexual theme or promoting homosexuality
- Nudity
- Racism
- Sex education
- Antifamily content

Where were these books most commonly challenged?

- Schools and school libraries (71%)
- Public libraries (24%)

Who challenged these books?

- Parents (60%)
- Patrons (15%)
- Administrators (9%)

The ALA's OIF both monitors and compiles reports from the field on this sort of activity nationwide, with annual updates, and provides you with loads of additional intellectual freedom information in their Web pages. Be prepared to sit down for a spell to navigate and digest all the information you'll find there. A few lists of challenged and banned books are made available, and you can purchase banned books resources with more comprehensive booklists that include detailed information.

So, what does all this mean to you when making classics connections with teens? First, as a professional who works with public and school communities, you should be aware of the sorts of reasons why literary content can be found offensive. Regardless of your own personal take on the matter, it will make you more professionally sensitive to the communities you serve.

Second, you should be aware of any controversies surrounding a classic you might like to promote in the schools or alternative educational environments. You may be more likely to have this awareness as an educator or school librarian than as a public librarian. If you are the latter, in advance of any school visits you may have scheduled, you should discuss with your school or alternative educational community if a particular classic is an appropriate selection to promote in that venue.

Public librarians might wonder if this is a censorship issue in itself. Is it? Not to my mind. You can promote any and all classics in the public library and in one-on-one interactions with teens in your personal and professional lives at large, hopefully using sound readers' advisory techniques! You can develop collections, displays, booklists, programs, informational brochures, and that sort of thing to help broaden teens' understanding of challenged and banned books and the issues surrounding reading and censorship. All that's super great stuff.

You should, however, respect the charge of school librarians, educators, and other adults who work with teens in more formal and defined environments, and remain aware that presenting certain sorts of books, classics or otherwise, without prior consultation may lead to a serious conflict for or with your colleagues. It's important to keep in mind that in the traditional educational environment, educators and school librarians are far more adversely impacted by literary content challenges than you as they play a very different role concerning our nation's youth. They act *in loco parentis*, assuming the role of parents to see to the all-around well-being of youth for the hours those youth are in school. They are held accountable. Laws and livelihoods are involved. Administrators, educators, school librarians, and parents take this quite seriously, and should.

The same respect applies with the alternative educational environments where parents are often educating their own teens or a small group of teens. These folks have usually chosen to teach their own youth for moral, religious, or lifestyle reasons that are of tantamount importance to them and will have strong opinions about appropriate reading selections for their youth. You've just got to keep that in mind and give it its due.

One other thing to keep in mind with banned books is that the plain fact that they are banned may actually motivate some teens to read them. Who doesn't remember seeking out taboo reading material in adolescent years, or being told that a certain book was "too mature," and then fervidly plowing through it?

When talking about banned books with teens, either in one-on-one readers' advisory interactions or to teens in groups, you have the option of passing on what you know about the book's controversial content if you feel it's important to do so. For example, when I'm called upon to booktalk Salinger's *The Catcher in the Rye* to 8th and 9th graders, which happens on occasion, I mention that there's lots of strong language in the book, and although some readers appreciate its use in a story, others just don't enjoy it. I let the teens know that if they don't like strong language, or their parents don't want them to read strong language, they have some decisions to make before picking up this classic. You might consider issuing these sorts of warnings in a neutral, low-key way, and at the end of a readers' advisory interaction or booktalk, so that the content of the book carries more weight up front. You might find this tactic more appropriate to younger teens in the middle grades than older teens in the upper grades.

Here's a short list of challenged and banned classics—just the tip of the iceberg—to give you the idea. Most are among the ten most frequently challenged books of the past decade (1990–1999). The remainder are on the OIF's list of the one hundred most frequently challenged books of the past decade. As mentioned above, you can use the ALA's Banned Books Week resources for more comprehensive lists of challenged and banned classics, and for all the background information you might need on them.

Challenged or Banned Classics

- *The Adventures of Huckleberry Finn,* Mark Twain (1884)
- *The Catcher in the Rye,* J.D. Salinger (1951)
- *The Chocolate War,* Robert Cormier (1974)
- *The Color Purple,* Alice Walker (1982)
- *Flowers for Algernon,* Daniel Keyes (1966)
- *Forever...,* Judy Blume (1975)
- *I Know Why the Caged Bird Sings,* Maya Angelou (1970)
- *Of Mice and Men,* John Steinbeck (1937)
- *The Outsiders,* S.E. Hinton (1967)
- *To Kill a Mockingbird,* Harper Lee (1960)

You might also take a look at a few of the more current books available regarding censorship issues, schools, and public libraries:

Foerstel, Herbert N. 2002. *Banned in the U.S.A.: A Reference Guide to Book Censorship in Schools and Public Libraries.* 2nd ed. Westport, CT: Greenwood Press.
    In this second edition, Foerstel provides an examination of censorship in schools and public libraries, including significant book banning activities in the United States, understandable information on the law and book banning

through history, updated interviews with authors of banned books, a look at the fifty most frequently challenged books between 1996–2000, and a bibliography.

Hull, Mary. 1999. *Censorship in America: A Reference Handbook*. Santa Barbara, CA: ABC-CLIO.

The title says it all. Hull's work is a complete look at the history and state of censorship in America, including book banning attempts, a timeline of critical censorship-related events, an introduction to important people in the censorship battle, significant censorship data, a directory of censorship-related organizations, and an annotated bibliography for further study.

Karolides, Nicholas J., Margaret Bald, and Dawn B. Sova. 1999. *100 Banned Books: Censorship Histories of World Literature*. New York: Checkmark Books.

The authors provide an in-depth look at one hundred books that have a history of challenges and banning in the United States and other countries. The books are arranged in sections that reflect the primary reasons for their history of censorship (political, religious, sexual, and social). Each entry includes full bibliographic information, literary form, and a detailed look at the text. This information is followed by a complete censorship history and a list of further readings.

Scales, Pat. 2001. *Teaching Banned Books: 12 Guides for Young Readers*. Chicago: American Library Association.

Although this book focuses primarily on upper-elementary school readers, it is a helpful resource for giving a fundamental introduction to the protections of the First Amendment and the issues of censorship and intellectual freedom from an educator's point of view. The book includes strategies for teaching young people about First Amendment rights and challenges, and for teaching twelve banned books in five thematic categories.

CLASSICS COMBOS

There are many ways to combine classics, and to combine classics with other types of book and nonbook materials to more successfully engage individual teens in your library or school and to make the most meaningful classics connections in the classroom or group environment. This section looks at nine "classics combos" that may make for more interesting and meaningful classics connections for teen readers, and also provides suggestions for finding and organizing your own "classics combos."

The first three classics combos look at combining classics with other classics by theme, by literary genre, and by different experiences of the same event or issue. The fourth classics combo proposes combining classics with their retold, "fractured," and rewritten versions (some of which are classics in themselves), from fairy tales to classical myths, from the Arthur Legend to Shakespeare's works. The remaining five classics combos suggest combining classics with other sorts of books and nonbook materials—from modern sequels to contemporary fiction and nonfiction, from comics and graphic novels to media formats.

You can use these combinations in one-on-one readers' advisory work with teens, to create interesting displays in your library or classroom, to make great booklists, in book discussion groups, and in classroom or group booktalking presentations.

#1: Combining Classics by Theme

This may be self-explanatory, but one of the most common classics combinations is by theme. In this case, your literature type is classics only and your theme is . . . hey, just what is your theme? Since there are classics of all kinds, the sky's the limit.

Something that might help you to pick a theme, and which works well for me on occasion, is to hark back to your own school years when you learned all that rudimentary stuff about larger themes in literature like "man versus man," "man versus himself," "man versus nature," and "man versus society." Can't say I truly approve of the gender specificity here, but that's how it was taught to me, and may ring a bell with you as well unless you are young enough to have a new version of that somewhere in your educational background. I wonder if it's now called "human versus human," or "person versus self"? Whatever the case may be, these broader concepts can help you develop themes when you aren't particularly inspired by something more specific.

Say you were leaning toward "man versus man" as a foundation for your classics theme. You certainly could pull together a group of classics about warfare. There's a list of those in Appendix C at the end of this book. You could also pull together a group of classics that demonstrate the misunderstandings and conflicts that build between people on smaller a scale—the Hatfields and McCoys sort of thing. Jack Schaefer's *Shane* and many classic works from Native American authors are good examples, many of which you'll also find in Appendix C.

If you were interested in "man versus himself," you could look at, say, J. D. Salinger's *The Catcher in the Rye*, Daniel Keyes's *Flowers for Algernon*, Mary Shelley's *Frankenstein*, and Robert Louis Stevenson's *Dr. Jekyll and Mr. Hyde*.

How about "man versus nature"? There are always survival classics like Jack London's *The Call of the Wild* and *White Fang*, or in a different sense, something like John Steinbeck's *The Grapes of Wrath*.

And "man versus society" certainly could lead you to Charles Dickens's *Oliver Twist*, Ken Kesey's *One Flew Over the Cuckoo's Nest*, Ralph Ellison's *Invisible Man*, Kate Chopin's *The Awakening*, and just about every single slave narrative and civil rights classic. And that's just to mention a very few of the more commonly known classics off the top of my head.

Many of the resources listed at the ends of Chapters 2 and 7 and in Appendix B that can assist you in selecting classics to read, will also provide themes for those classics. You might also look for themes as you are reading, and make a note of those you identify. Whenever I read a book I think teens might enjoy I save information about it in a database, and one of the fields I include is for theme. You might consider something similar, whether you use a database, index cards, or another filing system that works best for you.

Don't need or want to hark back to your school years for the "versus" stuff and still don't have a thematic inspiration? Okay, just skip that and head straight into a brainstorming session with yourself about the sorts of concepts or themes with high appeal to teens. Here's one that teens respond to: oppression. Here's another: revenge. How about sacrifice, alienation, heroic behavior, coming-of-age, depression, first love, racism, and friendship against the odds? Then there are the themes teens might not think are interesting, but are! Don't brainstorm only for themes you know will have high appeal to teens, brainstorm for themes that will create interest.

Just for an example, a theme that seems to cultivate interest just about every time I use it is "taking a trip through history," in which I collect a selection of classic fiction and nonfiction that reflects the way of life and course of events over a particular period of time in a particular place. I've used this to create displays, booklists, and in booktalking. This idea originally came out of an early American history assignment tie-in, and has worked well for other time periods ever since.

Another theme that seems to illicit a strong response from teens is character, that is, picking a predominant character from a classic and using that character for comparison or contrast with similar or diverse characters in other classics. Not so easy to do a display with, but great for a booklist and for booktalking. Teens, perhaps because they are in a self-oriented stage of life, can be strongly attracted to a character in a book when no other element would have drawn interest. Believe it or not, you can make some pretty interesting connections this way across a broad range of classics! I've even managed to get Schaefer's lone gun, Shane, and Doyle's independent operator, Sherlock Holmes, in the same booktalking presentation by making comparisons between them as characters.

Another way to approach themes is through current events. For example, if a trial has been receiving a lot of press, you could put together a selection of "classic courtroom mysteries." Or, if a war has been declared, you might use that theme to create a display of "war through the ages."

If you are having trouble coming up with themes on your own even after intensive brainstorming, ask your professional colleagues, and definitely ask teens in your library what sorts of subjects they like to read about, which themes are the most meaningful to them. They'll help kickstart you.

#2: Combining Classics by and across Literary Genres

You can promote classics in a specific literary genre, and in addition to highlighting specific classic titles, you can give teens an introduction to a genre they may not have known was out there and which may become a great joy for them as readers. Here are a couple of short starter lists of basic genres in which you'll find exceptional classics to share with teens. Don't forget that Chapter 7 provides starter lists of classics for most of the fiction genres and includes a list of genre guides at the end of the chapter. Appendix C provides starter classics lists for many of the nonfiction genres.

Fiction Genres	Nonfiction Genres
Adventure and Survival	Biography
Animal Fiction	Drama
Fantasy	Geography and History
Horror	Nature, Science, and Math
Mystery	Philosophy and Psychology
Romance	Poetry
Science Fiction	Religion and Myth
Short Stories	Social and Political Sciences
Western Fiction	

Even if they don't focus on the classics, you might also find the headings found in general readers' advisory resources useful, which often sort books into fiction, nonfiction, and subgenre designations.

Combining classics across literary genres can be a great way to introduce teens to a wide range of different literary types in a short booklist or dynamic booktalking presentation. This could work well with a sampler of miscellaneous classic works from a variety of fiction and nonfiction genres, but it seems to lend itself particularly well to a more focused theme. For example, let's say your theme is classic animal stories. You might promote James Herriot's delightful memoirs, *All Creatures Great and Small*, Richard Adams's novel, *Watership Down*, Stanley Kunitz's poem, "The Wellfleet Whale," and Joy Adams's true story, *Born Free: A Lioness of Two Worlds*.

#3: Combining Classics That Reflect Different Experiences of the Same Issue or Event

When making classics combinations that treat the same issue or event, do your best to include works from differing points of view. This shouldn't be too hard—most significant issues or events have inspired many great authors to write works from more than one angle in response.

Classic war novels are a good example of this. If you are going to promote Civil War and Reconstruction classics, you've got quite a range of viewpoints to represent, not just North and South! You've got classics like Margaret Mitchell's *Gone with the Wind*, that looks at the prewar and Civil War years from the perspective of a spoiled southern belle who is not equipped to face the coming change. You've got Irene Hunt's *Across Five Aprils*, which features a young man on an Illinois farm with a sick father who must grow up fast during the Civil War years. You've got Stephen Crane's *The Red Badge of Courage*, the first war novel written from the point of view of a common soldier. You've got Toni Morrison's *Beloved*, in which the main character's prior life of slavery, even after emancipation, leads her to commit a crime that haunts her.

You would be just as likely to find a wide range of classic novels about World War I, World War II, and the Vietnamese Conflict that treat their subjects from differing points of view, but don't just stop at wars! There are other significant issues and events that you can find classic works written about and that when introduced to teens, will offer them multiple entry points into the issue or event. With more than one entry point, you are likely to attract the interest of more readers.

#4: Combining Classics with Retold, "Fractured," and Rewritten Versions

There are numbers of retold or "fractured" classics that have high appeal to teen readers. Common among them are retold or "fractured" fairy tales, myths, and legends; rewrites of the Arthur legend (this gets its own mention just for sheer volume of retellings!); and rewrites of Shakespeare's works, but you can find a number of classic novels retold in one form or another as well. In Chapter 9 we talk about Bram Stoker's *Dracula* and the whole raft of retellings and adaptations that derive from it. We also look briefly at Dickens's *A Christmas Carol*. Keep your eyes open for other high-appeal derivatives of classic works. Once you start, you'll find them everywhere.

A great way to promote classics to teens and to more successfully legitimize them, is to combine the original classic with a selection of its retellings, "fractures," and rewrites in a booklist or booktalking presentation. You encourage the teens to explore the original works where all the high-appeal stuff came from, and make it okay for them to enjoy both.

Fairy Tales, Myths, and Legends

There's just something about fairy tales, myths, and legends that inspires a good retelling. Some are more than retold, they're "fractured": rewritten with a unique twist of some sort.

Many of the fairy tale retellings are written for teen audiences, from Robin McKinley's excellent *Beauty: A Retelling of the Story of Beauty and the Beast* to Donna Jo Napoli's numerous fairy tale retellings in novel form. Terri Windling and Ellen Datlow edited a few anthologies of fairy tale retellings for the younger set, including *A Wolf at the Door* and *Swan Sister*, as well as an adult series (older teens only on this one!) of dark and sometimes sexy fairy tale retellings, including *Black Heart, Ivory Bones*; *Snow White, Blood Red*; and *Ruby Slippers, Golden Tears*. The new Simon Pulse series features fairy tales rewritten into rollicking, adventuresome, and sometimes loosely associated narrative novel versions by well-known authors of teen literature and popular series titles. Among the titles in this "Once Upon a Time . . ." series are Cameron Dokey's *Beauty Sleep* (Sleeping Beauty) and *The Storyteller's Daughter* (The Arabian Nights), Debbie Viguie's *Midnight Pearls* (The Little Mermaid), and Tracy Lynn's *Snow* (Snow White).

You'll have no trouble finding retellings of Western classical mythology. Doris Orgel rewrites classic mythology in novel form, including *The Princess and the God*, a retelling of the Cupid and Psyche story. Some of her titles are a little young, but others are great for 7th and 8th graders. Priscilla Galloway's *Snake Dreamer* retells the Medusa and Gorgons story. Stephanie Spinner retells the Atalanta story in *Quiver*, a novel that was just published in 2002. Don't remember the Atalanta story? She's the young woman who wouldn't marry a suitor unless he could beat her in a race. Enter the gold apples. Okay, then you've got a 2003 book from Donna Jo Napoli called *The Great God Pan* about that wily and rambunctious goat man. Patrice Kindl rewrote the Theseus and Minotaur story from the point of view of the half sister of the Minotaur, called *Lost in the Labyrinth*. Then you've got retellings of the epic works, like Clemence McLaren's *Inside the Walls of Troy* and Adele Geras's *Troy* based on Homer's *Iliad*, and Clemence McLaren's *Waiting for Odysseus* in which Homer's *Odyssey* is reimagined from the point of view of the women—mortal and otherwise—in his life.

There is even a selection of nonwestern myths and legends represented in contemporary teen fiction, including Kara Dalkey's *Little Sister* and *The Heavenward Path*, which feature Japanese mythological characters, and Susan Fletcher's *Shadow Spinner*, which features the cripple, Marjan, Shahrazad, and the Sultan near the end of the thousand-and-one nights of death-defying storytelling. For another fictionalized Japanese legend, Noriko Ogiwara's *Dragon Sword and Wind Child* features a 15-year-old teen who finds she's the reincarnation of a Japanese princess of the underworld. To revisit *Beowulf*, there's Michael Crichton's *Eaters of the Dead*, a retelling that features a Muslim man named Ibn Fadlan who ends up helping Viking warriors against a flesh-eating evil. This, incidentally, was made into a film in 1999 called *The 13th Warrior*, starring Antonio Banderas.

And these just scratch the surface. Seek out some of the amazing number of fun retellings of fairy tales, myths, and legends to combine with classic originals, and you're likely to attract far more teen readers than you'd ever imagined. You might take a look at Gail de Vos's and Anna E. Altmann's 1999 *New Tales for Old: Folktales as Literary Fictions for Young Adults*. Despite the somewhat inscrutable title, the book takes nine major European folktales and provides a detailed look at each in its original and many derivative forms for use with teens. In 2001, the authors wrote a second volume called *Tales, Then and Now: More Folktales as Young Adult Literary Fiction*, which covers nine more tales in various iterations.

The Arthur Legend

How many teens do you think know something about the Arthur legend? I'd wager that most do. How many do you think know the earliest sources of the legend? Not very many. Even if they did, how many are likely to read a tome like Sir Thomas Malory's *Le Morte d'Arthur*? Maybe one or two, in the whole of the United States. All right, maybe a few more, but that's about it. I can admit I still haven't been able to handle it!

The Arthur legend is among the most popular and lasting of the classic legends of the Western world. And for good reason. All the scholarly stuff aside, you've got a young boy who believes himself to be of humble origins who it just so happens is really a king among men, and is acknowledged for it in his adolescence by both the everyday and supernatural worlds. He rises from young know-nothing to highly effective, highly ethical unifying king—with the aid of a great wizard. He's betrayed in love by his friend and wife, yet acts nobly. What could be better?

Wide appeal, no doubt. Perhaps especially to young men, who, as mentioned, want models in their reading materials and as we discuss later, want heroic models to boot. You might not be so likely to interest teens in Malory, but you certainly can interest them in any number of more accessible works that although derivative, are themselves considered classics. Just to throw a few titles out, you have *Sir Gawain and the Green Knight* (try J.R.R. Tolkien's translation), T. H. White's *The Once and Future King*, Roger Lancelyn Green's *King Arthur and the Knights of the Round Table* (for the younger set and struggling readers), Mary Stewart's Arthurian saga (*The Crystal Cave, The Hollow Hills, The Last Enchantment*, and *The Wicked Day*), and, even though a more alternative retelling from the women's points of view, Marion Zimmer Bradley's *The Mists of Avalon*. And these are just the book versions—there are also movies! You might also combine those with high-interest fiction, teen and adult, which are legion.

The Bard

Shakespeare in its original form can be a real challenge for high school readers, and is certainly outside the abilities and interests of most middle grades readers. But, like teen reader Jackie Lockerby told us in Chapter 4, the content of Shakespeare's works can be wonderfully appealing and exciting for teen readers—if only they could get past the unfamiliar and complex language. There are ample resources out there for educators to engage middle-grades teens in Shakespeare's works, including activities and contemporary retellings. I'm still hoping that wily librarian will come forth with his or her fabulous resource on sharing Shakespeare with teens through readers' advisory and booktalking, but until that time, librarians might make use of available educational resources.

You might also consider searching out retellings and derivative works to share with teens, and mention each original source without actually suggesting it in the original form. With Shakespeare, use your honesty-is-the-best-policy stuff. If you can attract teens to his stories but let them know that retellings are easier places to start, you can interest them with what they can reach now, and when they are ready or have an educator to help them through one of Shakespeare's original works, they've got a head start.

I won't spend too much time here, but you might consider books that retell Shakespeare's stories for younger audiences, like Charles and Mary Lamb's *Tales from Shakespeare*. You might share derivative works like that ever-present high school companion to *Romeo and Juliet*, *West Side Story* (the written versions—we'll talk more about film versions of classics in a following section), Julius Lester's *Othello: A Retelling*, or Sharon Draper's *Romiette and Julio*. You might also consider high-interest contemporary teen fiction titles that don't actually retell Shakespeare's works, but feature him as a character. A few examples of these would be Susan Cooper's *King of Shadows*, Gary L. Blackwood's *The Shakespeare Stealer*, and Lynn Kositsky's *A Question of Will*.

#5: Combining Classics with Their Modern Sequels

Combining classics with their modern sequels can bring something into the present that seems old and obsolete to teens. When they find out that a contemporary author was impacted so strongly by a classic work that he or she decided to continue the story, or write it from another character's point of view, or feature one of its characters in another book entirely, it may convince them to give that classic a chance.

There aren't many modern sequels out there with a twist on the same storyline (as opposed to continuations) as their classic originals, but there are a few, and it's a good idea to know about them and suggest or booktalk them together when you can. To mention two of the more well-known:

Charlotte Brontë's *Jane Eyre* and Jean Rhys's *Wide Sargasso Sea*
 Both of these classics feature Mr. Rochester, "the madwoman in the attic," and Jane Eyre. Brontë's 1847 work features Jane Eyre as the main protagonist with whom the reader feels connection and sympathy. Rhys's 1966 work places Antoinette Cosway (a.k.a. "the madwoman in the attic")—Mr. Rochester's first wife—as the main protagonist with whom the reader feels a connection.

Beowulf and John Gardner's *Grendel*
 The eighth-century Anglo-Saxon poem features the hero, Beowulf, who has come to the Danish court of King Hrothgar to rid him of the monster, Grendel, who is plaguing his kingdom. John Gardner's 1971 book tells the story from the point of view of the monster.

In case you don't have a familiarity with modern twists on and sequels of classics, here's a few more examples to give you the idea:

Classics and Their Modern Sequels

The Classic	The Modern Sequel
The Count of Monte Cristo, Alexandre Dumas	*The Revenge*, Stephen Fry
Gone with the Wind, Margaret Mitchell	*Scarlett*, Alexandra Ripley
The Hound of the Baskervilles and the Sherlock Holmes stories, Sir Arthur Conan Doyle	The Mary Russell mysteries, Laurie R. King
Moby Dick, Herman Melville	*Ahab's Wife*, Sean Jeter Naslund
The Phantom of the Opera, Gaston Leroux	*The Phantom of Manhattan*, Frederick Forsyth
Pride and Prejudice, Jane Austen	*Pemberley* and *An Unequal Marriage*, Emma Tennant
Rebecca, Daphne du Maurier	*Mrs. De Winter*, Susan Hill
The Strange Case of Dr. Jekyll and Mr. Hyde, Robert Louis Stevenson	*Mary Reilly*, Valerie Martin
The Time Machine, H. G. Wells	*The Time Ships*, Stephen Baxter
Treasure Island, Robert Louis Stevenson	*Return to Treasure Island*, Denis Judd
Wuthering Heights, Emily Brontë	*Heathcliff: The Return to Wuthering Heights*, Lin Haire-Sargeant

Although it isn't the only place to find modern sequels to classic works, the State Library of Tasmania has a set of Web pages dedicated to building a list of them by original author. Go to http://www.statelibrary.tas.gov.au/modernsequ/ to find "A select list of recent fiction that includes sequels to both old and modern classics. These titles also represent recent fiction that derives plot and/or character details from previously published works."

#6: Combining Classics with Contemporary Works in the Same Genre

This is another one of those self-explanatory classics combinations, but worth a brief mention regardless. Like combining classics with their modern sequels, combining classics with contemporary works in the same genre is a way to connect the old and the new for teens and to encourage the understanding that all these works are in a continuum, the older leading to the newer, and the newer reinforcing the value of the older within each genre.

Were you promoting National Poetry Month in April, for example, you could mix a selection of classic poems with contemporary, hip poems into a booklist, or build them into a booktalking presentation for a classroom visit. You might group them by theme, you might group them by type of poetry (like narrative, parody, lyric, verse, and ode), you might group them by poetic form (like haiku, limerick, sonnet, and epic), or any other sort of grouping that works to integrate classic and contemporary poetry together. You might combine classic plays in much the same way for a drama class with some information about newer Broadway plays, or combine classics biographies with some contemporary biographies in a display about famous people through the ages. You could do a "true stories" booklist or booktalk of nonfiction classics and current high-interest works for a particular era or period in history.

You certainly could combine seminal and vintage science fiction with contemporary science fiction by theme within the genre, or classic mystery fiction with current mystery fiction by subgenre. You might combine contemporary police procedurals with the classic Sherlock Holmes stories, or Private Dick mysteries with the classic Dashiell Hammett and Raymond Chandler noir mysteries. You might combine a "trip through history" with genre and, for example, create a dynamic display or booktalking presentation of classic and contemporary fiction that traces the evolution of the horror genre.

These are just a few ideas for putting classics works together with contemporary works in the same genre, but there are as many more possibilities as there are literary genres and subgenres.

#7: Combining Classics with Contemporary Teen and Adult Fiction

Combining classics with contemporary teen and adult fiction can be done in many other ways: by theme, by appeal feature, or in some way you'll think up on your own in the shower one morning that no one else has yet considered!

As new books arrive in your library, or as you read reviews of new books that you may be able to purchase for your library, keep in mind how those works might combine with the classics you've been reading or are about to put in your reading plan. For example, just over a year ago I reread Anne Frank's *The Diary of a Young Girl* for a biography and memoir booktalking presentation, and just this past year Cherie Bennett's *Anne Frank and Me*, a contemporary teen novel based on the play of the same name, landed new in paperback on my desk. Next time I booktalk Anne Frank's diary, you can be sure I'm going to combine it with Bennett's novel about a girl who gets pulled back in time from the Holocaust Museum in the present day to the Nazi occupation of Paris during World War II, and eventually ends up meeting Anne Frank. Keep your eyes peeled to the possibilities whenever you can.

You could also start on the contemporary side, and look for classics that combine well with the more popular themes and elements you're finding in the current teen and adult literature you're reading. When I worked with incarcerated youth in Grand Junction, Colorado, John Gilstrap's *Nathan's Run* was popular at the facility. If I'd been thinking about possible combinations between that book and the classics to turn into a booktalk, for example, I might have come up with a link to Charles Dickens's *Oliver Twist*. Both have kids on their own after being shafted by the system, who meet up with a series of characters—some good, some bad—and who eventually receive assistance from smart adults willing to believe in them despite appearances and willing to make a sacrifice or two.

They've also got interesting points of diversion. To mention an obvious one, Gilstrap's book features a young protagonist who is really quite savvy to his situation and how to go about resolving it, he just can't quite make it work without an adult advocate. Dickens's book features a pretty hapless kid. Is it the times? Possibly. Is it the intent of the author? Probably. Whatever the case may be, both Nathan and Oliver are good kids in bad predicaments in systems that don't seem inclined to help and may be motivated to hinder. In addition to tapping in to teens' attraction to themes of youth oppression and survival in an adult world, you've lots more to work with here to make a really attractive booktalking combination, and by pairing with other popular/classics combinations, could also create a great booklist.

It's not just the brand new fiction titles that make good combinations with classics. There's a whole magnificent universe of contemporary fiction out there to draw from. Keep in mind all those incredible teen and adult readers' advisory resources, both traditional and online, to help you select contemporary fiction to combine with classics. A couple of helpful resources specific to combining teen fiction with the classics are Sarah K. Herz and Donald R. Gallo's 1996 book, *From Hinton to Hamlet: Building Bridges between Young Adult Literature and the Classics*, and *Adolescent Literature as a Complement to the Classics*, edited by Joan F. Kaywell and published in four volumes between 1993 and 2000. Herz's book provides a great deal of practical information for educators and also includes a list of classics titles commonly taught at the secondary level with themes identified and lists of contemporary teen fiction titles linked to the classics by shared theme. Kaywell's book is also intended for educators who may want to teach the classics in combination with contemporary teen literature. Both resources, though, have content that readily adapts to youth services librarianship.

#8: Combining Fiction Classics with Nonfiction Works

Nonfiction often gets a short shrift with teens. It shouldn't! There are as many teen readers out there who prefer nonfiction as those who prefer fiction. I've often found it's easier to attract a reluctant teen reader to nonfiction than fiction, especially young males. I'm not sure precisely why that may be. Some of these teens may not have the patience for a story that's outside their possible reality, a story that hasn't really happened and is just imagined. Others may simply not care for fiction. Some may prefer their fictional stories to come from other media sources, like television and film, and are attracted to nonfiction because they aren't getting much, if any, of it through the media. Whatever the case may be, nonfiction is not only the preferred reading choice of many teens, it's one way to interest reluctant or disinterested readers. Although you can promote nonfiction works in a display or booklist or booktalking presentation—either all classics or classics combined with contemporary nonfiction—this would be more a theme than a combination, so let's focus here on combining fiction classics with nonfiction works.

You could combine classic fiction with classic nonfiction works, pairing, for example, Claude Brown's 1965 *Manchild in the Promised Land* with Nathan McCall's 1994 contemporary classic, *Makes Me Wanna Holler: A Young Black Man in America*. Both books, the first fiction and the second nonfiction, are classic works that immerse the reader in the experiences of young black men in America who pull themselves out of profound disadvantage and lives of crime to realize success. You might combine Alan Paton's classic novel, *Cry, the Beloved Country*, or Nadine Gordimer's classic novel, *Burger's Daughter*, with Nelson Mandela's classic biography, *Long Walk to Freedom*, or Desmond Tutu's nonfiction classic, *No Future without Forgiveness*, all of which address South African apartheid from multiple perspectives during its horrific reign and after its collapse.

You could combine classic fiction with current or high-interest nonfiction works. For example, you might combine Stephen Crane's classic novel, *The Red Badge of Courage*, with Clifton G. Wisler's *When Johnny Went Marching: Young Americans Fight the Civil War*, a nonfiction book written for young people that looks at forty-nine real teen participants, male and female, who stood out for their unique and courageous behaviors during the war. Or, you might combine one of Ambrose Bierce's Civil War short stories or Michael Shaara's classic novel, *Killer Angels*, with something like Harold Elk Straubing's book, *In Hospital and Camp: The Civil War through the Eyes of Its Doctors and Nurses*, which compiles a series of fascinating, visceral letters from the real people who took care of the Civil War's wounded and buried its dead. You'd be combining the fictionalized points of view of officers and soldiers with the real-life communications of field medical personnel of the time. What a great combo!

How about combining classic science fiction with science fact? You might promote Michael Crichton's 1969 classic novel, *The Andromeda Strain*, with Richard Preston's 1994 high-interest nonfiction work, *The Hot Zone*. Both are about outbreaks of deadly pathogens and the desperate efforts of scientists to identify and contain them. Both are edge-of-the-seat biological thrillers. One is speculative fiction about a space pathogen, the other the true story of the Ebola virus. Incredible stuff. You could make a link between Frank Herbert's science fiction classic, *Dune*, in which the Guild Navigators inhale spice (the most important commodity in the known universe and around which the entire story revolves) so they can fold space and ferry civilizations among the planets, with Stephen W. Hawking's *A Brief History of Time*, in which the preeminent scientist discusses for the layperson the current realities of time, space, wormholes, and the potential for travel among the vast reaches of the cosmos.

Or, to briefly mention another fiction genre, you might pair just about any classic mystery that starts with a single or multiple murder with Truman Capote's 1965 *In Cold Blood: A True Account of a Multiple Murder and Its Consequences*, the very first of the true crime genre.

All in all, you could go nuts with the possible combinations you might make between classic fiction and nonfiction of all kinds, and you'll be doing active and potential teen readers a favor by making combinations that offer a variety of possible entry points.

#9: Combining Classics with Other Media Formats

Because of the dynamic nature of most media formats, you can get some real buy-in from teens when you make use of them. Combining classics with other media formats makes for appealing booklists, displays, and engrossing booktalking presentations—whether in a classroom environment or in your school or public library as a special program for teens (see Chapter 8!). Not only does the integration of media formats bring a unique dynamic, mood, or "feel" to the classics, in this media-soaked world the use of media formats can also go a long way toward legitimizing both you and the value of what you're offering—the classics—to teens.

Recorded Books

Many classic novels and nonfiction works are available unabridged in a recorded book format. Not only can these be good stand-alone choices for some teens, they work well as a classics combo. Consider featuring the recorded classic with its printed version in your displays, include information for the recorded book format in booklists, and use recorded books in your classics booktalks. You'll give teens an additional choice for connecting with that classic. An alternative format like a book on tape can be the only appealing entry point to the classics for teens who have visual disabilities, poor reading skills, or just very little interest in the process of reading. Before using this media format in combination with original classics, it's a good idea to listen to a portion to assure yourself of the quality of the reader's presentation.

As a part of a classic booktalking presentation, you might select an action-oriented passage or pivotal scene, a revealing monologue by a main character, or a moving description to play for your teen audience. Teens are often more still and rapt when you read from a book than when you're just talking about one, and are even more engaged when someone with a wonderful voice and real skill as a performer reads to them on tape or compact disk. And, listening to a skilled reader as a part of your presentation may leave teens with a positive feeling toward that classic and toward your presence there as a promoter of classics, which bodes well for your future relationship with them and influence on their classics connections!

Music

Okay, music soothes the savage beast. Need I say more? All right, I'll say just a bit more. A cliché it may be, but music is the universal language, and teens speak it. Why not include it in your displays, booklists, and booktalks? You can actually play music in the classroom or to a teen group to set a mood and draw in even the most reluctant of souls to your classics booktalks—at least for a little while—which is better than for no time at all! You could combine classic music with classic literature from the same time period, or combine new and hip music with classic literature by theme. Rap music lends itself especially well to the latter. Why not combine it with a classic poem on the same theme? You could combine the music of a world culture with its classic literature. There are lots of choices available to you.

You might display the soundtrack of Andrew Lloyd Webber's Broadway production with Gaston Leroux's *The Phantom of the Opera*. You might include compact disks of South African drumming rhythms or Soweto street music on a booklist with Nelson Mandela's classic autobiography, *Long Walk to Freedom*, and Alan Paton's classic novel, *Cry, the Beloved Country*, and add in contemporary teen historical fiction about South African apartheid, like Beverly Naidoo's *Chain of Fire*. You could play the Tibetan Monks' intense multichord vocal chants when booktalking the Dalai Lama's autobiography, *Freedom in Exile*, which you could also combine with some fascinating nonfiction books about the monks' daily lives, spiritual practices, and beliefs.

The possibilities are almost endless on this one, and it really can work to pull a rich emotional response out of teens that they will, first, appreciate, and second, favorably associate with the classics.

Imagery

Imagery lends itself exceptionally well to displays and is an especially powerful tool in a classics booktalking presentation. When you can, connect teens with images that support and enhance the classics you are promoting. Images can immediately bring a situation or circumstance or concept to people with an impact and force words just won't provide in the same time frame and fashion. You could find a way to enlarge a high-impact or mood-setting image and have it on display with a selection of classics in your classroom or library's teen area. You might pass powerful images around the classroom or group to enhance classics booktalks.

Here are a few ideas of the sorts of images you might use in combination with the classics:

- *Prints of paintings by famous artists that illuminate a time period or tone of a classic*
  For example, John Singer Sargent's turn-of-the-century portraits of American women would meaningfully combine with an early American women's classic like Kate Chopin's *The Awakening*, or Charlotte Perkins Gilman's *The Yellow Wallpaper, and Other Writings*, so teens can more accurately visualize the protagonists in the formal and restrictive dress of their time.

- *Journalistic photos that support a classic*
  For example, the wrenching 1973 Pulitzer Prize–winning image of 9-year-old Kim Phuc, running naked in terror after stripping off her burning clothing when her South Vietnamese village was accidentally napalmed, would meaningfully combine with Walter Dean Myers's teen fiction classic, *Fallen Angels*, or Tim O'Brien's contemporary Vietnam classics, *Going After Cacciato* and *The Things They Carried*.

- *Sketches and drawings by fans of a particular classic*
  Fantasy and science fiction classics lend themselves well to this. For example, any number of extraordinary artists, such as Alan Lee, Ted Nasmith, John Howe, Greg and Tim Hildebrandt, and the author himself, have rendered J.R.R. Tolkien's fantasy works into lush imagery.

- *Vintage movie posters of classics made into films*
  These can be good, cheesy fun, and may be particularly fun to share with classics booktalks.

- *Literary maps that illustrate significant geographies or journeys represented in classics*
  Mary Ellen Snodgrass's *Literary Maps for Young Adult Literature* includes quite a selection of easily reproduced maps, including well-known classics like

Twain's *The Adventures of Huckleberry Finn*, Maya Angelou's *I Know Why the Caged Bird Sings*, Conrad Richter's *The Light in the Forest*, and Charles Portis's *True Grit*. Just for fun, you might take a look at the Library of Congress's book of literary maps called *Language of the Land*, which is full of prints of really fun vintage pieces from the Library's collections. You might also find books with maps of fantastical worlds described in classics, Tolkien's works being a good example yet again.

Comics and Graphic Novels

Teens and comics are a match made in heaven. But what do comics have to do with classics, you ask? Well, a significant number of comics are highly respected classics in their own right. In addition, some are based on classic literature. And many share meaningful themes with classic literature. Great combinations to be made here! You can attract a great deal of teen interest by including them in your readers' advisory suggestions, in your displays and booklists, and in your classics booktalking presentations—and by combining them with other classic works by theme or genre.

You might simply promote comics that are classics on their own terms. Nothing wrong with that, and you are likely to immediately engage teen interest, which can lead from comics into other classics. You have lots of choices with classic comics, including *Batman, Spider-man, Superman, The Flash, The Green Lantern, Aquaman, The Justice League of America, The Green Arrow, Wonder Woman, Captain America, The Fantastic Four, The Hulk, Thor*, and *The X-Men*, just to mention a very, very few.

You might combine classic comics with literary classics by theme. If you were exploring a reluctant hero theme, for example, you could include the original, brooding *Batman* comics or *Spider-man* comics with your literary classics selections. Jack Schaefer's *Shane* features a reluctant hero. J.R.R. Tolkien's two hobbit protagonists, Bilbo Baggins and Frodo Baggins, are the reluctant heroes of *The Hobbit* and the *Lord of the Rings* trilogy, respectively. So is Samwise Gamgee in the latter, come to think of it. You might contrast reluctant heroes with a gung-ho hero, and add in *Beowulf*. I mean, despite a one-track monster possessing sharp claws and a mean mother, Beowulf seems ever eager to enter the fray! You certainly could combine classic heroes from comics with classic heroes from literary classics. You'll find the heroic characters Hercules and Thor exist in both literary forms. If you had a good-versus-evil theme, you might combine *The Hulk* with Robert Louis Stevenson's *Dr. Jekyll and Mr. Hyde*. Both feature good men, scientific men, who physiologically morph from reasoned humans to raging monsters, and back again. And back again. . . .

There may be concept combinations you can make between classics and comics whether the comics are classics or not, say, between any one of the Arthurian classics and *Camelot 3000*, a DC Comics graphic novel by author Mike W. Barr and illustrator Brian Bolland. In this imaginative work, Arthur Pendragon, brought back to life in the far future, enlists the aid of the wizard Merlin and the soon-to-be reincarnated Knights of the Round Table to fight off invading aliens controlled by his archenemy Morgan La Fey. Or, you might simply link comics set in particular time periods to literary classics set in the same time periods, with or without any character, thematic or plot-oriented link. CrossGen Comics (an awesome publishing house) currently offers a slick, sexy comic mystery series called *Ruse*, featuring the brilliant-but-distant Detective Simon Archard and his assistant Emma Bishop, set in a twisted, alternative Victorian England. You might combine this lushly illustrated series with Sir Arthur Conan Doyle's Sherlock Holmes mysteries, or with Wilkie Collins's *The Moonstone* or *The Woman in White*, all mystery classics written and set in Victorian and early Edwardian England. You might combine Art Spiegelman's *Maus: A Survivor's Tale*—a classic itself—with other classic Holocaust titles.

By including classic and popular comics as part of your classics suggestions to teens, you are first acknowledging and demonstrating that classics come in many forms, not just the literary highbrow. Some of those classics forms are immediately appealing and accessible to teens, and are often just plain enjoyable for all ages. In my opinion, when introducing teens to classics, it's always better to be more rather than less inclusive. Secondly, you are introducing teens to fun reading that has strong connections to the literary classics. This is a great thing. You are chipping away at that "boring barrier" (which we'll talk about a little more in Chapter 9) and other unfortunate reputation issues classic literature has with teens, and showing them through a medium they know and enjoy that classics are full of all the right kinds of things—just like comics! Thirdly, you are boosting your credibility with your teens, who are more likely to come to you for other reading recommendations in the future if you've shown yourself to be savvy enough to promote the comics to them in the here and now! There's probably a fourthly and a fifthly and so on, but suffice it to say, there's just nothing bad to say about combining comics and graphic novels with other sorts of classics when making classics connections with teens.

Film and Television Programs

Just like recorded books, you can rely on teens to be more interested when you tie classics to films and television programs and give them an additional entry point. These media formats can go a long way toward making all classics more interesting, approachable, and meaningful for potential teen readers.

The possible combinations between classics, films, and television programs, by theme or genre, may nearly approach infinity! There's almost no end of film and television programs based directly on the classics alone. If you are making thematic or genre combinations between a classic and a film that is not based on that classic, make sure you have a super strong connection between the two. You don't want to confuse teens by stretching a connection too thin. The whole point here is to use this media format to attract the interest of potential teen readers to a classic work, not to distract them from it or confuse them regarding its themes or meanings with a loosely connected element. Even though you could draw some comparisons between the X-Men movies and Alexandre Dumas's *The Three Musketeers*—both are about groups of individuals closely associated by unique qualities and skills who fight and defend against a known evil—you might be stretching it a bit far!

Unlike unabridged recorded books, films and television programs are *adaptations* of the original. You really need to watch the film or television program in its entirety before promoting it in combination with an original classic to teens; you need to be certain of quality and appropriateness. As long as we're talking about watching the film or television program in its entirety, I implore you not to believe for even a moment that if you have watched the movie and feel it's a good one, you should promote it in place of the classic it's based on! Use films and television programs in combination with their original classics only. Even the truest of media adaptations are still just adaptations and are not equal to the classics themselves.

Avoid film or television adaptations that are not true to the theme or meaning of the original classic, and avoid poorly written, poorly acted adaptations. A perfect example here might be the relatively new television adaptation of *Dr. Jekyll and Mr. Hyde* starring John Hannah that aired on Bravo in October 2003. It was wretched! You wouldn't have known it from the advertisements, though. It looked like one of those awesome BBC productions of the classics, with great historical sets, costuming, stage actors, and all that good stuff. You know, horse-driven carriages on cobblestones, waistcoats with pocket watches, walking sticks, great coats and top hats, even mutton chop sideburns. Unfortunately, the look was not enough to cover the horrific rewrite, unfortunate casting, embarrassingly over-the-top acting, and all that bad stuff. Worst of all, it was just not true to the plot or theme or meaning of Stevenson's classic.

A year or two later, this version may be available on videocassette or DVD, and were you to put this on a classic combo booklist or show a part of it in a classroom as a booktalking presentation, it certainly might appeal to teens. There's lots of nutso behaviors going on, syringes full of bright blue liquid being injected into veins, blood and gore spraying about, and even a cameo by a dismembered hand. But there's also no trace of Stevenson's Mr. Utterson, the character Stevenson used to tell the tale, and there's a truly gratuitous and upsetting (although not graphic) rape scene, which is repeated a second time while the young victim is recovering from the first brutalization. A horrific mess of a production, one you would not want to use to attract interest in the classic that shares almost nothing but the same title and a very rudimentary concept.

Speaking of potentially upsetting sorts of scenes, you'll want to be sure even with a magnificent production that you don't promote a film or television program that's not appropriate to the age and stage of development of an individual teen or a teen audience. This is a little easier to manage in a booklist for a particular age range, or as a booktalker speaking to a particular group of teens. It's a little trickier when doing a bulletin board or display in your classroom or library's teen area. If a film version, you should know the rating the film originally received from the Motion Picture Association of America (MPAA). You most likely don't want to use a film that received an R-rating on a booklist or in a booktalking presentation for teens in the middle grades, nor do you want to feature it on a bulletin board in your teen area.

If showing a piece of film or television program as part of a booktalking presentation, be sure that you are not breaking any laws by showing a small portion in an educational setting. The laws around educational use of copyrighted materials are fairly generous, but do your homework first to be certain.

It's probably easy enough to come up with classics combinations between the original works and those high-quality BBC productions like Jane Austen's *Pride and Prejudice* and Dickens's *Great Expectations*. You won't have any trouble combining James Ellroy's contemporary classic noir mystery, *L. A. Confidential*, with the Academy Award–winning film of the same name starring Kevin Spacey, Russell Crowe, and Kim Bassinger. You might remember the Steve Martin comedy film, *Roxanne*, based on Edmund Rostand's play, *Cyrano de Bergerac*. It's obvious that you could combine Tolkien's *Lord of the Rings* trilogy with the truly incredible Peter Jackson film trilogy, or Patrick O'Brian's *Master and Commander* with its 2003 film version starring Russell Crowe (he gets around). But where do you get the not-so-obvious ideas for combining film and television programs with the classics?

You may have to do some research on your own using reference resources that group film and television programs by genre or story. Luckily for you, with just a minimum of effort lists upon lists of films based on the classics or on books of any kind can be at your fingertips. You'll find loads of lists of books on film and on television on the Internet. Just to get you started, the Morton Grove Public Library's Webrary Reader's Services pages has short lists of books to movies at http://www.webrary.org/rs/flbklists/Movies.html and books to television at http://www.webrary.org/rs/flbklists/TV.html. J. M. McElligot's Literature Awards site has a list of "Best Picture" Academy Award–winning films originally based on novels at http://www.literature-awards.com/books_on_film.htm. For a short list of great book sources to help you find classics on film, see the list at the end of Chapter 8.

FINDING AND KEEPING TRACK OF YOUR OWN CLASSICS COMBOS

How do you find the specific works you might use for all these classics combos, and when you do, how do you keep track of them all? You dig around, and you chart it all out!

As you're reading classics, ideas for one-on-one readers' advisory, displays, booklists, and booktalking combinations will just come to you and you can dig around for materials that might make those combinations work well. You can rifle through booklists, surf the Internet for ideas, look in reference resources, skim through poetry anthologies, search your library's online catalog, ask your professional colleagues, check teen literature listservs and online discussion groups, and that sort of thing.

What about the charting part? Well, you need some way to record all the titles and formats you're collecting into some cohesive whole. A chart is especially helpful for building master theme lists of classics and contemporary materials across all genres and formats. I usually build charts by theme—it's the most common sort of classics combination I use, both by my own design and by educator request. It's likely to be the most common sort of combination you'll use, too, but you should build your charts to best suit your needs.

Since it's hard to describe a chart and easy to show an example of one, see the example on pages 144–145. This is a good example of a layout, but it is on the simpler side. There aren't any legends or comics or that sort of thing listed. For some topics or themes, a chart of this sort will include a broad range of book and non-book combinations.

Once you read Chapter 9, it will become clear to you that I am fascinated by the plague! Just so you know I am not completely imbalanced, I have many of these theme charts, one of which is on good, old all-American baseball. It's just too long to fit in here. I've also got one on invisibility that's just too long to fit in, and that's because invisibility seems to be just about as fascinating to everybody as baseball! I doubt, however, that invisible baseball would provide much of an attraction.

You might set up your theme charts in a different fashion that makes more sense to you, but this setup works well for me with theme at the top, genres and formats down the left column, and the title, author, genre, subject, and simultaneous format of each work filled in from left to right in rows.

So, what does the fancy chart do that a hand-jotted list won't do? Hmmm. Good question. Well, it can allow you one complete, easy-to-read visual tool that contains enough titles and formats on a particular theme that when you narrow down to a selection of titles from within it, you've got all the information you need to build a cohesive display or booklist, or to craft a nice, tight booktalking presentation with a great balance based on the wider world of available choices. It also can be of great help to you in the future when you've forgotten just how you pulled together that last booktalk from two years ago on the same theme you've been asked to do again this year. You're way too busy to reinvent the wheel!

Another benefit is that the chart can be readily printed and handed out to teens who want to use it as a self-guided readers' advisory tool, and can add up to a handy readers' advisory tool for other library staff to use with teen readers when you are not present to offer your expertise. And even when you're not promoting the classics, your chart will have the lion's share of the other contemporary titles and formats on that theme.

Last but not least, your chart can prevent mistakes. If I had been in a hurry (which I usually am at work, and I'll bet you are, too) when I pulled together a classics combo by theme on the plague, I might have assumed that the plague in Europe was the plague in Europe. Not so! There were *two* incidents of the plague in Europe, about three hundred years apart. I'm still no expert on the plague, but I was even less aware of the historical specifics while building my chart and before reading the books I'd selected for a booktalking presentation. Had I not laid out all the title information, including subject and notes, in this easy-to-read format for myself, I would have missed that some of the listed titles are about the 1348 plague and some are about the 1666 plague. Huh. I could have read a few books, missed a neural link or two along the way, and not figured out that the books I was promoting were from completely different periods in history. That would not have been good for me, and would not have been good for my teen audience. Transmitting inaccurate information is bad for your reputation, and misinforming young people is a very bad thing, period!

On the brighter side (if there is one when talking about the plague), when looking at this chart with all the information laid out in a nice, neat grid, I got the idea to do a booktalk that used the titles from both time periods in a compare-and-contrast sort of way. That idea would not have been triggered without a clean, all-in-one-view of the titles I located on this theme.

SUMMING IT UP

As a teen services librarian or educator, once you have a familiarity with the many forms classics take, including the "must-know" classics, and understand the appealing ways you can combine them together and with other book and nonbook materials, you can more meaningfully draw teens in your library or classroom toward the wonders and relevance of these great works. By keeping a record of the classics combination you make by theme, genre and/or format, you have a tool to draw on in your work with teens over time.

Theme: Bubonic Plague

	Title	Author
Classics	*Doomsday Book*	Connie Willis
	The Plague	Albert Camus
	A Journal of the Plague Year	Daniel Defoe
Adult Fiction	*Bleak Midwinter*	Peter Millar
	Year of Wonders: A Novel of the Plague	Geraldine Brooks
	The Plague Tales	Ann Benson
	The Years of Rice and Salt	Kim Stanley Robinson
	A Plague on Both Your Houses	Susanna Gregory
Teen Fiction	*The House on Hound Hill*	Maggie Prince
	Nell of Branford Hall	William Wise
	A Parcel of Patterns	Jill Paton Walsh
	The Cure	Sonia Levitin
Nonfiction	*In the Wake of the Plague: The Black Death and the World it Made*	Norman Cantor
	Life During the Black Death (The Way People Live series)	John Dunn
	The Black Death (Turning Points in World History series)	John Nardo
	The Black Death (World History series)	Phyllis Corzine
	The Black Death	Tom McGowen
	When Plague Strikes: The Black Death, Smallpox, AIDS	James Giblin
	Epidemic	Brian Ward
	The Plague (Epidemics: Deadly Diseases through History series)	Holly Cefrey
Media	*The Black Death* (History's Turning Points video series)	The Learning Channel

Genre	Subject/Notes	Other formats?
Science Fiction	Time travel to England at onset of 1347-1351 plague	Audiobook
Fiction	Fictional North African plague	
Fiction	1665 plague in London	Audiobook
Fiction	Outbreak of plague in modern England	
Fiction	Eyam "The Plague Village" in 1666	
Fiction	Dual story of 14th century and 21st century bubonic plagues	
Science Fiction	Alternative history with Black Death decimating Europe and other countries coming into dominance	
Mystery	Middle Ages physican, Matthew Bartholomew works on a mystery in the time of the Black Death	
Science Fiction	Time travel to the 1665 London plague	
Fiction	1665 plague in London	
Fiction	1665 plague in Derbyshire village	Audiobook
Science Fiction	Time travel to 1348 Strasbourg during the Black Death and a time of anti-Semitism	Audiobook
	Tells individual life stories and the significant historical outcomes of the plague	Audiobook
	How the way people lived contributed to the spread of the plague and how affected survivors	
	A research book for teens with clear sections/essays on the plague, its occurences and its impact on human history	
	Causes and consequences of the 14th century Black Death	
	The Black Death from its start aboard an Italian ship to to its role in ending the Dark Ages and beginning the Renaissance	
	The stories of the three greatest plagues known to humankind	
	Dorling Kindersley Eyewitness Book with full-page color graphics describing epidemics and the fight against them, the Black Death included	
	Part of a series for teens, this volume takes the reader from flea to rat to human being, and beyond into the plague's effect on history	
	Follows the plague from an infected ship through Europe in 1347	

WORKS CITED

Attmann, Anna E., and Gail De Vos. 2001. *Tales, Then and Now: More Folktales as Young Adult Literary Fiction*. Englewood, CO: Libraries Unlimited.

Books on Film: An Alphabetical Listing. J. M. McElligot. Available online at: http:// www.literature-awards.com/books_on_film.htm (accessed 21 October 2003).

Books to Movies. Morton Grove, IL: Morton Grove Public Library. Available online at: http://www.webrary.org/rs/flbklists/Movies.html (accessed 21 October 2003).

Books to Television. Morton Grove, IL: Morton Grove Public Library. Available online at: http://www.webrary.org/rs/flbklists/TV.html (accessed 21 October 2003).

Brown, Max. 2003. E-mail exchange with the author. Bothell, WA: 2 October.

Challenged and Banned Books. Chicago: American Library Association. Available online at: http://www.ala.org/Content/NavigationMenu/Our_Associa tion/Offices/Intellectual_Freedom3/Banned_Books_Week/ Challenged_and_Banned_Books/Challenged_and_Banned_Books.htm# wdcb (accessed 29 June 2003).

De Vos, Gail, and Anna Altmann. 1999. *New Tales for Old: Folktales As Literary Fictions for Young Adults*. Englewood, CO: Libraries Unlimited.

Dr. Jekyll and Mr. Hyde. 2003. Burbank, CA: Bravo. Original Bravo movie broadcast on 18 October.

Herz, Sarah K., with Donald R. Gallo. 1996. *From Hinton to Hamlet: Building Bridges between Young Adult Literature and the Classics*. Westport, CT: Greenwood Press.

Kaywell, Joan F., ed. 1993–2000. *Adolescent Literature as a Complement to the Classics*. 4 vols. Norwood, MA: Christopher-Gordon Publishers.

Kunitz, Stanley. 1988. "The Wellfleet Whale." In *The Norton Anthology of Modern Poetry*. Edited by Richard Ellmann and Robert O'Clair. 2nd ed. New York: W. W. Norton and Company.

Modern Sequels. Hobart, Tasmania: State Library of Tasmania. Available online at: http://www.statelibrary.tas.gov.au/modernsequ/. (accessed 14 October 2003).

SELECTED ANTHOLOGIES OF CLASSIC AND "BEST" SHORT STORIES

The American Short Story: A Collection of the Best Known and Most Memorable Short Stories by the Great American Authors. 1994. Edited by Thomas K. Parkes. New York: Galahad Books.

The Best American Mystery Stories of the Century. 2000. Edited by Tony Hillerman. Boston: Houghton Mifflin.

The Best American Short Stories of the Century. 1999. Edited by John Updike and Katrina Kenison. Boston: Houghton Mifflin.

A Century of Great Western Stories. 2000. Edited by John Jakes. New York: Forge.

A Century of Noir: Thirty-Two Classic Crime Stories. 2002. Edited by Mickey Spillane and Max Allan Collins. New York: New American Library.

Children of the Night: The Best Short Stories by Black Writers, 1967 to the Present. 1995. Edited by Gloria Naylor. Boston: Little, Brown and Company.

No, but I Saw the Movie: The Best Short Stories Ever Made into Film. 1989. Edited by David Wheeler. New York: Penguin Books.

The Pushcart Book of Short Stories: The Best Short Stories from a Quarter-Century of The Pushcart Prize. 2002. Edited by Bill Henderson. Wainscott, NY: Pushcart Press; New York: Distributed by W. W. Norton and Company.

The Science Fiction Hall of Fame, Volume I: The Greatest Science Fiction Stories of All Time, Chosen by the Members of the Science Fiction Writers of America. 2003. Edited by Robert Silverberg. New York: Tor.

We Are the Stories We Tell: The Best Short Stories by North American Women since 1945. 1990. Edited by Wendy Martin. New York: Pantheon Books.

SELECTED ANTHOLOGIES OF CLASSIC POETRY

The 100 Best Love Poems of All Time. 2003. Edited by Leslie Pockell. New York: Warner Books.

The 100 Best Poems of All Time. 2001. Edited by Leslie Pockell. New York: Warner Books.

101 Classic Love Poems. 2003. Compiled by Sarah Whittier. Chicago: Contemporary Books.

101 Famous Poems. 2003. Compiled by Roy Jay Cook. Chicago: Contemporary Books.

The Best American Poetry. 1988–. Annual. New York: Collier Books; Scribner Poetry. (The 2000 edition edited by Rita Dove includes a list of the best poems of the century.)

The Classic Hundred: All-Time Favorite Poems. 1998. Edited by William Harmon. New York: Columbia University Press.

Committed to Memory: 100 Best Poems to Memorize. 1997. Edited and with an introduction by John Hollander. New York: Riverhead Books.

Great American Prose Poems: From Poe to the Present. 2003. Edited by David Lehman. New York: Scribner.

Ornaments of Fire: The World's Best 101 Short Poems and Fragments. 1994. Selected and edited by Edd Wheeler. Santa Barbara, CA: Fithian Press.

The Random House Treasury of Best-Loved Poems. 2003. Edited by Louis Phillips. New York: Random House.

Part Two

Making It Happen

6

DEVELOP, MAINTAIN, AND DISPLAY YOUR CLASSICS COLLECTION FOR TEENS

Teens are probably not lined up overnight on the concrete walkways outside your libraries in sleeping bags and pup tents, with jugs of Fierce Grape Gatorade and bags of jalapeno cheddar Fritos, waiting for the doors to open so they can rush in and get the best spot in the library—be the first to lay their hands on that highly coveted copy of a literary classic. Alas, your library just does not have the same allure as a popular band on national tour. This is not to say you can't do a great deal to attract teens to the classics in your library; you're just unlikely to have to step over young bodies bundled up in nylon and fleece to get to your doors in the morning. That's probably a good thing, anyway!

You can start by building good classics collections with teens in mind. You can make those collections look good and draw teens to them through outstanding display. You can bring your expertise to bear and make connections between teens and classics through sound readers' advisory practices, and you can make it possible for teens to help themselves to great classics through passive readers' advisory tools. Oh, and those same passive readers' advisory tools can win friends and influence your coworkers, who will be quite grateful for the assistance the tools will provide when you're off waiting in line yourself for concert tickets somewhere!

This chapter considers how to develop and maintain a classics collections in your library, from building a collection from scratch to maintaining a good-looking collection over time. It examines many ways you can attract teens to classics through display, both in the library and online.

YOUR CLASSICS COLLECTION

Some of you may have (or have access to) attractive, nicely balanced, well-maintained, discrete classics collections for teens in your libraries, but I'm going to guess that's only some of you. Or, maybe only a very few of you! Many public libraries may not have a separate teen collection of any kind, let alone a separate classics collection. Alas, but that is a topic for another book! Other teen collections aside, for those of you public and school librarians who don't already have a teen classics collection, discrete or interfiled with other collections, you should strongly consider building one. To attract teens to the classics in your library requires having great classics for them in your library.

Developing Classics Collections from Scratch

Don't have a classics collection created and maintained with teens in mind? Maybe you are a school librarian with just a few classic titles that meet curriculum needs interfiled in your run of adolescent fiction. You might be in a public library where classics are considered adult reading, and are purchased through adult budgets and interfiled in adult fiction and nonfiction collections. I'm in the first library system of my career that has teen classics collections in most branches, and generous budgetary resources to support them. I would suspect classics-free teen collections are more common than not.

If you are one of the librarians described above, or fit some other professional description but don't currently have a classics collection dedicated to serving teens, consider doing what you can to start one in or near your teen area. If you don't have a teen area and can't create one, get those classics in the library somewhere where they're accessible to teens! Are you in a very small library? Do you have a very small budget? One, or the other, or both? You can start a classics collection with just a handful of books and build it over time. The important part is that you begin to build a collection that has your teen community in mind, even if it only ever spans two feet of shelf space.

Why is this so important?

- It's my experience that when you demonstrate to teens that you are doing something specifically for them, you attract their attention and they appreciate both it and you. Good vibes all around! It might sound corny, but hey, it's true.

- Bringing together a collection of classics, regardless of the size of that collection, and putting it in an area dedicated to teens, makes it easy for them to get to these great books. This is a simple issue of access. Most teens aren't likely to hunt for classics that are buried in other collections (if it ever crosses their minds to hunt for such a thing in the first place) unless they are required to read them, and they aren't likely to notice them while on browsing forays through those collections, either. Classics aren't the first sort of book that just pops up in the selective viewing of a teen book browser.

- It's just good merchandising. If you want to attract a group of people to anything at all, emphasize that thing. If you want to connect teens to classics, emphasize those classics.

- The classics in the teen area of a public library are bound to be of a different makeup than the body of classics found in adult public library collections, and from the titles used to support curriculum typically found in school libraries. You'll have far greater success connecting teens to classics in your library if you have the right sorts of classics to connect them to.

How do you build a teen classics collection from scratch? It's not so hard! You determine the sorts of classics your collection should have, you make the best selections for it, and you make the best purchases you can within your budget.

Determining the Sorts of Classics You Should Have

How do you get started? First and foremost, learn about your teen community. Having a general sense of who they are, what they need, and what they might enjoy will give you a real boost when it comes time to select titles for a classics collection just for them.

If you are a school librarian, you know your teens. You know their age ranges, interests, cultural mores, and intellectual and social capabilities. That's a great place to begin.

If you're a public librarian, you'll have to do some assessment. First, speak with your colleagues in the schools and alternative educational environments. Which titles are being used in the classrooms? If you don't have much space or much of a budget (these two tend to go hand in hand), you might avoid those titles in your public library collection. Teens tend to equate assigned reading with misery, and if you can only keep a few select titles, select something else! If you are in a larger public library and have a reasonable amount of shelf space and a decent budget, consider having a few of those assigned titles for teens to check out who skipped class the day the books were handed out, or for that one teen who left the book in his locker and the school's locked up but the book report is due tomorrow. Sure, the misery factor is there, but the bounties of your classics collection will save that teen in a time of deep educational crisis, and you can only look good for that!

Ask your colleagues, both in the schools and in your library, if they have any ideas for types of classics, or suggestions for specific classic titles to include in your collection beyond those required for assignments. Which categories of classics do they think might engage teen interest? How would they recommend you balance the contents of your collections between younger and older teens? What are the general reading levels in local schools? High? Low? If the latter, would they recommend crossover and thin classics for your collections? Are there types of classic literature that teens might like to pursue on their own to tie in with subjects they're studying in, say, history or science classes?

Public or school librarian, you should ask teens. Sure, some may look at you with incredulity—there's a high probability of that! But others might have some good ideas for you, ideas you'd never have thought up in a million years. It was a teen who first suggested to me that I ought to include a copy or two of Hugo and Nebula award-winning science fiction classics in my teen classics area (mostly so he didn't have to go hunting through all the adult science fiction and fantasy books for them!). That was a great idea; most Hugo and Nebula award-winning titles truly are classics. I expanded the idea to include other genre award winners, and those books circulate like crazy from my library's teen classics collection, and bring teens in contact with other classics they might enjoy and would never have noticed otherwise.

You can talk to teens one on one, but you might use a homegrown classics survey of your teen community like we talked about in Chapter 4. Answers to some of the survey questions could be quite helpful in building a better classics collection for teens.

You might just give yourself the credit you deserve and apply your own knowledge of your teen community and its needs to classics collection-building in your library. You are a professional and possess an expertise! If you have a hunch, educated or otherwise, about the sorts of classics that would work in your collections, go with it.

How to Make the Best Selections for Your Classics Collection

You either know the needs and interests of your teen community already, or you've done some assessment to find out. You've thought professional thoughts. You now feel you have a good sense of how to build your teen classics collection. It's time to make real selections, title by title. Even if you jotted down some suggested titles from colleagues and teens during your assessment activities, or made note of your own ideas for great titles, those probably aren't enough. Look to classics lists for additional titles you might include in your classics collection. The lists at the ends of Chapters 2 and 7, and in Appendix B, are excellent places to start. You might also look at the starter classics booklists found throughout Chapters 5 and 7 for recommendations, and certainly take advantage of the Internet for ideas.

Once you've built your starter list of classics titles for purchase, you'll need to decide if you're going to purchase them in hardcover or paperback bindings. If your library has a policy about which binding types are purchased, that decision has been made for you. If it's up to you or up to someone you can strongly influence, I highly recommend you build your classics collection in paperback. Why? First and foremost, with a limited budget (who doesn't have one?) you can buy a lot more paperbacks than hardcovers. Circulation for circulation, paperbacks don't last nearly as long as hardbacks, that's true. But for the price, you are likely to come out about even, including occasional replacement of deteriorated copies. Also, if a teen loses or damages a paperback classic and your library enforces lost book payment, the fine is not as steep and that teen is not nearly in as much trouble with a parent or guardian, and is not nearly so turned off (or maybe even blocked from using the library) by fines and fees policies as would be the case with a lost or damaged hardcover.

Most importantly, teens usually prefer paperbacks, and you are far more likely to attract a teen to a paperback classic than a hardcover classic. The books are smaller and thus less visually overwhelming. They are lighter and easily fit in pockets, purses, and backpacks. Portability is important with teen readers. Paperback editions of the classics almost always have more appealing cover art and will draw in teens that hardcovers won't. You might consider mass-market paperbacks for most choices in your classics collection, but some trade paperbacks are excellent choices as well, just not quite as affordable and definitely not as likely to fit in pockets! With paperbacks, your school or public library may require you purchase a protective binding type or plastic coating. If so, do your best to have the cover art and descriptive text preserved to provide necessary allure for teen readers.

On to editions! Let's say you're focused at present on selecting a few time-tested and contemporary classics by women. If you are in a position to select which editions you'll purchase, you might not have any trouble finding the best paperback copy for your budget of Barbara Kingsolver's *The Bean Trees*, or Gloria Naylor's *The Women of Brewster Place*. Both are contemporary classic titles and are only available in one or two editions. But what about Jane Austen's *Pride and Prejudice*, or George Eliot's *Middlemarch*? You've got one publisher on top of another, all with multiple trade paperback and mass-market editions. What to do? Well, if you want the biggest bang for your buck, you could start by eliminating the trade paperback editions. They're bigger, nicer, and pricier. Still, you've got quite a choice left between all the mass-market editions. Price isn't going to decide it for you—they all cost about the same and are similarly discounted through book distributors.

What will decide it? Various physical characteristics will, especially appearance. You want to select the highest quality, most appealing, teen-friendliest editions with the best cover art you can find. Over time you will develop a familiarity with paperback classics publishers. You'll remember that the Aladdin paperback editions have pretty appealing covers, and include book discussion group questions in the back, but are printed on what looks and feels like the Big Chief Tablet paper you used in first grade. You'll remember that the Penguin classic paperbacks are quality editions, but have cover art with far greater appeal to adults and really small print that, even though their young eyes can handle it, may be a bit daunting to teen readers. You'll remember that Signet and Bantam classics are each a pretty good deal. Sure, they could have teen-friendlier cover art, but they're nice, compact, high quality paperback editions at the right price that won't turn teens off.

Until you develop this familiarity, though, rely on descriptions and examples of book covers found on Web sites and in online databases. You may have access to *Books in Print* through a library subscription or to a commercial book vendor's database, or you might just head off to one of the online bookstores to find descriptions of paperback classics editions and cover images. Most of the publishers of paperback classics editions have Web sites that list their titles, and many show at the very least a few examples of their editions' covers, which may help you make your selections as well.

Wouldn't it be great if there were a publishing house dedicated to putting out affordable quality paperback editions of the classics specifically for teens? A publishing house that chose to print the sorts of classic titles teens might be more interested in and capable of both understanding and enjoying, and produced them in a friendly typeface and font, and put covers on them with greater teen appeal? All right, I'm leading you on. There is only one publishing house to my knowledge that actively maintains a line of paperback classics intended for teen readers, and it's worth knowing about. You may already be familiar with this publisher for its long history in the science fiction and fantasy field—TOR Books. The Children's and Young Adult Division at TOR was founded on this classics line in the late 1980s, which over the years has become one of its staples, selling strongly in both the educational and retail markets.

The TOR classics line, almost one-hundred-titles strong, was conceptualized and launched by Kathleen Doherty, daughter of TOR founder, Tom Doherty, and Publisher of TOR's Children's and Young Adult Division. Ms. Doherty, a long-time supporter of children's and teen services librarians in their work with youth, explains this unique line:

> The idea behind starting the line was that as a kid my father would make me give him a book report a week. He would often have me choose from a selection of the "classics" i.e., *Tom Sawyer, The Scarlet Letter, White Fang*, and so on. I'd pick up one of these "classics" and think, "Oh, God!" They looked so boring and tedious—the covers were monochromatic, the type oppressive—everything that makes a kid say, "I hate reading." But, once I began the book, I would totally get into the story. I learned to love the classics (for the most part) but only because I was provoked to read them. I would never have chosen a classic off a bookshelf. So, when I had the opportunity to start a line for TOR, I thought, "Why not package the classics to appeal to the young adult reader?"
>
> These are great stories, why don't the covers reflect the wonderful, exciting content? If you look at the cover of TOR's *White Fang*—a dog showing its fangs and poised for attack, what kid (especially a boy) isn't going to say "Cool!"? I also recalled the introductions and afterwords in the classics to be boring, overly analytical and just not at all inspiring. I believed if you wanted to get the reader excited about reading the story, the introductions should be entertaining, a prelude for the excitement to come. So, I decided to hire well-known and popular young adult authors to write the intro-

ductions and afterwords. I gave the line an affordable price point (we are still very competitively priced against other lines) and the line continued to grow and establish itself.

We are now over 90 titles strong and the line has been a strong staple for the company since 1989. I've had a great deal of feedback over the years from customers, teachers and librarians who test the TOR line against other lines, and I have always been told that the kids show more interest in reading the TOR editions. It has been quite rewarding. (2003)

Should you buy from any one publisher exclusively? Probably not. Consider varying your selections, even if you buy more heavily from an excellent teen-oriented classics line like TOR offers. It's a good idea to select classics editions from more than one publisher so that you can provide more variety and better attract teen readers across age ranges, aesthetic preferences, needs, and interests.

Selecting Classics for Your Collection within a Budget

If you are a librarian working in either a school or public library, there is no doubt you are quite well versed in budgetary constraints, for collection development and for just about everything else. In a perfect world, money would be no object and you'd purchase at least one of each and every classic ever written that a teen could need or want in the best possible edition it comes in. As long as we're fantasizing, let's imagine you have all the shelf space it would take to hold these books in your brand-new teen area!

Especially if you are building a classics collection from scratch, you may want to sort your selected titles into priority purchasing lists. (We'll also revisit this in a following section when we talk about maintaining a good-looking classics collection over time.) You might have room for one shelf of classics but can only afford to purchase half a shelf of classics, or may have room for two full shelving units of classics, but can only afford to fill one unit this budgetary period. Whatever the case may be, you are likely to have created a classics wish list longer than your ability to purchase at any given time!

This being true, place priority on your selections as you're developing your classics wish list. You may want a copy of Steinbeck's *Tortilla Flat* to complete your collection of Steinbeck titles, but as it doesn't support the curriculum in your school library and money is of the essence, you place a lower priority on it. If there's any money left over after you've made your priority purchases, you can purchase *Tortilla Flat*. If you're a public librarian and you know the schools have multiple copies of William Golding's *Lord of the Flies* to support a yearly classroom assignment, maybe you don't need a second or third copy of it on your shelves despite how well it circulates, that is, unless the budget allows after all your higher-priority purchases have been made.

There are lots of ways to do this. Some folks make a long list and write a number next to each title indicating purchasing priority, "1" or "A" usually indicating highest priority, and on down the line. You might build a spreadsheet that sorts your titles into priority order. You might use index or note cards and sort them into priority piles. Do whatever works best for you, and helps you remain organized when trying to get the most for the least, given your budget, library size and type, and community needs and interests.

Why Your Classics Collections Should Look Good

This section is for all librarians who already have classics collections, either in their own magnificent little area or interfiled with other collections. You may not need to build a collection from scratch, but you will need to evaluate what you've got on a regular basis, maintain those classics in favorable condition, and enhance them when your budget allows so you can do your best to attract teen readers to those wonderful works.

Let's start with an exploration of why it's so important for your classics collections to look good. I imagine you've all heard the adage at least once in your life, "You can't judge a book by its cover." Without going into all kinds of socioanthropological mumbo jumbo about biological attractors and imperatives and survival of the fittest and strengthening the gene pool, let's just begin by saying that the less literal, more universal, meaning of this message carries rather little weight in the world of romance!

Just about any of us with any speck of honesty will admit we most certainly do judge potential romantic interests by appearance. We also judge by appearance each person who gets on the bus after we do, or who walks by in the mall, or sits next to us at the movie theater. We just can't help it. Human nature! Hopefully (at the very least in the world of nonromantic relationships) most of these are just initial judgments readily cast aside to move on toward the deeper, more important, and lasting features to be found in another human being. And, as we mature, we tend to make these sorts of judgments less often, or put less store in them, having developed compassion and having gained experience with the wonders to be found inside people rather than outside, and perhaps even having experienced painful judgments toward ourselves from others.

But that's the broader, human condition part of the adage. What about the literal, object part of the adage? Do we become less interested in good-looking *stuff* as we mature? Hmmm. When you burn out the heating element in your toaster, do you prefer a bright, shiny, new toaster to that slightly worn version your friend has in his garage and is willing to give you for free? I sure do, and I'll pay a veritable fortune for it, especially if it comes in a retro pistachio green and has a removable crumb tray. When you crack the block in your car engine and there's just no fixing it, do you want that reasonably priced well-running 1991 Honda Civic hatchback with only a few scratches on the driver's side door and with only a faint smell of barf in the back, or do you want a brand new Lexus 4-door sedan with heated cream-colored leather seats and a champagne sparkle paint job, despite a monthly outlay the size of some people's mortgages? Casting aside my tendency toward economy and my desire to stem the tide of environmental degradation, and casting aside my dislike of elite manufacturers, I would *so* prefer the Lexus!

Okay, the same holds true for books. When you, yourself, get that wonderful anticipatory feeling as a reader that it's time to immerse yourself in a classic high fantasy novel, or a stylish noir mystery, or a complex, edge-of-the-seat novel of the French revolution featuring Madame Guillotine, isn't there at least a twinge of disappointment when you go to the library to borrow a copy and the only one on the shelf has a cracked cover, torn pages, and something brown and crusty on the back (that you hope is chocolate and don't want to think about being anything else)? Even though I'm not much of a personal book buyer—too many years in a library, I guess—I might consider hitting a bookstore for a crisp, clean copy of that much-anticipated good read. I'm going to be holding that book in my *hands* for some time, after all.

Maybe it's not that bad. Maybe you get to the library and find a copy of Jack Schaefer's western classic, *Shane,* on the shelf, and it's not in too bad a condition. Binding's okay, pages are intact, seems stain-free. Wait a minute, though. The edition is from, oh, looks to be 1952. You're pretty sure the cover artist used those waxy colored pencils, the ones that are more likely to tear the page than leave a nice, rich mark. Your sketchy, unsubstantial Shane is a perfectly-coiffed blonde with underdeveloped pectorals and sloping shoulders. He's wearing a spanking-clean powder-blue pantsuit, and is quite nicely accessorized. Look at that saucily tied neckerchief! Is that Niles from *Frasier*? Wouldn't that gun on his hip tip him over?

Isn't Shane supposed to be a taciturn-but-sensitive, smooth-moving, lone wolf, reluctant-but-very-good-at-what-he's-forced-to-do gunslinger? Didn't Jack Schaefer write one of the most acclaimed models for every misunderstood "lone gun for hire" in literature and the media ever since? Shouldn't Shane look like Clint Eastwood in *Two Mules for Sister Sarah* (where he is, in my opinion, at his all-time most appealing)? What's he doing looking like, well, Niles? Now you've got that silly pant-suited man in your mind when you open the book to read about a highly effective and conscience-torn gunslinger, and may have to battle the unfortunate image for the entirety of the book. The cover has given you a poor first impression of the primary character in the work. What a turnoff.

Okay, so most of you don't like cruddy books with horribly outdated images on the cover. Neither do teens. You might pick up a book regardless (with a pair of surgical gloves or with a quick flip of the wrist to open the book and get past the unfortunate cover art), knowing with your greater maturity that despite rather disappointing outward appearances, it's really what's inside that counts. No disrespect intended in either direction, but teens aren't nearly so mature as you! They are a ruthlessly judging lot, and the majority of that judgment is happening at the visual level. You can't afford to have the appearance of your classics collection turn teens away.

You've got to admit if all of us had our druthers, adults and teens alike, most of us would opt for the cleanest, classiest, sexiest, neatest, freshest, slickest, newest stuff—books and their covers most definitely included. Why? Looks do matter.

Keeping Your Classics Collections Looking Good

Maintaining your classics collection is easy to do. Regularly yank the classics off your shelves that are in poor condition. This means dirt and grit, identifiable and not so identifiable stains and chunks, torn and yellowed pages, battered covers and broken spines, puffy and wavy pages from an unfortunate meeting with a full bathtub, a generally bad smell, and what have you. Get rid of the classics on your shelves that have ugly, outdated, and just plain ridiculous cover art from yesteryear. Even if they are in decent condition, classics on your shelves that look OLD (in the not-retro-hip uncool way) are a turnoff. Buy new books to replace them.

You might replace the titles you pulled, or purchase entirely new titles you think might be better additions to your collection.

Have a restricted budget for this sort of thing? Of course you do, you work in a library! You can do this in stages. Make a list of the titles you've weeded out of your classics collection based on poor condition and age. Break that list into smaller lists that can be phased in to your purchasing schedule over time, and give them priorities. Make an "A" list of the classics that have to be replaced first. These might be classics that best support curriculum, classics that you've read and feel you have an outstanding chance connecting to teens (if only your copies weren't in such poor condition), classics you intend to booktalk in the classroom or alternative educational environment, or the classics in the very worst physical shape. Make a "B" list, a "C" list, and so forth. As you can over time, squeeze these lists into your purchasing schedule to replace all those physically undesirable classics with slick, attractive new versions.

Your new classics can get ratty pretty fast themselves, particularly if they're checked out regularly, which yours will be as you encourage teens to read them! So set an ongoing schedule for evaluating your classics collection just as you would any other collection for which you are responsible. Once each year, or on a schedule that makes sense given the size of your classics collection and the time you have to engage in this sort of thing, pull all your classics off the shelves and examine them for condition, general appearance, and circulation. Make notes as you go along about which weeded titles you feel you should replace, and which you could or should do without. You've got to make room for the books teens will read.

As you evaluate your classics collection title by title, you should also note the general balance of the collection. Do you need more classics selections for younger teens? Are you short on classics by and about women? Have you got a good basic selection of world classics, not just those by Americans and Europeans? Is there a good balance between fiction and nonfiction classics in your collection? What about genre classics, themed classics, outstanding classics not used in the curriculum (and there are loads of these!), or lesser known but magical classics that you've read and want an opportunity to share with teens as time goes on? Are there enough copies of Orwell, Twain, and Steinbeck titles to meet teen needs for reading assignments? If you can only afford three to five titles a year, which ones would create the greatest breadth for your collection given what you've already got? The answers to these questions will provide you with ideas for further exploration to enhance your classics collections beyond just the replacement process.

If you do this sort of evaluation on a regular cycle, it will be a simple, quick task to keep your classics collection up to snuff and continually improving, it will keep you from ever harboring a book with a ridiculously outdated appearance, and it will keep you continually in touch with what you have on your shelves—always a good thing for one-on-one interaction and readers' advisory with teens.

DISPLAYING YOUR CLASSICS

Books are really on display all the time in the library. They're on open shelves, all lined up looking smart and weird and fascinating and sexy and sad and frightening and all those things books are. They're just waiting there for readers to pull them off, open them up and experience what they have to offer. Your classics books will be on display just by virtue of their presence in your library. Does that mean they are displayed to their best advantage, to teens' best advantage? Probably not.

You picked them, you purchased them, you've got those excellent classics right there in your library to share with teens. Now show them off! Draw teen attention to these outstanding reading choices. From where your classics collections are located to how they're filed, from classics signage to merchandizing and special display—in your library and online—there are many ways to make your classics collections the stars of their own show—visible, attractive and exciting to potential teen readers.

To Interfile, or Not to Interfile?

If you're in a small public library, or have a small collection of classic works, you may not have them separated out into a section of their own. For that matter, even if you're in a larger public library with a greater number of classic works in your collections, you may not have them separated out. If your contemporary teen fiction and nonfiction titles are either interfiled with children's materials (the horror!) or with adult materials (not great, either), you certainly are unlikely to have a separate classics collection just for teens. If you're in a secondary school library, you don't have children's or adult collections to worry about, but your classics collections may still be petite and interfiled with other materials. Although the Dewey Decimal classification system still predominates in public and school libraries, many of you may work in libraries with unique filing systems and arrangements that have been developed over time to best suit your community's needs.

All that said, here's the question: when your goal is to promote the classics with teens, to help them making rich, meaningful connections with the contents of those great works, should you interfile them with other collections, or should you separate them out? I'll bet you know what I'm going to say! In my opinion, you should separate them out. To separate them is to feature them as unique and worthy, which they are. To interfile them is to hide their collective lights under a bushel.

If you are a school librarian or if you have a discrete teen area in your public library, put classics in their own area within it. If you don't have a teen area, put those classics in a high-profile location or in an area where teens hang out in your library, with jazzy signage that promotes them specifically to teens. Make it clear that these books are singular and special. Make it easy to get to them, for teens to browse them for good personal reading matches. Make it easier for yourself and your professional colleagues to promote classics to teens in your library. Make it easier on you to "merchandize" those classics and to build displays around them.

Merchandize, with Modification!

Did someone really say "merchandize"? Oh, was that me? What an annoying word that is! You may be among the many fine librarians who find the current, trendy administrative overuse of retail terms in the not-for-profit sector irksome in the extreme. If so, you are in good company! There are, indeed, enough significant differences between what librarians do and what people who exchange products and services for monetary recompense do, that this retailing concept is, well, irksome.

But, hey, when the concept fits . . . or almost fits . . . According to the *American Heritage Dictionary*, second college edition, "merchandise" as a noun means "commodities or goods that may be bought or sold." The verb form means, "to promote the sale of, as by advertising or display" (1982, 786). All about financial profit, isn't it? I'll bet, though, if you were to rewrite that verb form in your mind as "to promote use, enjoyment and enrichment, as by advertising or display" and got rid of that pesky buying and selling business, you could accept this m-word as representing a highly important concept for libraries, librarians, books, and readers. Through advertising and display, you are far more likely to draw attention to your "goods"—those wonderful stories and fantastical imaginings, those historical accounts and life philosophies, those myths and legends of the world's cultures, and so on—than you are without it. Teens need you not only as a direct connection between the classics and themselves as readers, but indirectly as the behind-the-scenes mastermind who sets up ways for teens to more successfully make their own connections with classics.

Merchandising can take many forms. The first and most important form is featuring your books as a unique set of "goods." The second most important form is signage. Got to have it for your classics collection! Think about this from a teen's eye view. What does a teen see when she walks into a library, small or large? Books. Lots of them. They're all lined up spine out on shelving units that are probably arranged on the square. It's just one large, rapidly blurring field of book spines on shelves at right angles. Which ones are which? Not easy to tell. Not only is it not easy, it can be a complete barrier. Oh, but wait! There's a hip, colorful sign over there by that section of books. What's it say? "Classics for Teens." Okay, there's no longer a complete barrier. One area has been identified, and with a straightforward, eye-catching, colorful sign. Even though classics are surely gross, musty old boring books, maybe she'll take a closer look. After she uses the computers . . .

Even better, what if that teen makes her way over to that easily identified teen classics collection, and the books there aren't gross, musty and old. What if they're new, slick, attractive classics? Hey, you just bought those to attract this teen's interest, and all the others like her. Good for you! And, what if they aren't all spine out in a row on the shelves? What if you've faced several of them out so she can see those appealing covers without having to lift a finger? Facing books out is another form of merchandising, and a great one for use in your classics collection. First, you break up that blurring visual field effect. Books that are faced out become featured titles, a sort of smaller menu out of all the possible reading selections the library offers teens, which can reduce what I call "options overload" and allow them to make an easier connection with a book. In this case, with a classic!

Classics on Display

Display is a form of merchandising, too, but because it's so cool, it gets it's own header! If you have a display area in your library that is either dedicated to teens or can be used on a rotation for teen displays, make good use of it for promoting the classics. Whether that display area is just a shelf, a bulletin board, or a deep glass case you can build a whole little world in— you can make good use of it to attract teens to great classics reading choices.

Unfortunately, there aren't any current books in library literature on the basic techniques of traditional display making for teen audiences. You've either got the fairly current tiny-tot stuff or a couple of odd, old books on displaying "realia" on cardboard boxes covered with crumpled tablecloths. With the exception of Mary Ann Nichols's chapter called, "Targeting Teens: Marketing and Merchandising Young Adult Services" in *Young Adults and Public Libraries: A Handbook of Materials* (Nichols and Nichols 1998), you might look beyond library-related resources and dig up display principles, techniques, and ideas from retail resources, home-décor books, entertaining and holiday books and magazines, and just about every Martha Stewart thing you can lay your hands on.

Given the lack of resources, a few general do's and don'ts for book-related display-making might be useful here:

Do's and Don'ts of Displays

Do:

- Match the display style to the audience
- Clearly identify the theme of the display in its design
- Place important information at your audience's eye level if possible
- Fill the available space
- Use bright, contrasting, eye-catching colors
- Use bold, simple designs
- Keep related books well-stocked in or near the display
- Provide a brochure or handout of annotated titles associated with the display

Don't:

- Use a juvenile display style in a teen or adult area
- Leave large, vacant areas in your display
- Overcrowd the space
- Use typefaces and fonts that are difficult to read (regardless of how hip, grungy, or edgy they are!)
- Create an alluring display about titles not available to check out in the library
- Leave a time-specific display (like Banned Books Week, for example) up past its relevant dates

---

Although how you display the classics for teens in your library will depend on the sort of space you have in which to do so, here are a few basic ideas you might use as starting points:

- Display a selection of classics you particularly liked and think teens will also enjoy, a sort of "classics top picks" list. Provide prints of book covers accompanied by readable annotations in a nice arrangement on a bulletin board or in a brochure format.

- Gather together a collection of props and artfully arrange them around the classic titles they represent, with a selection of those books nearby for teens to check out.

- Tie a classics display into timely events, like some relevant topic in the news, a new film release based on a classic work, a classic author's death, a classic author receiving a major literary award, and so forth.

- Include classic works in larger display themes like Black History Month, Women's History Month, or Poetry Month.

- Build classics displays around themes or genres. The starter booklists and resources listed in and at the ends of Chapters 5 and 7, many of which divide classics into themes and genres, and the classics fiction and nonfiction lists in Appendix C may be of use to you here.

- Combine classics with other reading materials and media formats, by theme or genre. The ideas in Chapter 5 for "classics combos" make for some good book display ideas of this sort.

- Build a display around teen book reviews of the classics.

- If you are a public librarian, coordinate with your school librarians or educational colleagues to bring a classics display from the public library to the school before a classics booktalking presentation, or simply to advertise public library resources in a location regularly frequented by teens.

Displaying Classics Online

Traditional displays happen in the library building, but you can also display classics to teens beyond your library through online technology. With as many teens as use computers, surf the Internet, and remotely access library information, you should consider your Web pages prime display space. If your library has a Web site, consider providing a section that describes services and collections to teens. You can mention here that your teen collections feature a selection of excellent classics, and a librarian is available to help teens make great classics reading connections.

Remember that looks matter and have your library's Webmaster or IT staff provide a good-looking, teen-friendly Web design for your online classics display. You may have a teen section already where you can post your online displays and booklists, but if not, find an easily accessible area in your library's Web site for them. You can use many of the same ideas you use for traditional display in the library, minus props! Provide appealing cover images and annotations. Provide easy-to-print booklists. You might even consider featuring a single classic title now and again with a written booktalk. And, you most certainly should post teen book reviews of classics on your Web pages when you've got them—there's some instant buy-in for other teen readers. Advertise your online displays with teens and with your professional colleagues. You might even ask the latter to put a link to your displays on their Web pages. Pretty neat, using the technology of today to connect teens with their long-time literary heritage!

SUMMING IT UP

Regardless of your budget and collection size, a discrete classics collection that is developed and arranged to meet needs and spark interests, will greatly assist you in making meaningful classics connections with the teens in your community. Through regular maintenance and through appealing merchandizing and displays, both in the library and online, you can feature your classics collection in appealing ways to entice teen readers.

WORKS CITED

American Heritage Dictionary. 1982. Second college edition. Boston: Houghton Mifflin.

Doherty, Kathleen. 2003. E-mail correspondence with the author. New York: 24 February.

Nichols, Mary Anne, and C. Allen Nichols, eds. 1998. *Young Adults and Public Libraries: A Handbook of Materials and Services.* Westport, CT: Greenwood Press.

7

BE A SUCCESSFUL CLASSICS READERS' ADVISOR WITH TEENS IN YOUR LIBRARY OR SCHOOL

As a readers' advisor, you are the single greatest element in connecting teens to classics in your library or school. Although readers' advisory involves some passive tools (which we'll look at in the last section of this chapter), it is primarily a direct practice of matching a reader to books that reader is likely to enjoy. In your case, that reader is a teen, and those books are classics. Just how does this happen? Through your knowledge and understanding of teens, your knowledge and understanding of the classics, and some sense of how to best connect the two!

From intellectual foundation to direct practice, readers' advisory is as important in making meaningful classics connections for teens as everything else we've talked about so far—maybe even more so. A strong readers' advisory interaction with a teen will still be a success, and can pave the way for a long-lasting open dialogue between you and that teen, even if you aren't absolutely brilliant on the subject of classic literature and even if you don't have more than a handful of classics in your library or classroom. Conversely, it won't matter how well you know and love classics and it won't matter how many wonderful classics choices you have available for teens, if you don't use good readers' advisory skills to promote meaningful matches.

An understanding of the basic elements or "appeals" in literature that attract readers of all ages, a familiarity with common and well-loved literary genres and why those genres may appeal to teens in particular, how classics fit in to those genres, and an awareness of the diversity of teen readers, are all essential to your classics readers' advisory work with teens. All of this knowledge, coupled with the practice of strong direct readers' advisory techniques—getting what you need from teens and giving what you've got to teens—are critical in making meaningful connections between teens and the classics, and can be highly satisfying, both for you and for the teens you serve.

This chapter begins with a brief overview of the rudiments of readers' advisory, including appeals, genres, and the diverse characteristics of the teens you will work with; and follows with an exploration of both general and classics-specific readers' advisory techniques you can use with teens as either a librarian or an educator. This chapter assumes that you'll be in a library when providing readers' advisory services to teens, but you can translate most of the information you find here to other educational environments where there are teens and books. Oh, and you! You'll find some short and sweet classics booklists to give you a leg up along the way, including an expanded list of thin classics and a list of genre guides—most of which focus on genre classics—at the end of the chapter. The chapter concludes with a look at some of the more common passive readers' advisory tools you can provide for teens, parents, and staff in your library or educational environment. It is assumed that the readers' advisory work you are doing is classics-related, but the information here is often of a general nature and has a broad application in making matches between teens and any sort of good reading.

THE RUDIMENTS OF READERS' ADVISORY

If you are a teen services librarian, you'll be doing lots of readers' advisory during your career as a professional who values the classics and wants to share them with teens. If you're an educator, you can also play a meaningful readers' advisory role and partner with librarians to bring teens and classics together. A basic understanding of current readers' advisory principles and techniques is an essential starting point. You'll get a rudimentary look at them in this section, but I recommend you check out Joyce G. Saricks and Nancy Brown's 1997 book, *Readers' Advisory Service in the Public Library*, for a more in-depth look. Theirs is not the only book on the subject, but it's one of the best for the nuts and bolts of readers' advisory work in libraries. Although this slim volume is not specific to teens or to classics and is specific to fiction readers' advisory, it does provide a clear look at readers, books, and how to make the best possible connections between them. The authors' framework for thinking about books and interacting sensitively and respectfully with readers in the library can only benefit you in your work with teens. Oh, and don't worry about the title. The principles outlined in the book have a broad application.

Understanding Appeals

At the heart of current readers' advisory theory is the assertion there are identifiable factors or elements in books that draw readers to them. By asking the right questions and carefully listening for clues, you can find out just which factors or elements attract a particular individual to a particular book or type of book and can make more successful reading suggestions based on that knowledge. What are those factors or elements? According to Saricks and Brown—who call them "appeals"—they are pacing, characterization, storyline, and frame. Let's take a brief look at how the authors define these elements (I've paraphrased):

Pacing

This appeal describes how fast a book moves along. A book with a faster pace will usually have more obvious, action-oriented characters, lots of dialogue, a straightforward plot that reveals itself early and resolves itself within the work, and a lighter, more concise writing style. A book with a slower pace will have more slowly revealed, psychologically-defined characters, less dialogue and more descriptive text, a complex or slow-moving plot (or no real plot at all), the potential for the story to remain unresolved, and a denser writing style.

Characterization

This appeal describes the qualities of the characters found in the book. Some books feature characters who simply move the plot along and are perhaps even stereotypical, others feature fascinating, complex characters who may be hard to figure out. Some books focus on one character, others on many characters and how they relate to one another and the plot. Some books are told from the point of view of a character or a collection of characters, others are told in the "third person." Some books are all about the characters, some use characters merely to carry the plot. Some characters are meant to be identified with, others just fill a place in the story.

Story Line

This appeal describes the overall characteristics of the story itself. Some story lines focus on people, some on situations, some on events. Some story lines are meant to be serious, others comic. Some story lines are more introspective and intellectual, others are more outward and driven by action.

Frame

This appeal describes the elements surrounding the story and their effect (or lack of one) on the story, such as sketchy or densely constructed background or time period, and the mood or tone an author sets for a book.

Understanding Genres

Appeal features are good ways to think about books, especially for books that aren't easily categorized into genres, but the most common way readers seek books (after author) is by genre. Genres are usually applied to popular fiction, but there are classics to be found in each and every genre, and it would behoove you to have a rudimentary understanding of each to connect teens with the classics that will most likely engage their personal reading interests. There are many readers' advisory resources that examine the various genres and provide annotated lists, from general resources like Diana Tixier Herald's *Genreflecting: A Guide to Reading Interests in Genre Fiction* (2000) and *Teen Genreflecting: A Guide to Reading Interests* (2003), and Joyce Saricks's *Readers' Advisory Guide to Genre Fiction* (2001), to more detailed explorations in resources like Libraries Unlimited's Genreflecting Advisory Series or Gale's What Do I Read Next? series, with titles focusing on such individual genres as mystery, adventure, fantasy, science fiction, horror, and Christian fiction. You'll find many of these and other resources listed at the end of this chapter in the "Genre Guides."

For now, though, here are a few of the well-loved genres that appeal to teen readers, with a few short and sweet classics booklists thrown in to help you get started in your readers' advisory work with teens.

Adventure and Survival

Adventure fiction usually involves a highly sympathetic character or group of characters who are facing a conflict (often in the form of a clever and devious villian!) or who are charged with solving a problem (sometimes as basic as simple survival)—and do so in dramatic, risk-filled, and thrilling ways in unique and interesting places.

Adventure classics can be compelling reads for any teen, and may be especially strong choices for teens who enjoy action-oriented, quick-paced, highly imaginative books with satisfying resolutions. You'll find loads of adventure and survival classics out there, a few of which are listed for you here.

Adventure and Survival Classics

- *20,000 Leagues under the Sea*, Jules Verne (1870)
- *The Adventures of Huckleberry Finn*, Mark Twain (1884)
- *The Call of the Wild*, Jack London (1903)
- *Captains Courageous*, Rudyard Kipling (1897)
- *Kidnapped*, Robert Louis Stevenson (1886)
- *Kim*, Rudyard Kipling (1901)
- *The Lost World*, Sir Arthur Conan Doyle (1912)
- *Tarzan of the Apes*, Edgar Rice Burroughs (1914)
- *The Three Musketeers*, Alexandre Dumas (1844)
- *Treasure Island*, Robert Louis Stevenson (1883)

Fantasy

Fantasy fiction tells stories with magical, mythical, supernatural elements—including powers and creatures. Fantasy stories may take place in our own world with impossible elements added in, or may take place in another fantastical time and place entirely. The genre has numerous subgenres which are ever expanding, from sword and sorcery to humorous fantasy, from romantic fantasy to animal-oriented fantasy (you know, talking badgers in tunics and that sort of thing!).

Fantasy is often compelling to teens simply for its rich, strange, and imaginative creations, for its plot- and goal-oriented structure, for its predominant elements of good triumphing over evil, and for its heroic qualities, just to name a few. Of great good fortune to fantasy lovers, there are many, many extraordinary works of fantasy acknowledged as classics—especially now that the Harry Potter books have convinced publishers to release new fantasy titles and reissue fantasy classics. Here are just a very few to get you started.

Fantasy Classics

- *Alice's Adventures in Wonderland*, Lewis Carroll (1865)
- *The Forgotten Beasts of Eld*, Patricia A. McKillip (1974)
- *The Hobbit*, J.R.R. Tolkien (1937)
- *The Jungle Books*, Rudyard Kipling (1894–1895)
- *The Last Unicorn*, Peter S. Beagle (1968)
- *The Once and Future King*, T.H. White (1958)
- *The Princess Bride*, William Goldman (1974)
- *Through the Looking Glass*, Lewis Carroll (1871)
- *Watership Down*, Richard Adams (1972)
- *Witch World*, Andre Norton (1963)
- *The Wizard of Oz*, L. Frank Baum (1900)

Classic Multi-volume Fantasy Works

- *The Arthurian Saga: The Crystal Cave, The Hollow Hills, The Last Enchantment, The Wicked Day*, Mary Stewart (1970–)
- *The Chronicles of Narnia: The Magician's Nephew; The Lion, the Witch and the Wardrobe; The Horse and His Boy; Prince Caspian; The Voyage of the Dawn Treader; The Silver Chair; The Last Battle*, C.S. Lewis (1950–)
- *The Chronicles of Thomas Covenant: The Unbeliever: Lord Foul's Bane, The Illearth War, The Power That Preserves*, Stephen R. Donaldson (1977–)
- *The Dark is Rising: Over Sea, under Stone; The Dark Is Rising; Greenwitch; The Grey King; Silver on the Tree*, Susan Cooper (1965–)
- *The Earthsea Cycle: A Wizard of Earthsea, The Tombs of Atuan, The Farthest Shore, Tehanu*, Ursula K. Le Guin (1968–)
- *The Gormenghast Trilogy: Titus Groan, Gormenghast, Titus Alone*, Mervyn Peake (1946–)
- *The Lord of the Rings Trilogy: The Fellowship of the Ring, The Two Towers, The Return of the King*, J.R.R. Tolkien (1954–1955)

(continued)

(continued)

- *The Time Quintet: A Wrinkle in Time, A Wind in the Door, A Swiftly Tilting Planet, Many Waters, An Acceptable Time*, Madeleine L'Engle (1962–)

Horror

According to Anthony J. Fonseca and June Michele Pulliam, authors of *Hooked on Horror: A Guide to Reading Interests in Horror Fiction*, the defining characteristic of the horror genre is the monster. That monster could be a Freddy Kruger–type of character, a virus, a serial killer or the main character's own psychological state. But monster it is, and one that might be defeated.

There are many reasons why the horror genre appeals to readers, teens included. Pulliam suggests, "life is scary and uncertain, and horror at least allows us to experience the emotion of fear in a controlled setting" (Fonesca and Pulliam 2003, xv). That is, horror helps readers vicariously deal with real fears, both personal and societal, that have no immediate direction. Others may enjoy horror as a form of extreme sport or thrill-seeking behavior. This is certainly common among teens, especially boys. Some folks enjoy reading horror for the more intellectual concepts it often explores. Others like the excitement and edge-of-the-seat plotting. Horror fiction can contain an element of mystery and may appeal to readers who like high suspense.

Whatever the reason may be, horror is known to appeal to teens, again, especially males. Does this make them creepy young people, obsessed with the dark side? No! Remember Fonseca and Pulliam's words when working with horror-loving teens: "Librarians should also keep in mind that these readers are not disturbed individuals who need counseling but are simply people who enjoy curling up with a scary or thought-provoking book" (2003, xvii).

The genre has a history of original and seminal works associated with it, so you will not have any trouble finding classics to suggest to teens. Here's a couple of short lists to get you going.

Classic Horror Novels

- *Conjure Wife*, Fritz Leiber (1943)
- *Dracula*, Bram Stoker (1897)

(continued)

(continued)

- *Frankenstein*, Mary Wollstonecraft Shelley (1817)
- *The Haunting of Hill House*, Shirley Jackson (1959)
- *I Am Legend*, Richard Matheson (1954)
- *The Invisible Man*, H.G. Wells (1897)
- *Something Wicked This Way Comes*, Ray Bradbury (1962)
- *The Strange Case of Dr. Jekyll and Mr. Hyde*, Robert Louis Stevenson (1886)
- *The Turn of the Screw*, Henry James (1898)
- *The Werewolf of Paris*, Guy Endore (1933)

Short Story Collections by Classic Horror Writers

- *The Best Ghost Stories of Algernon Blackwood*, Algernon Blackwood (compiled 1973)
- *The Best Ghost Stories of J.F. Lefanu*, J.F. Lefanu (compiled 1964)
- *The Best of H.P. Lovecraft: Bloodcurdling Tales of Horror and the Macabre*, H.P. Lovecraft (reissued 1987)
- *The Books of Blood*, Clive Barker (1986–)
- *The Collected Ghost Stories of E.F. Benson*, E.F. Benson (compiled 1992)
- *Ghost and Horror Stories of Ambrose Bierce*, Ambrose Bierce (compiled 1964)
- *The Ghost Stories of Edith Wharton*, Edith Wharton (compiled 1982)
- *The Lottery and Other Stories*, Shirley Jackson (1949)
- *Tales of Mystery and Imagination*, Edgar Allan Poe (1845)
- *Twice-Told Tales*, Nathaniel Hawthorne (1839–)

Mystery

Mystery is one of the most prescribed of the genres and also among the most popular. Gary Warren Niebuhr, in *Make Mine a Mystery: A Guide to Mystery and Detective Fiction*, states, "A mystery is a work of fiction in which the reader is asked to help solve a puzzle. The essential ingredients are an element of crime mixed with an element of detection" (2003, xiii). Despite a number of subgenres with their own slight twists on these essential ingredients, there are rules or conventions that generally hold true for all. The crime must be intriguing and compel both the investigating character (who may be flawed but must be likable) and the reader to discover the truth. The investigation must involve more than one suspect and must lead ultimately to the truth. Niebuhr describes the mystery reader as one who is "playing a structured game with specific rules" (2003, 6).

What's the appeal in mysteries, and what makes them attractive to teens? First, they are an exercise in problem solving, in tracking details and puzzling them out. Many teens enjoy this sort of mental challenge, and many are rather good at it! Mysteries feature investigators made sympathetic and engaging through both flaws and strengths, giving teen readers a good hook and reason to become involved in the story. Some teens will be attracted to literary style, which is a signature of some mystery writers, especially the classic writers of the 1930s and 1940s like Raymond Chandler and Dashiell Hammett. Cozy or tough, grandmotherly investigator or hate-filled cop unjustly suspended from the force, murder or heist or caper, there are mysteries to match the interests of any reader of this genre, classics included.

Here's a short list of classic mysteries that represent several of the more popular subgenres to get you going.

Mystery Classics

- *The Big Sleep*, Raymond Chandler (1939)
- *Green for Danger*, Christianna Brand (1945)
- *The Hound of the Baskervilles*, Sir Arthur Conan Doyle (1902)
- *The Innocence of Father Brown*, G. K. Chesterton (1911)
- *The Maltese Falcon*, Dashiell Hammett (1930)
- *The Moonstone*, Wilkie Collins (1868)
- *Murder on the Orient Express*, Agatha Christie (1934)
- *The Phantom of the Opera*, Gaston Leroux (1911)
- *The Name of the Rose*, Umberto Eco (1980)
- *The Spy Who Came in from the Cold*, John Le Carré (1963)

Romance

A romance is a love story centered around two main characters and no matter what else happens, it's secondary to that love story. There has to be an attraction, at least one conflict, and a resolution of the conflict that results in a "happily ever after" ending. The reader experiences the romantic attraction, the development of a relationship, the conflict that threatens it, and its satisfying resolution along with the main characters.

What makes the romance genre appealing to readers? Kristin Ramsdell, in *Romance Fiction: A Guide to the Genre*, states that romance "attracts readers for diverse reasons that include emotional involvement, female empowerment, the promotion of moral values, the celebration of life, the ultimate triumph of love, and a sense of unflagging optimism" (1999, 18).

Who reads romances? Females, mostly. Teens read romances to vicariously experience the adult world of romantic relationships in a positive, safe, formulaic way. These readers may be brand new to the idea of close interpersonal love relationships with the same or opposite sex and are intrigued by it, they may be in a topsy-turvey adolescent relationship they're having trouble navigating and are looking for ideas, they may just like the titillation of a good love story, regardless of their own personal situations.

There are a lot of different kinds of romance fiction out there, classics included, so don't assume when connecting a teen with a romance that, oh, *Wuthering Heights* will do. Find out what sort of romance that teen may be interested in. Historical? Gentle and clean? Spicy and wild? Gay or lesbian? Suspenseful? Gothic? Time traveling? Maybe even written for the stage?

Here's a short list of classic romance fiction crossing a few of the common subgenres and literary forms to help you get started.

Classic Romances

- *Cyrano de Bergerac*, Edmund Rostand (1897)
- *Dragonwyck*, Anya Seton (1944)
- *Gone with the Wind*, Margaret Mitchell (1936)
- *The Importance of Being Earnest*, Oscar Wilde (1895)
- *Jane Eyre*, Charlotte Brontë (1847)
- *Pride and Prejudice*, Jane Austen (1813)
- *Rebecca*, Daphne du Maurier (1938)
- *The Scarlet Pimpernel*, Baroness Orczy (1905)
- *Sylvester, or the Wicked Uncle*, Georgette Heyer (1957)
- *Wuthering Heights*, Emily Brontë (1847)

Science Fiction

"In this genre just about anything can happen—as long as science or technology rather than magic or the fantastic is involved," say Di Herald and Bonnie Kunzel in their 2002 book, *Strictly Science Fiction: A Guide to Reading Interests* (xii). Science fiction is a highly imaginative genre in which the only rule is that real or speculative science is center stage in the story. Times, places, characters, and themes vary, but science is always present and essential to the plot. Although the genre can be based in science fact, it isn't called science *fiction* for nothing! Stories can feature believable elements of real science, but they can also feature some real far-out science ideas. Science fiction can be idealistic and hopeful, it can be dark and frightful. There are two predominant styles: hard science fiction is all about the science and its impact on individuals and societies; soft science fiction tends to focus on psychological or social concerns.

There are as many reasons why readers enjoy science fiction as there are stars in the sky. Well, probably not quite that many! Let's look briefly at just a few of them. First, being a genre with almost endless possibilities for theme, setting, and so forth, science fiction appeals to readers who like to immerse themselves in—escape to—worlds not their own. There are lots of teens who like to do that! Second, science fiction engages readers intellectually and can help them ponder possibility and change. It has been known at times to actually presage technological and societal change. Third, science fiction imagines life beyond what is currently known and understood, and in doing so can not only entertain, but may provide food for thought on the fundamental questions of life in the here and now. There are many teens who like to ponder things, who like to think about the question Betty Rosenberg stated in the first edition of *Genreflecting* as defining the science fiction genre—"What if . . . ?" (Herald and Kunzel 2002, xi).

Science fiction is a relatively new genre, with its roots in fantastic stories. So, there aren't many science fiction titles that date back to ancient times! Here's a list of vintage science fiction classics to help you get started, but there are many fine contemporary classics from the 1970s, 1980s, and even the early 1990s you might seek out to promote to teens. For additional classics from the full range of science fiction as a genre, the genre guides at the end of this chapter will be of great help to you.

Golden Age Science Fiction Classics (the 1950s and 1960s)

- *1984*, George Orwell (1949)
- *2001: A Space Odyssey*, Arthur C. Clarke (1968)

(continued)

(continued)

- *The Andromeda Strain*, Michael Crichton (1969)
- *A Clockwork Orange*, Anthony Burgess (1962)
- *Dune*, Frank Herbert (1965)
- *Fahrenheit 451*, Ray Bradbury (1953)
- *The Left Hand of Darkness*, Ursula K. Le Guin (1969)
- *The Man in the High Castle*, Philip K. Dick (1962)
- *The Stars My Destination*, Alfred Bester (1957)
- *Stranger in a Strange Land*, Robert A. Heinlein (1961)

Looking for the Hooks

When promoting classics to teen readers, make a conscious effort to find ways to connect the books to teen interests. Although teens are individuals with diverse likes and dislikes (as we discuss in the next section), there are some principles that apply broadly. As you choose books to promote to teens, keep the following interests in mind and try to find books that fit in with these interests, and be sure to make teens aware of features they might find appealing.

All About Me

Self-consciousness and consciousness of the self are major preoccupations of the teen years. Finding classics with characters teens can relate to is crucial. What matters? Besides age (for both girls and boys) and gender (especially for boys) of the characters, there are personality traits and qualities that may resonate with your teen readers. Rebellious protagonists who question authority, outsiders, unlikely heroes, and teens who feel misunderstood or underappreciated by their families, their peers, or by the system—these are compelling characters for teens. Books with realistically portrayed teen characters hold special appeal for this group; when you're describing the books to teens, this is something to keep in mind.

The Great Escape

Teens, like adults, lead very stressful lives. Sometimes an escape into the world of books offers great relief. The popularity of fantasy titles as well as historical fiction speaks to this. What if dragons are real, and they fly high up in the sky protecting us by fighting evil? What was it like to live in the Stone Age? Or Edwardian England? During the American Civil

War? Teen readers enjoy stretching their imaginations, and yes, getting away from it all. Help them connect with classics that allow them the right kinds of escape.

The Material World

Let's face it, we live in a material world. Teens are accustomed to being bombarded through all of their senses. So, when promoting classics, don't restrict yourself to the verbal. Show the cover (providing it's visually attractive, which it should be), hand the book to the reader and let him or her page through it (retailers use this technique because it works). Think of ways to stimulate the senses. Use music to set the stage for your book-talks, or use props (see Chapter 9 for details). You might even be able to tie into the olfactory sense with scented candles; or create a taste sensation—serve fortune cookies at a book club discussion of *The Woman Warrior*, or offer slices of mango before booktalking *The House on Mango Street*.

Pop Culture

Teens are products of the culture they are raised in, and popular culture connections to classic literature can whet a teen's appetite for a book that might otherwise seem distant or remote. By tying into current events, film, music, superstars, fashion, or even contemporary authors and books, you'll generate more teen interest in classic literature. Did a teen enjoy the movie *Master and Commander*? Perhaps he would enjoy Patrick O'Brian's original book version. Is she fascinated with body art? She might enjoy Tennessee Williams's play, *The Rose Tattoo*. There are scads of ways to connect classics with pop culture—the "Classic Combos" in Chapter 5 gives you ideas for accomplishing this, as does Chapter 9 on booktalking the classics to teens.

Reality Rules

What's the story, the real story? Teens want to know. They are not interested in a white-washed, sugar-coated version of historical or current events—they want the truth. When recommending classics, keep in mind that titles that reveal gritty realities and alternative perspectives are likely to be hits with teen readers. And remember, when working with teens, be real, be sincere—don't be a phony.

Peer Pressure

For better or for worse, when it comes to reading advice (and lots of other advice), teens may or may not listen to their parents, their teachers, or any other adult; but they generally take very seriously the comments and recommendations of other teens. You can take advantage of peer involvement by quoting other teens when you're booktalking or shelftalking; by posting or quoting teen book reviews in your library newsletter, on your Web site, or in book displays; and by encouraging teens to talk about favorite classics to each other—in book clubs or just informally after you've finished a booktalk.

Tech Times

You've heard the stories—the 13-year-old who solved the library's computer network problem when no one else could, the 15-year-old who set up the computers at her father's business. The fact is, today's teens are generally more computer-literate than most adults. They've grown up with the Internet, and they spend as much or more time on the computer as they do watching TV. So, use your library Web site to connect to teens, and to connect teens to classic literature. Post reading lists and reviews on the Web, not just on paper handouts or posters at the library. On your teen page, list Web sites that offer access to e-classics or that support conversations about classic literature. (See Appendix A for a list of Web sites where full-text classics can be found.)

Weirdness

Teens are fascinated by the unusual, the strange, or the unbelievable. There's plenty of weirdness in the classics—and in a lot of the authors who wrote them. Sharing a few anecdotes about the life of Edgar Allen Poe before booktalking "The Tell-Tale Heart" is sure to get teen attention. Or you might incorporate weird facts into a review posted on your library's online teen page. The strange story of Vlad Dracul, the historical figure whom the Dracula character is based on, will likewise peak interest. (You'll learn all about the bizarre and nasty Vlad and find some suggestions on where to find this type of background material in Chapter 9.)

Understanding Teen Diversity

Lots of folks lump all teens together into a single collective. You've got a gaggle of geese, a pod of whales, an exaltation of larks, a skulk of foxes, a pride of lions, a culture of bacteria, a nest of hornets—and then you've got TEENS. They come in packs, cliques, and gangs. Huh . . . If we were to rightly label teens with any collective terminology, it should be a *diversity* of teens. Teens are no more homogenous than the rest of the world's populations: ethnically, physically, socioeconomically, morally, academically, spiritually, psychologically, and just about any other "ly" you can imagine.

An awareness of and sensitivity to the diverse characteristics and qualities that make up each individual teen who comes into the library, coupled with a familiarity with teen developmental stages and the general characteristics of teens as readers (we talked about these in Chapter 4), are indispensable in your readers' advisory work. How can you develop this awareness and sensitivity? You can start by practicing keen powers of observation when interacting as a classics readers' advisor with a teen. You can ask good questions, you can listen intently to the answers. And you can keep in a mind some of the general ways in which one teen might be unique from another. What might those be?

- Age and grade
- Educational achievement/ability
- Ethnic/cultural identity
- Living environment
- Gender
- Sexual orientation
- Belief systems
- Physical challenges
- Interest in reading

Let's take a closer look at a few of those you'll find significant in your classics readers' advisory work.

Age and Grade

This one's easy! When you know the age and grade of the teen you're advising, you can make appropriate classics recommendations that better match reading level, general interest, and developmental maturity. Don't forget Chapter 4 includes this information in the section on adolescent developmental characteristics by age and grade, and includes a short list of resources for further exploration. Keep in mind that everyone matures at different rates (emotionally, physically and intellectually), so use age and grade as a broad guide, but consider the individual.

Remember that regardless of a classic's worth, it may not be an appropriate selection for teens in a particular age and grade. You might revisit Chapter 2 where we talked about reading to make informed recommendations to teens. You want to suggest classics that are of interest and are accessible to that teen. You don't want to insult with books that are too young or overwhelm with books that are too complex or sophisticated. You do want, though, to suggest classics that challenge and excite an advanced reader. Also keep in mind our earlier discussion, also from Chapter 2, that the length of a book does not equal its intellectual challenge. Don't assume that the shorter a book is, the more accessible it will be to a young reader in an earlier grade.

Speaking of young readers in earlier grades, in my experience, connecting younger teens—between the ages of 12 and 14 and in the 7th and 8th grades—to classic literature can be a real challenge. These teens have often read (or had read to them) most or all of the children's classics or may just consider them too young, and they are not ready for the majority of so-called adult classics. Keep crossover classics in mind for these teens.

What does "crossover" mean? It simply refers to books that cross over between childhood and adolescence. Crossover books can be read and enjoyed by advanced readers in 5th grade, they can be read and enjoyed by struggling and/or reluctant readers in 9th grade, and by every teen in between. Crossover classics are considered by some to be children's titles; others think of them as teen titles. These classics often have savvy, complex older child or younger teen protagonists and content that appeals to both children and teens. They're great reading all around, and may be great choices for reluctant readers in particular. Here's a short and sweet list of crossover classics to help you get started in your readers' advisory work with younger teens:

Crossover Classics

- *The Adventures of Tom Sawyer*, Mark Twain (1876)
- *Anne of Green Gables*, L. M. Montgomery (1908)
- *Jacob Have I Loved*, Katherine Paterson (1980)
- *Johnny Tremain*, Esther Forbes (1943)
- *Little Women,* Louisa May Alcott (1868)
- *Rifles for Watie*, Harold Keith (1957)
- *Roll of Thunder, Hear My Cry*, Mildred D. Taylor (1976)
- *Smoky, the Cowhorse*, Will James (1926)
- *A Wrinkle in Time*, Madeleine L'Engle (1962)
- *The Yearling*, Marjorie Rawlings (1938)

Classics of teen fiction—or YA literature, as it is often called—can also be good choices for the younger set. They feature adolescent protagonists, they have characters and plots that appeal to younger teens, and they are at a reasonable reading level for most of them. For a larger number of teen books that might be considered classic, check out the booklists and book awards section of the YALSA Web pages at http://www.ala.org/yalsa/booklists/. Pay particular attention to the list on the Professional Development Center pages at http://www.ala.org/ala/yalsa/profess sionaldev/whatbooksshould.htm. Called "What Books Should Anyone Working with Teens Know?," the list is the result of a question submitted to numerous children's and teen services librarians' listservs and teen literature experts, and includes a number of titles considered among the best of the best—a.k.a. classics.

Also take a look at the millennial "Best of the Best Revisited" list, which is in the members-only section on the YALSA Web pages. The titles on the list were selected by librarians as the top one hundred titles written for teens from all the Best Books for Young Adults lists since the program's inception in 1966 through 2000. It updates the top one hundred list selected in 1994. Many other reputable groups have created all-time "bests" lists of teen literature, which you can sort through by searching on the Internet combining such key words as "best," "literature," "young adult," "teen," and so forth. Many of the books that appear on these lists are unquestionably classics in their own right.

Here's a short list of teen fiction classics to help you get started with the younger set. Fair warning: unlike most children's and crossover classics, teen fiction classics are not necessarily "gentle" or "clean." If you are working with a teen who prefers his or her books be just that, make your suggestions based on books you have read, or pass on the fair warning to that teen.

Classics of Teen Fiction

- *Annie on My Mind*, Nancy Garden (1982)
- *The Chocolate War*, Robert Cormier (1974)
- *Deathwatch*, Robb White (1972)
- *Forever...*, Judy Blume (1975)
- *Go Ask Alice*, Anonymous (1971)

(continued)

(continued)

- *A Hero Ain't Nothin' but a Sandwich*, Alice Childress (1973)
- *The Outsiders*, S. E. Hinton (1967)
- *The Pigman*, Paul Zindel (1968)
- *Summer of My German Soldier*, Bette Greene (1973)
- *A Tree Grows in Brooklyn*, Betty Smith (1943)

Need a little additional assistance with the sorts of reading experiences teens may be interested in based on their age and grade? Arthea J. S. Reed's 1988 *Comics to Classics: A Parent's Guide to Books for Teens and Preteens*, although intended for a slightly different audience and not specifically targeting classics reading, has clear and illuminating chapters called "The Preadolescent and Reading," "The Early Adolescent and Reading," "The Late Adolescent and Reading," and "Encouraging Teens and Preteens to Read" that may be useful to you.

Ethnic Identity

Although classics often receive their status as such because of their universal relevance and appeal, you should nonetheless consider the ethnicity of the teen you're advising and include works that may be of more immediate interest based on cultural connections. When you acknowledge and value a teen's cultural identity enough to promote his or her culture's great literary works you not only gain that teen's respect, but may also allow that teen to let down any cultural defenses and show greater interest in classics outside his or her own life ways.

All right, so let's say you know that the teen in front of you is Hispanic. Among other classics suggestions, you can include great works to share with that teen written by authors who share and describe her cultural identity. But you don't have quite enough information yet to do that. The devil is in the details! Are you sure you know just what "Hispanic" means here?

If you are an individual raised in a mostly homogenous environment, unexamined assumptions and generalities about other cultural identities may hold sway. There may be considerably less understanding of the nation's cultural cornucopia for those of you who come from those more homogenous areas or simply have less exposure to other cultural communities in your area. Whoever you are and wherever you've lived your life to date, it's profoundly important to educate yourself about the unique cultures you'll find represented by teens.

Let's say you didn't have any understanding of the variety of Hispanic cultures represented in your library. You work in a library in a central- or southwestern state somewhere, and make the assumption that this Hispanic girl is of Mexican descent. In an attempt to be culturally sensitive you recommend Carlos Fuentes's *The Old Gringo*, Rudolfo Anaya's *Bless Me, Ultima*, and Richard Rodriguez's *Hunger of Memory*. These are all exceptional classics that richly describe and represent life for Mexicans and Mexican Americans and explore race relations with Anglo society. To expose anyone to these books is a wonderful thing. However, this teen is not of Mexican descent! Turns out you are talking to a teen of Cuban descent who recently relocated with her family to your area. As wonderful as the classics you've suggested are, as awesome a reading experience as they can be for any teen of any background, you were specifically trying to engage the interests of and demonstrate a respect for that teen's ethnic population. You missed the mark! You've actually gone in the other direction by demonstrating ignorance, which although well intended, is never a good thing.

So, when considering the ethnic identity factor in making classics connections with teens, do not rely on generalities and assumptions. Knowing the ethnic composition of your community is a good start, but respectfully querying your individual teen patron to learn about his or her cultural heritage is your best bet when considering ethnic identify in readers' advisory work. And as it's worth mentioning more than once, don't assume that teens only want to read about their own cultural background and life ways. Honor cultural identity, but foster expansion of thought and experience in your classics recommendations to teens.

In Appendix C you will find a few short lists of classics that represent the ethnic experience in classic fiction to help you get started. If they were comprehensive, including nonfiction as well, these lists might just make a book in and of themselves. Just know that you—and teens—have many, many superb choices with the classic literature that represents this nation's and the world's ethnic identities and realities.

Gender

Obvious yet important, teens come in both genders! You should keep this in mind to better suggest classics that meet the interests of both male and female teens. You would not make the best literary connections, for example, if you suggested a number of classics to a young woman in the

10th grade and not one of them had a female protagonist or centered around issues of great relevance to women, or suggested a number of outstanding classics to a 14-year-old male that feature female protagonists! Remain aware that by suggesting a balanced selection of classics that include that teen's gender, you will help a greater number of teens find literary connections that are meaningful to them.

Although they are subject to debate and can result in stereotyping, you might familiarize yourself with some of the commonly held beliefs about male and female readers. They're commonly held because they often prove true.

Teen Readers by Gender

Teen males:

- Are less likely to read for fun than females
- Comprise the majority of reluctant readers
- Find nonfiction appealing
- Enjoy alternative reading materials, such as magazines and graphic novels
- Are not encouraged to read by family and society as much as females are
- Do not have strong male role models who read
- Want to read about heroes to emulate
- Want more action in books
- Don't like to read about girls
- Are reluctant to discuss what they read

Teen females:

- Are much more likely to read for fun than males
- Generally prefer fiction to nonfiction
- Find the development of characters and literary style as appealing as plot and action
- Seek emotional extremes through reading
- Will read books with male protagonists
- Enjoy discussing what they read

Classics for Teen Males

You've already got a few great short and sweet classics lists you can make good use of with teens of the male persuasion. The adventure/survival, fantasy, horror, and science fiction genres have high appeal with teen males. As teen males routinely show interest in nonfiction, there's also a nice list of nonfiction classics by subject in Appendix C for your use. It has also been my experience that most teen males demonstrate great enthusiasm for war stories. You'll find a list of classics of war fiction in the same appendix, arranged chronologically by war. A little further on in this chapter, you'll find a list of thin classics for reluctant readers, who we've already noted are predominantly male, and at the end of the chapter you'll find an expanded list. You can make good use of these lists with the teen males in your library.

All that said, here's another short list of male-friendly classics titles to accompany those genre, nonfiction, war fiction, and thin classics lists, with emphasis on high-appeal elements—challenge and problem solving, action, and heroics.

Male-friendly Fiction Classics with Lots of Challenge, Action, and Heroics

- *The Chocolate War*, Robert Cormier (1974)
- *Dune*, Frank Herbert (1965)
- *Ender's Game*, Orson Scott Card (1985)
- *The Hobbit* and the *Lord of the Rings* trilogy, J.R.R. Tolkien (1937, 1954–1955)
- *Hondo*, Louis L'Amour (1953)
- The Horatio Hornblower series, C. S. Forester (1937–1967)
- *The Prince and the Pauper*, Mark Twain (1882)
- *Riders of the Purple Sage*, Zane Grey (1912)
- *Treasure Island*, Robert Louis Stevenson (1883)

Classics for Teen Females

As with teen males, you can make great use of the genre classics lists provided above with teen females as well. Genre readers are genre readers, regardless of gender. That's almost a tongue-twister. As teen females read more frequently and broadly, just about every classics booklist and resource you'll find throughout this book will be useful in your readers' advisory work with teen females. Of particular note, Appendix C also includes a couple of short lists of classic fiction by and about women for those interested in reading about women and women's issues in particular.

That said, it never hurts to have another short list of high-appeal titles to suggest to teen females. Here's one that includes classics with strong and memorable characters—mostly female with a couple of males thrown in—in compelling stories with high emotional appeal.

Female-Friendly Fiction Classics with Strong Characters and Moving Stories

- *The Color Purple*, Alice Walker (1982)
- *The Dollmaker*, Harriet Louisa Simpson Arnow (1954)
- *Dragonsinger*, Anne McCaffrey (1977)
- *Flowers for Algernon*, Daniel Keyes (1966)
- *The Last Unicorn*, Peter S. Beagle (1968)
- *Little Women,* Louisa May Alcott (1868)
- *To Kill a Mockingbird*, Harper Lee (1960)
- *Their Eyes Were Watching God*, Zora Neale Hurston (1937)
- *True Grit*, Charles Portis (1968)
- *Wide Sargasso Sea*, Jean Rhys (1966)

Keep in mind that although they may hold true at large, sweeping gender generalities do not accurately define each individual's reading interests. More important than any gender tendency is the individual in front of you, so get to know that teen you're connecting to the classics!

Sexual Orientation

Teens are encouraged to take pride in and model great adult achievers who share their ethnic and cultural backgrounds, young music students are encouraged to study musicians accomplished on the instrument they are learning, young sports players are encouraged to look up to major sports figures, and so forth. Teens don't just look to these adult role models that are like them or share their interests because society encourages it, they do it on their own; it is an important part of the adolescent maturation process.

Don't deny GLBTQ (gay, lesbian, bisexual, transgendered, and the "Q" is for questioning) teens the same role models. How many teens struggling to understand what mainstream society considers an alternative at best, and deviant at worst, sexual orientation, know that the great literary wit, Oscar Wilde, was gay? How many know that Leonardo da Vinci, perhaps the greatest thinker, artist, and writer in our recorded history was a man denounced at one time for homosexuality? Through this exposure, you allow these teens a connection to accomplished writers of great literary merit who may share a similar sexual orientation and who achieved their own forms of greatness regardless of the minority status of that sexual orientation. And, you can expose teens in general, regardless of sexual orientation, to the many life ways out there, to the variety of fashions in which people are formed and live their lives.

This may be a tough one for some of you. You could have personal beliefs that make it hard for you to feel okay with nontraditional sexual orientations, let alone talk openly about them with teens in your library. It is also true that many GLBTQ teens in your library may also not be comfortable with and won't talk openly about their sexual orientations. For you and them, a GLBTQ classics booklist in your teen area is a good idea.

For those teens who have been open with you in this regard, and for those of you who are more comfortable with alternative sexual orientations, engage in a readers' advisory conversation and head in the right directions. Something to keep in mind here is that there is a difference between GLBT authors and GLBT content. There are many, many authors out there with nontraditional sexual orientations who do not write about it. There are a few heterosexual authors who write GLBT characters and storylines. And, there are GLBT authors who write GLBT content. Find out what the teen you are working with is interested in before heading off to make these sorts of reading connections!

Another thing to keep in mind: not only GLBTQ teens read GLBT authors and GLBT content. Don't count out a great GLBT author or classic as a recommendation to a heterosexual teen if it seems to meet the reading interests you've identified in your readers' advisory interaction. It may only take a brief mention or a built-in remark as you are describing something else interesting about an author to clue a teen in that either author or content is GLBT. You don't need to make a huge deal of it. Sexual orientation is just a part of a total being, after all, and sexuality is a mostly personal thing in any life. It would seem pretty weird were you to just blurt out while suggesting a particular classic, ". . . and this author is gay," or when introducing a book remark that the author is "a lesbian, you know." On the other hand, you might, for example, mention when suggesting Gertrude Stein's *The Autobiography of Alice B. Toklas* to a teen, that the title character is based on the author's real life live-in lover.

It may not be as easy to find classics that represent gay, lesbian, bisexual, and transgendered life ways as it is to find other sorts of classics, but there are a number out there. A larger number of the world's great writers than you may know were and are homosexual and bisexual, and you can readily find out about their lives in the resources we discussed in Chapter 3. Although not provided here, you might pursue contemporary GLBT classic titles. The 1980s and 1990s were dynamic decades in the gay and lesbian literary world. You can learn about these contemporary classics through a variety of readers' advisory resources and on the Internet.

Well, we're really more focused on the "GL" part, but what about the "BT" part? I've got to be honest with you—I just could not find any classics by authors who identify themselves as either bisexual or transgendered, or many classics with content focused specifically on bisexual or transgendered issues. Were you to receive a request for a gender-bending classic, or feel the need to recommend one, one idea might be to recommend a classic like Ursula K. Le Guin's *The Left Hand of Darkness* (1969), which is a science fiction classic that explores androgyny and flexible sexual identity.

Here's a couple of short lists of modern gay and lesbian fiction classics—mostly by gay and lesbian authors writing about the gay and lesbian experience—to help you get started. Be forewarned: because these are seminal novels in their subject predominantly by people who lived or live the life, many deal with controversial, difficult, and mature themes. They are not necessarily "clean." You may want to read a few first or learn about them through the resources we discussed in Chapter 3 before recommending them to teens, or at least give teens a heads-up so they can make their own choices with some advanced knowledge.

Classic Gay Novels

- *The Berlin Stories*, Christopher Isherwood (1954)
- *A Boy's Own Story*, Edmund White (1982)
- *The City and the Pillar*, Gore Vidal (1948)
- *Death in Venice*, Thomas Mann (1912)
- *The Front Runner*, Patricia Nell Warren (1974)

(continued)

(continued)

- *Giovanni's Room*, James Baldwin (1956)
- *The Kiss of the Spider Woman*, Manuel Puig (1976)
- *Maurice*, E.M. Forster (1971, published posthumously almost fifty years after written)
- *The Persian Boy*, Mary Renault (1972)
- *Tales of the City*, Armistead Maupin (1978)

Classic Lesbian Novels

- *The Autobiography of Alice B. Toklas*, Gertrude Stein (1933)
- *Desert of the Heart*, Jane Rule (1964)
- *Loving Her*, Ann Allen Shockley (1974)
- *Mrs. Stevens Hears the Mermaids Singing*, May Sarton (1965)
- *Nightwood*, Djuna Barnes (1936)
- *Orlando*, Virginia Woolf (1928)
- *The Price of Salt*, Patricia Highsmith (1952)
- *Rubyfruit Jungle*, Rita Mae Brown (1973)
- *The Well of Loneliness*, Radclyffe Hall (1928)
- *The Woman Who Owned the Shadows*, Paula Gunn Allen (1983)

For those teens who may want gay and lesbian classics from deep history, you might direct them to works from ancient Greece and Rome, such as Sappho's poetry, Plato's dialogue, *Phaedrus*, and Plutarch's biography of Alexander (in *Plutarch's Lives*), all of which reflect homosexuality as a natural aspect of human life and society.

Belief Systems

Just about everyone subscribes to some sort of belief system, be it an informal and personal sensibility, or a formal and organized doctrine. Informal, personal beliefs are not likely to enter in to your readers' advisory interactions all that much, but do respond with respect and sensitivity to individual beliefs if they are revealed. Teen followers of more formal, organized doctrines who may be in certain types of home-schooled groups or who may attend religious schools and use your library, will require special attention. It is essential that you find out what type of content may be attractive or objectionable to them. These teens are highly likely to clue you in right away, sometimes with a statement like, "I want a nice love story but it can't have any of the bad stuff," or, "I can't read anything that has wizards or magic in it."

It's not uncommon for parents to accompany teens with these religion-based reading restrictions to communicate to you what content is and is not acceptable. Parental involvement can be good, but it can also make your job difficult! The section below called "The Parent Barrier: Breaking through It" might be of assistance here. There will be times, though, when parents aren't present and teens don't really know how to communicate their reading restrictions to you, so listen for any clues they may be giving you before making classics reading connections. They usually come after a recommendation that is unacceptable to them! You might consider as a regular part of your readers' advisory work with teens, to just ask a simple question, like, "Are there any types of books that it's best for you not to read?"

No matter how wonderful a classic may be, and no matter how strong your own personal feelings about a teen's formal belief system, under no circumstances should you recommend a book with content in opposition to that teen's stated needs. Is this some form of censorship? No way, it's respect for and sensitivity to the life ways of others. Your goal is to connect teens of all walks of life with classics that will be meaningful to *them*, and how you do that is by recommending books they can accept and appreciate.

Religiously themed classics may be uplifting, inspirational, spiritual, gentle, and clean sorts of titles. They can also be cynical and questioning rather than affirming, or even quite brutal, showing hypocrisy and corruption in religion. Yet again, another reason to know your classics, either by reading them or learning about them! You would not want to recommend to a fundamentalist Christian teen, say, Nikos Kazantzakis's *The Last Temptation of Christ*, a classic novel in which Jesus debates whether or not to die on the cross, and instead thinks about marrying Mary Magdalene and living a long, peaceful, and ordinary life.

If you do not read Christian literature but do work with Christian teens in your library, you might look to John Mort's book *Christian Fiction: A Guide to the Genre* (2002). This resource provides an overview of the genre, including its history and early classics, and notes works of particular impact and quality in each subgenre category. There is also a separate chapter on teen titles. Of real value in your readers' advisory work with teens, Mort notes controversial content for those readers who prefer gentle and affirming books over controversial or heavy books.

This short starter list of "gentle" Christian classics strongly represents the more conservative and/or fundamentalist Christian belief systems, as they are predominant in Western life and literature. Keep in mind that many teens reading religiously themed classics will not need "gentle" titles, though, and teens of other faiths—Judaism, Islam, and Buddhism, for example—may have specific needs when it comes to reading material.

A Few Gentle Christian Classics and Classics Series

- *Christy*, Catherine Marshall (1967)
- *The Chronicles of Narnia*, C. S. Lewis (1950–)
- *I Heard the Owl Call My Name*, Margaret Craven (1973)
- *The Lilies of the Field*, William Barrett (1962)
- *Love Comes Softly* (multiple volumes in the series), Janette Oke (1979–)
- *The Time Quintet*, Madeleine L'Engle (1962–)

Interest in Reading

It's important to know a teen's general interest in reading so you can better make classics connections with both the high-interest teen and the disinterested teen. As a basic and probably obvious rule, interested readers are more responsive in the readers' advisory interaction. They already like books. They are willing to stretch intellectual boundaries, read beyond their experience of life, relish a reading challenge, and that sort of thing. As another basic rule, disinterested readers are not the most enthusiastic you'll experience in the readers' advisory interaction! They do not like books (or think they don't), and are not willing or currently able to stretch and challenge themselves through reading. If you can engage them at all, they are more likely to show interest in a book if it's a quick and easy read about something they find relevant to their own lives or about something currently hip or full of shock appeal that ties in to their current developmental reality.

Do not, however, assume that the classics have no power to attract disinterested or reluctant readers. Some youth services librarians, even some whose articles or books you may have read, discard the classics out of hand when working with these teens. That's just nuts! I don't, and sure hope you won't. Great literature can appeal to reluctant readers regardless of the reasons for that reluctance, and there are ways to help these teens engage in it, and having done so, enjoy a meaningful reading experience.

In addition to crossover classics and classics of teen fiction, which can be excellent suggestions for struggling and reluctant readers as well as those younger teen readers, and in addition to short story classics (which we talked about in Chapter 5), coming-of-age classics, classics that feature teen protagonists, and thin classics can provide appeal.

Coming-of-Age Classics

Teens are right in the middle of their "coming-of-age," that time between childhood and adulthood in which the broadening experiences of life, not all of which are pretty, are building knowledge, understanding, and maturity for adult lives. A great way to make classics relevant to teen readers, and especially to reluctant teen readers, is by sharing those that explore or focus on coming-of-age experiences.

Coming-of-Age Classics

- *The Adventures of Huckleberry Finn*, Mark Twain (1884)
- *Black Boy*, Richard Wright (1945)
- *The Catcher in the Rye*, J. D. Salinger (1951)
- *I Know Why the Caged Bird Sings*, Maya Angelou (1970)
- *Little Women*, Louisa May Alcott (1868)
- *The Member of the Wedding*, Carson McCullers (1946)
- *The Outsiders*, S. E. Hinton (1967)
- *To Kill a Mockingbird*, Harper Lee (1960)
- *A Tree Grows in Brooklyn*, Betty Smith (1943)
- *The Woman Warrior*, Maxine Hong Kingston (1976)

Classics that Feature Teen Protagonists

In my experience, many teens are reluctant to read because they think there is nothing of interest or relevance to them in books, especially in classics—which they've been exposed to in the classroom and which may, in all fairness, not have interested them or seemed relevant to their lives. A good way to engage reluctant teens in reading is by providing them with books that feature interesting people in unique situations who are their own age. You might directly link these teens to excellent classics with teen protagonists, or you might bridge from contemporary teen titles to the classics.

Classic Novels that Feature Teen Protagonists

- *The Adventures of Huckleberry Finn*, Mark Twain (1884)
- *Captains Courageous*, Rudyard Kipling (1897)
- *The Catcher in the Rye*, J. D. Salinger (1951)
- *The Chosen*, Chaim Potok (1967)
- *A Clockwork Orange*, Anthony Burgess (1962)
- *Go Tell It on the Mountain*, James Baldwin (1953)
- *The Heart Is a Lonely Hunter*, Carson McCullers (1940)
- *The Light in the Forest*, Conrad Richter (1953)
- *Red Sky at Morning*, Richard Bradford (1968)
- *A Separate Peace*, John Knowles (1959)

Thin Classics

It's often the sheer size of a book that overwhelms a reluctant or struggling teen reader. These teens are not in a warm and friendly relationship with books. They are unlikely to have experienced how a book that at first seems to be a thick, heavy dreadnought can in a matter of pages become a world of wonder for them. And you'll never convince these teens that, no, really, this 792-page classic is really, really awesome! They just can't get past the size. Thin classics are a great way to introduce reluctant and struggling readers to great literature and to pave the way for a more positive attitude toward longer works.

There are probably as many definitions of "thin" books as there are people providing the definitions. For our purposes, a thin classic is one under two hundred pages (editions vary, so give or take a few pages). Many are considerably less than two hundred pages. Remember, not all thin classics are easy reading. The classics on the list below are higher-interest, easier-access titles, but they aren't high-low titles. Another reminder: at the end of the chapter you'll find an expanded list of thin classics.

High-Interest, Easy-Access Thin Classics

- *The Bridges at Toko-Ri*, James Michener (1953)
- *The Call of the Wild*, Jack London (1903)
- *A Christmas Carol*, Charles Dickens (1843)
- *Fahrenheit 451*, Ray Bradbury (1953)
- *The House on Mango Street*, Sandra Cisneros (1984)
- *I Heard the Owl Call My Name*, Margaret Craven (1967)
- *The Pearl*, John Steinbeck (1947)
- *Shane*, Jack Schaefer (1949)
- *The Sound of Waves*, Yukio Mishima (1956)
- *The Time Machine*, H. G. Wells (1895)

READERS' ADVISORY TECHNIQUES WITH TEENS

You've got a few appeals to keep in mind—those broad elements found in books that attract readers to them—when making connections between teens and the classics. You have a basic understanding of the popular literary genres and why they might appeal to teens. You have a few classics starter lists within those genres. You're thinking about the wonderful and diverse lot of individuals that make up the teen population in your library and have some starter lists of classics that might appeal across a broad range of teen interests. Now what? You've got to gain some knowledge of the unique characteristics of the teen in front of you and find out just which of those appeals, which of those genres, will draw that individual to the wonders of the classics. All of this involves a personal touch! After getting what you need from a teen (not always an easy task), you've got to give him or her what you've got—great suggestions delivered with just the right sort of emphasis and enthusiasm.

The Interview: Getting What You Need from Teens

We've been talking about the basic concepts behind readers' advisory and about elements in books that appeal to readers, and we're about to explore a form of interaction that attempts to draw out of teens information needed to make strong connections between them and classic litera-ture. This is all great stuff, but let's stop for just a moment and talk from a less "professional" place. The bottom line in connecting teens to great classics is this: care about their reading experiences, enjoy interacting with them, encourage them to talk to you, listen to what they say, and respond honestly. You can't go wrong with this approach.

You may be one of those sorts who rely on intuition and spontaneity to conduct successful readers' advisory interviews with teens in the li-brary. You might be the sort who gets all the information you need just by shooting the breeze with a teen. Right on for you, you're a natural! This begs the question: is it lonely at the top? For the rest of you, a few tips will come in mighty handy when conducting a readers' advisory in-terview with teens.

First, how about a definition of just what your job as a readers' advi-sor *is* from Saricks and Brown's book? "The job of the readers' advisor is to suggest books, based on information received from readers about their reading tastes and moods" (1997, 58). Simple! You're already reading clas-sics, so your ability to suggest titles is well underway and will build over time. You've already demonstrated your dedication to teens as readers by virtue of your choice of profession, and as readers of the classics in spe-cific (you are at this very moment reading a book about just that!).

Now that that's done, how about a quick and dirty list of teen readers' advisory tips before we move on in more detail? Angelina Benedetti's chapter in *The Readers' Advisor's Companion*, edited by Kenneth D. Shearer and Robert Burgin (2001), is a good place to go for this. In "Leading the Horse to Water: Keeping Young People Reading in the Information Age," you'll find a numbered list of readers' advisory skills you should prac-tice to make the best reading connections with teens in the library. These tips are no less true for classics than for more popular reading connec-tions. For the full effect, read the chapter, but here's a distillation of her eight tips for successfully "talking with teen readers" (Benedetti 2001, 242–244):

1. Begin with an easy question.
2. Listen to everything the teen has to say.
3. Refine your search.
4. Narrow your age range.
5. Assess the situation. Is the teen alone? With a parent? With friends? Be aware of how these factors affect the interview.
6. Be real.

7. Be honest.

8. Do not oversell.

Seeking Teens Out and Making Yourself Available

You know what your job is and you have some basic tips for readers' advisory interviews with teens in the library. You're ready to get started. So where are the teens? Don't wait for teens to come to you unless your goal is to interact with only those working on schools assignments, which is far fewer of them than you should! Start by casually seeking out teens in the library who are browsing the shelves and may look a little lost. Go to them, but don't push yourself on them. I've often approached teens while floating around the library (which is a cool thing to do), to find that within one or two words out of my mouth, they jump like startled deer and take off. Happens! It could be I wasn't sensitive to an intense focus that I interpreted as a lost condition, it could be I came across an antisocial teen or two, it could be any number of things. Don't let that worry you. As long as you do your best to be sensitive in your approach, and don't stick around when it's clear you're an intruder, you are doing all you can do on that front.

A quick note here: if you seek out teens in the library to help with reading connections, be open to what it is they truly want. Although we're talking about making classics connections through readers' advisory principles and practices here, I wouldn't for a moment want you to think that any time you approach a teen in the library, you will need to make classics suggestions a part of that interaction.

Starting with a Broad Question

The first part of your readers' advisory interview is to gather information. You might start with a broad question to identify just what that teen has in mind, what he or she is looking for, like, "Are you looking for a book for a school assignment, or just something to read?", "Do you have a sense of what you might like to read next?" or "Are there any books you have enjoyed reading recently?" Yes, this seems awfully open-ended and vague, but it really can be quite useful. You can get a pretty good start matching a teen to a good classic from responses like, "I don't know, I just really like books that have, um, women who, like, stand up to stuff." You could go a long way toward making great reading suggestions on this one.

In the case of a reticent teen who seems to have a hard time articulating what he or she enjoys, taking the opposite approach might be more revealing. "Have you ever really hated a book?" In describing books they did not enjoy, teens will often give clues about what they'd like to experience in a book.

Filling in the Details

Whether or not you got a revealing response to a broad question, there are more specific readers' advisory questions that can help you get a bead on a teen's reading interests. Ask those questions that help identify specific appeals. You could ask if a teen really likes edge-of-the-seat thriller type plots or books that look inside people and explore how they feel and react. You could ask if a teen prefers it when the characters talk to each other a lot or when the author describes a character's feelings and responses. You could ask if a teen likes it when a character tells the story. You could ask if a teen wants a book that makes him or her cry or laugh. You could find out if a teen enjoys books that are set in the present or likes to read books set in other historical time periods—including the future! Beyond appeals, you could ask what genres a teen likes (maybe not using the word "genre"). You could ask if a teen likes books with stories that could really happen, or prefers mysteries, horror, or fantasy books with magical plots and creatures.

Remember, not all classics are full-length novels. Ask if a teen prefers novels, nonfiction works, short stories, plays, poetry, myths and legends, and so on. There are classics in just about every literary form imaginable and you may make the best connection between a teen and an extraordinary classic work by finding out that that individual has always loved plays and the theater and would way prefer to read *The Miracle Worker*, William Gibson's classic play about Helen Keller's life, than Helen Keller's classic biography, *The Story of My Life*.

There are other facts to gather in beyond those that define reading preferences. If you don't already know—because the teens in the library aren't part of a specific group or classroom you are well acquainted with as a librarian or educator—find out what age and grade a teen is in, try to get a teen's honest assessment of how well he or she reads, how interested he or she is in reading. Use the categories that define teen diversity in the section above as a guide. Worried that asking these sorts of questions will seem like the third degree and feel insulting? I used to, but I can honestly say I've never had a negative teen response to these sorts of questions. You are demonstrating your interest in teens, and they usually respond well to that.

It is good to avoid questions that are too broad for them to answer easily or that imply any value judgment. When asking for an assessment of reading level, you might not ask, "How well do you read?" Instead, you might ask, "Do you consider yourself a strong reader, or do you struggle a little?" Avoiding judging words like "good" and "poor" can also help with any sensitive feelings.

If you don't get all the information you need from these sorts of questions, probe for a little more. Although certain kinds of open-ended questions can work well in readers' advisory work, you can also have success in asking teens to choose between things—or give them the opportunity to choose none of them and more specifically describe their needs. An example might be, "If you were going to read a book about a woman who stood up to something, would you rather it be that she stood up to someone in her family, or that she stood up to an unfair rule of some kind, or that she stood up to a disease she was just diagnosed with?"

Confirming the Facts

Once you think you've gathered enough information from a teen reader and have pulled it together in your mind, repeat it back. You might say something like, "Okay, so you really like books that feature relationships between animals and people, and it doesn't really matter to you which time period the book is set in, and you'd prefer the main character to be a female, and it could either be a true story or a novel. Did I get that right?"

The Approach: Giving What You've Got to Teens

Once you've got the information you need from a teen reader and have confirmed that you've got it right, you get to do the fun part and make classics reading suggestions! Before going on, readers' advisory suggestions (sometimes known as "shelftalking") and "booktalking" are synonyms for some folk. For the purposes of this book, though, they are merely closely related! Readers' advisory or "shelftalking" is a more personal, less formal one-on-one interaction about books between yourself and a teen. "Booktalking" is a more formal presentation or promotion of books to a group of teens. We'll take a close look at booktalking the classics in Chapter 9.

Okay, back to those classics reading suggestions. It won't just be *what* you're suggesting, but *how* you're suggesting it that can convince a teen to try a classic. Here are some tips when making classics suggestions to teens:

- Suggest a few classics to choose from (but don't make the menu too big). One is not enough! A teen may not feel attracted to a particular work regardless of how well it might seem to match his or her interests.

- Provide a brief synopsis or "hook" of each classic you're suggesting, without revealing anything a reader should experience on his or her own. It's not necessary to "booktalk" in one-on-one readers' advisory. In fact, if you do, you may overwhelm your teen reader. Just talk the book off the shelf, or, "shelftalk."

- If you can, make connections between other books a teen has mentioned he or she loved and the classics you are suggesting, or suggest a popular teen title in tandem with a classic (we talked about classics combos in Chapter 5).

- Share favorite classics of other teen readers.

- Mention briefly why each classic might be a good reading match based on a teen's stated interests. You can do that by any number of factors—appeals, genre, literary form, and so forth.

- Share any fun or unique information you might have unearthed about the book or author in your own reading of that classic. You may have stumbled across a few fascinating facts in those great resources described in Chapter 3! (We'll talk more about using fascinating facts to draw teen readers to classics in Chapter 9 on presenting great classics booktalks.)

- Share your honest (positive only) responses as a reader to classics you're suggesting, but only in brief and with care not to unduly influence a teen's personal response to that classic.

- Be honest about whether or not you've read a classic you're suggesting. Unlike booktalking, you don't have to have read a classic first to suggest it as a possibility in a readers' advisory interaction.

- Mention any reading roadblocks a teen might experience with that classic. An example would be, "It takes a chapter or two to really get going, but once it does, it never stops," or "You might have trouble understanding the dialect at first, but if you stick with it, it'll just suddenly click into place, and it's worth it."

- Suggest a few classics that aren't right on the money given your readers' advisory interview, but you just think are great reads and have a hunch might engage a particular teen reader.

- Leave the teen alone with the suggested classics to make a reading selection (or not!). Before doing so, let that teen know that you are there to help at any time, that you are interested in knowing if a suggested classic worked out or didn't, and that there are always more suggestions you can make in the future.

If a teen doesn't leave the library with one of your suggested books in hand, should you feel you've failed? No, no, and no! You care about the power of reading, and the power of reading classics in specific, in teens' lives. You are reading classics on your own to better help teens make meaningful connections with great literature. You sought out teens in the library to help with their classics reading selections, you asked a lot of great questions and listened carefully, you brought many fine books to their attention.

Those teens you interacted with now know, first of all, who will give them the time of day. This is more important than you can imagine. They now know that you will listen to their preferences and that you know things and can help them find good stuff to read. Last but not least, they now know there's no pressure or negativity in interacting with you—it's okay if they don't take a book that day, and they're welcome to come back and ask for your help again, regardless. There's no failure in that!

The Parent Barrier: Breaking through It

Everything to this point has assumed a one-on-one readers' advisory interaction with a teen. As with all assumptions, this one is flawed! If you work in a public library, as often as you engage in a one-on-one readers' advisory interaction with a teen you will be engaged in a one-on-one readers' advisory interaction with a teen's parent—usually while the teen stands nearby looking miserable. To be fair, there's the happy middle ground with a teen, an engaged and supportive parent, and you—all in a great readers' advisory interaction that's easy and fun and smooth, and where the parent plays a valuable role in the connections made between his or her teen and a great book. That does happen, and it's an excellent experience for everyone. But now that I've been fair, let's get back to that miserable teen standing nearby!

Most parents mean well, but in their eagerness to help their teens interact with staff and get the best service in the library, they can tend to take over. They often feel compelled to act as spokespeople for their teens, and in my experience, their teens are usually none to happy about it. So, what's wrong with that? Well, even a young teen is old enough to express him or herself, to answer questions and share opinions about books and reading—which is probably why that teen is so unhappy with a parent doing it in his or her stead.

Barring acute shyness or a disability that prevents it, you should encourage teens to interact directly with you; it cements their relationship to librarians and to the library as a benevolent institution, it allows them a safe experience as emerging independent beings, it gives them a much needed voice, it allows them to practice social and communication skills (a significant part of the maturation process), and it gives you a shot at the information you need to do a good job connecting them to great books—which will do wonders for them in other ways. None of this can happen with mom or dad doing all the talking!

What to do? You have a few choices. You can just let mom or dad seize the day. Or you might carefully and respectfully, with no tone of disapproval or disrespect, ask a parent if you might interact directly with the teen, explaining that you just know with the answers to a few quick questions you'll be able to find just the right sorts of books for him or her to choose from.

Or you might simply direct your attention to the teen when a parent approaches you. A good tactic here is when a parent says something like, "My daughter needs to read a classic novel set in America some time before 1900," you can direct any remarks you might need to make straight to the teen. You might ask, "Can you go back to the revolutionary period, or is your assignment just since we became the United States?" Or, "Is there any particular time period you would prefer to read about?" or "How about the Civil War years? There are loads of great classics novels about that time period." Most of the time, parents just sort of step back a pace or two and listen while their teen responds to your questions, and now you're in a direct interaction with the real, live teen.

All this said, the bottom line is connecting teens with great reading choices. If you have to do it through a parent, do it through a parent. But if you have an option of finding a respectful way around that parent to connect directly with a teen, don't hesitate to do it!

OTHER READERS' ADVISORY TOOLS FOR TEENS

You can't be on call all the time (as much as it may feel like you are!), available to help teens make excellent classics reading selections. There may be a considerable number of teens who, even when you are there, don't want to interact with you—they just want to find something good to read without having to talk to anyone about it. That's their preference and their right. And, what about the teen who comes to the library service desk when you're at lunch or at home with the flu, and asks for assistance from one of your colleagues—your wonderful school library assistant, an educational colleague, a substitute teacher, or a public librarian who specializes in business and investment resources? Uh-oh!

For teens who prefer to help themselves, and for other library and educational staff who don't specialize in either literature or service to teens but who are called on from time to time to assist them, you can and should provide what in the library profession is called "passive readers' advisory tools"—that is, books, booklists, readers' advisory binders, and book reviews—even those written by teens themselves. "Passive" is a silly sort of descriptor, but it means those tools that just sort of lay there. They don't run around looking for excitement, but they can generate it when they're picked up and used!

Published Classics Readers' Advisory Resources

To my knowledge, there aren't many published readers' advisory resources that specifically support making reading connections between teens and the classics, with the exceptions of Hazel Rochman's 1987 *Tales of Love and Terror: Booktalking the Classics, Old and New* and, of course, this book! There are, however, many readers' advisory resources that include or feature the classics for adult readers, and as most classics are for readers of all ages, these can be of great use with teens—especially at the high school level. Many of the books listed at the end of this chapter and at the end of Chapter 2 can serve as teen readers' advisory resources. You might take a look at a few of them and purchase one or two for your library or classroom that might best suit your community's needs for use in readers' advisory work with teens.

Print and Online Classics Booklists

Having one or more classics booklists displayed prominently in your library (or in classrooms) can make classics attractive to teens who otherwise may not have considered reading them, and gives teens who are actively seeking out classics something to help them make better selections to match their needs and interests. You can display these booklists with your classics collections, you can put them in other collections or areas of the library teens might go, and you can put them in a prominent place or common area in a classroom. You certainly could post them on your library or school Web site for teens using your resources from home.

Some classics booklists might be long booklists of teacher-accepted classics for reading assignments. Others might be short and sweet by genre or theme. Those long booklists serve a great purpose. My library system, the King County Library System, has two longer booklists,

MegaLit: Fiction and *MegaLit: Nonfiction*, developed to provide teen and adult readers with a more extensive list of classics reading selections and to support literary reading assignments in the schools in our county. Many school libraries have similar booklists. In the interest of providing teens with smaller menus, though, I encourage you to also provide at least one or two classics booklists in your library or on your Web site that are of the short and sweet sort. Some teens want a meaty booklist from which to make their selections, others need a quick and easy access point through just a handful of classics titles. And be sure to include classics with popular contemporary titles, if you're producing thematic booklists.

There are a few solid rules of thumb when creating booklists of any kind:

- Make the booklist as attractive as you can. Just like displays, how you use the space you have makes a difference in how well it will appeal to teens. Use simple (and not too juvenile or corny!) images, rich colors, readable typefaces and fonts. Leave adequate "white space" so your pages don't appear overcrowded with words.

- Make the booklist a size that's easy to pick up and stick in a purse, book bag, backpack, or pocket. Consider a bookmark, or a folded or brochure format rather than a full-page format.

- The booklist must have a visible title. It doesn't need to be flashy, but it does need to be immediately apparent.

- If the booklist's title is not descriptive of its contents, the booklist should include a statement of purpose or a description of its contents adjacent to its title. For example, the King County Library System's *MegaLit: Fiction* booklist includes a descriptive statement that reads, "Novels, collected short stories, and narrative verse of outstanding literary merit from around the world and across time." The *MegaLit: Nonfiction* booklist includes a descriptive statement that reads, "Selected significant writings in philosophy, science, poetry, drama, history and other disciplines from around the world and across time."

- The booklist should only include titles available in your library.

- All booklist entries should include the same information, and should be arranged and formatted consistently.

- The booklist should be annotated briefly with its intended audience in mind, in a language they can relate to.

- The booklist should be dated (for future evaluation and updating) and the owning or creating library or school should be identified by logo (if you have one) and include full contact information.

- It never hurts to include a statement suggesting that there are many more choices than found on a particular booklist, and to ask a librarian or educator for further assistance.

- And last, but certainly not least, before printing the list should be reviewed for any errors.

What sorts of short and sweet booklists might you do? You could do seasonal booklists of classic stories set in the deep dark of winter or at a winter holiday, classics set in the height of summer when gentle breezes are blowing, and that sort of thing. You might make a booklist that ties classics to their film versions. Here's a great idea: how about making a classics booklist of titles that have garnered great responses from teen readers in the past, and include a pithy teen remark or two with each? Or, even better, how about having a group of teen readers do a list of their favorites for you?

You could also do some quirky classics booklists. Carol Jago includes a few at the end of her book, *With Rigor for All: Teaching the Classics to Contemporary Students*, one of which is, "10 Classics for Girls Certain They Will Never Meet Prince Charming," which includes greats like Jane Austen's *Pride and Prejudice*, Carson McCullers's *The Heart Is a Lonely Hunter*, Margaret Mitchell's *Gone with the Wind*, and Yukio Mishima's *The Sound of Waves*. Another fun one is, "10 Classics for Boys (and Girls) Who Love Action and Hate Long Descriptions of Drawing Rooms and Landscapes" (Jago 2000, 153).

You could make some neat booklists using those readers' advisory appeals we discussed earlier. You might develop classics booklists with titles like, "Action-Packed Page-Turners," "If you like interesting characters in books, you might like . . . ," "If you like books steeped in history, you might like . . . ," or "If you like scary books (or any other genre), you might like. . . ." There's just about no end to the ideas you could come up with for appeals.

Where do you find the classics to support your booklist ideas? You most likely haven't read enough classics and retained all their details to do it off the top of your head! Draw from all those great classics resources lists found at the end of Chapter 2 and from the genre guides list at the end of this chapter. Ask colleagues, post to a literature-related listserv or online book discussion group (we talked about a few of those in Chapter 2), dig around on the Internet. You might also check out the classics booklists in this book for some titles.

Don't forget to share the wonderful classics booklists you create with your colleagues in the community. If you are a public librarian who's just created a great classics booklist, send multiple copies to other branches in your system and to school librarians and educators in your community. If you're a school librarian or educator, you will be doing your public librarians a great service to send them copies of the booklists you've generated to use with teens who seek out titles from your lists in their local public library.

Classics Readers' Advisory Binders

Most of you collect teen-related booklists. You may get them from your colleagues, you may collect them at conferences or workshops. You might be on a listserv or two that discuss books and you occasionally pull lists from postings, or you might pick them up when you visit other schools, school libraries, or public library systems. You might get them from reviewing sources, you might unearth them in general Internet searching.

Include the classics in your booklist collection activities as well! Start collecting all the classics-related booklists you can find. You might add them to an existing teen readers' advisory binder, or might arrange them in their very own classics readers' advisory binder. What's a teen readers' advisory binder? It's simply a three-ring binder in which you have collected lists of books and media materials of interest to teens in a variety of categories, like, oh, adventure/survival stories, alternative lifestyles fiction, biography for teens, books for grieving teens, great audiobooks for teens, historical fiction, humor for teens, movie tie-ins, science books for teens, and so on. The sky's the limit on the sorts of lists you can collect into a binder to help teens, parents, and other colleagues in your working environment find great stuff for young people to read, listen to, watch, and so forth. Whether you include classics as a category in a broader teen readers' advisory binder or in a dedicated binder, it's not a bad idea to make copies both for staff use and for teen use.

In Chapter 5 we looked at types of classics you should know about to make strong reading connections with teens, among which are award winners. Another idea for a readers' advisory binder is one that lists award winners that might be considered classics, crossing from teen to adult literature. You might have a tabbed section for each award, and in each section a description of the award followed by a list of its winners and honor books through time. You can find a list of reference resources that list both teen and adult literary awards at the end of Chapter 2 in "Resources to Help You Choose Classics to Read," and will find many Web sites on the Internet that do the same thing, including many of the major online booksellers.

Teen Classics Book Reviews

Teen book reviews can be great readers' advisory tools. If you have a reading incentive program of some kind during the summer or school year and collect book reviews, get permission from teens who've written particularly fun, witty, or interesting reviews of classics to display those reviews in your library or classroom. You might have a bulletin board you can post these on, or acrylic display holders to put them in. Or, you may have space constraints and choose to put them in a binder somewhere within easy reach. Whatever the case may be, you can draw teens to classics through the opinions of other teens (far more credible to them!) who have already read and enjoyed them. And, in my experience, this sort of passive readers' advisory tool not only attracts teens to reading the classics, it attracts them to writing reviews themselves, which just keeps the whole thing going!

SUMMING IT UP

Your role as a classics readers' advisor is essential in making meaningful connections between teens and the classics. With an understanding of the theoretical and practical basics of readers' advisory work, including appeals and genres, and with specific attention to the skills you might employ to make the best matches between teens and classic literature, you are better equipped to make those reading connections meaningful. In addition to direct one-on-one work with teens, you can provide a wide variety of passive readers' advisory tools to both teens and other staff who may work with teens when you are not available to provide expert assistance!

WORKS CITED

Benedetti, Angelina. 2001. "Leading the Horse to Water: Keeping Young People Reading in the Information Age." In *The Readers' Advisor's Companion*.

Edited by Kenneth D. Shearer and Robert Burgin. Englewood, CO: Libraries Unlimited.

Booklists and Book Awards. Chicago: Young Adult Library Services Association. Available online at: http://www.ala.org/yalsa/booklists/ (accessed 28 February 2004).

Fonseca, Anthony J., and June Michele Pulliam. 2003. *Hooked on Horror: A Guide to Reading Interests in Horror Fiction.* 2nd ed. Englewood, CO: Libraries Unlimited.

Herald, Diana Tixier. 2000. *Genreflecting: A Guide to Reading Interests in Genre Fiction.* 5th ed. Englewood, CO: Libraries Unlimited.

———. 2003. *Teen Genreflecting: A Guide to Reading Interests.* 2nd ed. Westport, CT: Libraries Unlimited.

Herald, Diana Tixier, and Bonnie Kunzel. 2002. *Strictly Science Fiction: A Guide to Reading Interests.* Greenwood Village, CO: Libraries Unlimited.

Jago, Carol. 2000. *With Rigor for All: Teaching the Classics to Contemporary Students.* Foreword by James Strickland. Portland, ME: Calendar Islands Publishers.

MegaLit: Fiction. 2002. Staff-generated booklist. King County, WA: King County Library System.

MegaLit: Nonfiction. 2002. Staff-generated booklist. King County, WA: King County Library System.

Mort, John. 2002. *Christian Fiction: A Guide to the Genre.* Greenwood Village, CO: Libraries Unlimited.

Niebuhr, Gary Warren. 2003. *Make Mine a Mystery: A Reader's Guide to Mystery and Detective Fiction.* Westport, CT: Libraries Unlimited.

Professional Development Center: Knowledge of Books: What Books Should Anyone Working with Teens Know? Chicago: Young Adult Library Services Association. Available online at: http://www.ala.org/ala/yalsa/professsionaldev/what booksshould.htm (accessed 28 February 2004).

Ramsdell, Kristin. 1999. *Romance Fiction: A Guide to the Genre.* Englewood, CO: Libraries Unlimited.

Reed, Arthea J.S. 1988. *Comics to Classics: A Parent's Guide to Books for Teens and Preteens.* Newark, DE: International Reading Association.

Saricks, Joyce G. 2001. *The Readers' Advisory Guide to Genre Fiction.* Chicago: American Library Association.

Saricks, Joyce G., and Nancy Brown. 1997. *Readers' Advisory Service in the Public Library.* 2nd ed. Chicago: American Library Association.

GENRE GUIDES
General

Herald, Diana Tixier. 2000. *Genreflecting: A Guide to Reading Interests in Genre Fiction.* 5th ed. Englewood, CO: Libraries Unlimited.

Christian

Mort, John. 2002. *Christian Fiction: A Guide to the Genre*. Greenwood Village, CO: Libraries Unlimited.

Horror

Bloom, Harold, ed. 1994. *Classic Horror Writers*. New York: Chelsea House.

Fonseca, Anthony J., and June Michele Pulliam. 1999. *Hooked on Horror: A Guide to Reading Interests in Horror Fiction*. Englewood, CO: Libraries Unlimited.

———. 2003. *Hooked on Horror: A Guide to Reading Interests in Horror Fiction*. 2nd ed. Englewood, CO: Libraries Unlimited.

Jones, Stephen, and Kim Newman, eds. 1998. *Horror: The 100 Best Books*. New York: Carroll and Graf.

Mystery

Bloom, Harold, ed. 1994. *Classic Crime and Suspense Writers*. New York: Chelsea House.

Bloom, Harold, ed. 1995. *Classic Mystery Writers*. New York: Chelsea House.

Dubose, Martha Hailey. 2000. *Women of Mystery: The Lives and Works of Notable Women Crime Novelists*. New York: St. Martin's Minotaur.

Keating, H.R.F. 1987. *Crime and Mystery: The 100 Best Books*. New York: Carroll and Graf.

Kelleghan, Fiona, ed. 2001. *100 Masters of Mystery and Detective Fiction*. 2 vols. Pasadena, CA: Salem Press.

Niebuhr, Gary Warren. 2003. *Make Mine a Mystery: A Reader's Guide to Mystery and Detective Fiction*. Westport, CT: Libraries Unlimited.

Romance

Ramsdell, Kristin. 1999. *Romance Fiction: A Guide to the Genre*. Englewood, CO: Libraries Unlimited.

Science Fiction and Fantasy

Bloom, Harold, ed. 1994. *Classic Fantasy Writers*. New York: Chelsea House.

Bloom, Harold, ed. 1995. *Classic Science Fiction Writers*. New York: Chelsea House.

Bloom, Harold, ed. 1995. *Science Fiction Writers of the Golden Age*. New York: Chelsea House.

Herald, Diana Tixier. 1999. *Fluent in Fantasy: A Guide to Reading Interests*. Englewood, CO: Libraries Unlimited.

Herald, Diana Tixier, and Bonnie Kunzel. 2002. *Strictly Science Fiction: A Guide to Reading Interests*. Greenwood Village, CO: Libraries Unlimited.

Masterpieces: The Best Science Fiction of the Century. 2001. Edited by Orson Scott Card. New York: Ace Books.

Pringle, David. 1989. *Modern Fantasy: The Hundred Best Novels*. New York: Bedrick Books.

———. 1985. *Science Fiction: The 100 Best Novels: An English-Language Selection, 1949–1984*. New York: Carroll and Graf Publishers.

Lots More Thin Classics!

You never can have too long a list of thin classics. Over time, it will be worth its weight in gold. So here's that short list from earlier in the chapter plus lots more to share with teens.

- *Alice's Adventures in Wonderland* and *Through the Looking Glass*, Lewis Carroll (1865, 1871)
- *Animal Farm*, George Orwell (1945)
- *Annie John*, Jamaica Kincaid (1985)
- *The Awakening*, Kate Chopin (1899)
- *Billy Budd*, Herman Melville (1924)
- *The Bridge of San Luis Rey*, Thornton Wilder (1927)
- *The Bridges at Toko-Ri*, James Michener (1953)
- *The Call of the Wild*, Jack London (1903)
- *Candide*, Voltaire (1759)
- *A Christmas Carol*, Charles Dickens (1843)
- *Daisy Miller*, Henry James (1878)
- *The Death of Ivan Ilyich*, Leo Tolstoy (1884)
- *Ellen Foster*, Kaye Gibbons (1987)
- *Ethan Frome*, Edith Wharton (1911)
- *Fahrenheit 451*, Ray Bradbury (1953)
- *Go Ask Alice*, Anonymous (1971)
- *Grendel*, John Gardner (1971)
- *Heart of Darkness*, Joseph Conrad (1902)
- *The House on Mango Street*, Sandra Cisneros (1984)
- *I Heard the Owl Call My Name*, Margaret Craven (1967)

(continued)

(continued)

- *The Invisible Man*, H.G. Wells (1897)
- *The Island of Dr. Moreau*, H.G. Wells (1896)
- *Laughing Boy*, Oliver La Farge (1929)
- *The Legend of Sleepy Hollow*, Washington Irving (1820)
- *The Light in the Forest*, Conrad Richter (1953)
- *Lord of the Flies*, William Golding (1954)
- *The Man Who Fell to Earth*, Walter Tevis (1963)
- *The Member of the Wedding*, Carson McCullers (1946)
- *The Metamorphosis*, Franz Kafka (1915)
- *Night*, Elie Wiesel (1956)
- *Of Mice and Men*, John Steinbeck (1937)
- *The Old Gringo*, Carlos Fuentes (1985)
- *The Old Man and the Sea*, Ernest Hemingway (1952)
- *One Day in the Life of Ivan Denisovich*, Aleksandr Isaevich Solzhenit-syn (1962)
- *The Pearl*, John Steinbeck (1947)
- *The Red Badge of Courage,* Stephen Crane (1895)
- *The Red Pony*, John Steinbeck (1937)
- *Rip Van Winkle*, Washington Irving (1819–1820)
- *The Sea of Grass*, Conrad Richter (1937)
- *A Separate Peace*, John Knowles (1959)
- *Shane*, Jack Schaefer (1949)
- *Siddhartha*, Hermann Hesse (1922)
- *The Sound of Waves*, Yukio Mishima (1956)
- *The Stranger*, Albert Camus (1942)
- *Things Fall Apart*, Chinua Achebe (1958)
- *The Time Machine*, H.G. Wells (1895)
- *The Turn of the Screw*, Henry James (1898)
- *Wide Sargasso Sea*, Jean Rhys (1966)

8

✦✦✦ ✦✦✦ ✦✦✦

FIT CLASSICS INTO TEEN READING PROGRAMS AND OTHER ACTIVITIES

As a librarian or an educator, you can develop and provide reading activities and programs for teens that can engage their interest and cultivate a positive relationship to the classics. From traditional after-school classics book discussion groups to classroom visits by contemporary classics authors; from reader's theatre programs to professional performances based on the classics; from classics movie nights to classics trivia games—you have opportunities galore!

This chapter will look at a selection of those reading activities and programs that you can provide through your public or school library, or as part of your classroom activities if you're an educator, to encourage even greater connections between teens and the classics. As for booktalking (promoting wonderful books to an audience), which certainly could be described as a program or an activity designed to attract teens to the classics and which is traditionally done in schools or with supervised groups of teens in other venues, we'll devote the next chapter to it.

CLASSICS BOOK DISCUSSION GROUPS FOR TEENS

Book discussion groups are great things, especially for teens. They provide a regular time and place for teens to talk about their reading experiences with interested peers in a nonjudgmental way, often outside of the formal classroom experience yet in an environment that has enough structure to hold their interactions together.

A teen classics book discussion group can take several forms. You may be imagining an all-teen book group that meets once a month or so after school hours in your school or public library, or in your classroom, in which you serve as a moderator for book selection and discussion. That's a fairly common sort of book discussion group. You might also think about forming and moderating a parent-teen book group, especially for the younger teen set who may appreciate parental involvement to create stronger social and literary connections (you may prefer their involvement, as well!). Parent-teen book discussion groups are all the rage, and they're generally quite successful. You might want to try an older teen-younger teen book discussion group in which older teens comoderate with you (to fulfill community service hours or get extra credit in a language arts class or just because they want to) to introduce younger teens to great classics and how satisfying it can be to discuss them with others.

You might simply be the mastermind behind a teens-only book discussion group, comprised solely of teens who rely on you for access to a workable meeting space and to behind-the-scenes support and advice. This sort of book discussion group may grow out of a moderated group, but you may find when you advertise your willingness to help start a teens-only book discussion group, that a highly motivated bunch of teens approach you right away for your support. Hey, it could happen! Lest you think teens aren't capable of maintaining a book group of their own, even if they demonstrate enthusiasm for the idea, perhaps teen market publisher and author, Marc Aronson, will inspire you to think otherwise. From an article entitled, "The Myths of Teenage Readers," Mr. Aronson asserts:

> Whenever teenagers get to books, and get to talk about them, the results are amazing. I think that, with a little bit of organization, we could have a revolution on our hands, as groups of teenage readers around the country read books, discuss their reactions in person or by email, and create a national conversation in which the prejudices of adults have almost no role. When they read and talk, our most firmly held myths simply evaporate. (2000, 9)

Planning and Promoting a Classics Book Discussion Group

Whether you'll be directly involved as a moderator or will play an organizational and support role behind the scenes, how do you get a teen classics book discussion group started? Sit down in a quiet place and think about just what sort of group you'd like. Do you feel your younger community of teens, those in middle and junior high school, will be more responsive to a classics book discussion group, or do you feel those high schoolers are a better bet? Do you have the time, energy, and resources to offer a book discussion group to both? Just an aside here—unless you are specifically forming an older teens–younger teens mentoring sort of discussion group, I wouldn't recommend a classics book discussion group that spans the full range of teen years. It could be difficult to find a classic that would be accessible and appeal across all teen ages and developmental stages, and social problems can develop in teen groups that are too disparate in maturity.

You will need to determine a time and place for the book discussion group. The time needs to be a good match for the community you're hoping to appeal to; you wouldn't want to promote a parent-teen book group before most parents are off work for the day, or during the dinner hour on weeknights, for example. As for place, if you're a school librarian or educator, you have a ready-made space in your library or in a classroom after school hours for a librarian-moderated or teens-only book group. If you're a public librarian, you'll need to determine a regular meeting place either in your library, if there's room, or in a nearby community meeting space—maybe in a school somewhere. You'll also need to think about how often the book group can successfully meet. Once a month, twice a month?

You'll need to identify any costs that might be associated with the book group. Does your library or educational organization have the resources to support snacks and drinks, hoagies or pizza during each meeting? Food is a big draw with teens. Will you be able to provide multiple copies of the titles selected for discussion, either through your library's collections, another community resource, or through a budget to purchase copies from a bookstore? Or, will book discussion group participants need to come up with their own copies?

Once you've conceptualized what your book group will look like, and where, when and how frequently it will meet, as well as what budgetary responsibility you can assume for it, you can put it all into motion:

- *Come up with a name for your classics book discussion group.*
  This could be simple and descriptive, like "Classic Book Discussion Group for Teens" or "Parent-Teen Classics Book Club." It could be a little more alliterative or snappy, like "The Cool Classics Club" or "The Classics Clique" or

"Connect with a Classic." You might do better than these, but they give you the idea! If you intend to encourage a teens-only classics book discussion group, don't get too attached to the name you use to promote the concept. Allow teens to pick their own name once their book discussion group is up and running.

- *Determine the date you'd like to kick off your classics book discussion group and set a regular time for ongoing meetings.*

  If you're a school librarian or educator, you most likely have your finger on the pulse of teen activity in your educational environment during the school year. Find the best time to kick off a book discussion group for teen interest and availability. If you're a public librarian, I suggest you don't start a classics book discussion group at the beginning of the summer. You'll have greater success if you wait until late summer when teens are bored, antsy, and looking for structure, or even better, for the fall, after school has settled into a routine and you can get buy-in from your educational colleagues. As for a regular meeting time, you might, for example, decide the book discussion group will meet on the first Thursday of each month at 4 PM, or the third Saturday morning of each month at 10 AM.

- *Develop flyers and posters promoting your classics book discussion group and prominently display them in your library and in other community agencies frequented by teens.*

  As with all display materials, make sure these are attractive and readable. You might take a look at Kirsten Edwards's book written for the Greenwood Professional Guides for Young Adult Librarians series, *Teen Library Events: A Month-by-Month Guide* (2002). The author provides a number of examples of high-appeal promotional art to use when starting a book discussion group, and also describes a number of the steps you can take to more successfully kick off a teen book discussion group. Because you are promoting a book discussion group for a type of literature not commonly thought of as fun by teens, you might think up a neat promotional statement to waylay concerns. Something like, "Sure, some classics are boring, but other classics are COOL. Want to test your limits? Join our classics book discussion group to read and talk about classics that can suck you in, break your heart in two, make you spitting mad, make you laugh until your guts ache, and cause you think about things you've never thought about before!"

- *Submit your classics book discussion group promotional materials to local newspaper and radio stations.*

  You may need to reformat those materials in press release form or other formats required by the media, but it's worth it if you get your teen classics book discussion group featured in the events page of the newspaper, or mentioned every couple of hours for a week or so on a local radio station that teens listen to.

- *If you are a public librarian and your classics book discussion group is starting during the school year, inform all your educational colleagues: school librarians, language arts teachers, and your home-schooling connections.*

  Provide your colleagues with your promotional materials and request they display them. Find out if they can advertise the book discussion group with the morning announcements for a period of time. Set dates to visit classrooms or alternative educational environments to talk up the book group directly with teens. You might also explore if teen participation in a classics book discussion group would fulfill a school's teen community service requirements, or might be tied in to extra credit opportunities in language arts classes.

- *Plan out the first classics book discussion group meeting if serving as a moderator.*

  Your first meeting will not be a discussion meeting as much as a business meeting. In this case, business and pleasure should mix, so put in some elements that will appeal to teens. You might provide food and drink and entertainment of some sort—a small kick-off celebration, if you will. That entertainment doesn't need to be anything fancy, but you might consider showing a short and dynamic piece of a film based on a classic, or create your own computer slide show of a fascinating classic and its author—something to whet reading appetites while you're satisfying culinary appetites! Pull together a short annotated list of classics for the book discussion group to choose from for the first reading selection. Here's a great idea: prepare booktalks for a few of the classics from the list you think might work well with your group and present them at your kick-off meeting.

- *Select a meeting time with teens who want to start a teens-only classics book discussion group with your assistance.*

  This one is pretty self-explanatory, but do remember that even highly motivated teens can be difficult to gather together for a meeting, or can lose their enthusiasm in what seems to you an incredibly short time, so you can do them a great service by carrying the burden of organization and providing lots of positive energy early on.

Leading a Classics Book Discussion Group

You may already have some experience working with groups of teens, either as a school librarian or educator, or as a public librarian who's been in the trenches for a while. If so, this section may be "old hat" to you. For those of you who haven't hosted teen programs or led teen book discussion groups of any sort before, a few pointers might be helpful to you to get started.

When working with teens in groups of any kind, remember that you really are a sort of benevolent dictator! If it weren't for your skills and activities as a professional, the classics book discussion group wouldn't come together, and it will take those skills and activities to keep it together. No matter how mellow or collegial a character you are, you will have to take charge and build a working structure for teens as its book discussion group leader. If you are not a mellow or collegial character, make sure you keep in mind at all times that the mission of your book discussion group is to meaningfully connect teens with classic literature, not lord it over them and minimize their pizza consumption! Your role is indeed one that will require real leadership to make your book discussion group work, but it is most certainly benevolent.

There are lots of books you might refer to for additional assistance in starting and leading a book discussion group, even though they are predominantly written for adult groups. Although not comprehensive by any means, here are a few do's and don'ts that might help you, for starters.

Do's and Don'ts in Leading a Teen Book Discussion Group

Do:

- Set a regular agenda that you more or less stick to at each meeting. Believe it or not, teens like some structure and like to know what to expect. Routine can attract them, as long as you're flexible to change when they indicate the need for it.

- Have teens introduce themselves each month and share something, if desired, about their lives since the last time the group met.

- Keep each meeting to a reasonable length of time. Teens who feel trapped in a room past their attention span may not come back.

- Include a diverse list of classics on your annotated list for teens to choose from. Don't forget short stories, plays, myths, legends, and so forth, as possible selections for the group to read and discuss, or classics with themes that match a particular time of year or season (i.e., creepy classics or holiday classics).

- Allow teens to pick the classic they'd like to read and discuss for the next meeting. You may also like to hear their opinions on whether the whole work can be read and discussed in a month, or whether they'd like to read and discuss it in pieces over two or more months.

- Prepare a series of discussion questions about each classic to guide the upcoming book discussion. You can create them yourself, and you can find them all over the place—on the Internet, at classics publish-

(continued)

(continued)

ers' Web sites, in the backs of some classics themselves, in reference and readers' advisory books on book group titles. A couple of good questions to include with the classics are, "Why do you think this book is considered a classic?" and "Do you think it *should* be considered a classic?" Remember to gear the discussion questions for the developmental level of the teens in your group.

- Prepare background information (pictures are always good to include) on the author or the time and setting of a classic to share with teens in your book discussion group if it might lend itself to their understanding or appreciation of it.
- Include other media formats in your book discussion group now and again for a change of pace. Have the teens listen to a passage of a classic on a recorded book format or watch a classic on film, and encourage them to respond to how closely the reader/actor's interpretation matched their own as readers.
- Demonstrate your enthusiasm for the classics.
- Demonstrate your appreciation of the teens.

Don't:

- Dominate the discussion.
- Correct teens' interpretations or opinions of a classic.
- Disagree with teens' responses to discussion group questions.
- Assert unnecessary authority.

All in all, through effective group leadership you can provide a wonderful opportunity for teens to read, appreciate, and respond to the classics in a relaxed and nonjudgmental environment that provides enough structure to channel their reading experiences into positive intellectual engagement and social interaction. Good stuff!

Advising a Teens-Only Classics Book Discussion Group

When assisting a teens-only classics book discussion group, you can make good use of most of the information already provided for moderated classics book discussion groups. Instead of serving as group leader, though, you will be serving as group advisor, which is a slightly more distant role that may actually require lots more effort from you!

You'll first need to decide what level of support you'll be providing these teens. Are you simply going to provide a meeting space at a designated time? Will you be developing publicity for the group, or if developed by the teens themselves, will you put it through your channels to reach the community? Are you going to help them make classics reading selections and develop questions to discuss among themselves? Will you fund their snacks? Will you help them set up audiovisual equipment if they want to use it at a meeting?

How do you decide what level of support to provide? That may depend in part on the organization you work for. Find out if it's acceptable for teens to meet without adult supervision in your educational environment, school library, or public library meeting room. There can be liability issues there. If not, you may have to commit to being in the corner of the room with your own project for each meeting. Find out if your organization has any rules about groups receiving funding, even if only for chips and dip, without direct organizational sponsorship or staff hosting an event. Find out if you can foot the bill for promotional materials for a teens-only group. Find out what level of responsibility you have for things going south in a teens-only group, say, when one teen expresses something deeply hurtful or damaging to another, or makes a remark construed as racist or sexist or against a deeply-held spiritual or religious belief. This stuff is important to know, and you should know it as soon as possible so you don't get teens excited about a group that ultimately looks very different from how they originally imagined it.

If you are in a position to offer full support to a teens-only classics book discussion group, despite possible problem spots, you've got your work cut out for you! You will have to meet with those interested teens to iron out quite a few things in advance, and will have to meet with them regularly thereafter to evaluate the strengths and weaknesses of the book discussion group.

First, you should make it clear what your role will be and what authority you have as their advisor to address issues and resolve problems. You might select one or two teens (or ask for volunteers) as your "point people" to work with more closely, if you feel that would work better than always interacting with the larger group. You should also develop a list of expectations or a code of conduct for the group. For example, you expect that they will come—and on time—each month, will use the time and space for its intended purpose, will openly and graciously welcome new participants, will treat each other with respect, will leave the room in the same condition they found it, and that sort of thing.

You might, after sitting down in a quiet place and brainstorming about the sorts of things you would do to create and lead a successful book discussion group, write those down to share with the group. It's guaranteed they won't know or do those same things without your guidance. The same information we've already explored in planning, promoting, and leading a teen classics book discussion group could be modified here for a teens-only group.

If a younger teens-only group, you may need to get written permission from parents or legal guardians as the advisor of that group, making certain they understand their teens may be unsupervised for an hour or so in your library or classroom. You may also feel the need to collect the names and contact information of the parents or legal guardians of the teens in your starter group.

Lots to think about and lots to do if when you advertise your willingness to help start a teens-only book discussion group, you get a positive response. It will be worth all your effort, though, to know you are helping teens help themselves to great classics—and to learning how to think about them and discuss them with their peers. Awesome!

If for some reason you are not capable of supporting a teens-only classics book discussion group, you might put together a brochure or flyer teens can pick up in your library that helps them start their own book discussion groups without library sponsorship. For example, a good place for you to direct them is at http://www.teenreads.com, a Web site that provides information to teens on how to start and run a book group and provides numerous reading guides with discussion questions on popular adult fiction and classics. You might include some of the adult book discussion group resources and other Web sites as you find them.

OTHER CLASSICS PROGRAMS FOR TEENS

Rick Duffield, the creator and executive producer of the *Wishbone* television series, decided to provide a missing link between children and the stories and themes of the classics through a lovable Jack Russell terrier named, yes, Wishbone. According to Duffield in a *Seattle Times* article, Wishbone's job, which began in 1995 and continued for forty episodes, was to expose children "to the primary ideas from each story" and "come away prepared to explore these stories more fully later in life" (Green 1995, H6). Hey, that's awesome, and the series was a smashing success. If a Jack Russell terrier and a wide range of children's theatrical performances and book-related programs can introduce children to great classics, why wouldn't programs developed for teen audiences do the same?

Although a topic for another book, teens are to some degree the forgotten audience. It's often assumed they'd rather be in front of MTV or a reality show than watching a PBS great books series or a live theatrical performance of some sort, that they'd rather hang out with their friends staring into space than participate in a reading incentive program. Cast aside those assumptions and give teens something else to engage in!

Classics programs for teens can be an excellent way to engage their interest in the wonders of great literature. Programs can range from author visits to brown-bag or lunchtime programs, from movie nights to professional performances based on the classics, to read-aloud programs. We'll look at a few common examples of classics-related programs for teens, but don't stop at these by any means. There are probably as many ideas for programs that meaningfully connect teens with classics as you've got the time to think up!

Contemporary Classics Author Programs

If you have the funding and the connections, either on your own or through a public programming department in your school district or public library, you can bring in authors of contemporary classics to speak to teens. You might consider authors of contemporary teen literature, like say, Chris Crutcher, Walter Dean Myers, Louis Sachar, and Virginia Euwer Wolff. You might consider authors of contemporary adult literature, like Michael Crichton, Ernest J. Gaines, Barbara Kingsolver, or Amy Tan. Yes, it can be difficult to afford these sorts of authors, especially the latter group, but it can be done and has been done, and I'd be remiss not to mention it for those of you who might be able to make such a wonderful thing work! For some, there may be local authors who are more accessible and affordable.

This sort of programming can work well when schools and public libraries work together to cosponsor the event. Funding comes from more than one source, the best possible venue can be located for the author visit between the two types of organizations, the greatest number of teens and parents of teens can be reached through promotion and publicity, the overall support system for such a significant event is comprised of a greater number of people, and so on.

Most importantly, the public library and school groups can work together to create the best possible audience for that author visit. As a school or public librarian, you can encourage your educational colleagues to read aloud from an upcoming author's works to teens in the classroom, or assign one of that author's books for classroom reading in advance of the visit, or give extra credit to teens for attending the author visit. If you're an educator in charge of your own classroom, you can do some of these things on your own, and work in tandem with other educators and librarians in your school and larger community to successfully connect teens with a visiting author.

Author visits allow teens an opportunity to put a face with a name, to experience the human being behind the great writing, to get some insight on why that writer writes, what's important to him or her and what he or she is trying to accomplish through the written word. It makes the world of books—writing them and reading them—more immediate and real. And, if you're lucky, you'll get an author who's a truly wonderful public speaker, who makes strong connections with the audience, and who understands the impact both the work and its author can have on young minds.

Brown-Bag/Lunchtime Classics Programs

A brown-bag or lunchtime program is something that could work well in an empty classroom, school library, or school cafeteria. Basically, a brown-bag program is a regular, short program that takes place during lunchtime when teens are eating, well, lunch. Educators and both school and public librarians willing to plan and present a low-key lunchtime program could make this work at a school. You might read aloud from a classic every Tuesday during the first and second lunch periods in a designated corner of the cafeteria or in the school library. You might present classics booktalks on the first and third Fridays of the month in the cafeteria or school library. You might actually show a short film that is based on a classic book or short story in one lunch period or over a few brown-bag sessions.

There are all sorts of ideas for short programs that might draw in teens to a different sort of lunchtime experience. It all depends on the teens, on the school, and on the length of lunch periods, but it's certainly a positive option for making classics connections in a short time without gobs of effort or any additional financial commitment.

Classics Movie Nights

If you are a public librarian and have open hours in the evenings, or if you are an educator or school librarian who can open up the school library or a common area for special events, you might consider a regular classics movie night in your library. The idea here is to show a movie in a space where teens can have snacks (don't forget the wonders of microwave popcorn!) and make themselves comfortable for the duration.

How do you find classics on film? There's a list of books at the end of this chapter for you! If you choose to do a classics movie night, look into copyright restrictions and public performance rights. Being no lawyer, I won't go into too much detail here, but be certain that the films you decide to show are either being used in full compliance with copyright law or were purchased with public performance rights.

You could just show the films as a way to introduce teens to a classic plot or theme in an entertaining way and leave it at that. Or, you could tie the classic book into the film based on it, either before the film begins (a good idea) or after the film ends (teens might be tired and ready to go, so maybe not as good an idea). You might provide some fascinating facts about the film, the classic it came from, or the author who wrote it. You might do a few booktalks of classics with related themes or plots, or that are set in the same time period. You certainly should have copies of the book the movie is based on for teens to check out if they so desire, and might also provide a handout that lists full information about the movie, the book, and any other related information you think a teen either might enjoy knowing or that might enrich his or her experience of that classic.

We've talked about this in earlier chapters, and will visit it again in Chapter 9 when we look at using media formats to promote the classics as a booktalker, but suffice it to say here that teens are a visual lot, they are attracted to media formats, and you can use this to great advantage to encourage connections between teens and the classics.

Professional Classics-Based Performances

You may have the good fortune of living in an area, be it large or small, rural or urban, with a strong arts community. If you have access to community performers, see if they can marry (or already have married) their performance skills with the classics. There are lots of possibilities, a few of which are:

- *History performances that tie in with classics from time periods and settings*
  In the Seattle and Tacoma areas, for example, a wonderfully engaging performer named Tames Alan does what she calls "Living History Lectures," which she is more than willing to adapt for teens, even to the extent that young

men in her audience get to serve as bedposts for her to hang on to while young women in her audience lace up her corset unbelievably tight! Ms. Alan then proceeds to put on volumes of clothing in a multitude of layers, and whites her face before talking about what it was like to be an upper class woman in Elizabethan England. And that's only one of the time periods she does! Just for the fun of it, even if you live in the Carolinas somewhere, check out Ms. Alan's Web site at http://www.oz.net/~tamsalan/histmain.html.

- *Performers who play famous authors or characters from classic works*
  Again, in the Seattle and Tacoma areas, as an example, a gentleman performer by the name of Jake Esau acts out Charles Dickens reading from his own works, and has been known to perform as Edgar Allen Poe and make occasional appearances, on stage and television as well, as Count Dracula (just wait, you'll hear loads more about the ever-present Count in Chapter 9!).

- *Performances of drama classics*
  How about providing a real live performance of a bona fide classic dramatic work—like William Gibson's *The Miracle Worker*, Edmond Rostand's *Cyrano de Bergerac*, or August Wilson's *Fences*—in your school or public library meeting space? You might keep your eye on local theatrical performances and when a classic drama is being performed, and explore whether that program can be brought to teens in your school or public library. If it's not feasible to bring an entire play with all set pieces, props, and actors, it may be possible to have a significant scene or two performed by a handful of actors in costume but without the larger accoutrements of the theatre. Or, if possible, you might find a way to get a group of teens to the theatre for a weekend matinee performance followed by a discussion of the play in a local eatery (I know, that's definitely a tall order!).

- *Performances of literary classics adapted to theater*
  Seattle has an excellent community of local theater groups, one of which is Book-It Repertory Theatre. This theatre regularly develops dramatic productions based on the classics. In fact, among their recent productions are stage adaptations of Austen's *Pride and Prejudice*, Kate Chopin's *The Awakening*, Charles Dickens's *Hard Times*, and Bram Stoker's *Dracula*. This theatre group not only performs these stage adaptations in their own venue, they are dedicated to working in schools and public libraries, and are willing to take their productions on the road. You may very well have a theatre group that does or will do a stage adaptation of a classic that you can bring to teens in your library or local community. Take advantage of the wonder of theatrical performances to bring classic works alive to teens and to intrigue them to read the complete work.

- *Professional book readers/performers*
  Some of the same sorts of people who read for recorded book companies do live readings of books. Look in your community for folks who do this and con-

sider inviting them to the classroom or to your school or public library to read for teens. You might ask a professional reader in for Banned Books Week, to read aloud from a single challenged or banned book, or to read critical passages from a series of banned books. You might have a reader come for Black History Month, Women's History Month, or National Poetry Month to read from classic books by African American writers, female writers, or poets. You might position the reader in a central location in your school or school library, or in the teen area in your public library, or you might set up a sort of coffee house in a meeting space where teens can get a drink and a snack, sit down at a table, and listen in. You could provide multiple copies of the books the reader is reading from for teens to check out. There are probably many more ideas here, but this gives you the idea.

All these sorts of folks can cost you, but nothing near what you'd have to come up with for a contemporary classics author. It's been my experience in more than one community I've worked in that a large percentage of professional performers are more than willing to give you a deal as a librarian or educator who is trying to help teens make connections with great literature. Most artsy folks have a great appreciation for people like you! That said, don't take even the sweetest of deals from a professional performer unless you've seen the performance yourself first. You can either attend a performance of the same material in a different venue, or request a sample of the performance from the individual or group you're considering.

Why do you need to see it first? Because it must be good. If it's not good, if the program or performers are subpar, you might go a long way toward convincing teens that classics stink. They will not know to separate out a performance that stinks from the classic it's based on. You do not want that to happen. On the other hand, when programs and performers are magical and entrancing, you have made great strides in forging meaningful links between classics and teens. On top of that, you've supported performers in your community, and have brought a wide demographic together to experience something entertaining and rich regarding the classics. Classics are good things and just keep on giving!

Classics Read-Aloud Programs

Folks read aloud to children all the time, it's considered highly beneficial to them for a variety of reasons. It provides them with a time to sit still and be taken away by a good story, it fosters the imagination, it prepares them for the joys of reading, and it increases listening skills, to name only a very few. I wonder why we stop reading aloud as much when young people reach the middle grades? Sure, they're supposed to be reading well on their own by then. They're *supposed* to be, but lots aren't doing so well in the middle and high school years, even beyond. And even if teens in the middle grades and high school are great readers, why would that rule out any enjoyment of a great book being read aloud? Everybody likes to be told a good story, teens included.

We'll talk a bit about the benefits of reading aloud in your booktalking presentations in Chapter 9, but you might also create a regular program in which you read a classic aloud to teens, chapter by chapter if a book, or all of a piece if a shorter work like a short story or long poem. This could be a wonderful way to introduce teens to classics in a relaxed, non-pressured way. They don't have to remark on it, they don't have to take a test later, they just get to hang out and listen. You may bring a classic story alive to a reluctant or struggling reader in this way and make the link that teen needs to proceed with reading on his or her own.

A good idea if you decide to start a read-aloud program is to hold it in a space where teens can be comfortable. A classroom with desks all in a row facing the front of the room may not be a good place for this sort of program. A nook or corner of a library with an open space and big pillows or comfy chairs, even just a carpeted floor to lay on, is a better bet.

You'll want to pick classics that are short enough to be finished in one session or over only a few sessions. Do not select Tolstoy's *War and Peace* to read aloud! The classics you intend to read should be accessible to teen intellects and exciting or active enough to draw in a listener. I wouldn't suggest the slower paced, psychological sorts of classics for this type of program. You'll need to select classic works that you will feel comfortable reading aloud. If a classic has lots of dialogue and unique voices, make sure you're capable of handling all that in a way that makes sense to a listener. Practice a bit ahead of each program to be certain the chapter or piece fits well with teen attention spans, and to be certain you are reading at an acceptable volume and pace.

A read-aloud program not only allows teens some needed "down time" to sit still and be introduced to a great classic with all its inherent benefits, it requires very little preparation and has no real associated costs. All you need is a great classic, a comfortable space, and a relaxed teen audience!

CLASSICS ACTIVITIES FOR TEENS

Programs can introduce teens to the classics in an engaging, entertaining way, but activities designed to involve teens may work even better. Teens are in a highly active stage of life, and their intellects and imaginations are well served by participatory activities and programs. There are probably many more wonderful and creative ideas for activities that can attract teens to the classics, but among the more common are classics reading incentive programs, classics review writing contests, classics trivia games, live action role playing games, teen drama performances, teen drama workshops, and teen reader's theatre.

Classics Reading Incentive Programs

Just what are reading incentive programs? They are, simply, programs that motivate people to read. Most children's and teen summer reading programs are incentive programs; most include some kind of prize or award each week as young people reach reading goals and may include some sort of grand prize at the end of the summer.

Summer reading programs aren't the only sorts of reading incentive programs available. You might consider a year-round program that gives teens incentive to read classics as they have the time. Depending on your incentive, teens may make the time! The King County Library System where I work just started a pilot program funded in part by a generous Library Foundation grant in a handful of its libraries called, *Read 3, Get 1 Free!* Although not specific to classics, this program could be modified to be a classics-only incentive program. The rules are: read three books, write three thoughtful reviews, and select a prize book to take home free. Easy as can be! A program of this sort almost runs itself. Sure, you have to create the program with its rules and incentives, design a form of some kind, and provide prizes (the most common form of incentive) or work out some other incentive. After that, you have to promote it to teens. But, that's the bulk of it. And the only expenses are multiple copies of a review form and prize books. What's not to like?

In addition to prize books, the *Read 3, Get 1 Free!* program also has another incentive. Teens are given a space on their review form to note if they'd allow the library to publish their reviews, either at their local library branch or online. I have not yet had a teen turn down a chance at this sort of fame! So, a free book to foster more reading, and a chance at being in the limelight for their opinions about what they've read. How cool is that?

Either as an educator, as a school librarian with a ready-made connection to educators, or as a public librarian pursuing relationships with educational colleagues to foster great community partnerships of benefit to teens, you might try to tie in a reading incentive program to classroom credit. Teens may earn extra credit points from their language arts teacher, for example, for participating in a classics reading program, or may fulfill community service hours for doing so if their reviews are ultimately published and made available to their peers.

In addition to creating your own reading incentive programs, you can refer teens to other programs when you stumble across them. Many local newspapers do incentive-based reading programs, and there are organizations that foster a love of reading using incentive programs of various sorts. An example here is the Annual Signet Classic Scholarship Essay Contest for teens, now in its eighth year. A classic work is selected each year by the publisher (a recent title is Oscar Wilde's *The Picture of Dorian Gray*), and high school juniors and seniors can write an essay on one of four selected topics (made available through the Signet Web site at http://www.penguinputnam.com/static/html/us/academic/essay-home.html). Five teens each win a $1,000 scholarship and the school library receives a complete Signet Classics library. As an additional incentive, the winning essays are posted on the Signet Web site.

Classics Review Writing Contests

The July-August 1999 *Book* magazine article mentioned in Chapter 4 includes responses from surveyed teens regarding book advertisements and reviews. The article mentions in a marketing world gone mad catering to teens it seems peculiar that "the adults running the media and deciding how to spend ad dollars seem convinced there's no market for marketing books" (Kloberdanz 1999, 35). This is especially odd given the remarks teens provided to the magazine. *Book* reported that teens want books—both teen and adult titles—reviewed with their age range in mind. Adam Lane, an 18-year-old from Illinois said, "If there was a book ad for every movie ad, there'd be a lot more kids reading," and "I'm sure teens could enjoy any adult book, but they aren't aware that it's out there" (Kloberdanz 1999, 38).

You might say to yourself, "Hey, I can do that for teens. I can read great books and write compelling reviews to entice teen readers, let them know what's out there." That's great, and you should go for it! But, how about this? You could run a regular contest, in which teens read and review books, in this case the classics, for their peers. This really is another form of a reading incentive program, just organized as a contest. You pick a first, second, and third place winner for best reviews of classics works during a particular period of time. What's the incentive? Public acknowledgment. A certain sort of fame. Very important stuff to most teens!

The teens who "place" could be featured for a month or so on your library or school Web site or on a public bulletin board (or both), with a portrait (if so desired), a brief biographical sketch, the review, and maybe even a print of a good-looking cover of the reviewed classic to accompany the review. You could collect a few copies of each reviewed title and have them near the display for other interested teen readers to check out. And, if you were able to make a successful program of this sort of contest and did it regularly, say, every month or two, or once a quarter, you could eventually publish each year's winners in a pamphlet or brochure format.

In addition to providing teens with incentive to read and review the great books for their peers and for community acknowledgment, you are providing an opportunity for those teens to really think about what they read, to evaluate their reading experiences, and to share that with others through their own written words. That's great for personal development and can contribute to a richer relationship with books and reading throughout life. And, one good incentive leads to another: You may help get the word out to other teens who may only connect to classics that have been "advertised" or "marketed" to them in this way, the same way they may rely on ads to help them choose what music to listen to and what clothes to wear.

Classics Library Games

Most people like a good game. Games are used throughout childhood to engage young minds and bodies, to educate through pleasurable experiences, to foster a relationship between learning and enjoyment, and to just plain old entertain young people and show them a good time. With the exception of organized sports, adult involvement in game playing tends to end in early adolescence. That could be because teens don't want to hang out with adults or because the sorts of games that interest teens don't interest adults; it could be all sorts of things. In some ways, this is a natural separation. In others, it's a bit of a shame. Adults who haven't lost the sense of play themselves can show teens a lot of ways to have a good time.

You might think that classics don't lend themselves to games. They may not be the most obvious choice, that's true! But you can find ways to foster a positive relationship to the classics through games in the library or classroom. We'll talk here about live action role-playing games, scavenger hunts, and trivia games, but these aren't the only possibilities for classics library games—just a few of the more common. Use your sense of play (which I'm sure is well developed!) to think up other games that might work to provide teens with a pleasurable experience that also exposes and attracts them to the classics.

Role-Playing Games

Most teens are familiar with fantasy role-playing games, even if they don't play them. For those teens who aren't interested in wizards and dungeons and heroic quests and the like, but who might enjoy trying on a role once in awhile for a short time, you might think about developing a role-playing game built around classic literature as a program in your library. There may be as many possibilities as your imagination can come up with, but we'll talk about just two of the more common sorts of role-playing games.

The first is really a form of charades. You might call the game "Charades from the Classics," or come up with something infinitely wittier! Your job is to write down dynamic scenarios from classics featuring one or two significant characters (who either feature prominently in the story or serve to set it up) that will be easy and fun for teens to act out, but not too easy for the audience to guess. A clarification here: teens are to guess about what's happening, not the classic work the scenario comes from! How could they know that—yet?! You will also need to prepare booktalks of the classics from which those characters and scenarios come, to present at the end of each charade.

How does it actually work? Teen participants are divided into two teams, and a volunteer is recruited to time the charades and record the times for both teams. In a designated period of time (three to five minutes would be good), a teen (who has been given a scenario by you and has had a moment or two to think about it) has to act it out silently in front of his or her own team. Team members guess at what's being acted out. You determine which elements from the scenario are to be identified. If an accurate guess is made during the designated time, the timekeeper records how long it took. If an accurate guess is not made, the timekeeper records the full time when it runs out. You then reveal the classic the scene came from and present your booktalk. The next round then starts with the other team. The team with the lowest total time at the end of the game, wins. You might award small prizes, but that's up to you.

Scenarios don't have to be, and probably shouldn't be, too elaborate. You only need to provide the setting of the scene, a general description of the character (age, size, other physical attributes), the emotional and psychological condition of the character (sad, frightened, obsessed, gleefully diabolical, etc.), and the scenario to be enacted. Robert Louis Stevenson's *Dr. Jekyll and Mr. Hyde* makes for a good example:

The setting: A London street in the early hours of the morning.

The character: A young girl running across the street.

The emotional/psychological condition of the character: Frightened and screaming.

The scenario to be enacted: When the young girl and a man collide, the young girl is knocked down and trampled by that man, who doesn't even look back as he continues on his way.

What a dynamic scene to act out, with all sorts of movement and emotional content! This one could be done with just one player as the young girl, or with two to enact the trampling. Another good example might be Chaim Potok's *The Chosen*:

The setting: A baseball diamond on a Sunday afternoon.

The character: A young man on the pitcher's mound.

The emotional/psychological condition of the character: Intensely competitive with the young man at the plate whom he thinks feels superior to him, and feeling a little malicious.

The scenario to be enacted: The young pitcher throws a fastball that the batter hits right into his face, smashing his glasses and knocking him off his feet.

Again, this could be acted out with just one player as the pitcher, but two could work well also.

You should also provide multiple copies of the classics used for the charades for teens to check out, as well as an annotated list of those classics for teens to use as a reminder for future reading selections.

Another role-playing game works well with mystery classics. You may have heard of a "Murder in the Library" program before, in which a crime has been committed by someone within a group of characters, and clues are provided to help the participants track down "whodunit." This would be that same type of game, either with all the bells and whistles or in a more simplified form, just using a classic mystery instead of an original story you've written yourself, borrowed from a colleague, or found in a prepared program kit. The full-on bells and whistles version can be work-intensive, both in the preparation and the hosting, so if you choose to go that route, you might find someone in the community who does this type of program, or might pair up with a colleague or a group of colleagues to offer it in your own school or library. The more simplified form, which we'll take a look at here, is something you can do on your own, requiring only some time to think and prepare all the pieces you'll need.

The idea is this: you select a classic story or novel you think has some appeal to teens in which a character has been murdered, or in which a heist has been successfully pulled off. The Sherlock Holmes stories are good choices. So is an Agatha Christie mystery in which the murderer occurs among a defined group of characters in a restricted location, like *Murder on the Orient Express*. You work up an overview or synopsis to set up the necessary elements of the story to present to your teen participants at the beginning of the program. You write character profiles to assign to teen participants and provide character name tags. One of those characters will be the murderer or sly mastermind who pulled off the heist (only you, and he or she will know this). Each teen, after hearing the setup for the story, will spend a few minutes with his or her character, and then will mill around in character (as best they can after spending only a few minutes with their profiles) asking questions of all the other characters to try to determine who did the dirty deed.

You are responsible for organizing and hosting the event and for helping characters interact with each other and have a good time asking crafty questions in their search for the culprit. At a designated time, everyone stops and in turn takes a guess at who did it, telling why they think so. Eventually, the "real" criminal stands up and confesses to the crime, explaining why he or she committed it. After the confession, you get to do some great booktalks of that classic and similar sorts of classics, both mysteries and books from other genres with mystery or suspense elements. You'll want, as always, to have copies of the book used for the program for teens to check out, even if they already now know the ending or have solved the mystery, and copies of the others you've booktalked. It never hurts to provide an annotated list of booktalked titles for teens to pick up.

Does this sound a little like the vintage board game, Clue? That's because it is. Just the real, live, 3-D version! But instead of Colonel Mustard doing it in the billiard room with the lead pipe, teens have the opportunity to act out the characters and seek the murderer in, say, Agatha Christie's mystery on the Orient Express as it chugs from Istanbul to Paris!

Scavenger Hunts

You might develop a classics scavenger hunt. This sort of scavenger hunt does not involve finding pens that write in purple ink, spools of yellow thread, a plastic fork, a burnt umber crayon, and an embroidery hoop, but information instead! A classics scavenger hunt could introduce teens not only to the classics themselves, but also to all the awesome resources in the library (and online) that help teens explore them and understand them more fully. A couple of neat things about scavenger hunts is that they can be customized to meet specialized needs, and they don't require much more than your brain power, some paper, and possibly a few prizes, to work well.

The idea isn't quite the same as an old-fashioned scavenger hunt. Teens wouldn't be running around in teams trying to gathering up real objects before their competitors do. An informational scavenger hunt can be more of a worksheet or a pathfinder to information, or can be a little more open-ended, with only a brief clue to give direction toward an informational resource or Web site. You might design the former for younger teens, and the latter for older teens. For example, as a librarian or an educator teaching library and information-seeking skills, you might have a question like this on a classics scavenger hunt for younger teens:

> The novels in the teen classics section are in alphabetical order by author. Find Stephen Crane's *The Red Badge of Courage*. Somewhere in the first few pages you'll find a brief biographical sketch of the author. Where and when was Stephen Crane born? What else did he write? When did he die?

This introduces younger teens to where classics are in the library and how they are arranged and that they often contain brief facts about their author in the front matter. For older teens, you might have a question like this:

> The books in the reference section on dramatic works are in the 812 to 820 Dewey Decimal call number areas. Find and note the reference book that includes this information about Arthur Miller's play, *Death of a Salesman*:

- Biographical information about the author
- An essay about the importance of the play
- A list of major characters
- A description of the story

This requires older teens to browse an appropriate Dewey Decimal area in the reference section and shows them that reference resources can contain a great deal of useful information. If you have any online databases that include information on classics authors and works that you'd like older teens to know about, you might include a question like this on your library scavenger hunt:

> Using the Literature Resource Center, note the three biographical resources in which information on Arthur Miller can be found. Find the overview of *Death of a Salesman* written by Louis Charles Stagg. Which resource was this overview originally published in before being included in the Literature Resource Center database?

This introduces teens to an online database as opposed to the general Internet (which they head straight for without an introduction to your subscription-based online products), and requires they navigate a bit to find the information requested. It demonstrates that lots of great resources originally published in print are pulled together into databases that can be accessed through a simple search.

If you get stuck or need examples, the Internet is loaded with educational and Internet scavenger hunts for a range of ages, which you could easily modify to the classics.

Librarians and educators can collaborate and use a classics scavenger hunt to introduce teens to a range of reading choices and reference resources for upcoming assignments in a literary unit. Librarians could work with a teacher of an Advanced Placement class to design a classics scavenger hunt for classic works to be studied during the school year, that introduces teens to resources containing more detailed information about authors, plots, characters, themes, writing styles, historical contexts, and so forth.

You could just offer the scavenger hunt as a stand-alone contest in your school or library. Teens who complete the hunt turn in their accurately completed forms (you'll have to check and remove inaccurate forms from the prize drawing), and at a designated time, you draw winners from the completed forms to receive a prize. You might give out tickets to a great local theatrical production, or, you might give out shiny, new paperback classics!

Trivia Games

In her book, *Teen Library Events: A Month-by-Month Guide*, Kirsten Edwards admits that to host a teen trivia game requires you "be a bit silly in public" (2002, 56), and that more reserved sorts might, well, do something entirely different. If you don't mind being a bit silly in public, you could build a trivia game around the classics! This could be a standard sort of trivia contest, or it could be built around a game show like "Jeopardy" or "Who Wants to Be a Millionaire?"

A standard trivia contest could be played between individuals or teams, either in a classroom as part of a literary unit or in the school or public library as an after-school program for interested participants. A question is asked, and either the first person to raise a flag or hit a buzzer (or whatever fun thing you come up with) gets a stab at answering it. Points or prizes are earned for correct answers, and either no points or prizes are earned or are subtracted for incorrect answers. At the end of the contest, the individual or team with the most points or prizes has won. You would need to develop the questions and answers, and provide the meeting space (if not played during a class period) and prizes. Even if the contest is played to earn points, there has to be some sort of payoff for teens at the end that's a whole lot less abstract. You'll have to determine some way for all participants to get something, and for the winners to get something extra. Candy is always a good bet.

Who might a classics trivia contest work best with? Teens in the middle grades may be the most receptive, but I do think with the right energy you could easily pull this off with high schoolers, and they are more likely to have a greater familiarity with more classics. This might work best in a school environment, particularly a classroom, but don't rule out a school or public library classics trivia contest after school hours or in the evening, and it would be a great idea to encourage a gathering of home-schooled teens for a trivia contest in the public library.

Because not that many teens are likely to know the answers to loads of classics trivia questions, you'll want to pay special attention to the sorts of classics you use and the questions you ask! You might build trivia questions around classics that are particularly popular and well known to most teens. Crossover classics like Jack London's *The Call of the Wild*, Robert Louis Stevenson's *Treasure Island*, and Mildred D. Taylor's *Roll of Thunder, Hear My Cry* could work. Teen classics like Robert Cormier's *The Chocolate War*, S. E. Hinton's *The Outsiders*, and Gary Paulsen's *Hatchet* could work well, too. Or, you might use well-known adult classics like Mary Shelley's *Frankenstein*, Shakespeare's *Romeo and Juliet*, and Alexandre Dumas's *The Three Musketeers*. The classics you pick to build trivia questions around will vary to some degree depending on the age of the teen players, of course.

What sorts of questions would you ask? A few examples might be:

- "Which classic novel of adventure and survival features a family dog that gets shipped to the Klondike to be trained as a sled dog?" Answer: *The Call of the Wild*

- "Which classic novel of adventure and intrigue on the high seas features a young man who pits his skill and intellect against a one-legged pirate named Long John Silver?" Answer: *Treasure Island*

- "Which classic novel for children and teens describes an African American family in the rural south trying desperately to hold on to their land during the 1930s Great Depression?" Answer: *Roll of Thunder, Hear My Cry*

- "What is the name of the classic teen novel in which a high school student refuses to be bullied into selling chocolate for the annual fund raiser?" Answer: *The Chocolate War*

- "Who wrote the book considered the first horror novel ever, about a doctor who creates a new being from the body parts of dead people?" Answer: Mary Shelley (for *Frankenstein*)

You could mix popular culture references with your classics questions to encourage a bridge between them. A few examples might be:

- "What is the title of the classic science fiction novel that the film *Blade Runner*, starring Harrison Ford, was based on?" Answer: *Do Androids Dream of Electric Sheep?* (by Philip K. Dick)

- "Which Greek mythological hero was the long-running TV series starring Kevin Sorbo based on, and what was that hero famous for?" Answer: Hercules and strength/courage

- "Which Broadway show from the 1950s, made in to a movie in the 1960s, retold Shakespeare's *Romeo and Juliet* in New York gang territory?" Answer: *West Side Story*

- "Who wrote the book that the movie, *Clueless*, was based on?" Answer: Jane Austen (for *Emma*)

- Which classic opera was MTV's 2002 Hip Hopera, starring Mekhi Phifer and Beyonce Knowles, based on?" Answer: *Carmen* (by Georges Bizet)

Librarians and educators might consider working together to offer a classics trivia contest focusing on the works studied in a literary unit.

After each question is successfully answered, or once you've provided the answer, you can booktalk that classic title and pass on any interesting facts about the author or title. It wouldn't hurt to have multiple copies of the classics you've included in the trivia contest for teens to check out once the game has ended.

Game show–style trivia games are a lot of work and can be well worth it. We won't go into any depth regarding them in this book, but in her book Kirsten Edwards provides full details on the way game show–style trivia contests (one of which she calls, "Who Wants to Win a Candy Bar?") can work in a library or classroom environment. You could easily modify her ideas for a classics contest. Edwards even provides handy lists of the materials required and sample booktalks for inserting into the game. If you're interested in this sort of thing, her book is an invaluable resource, and I recommend you take a look at it.

Teen Drama Performances

Teens can be attracted to classics through involvement in bona fide dramatic performances that they might perform for their peers, for younger kids, or for the community. They might receive class credit for their participation or fulfill community service hours. We're talking about a real classic play or critical scenes from a classic play, or a stage adaptation of a classic work with memorized lines, costumes, sets, and props—the whole works. To pull off something this big, you'll have to be willing to give up a lot of your free time (and probably get some financial commitment from your organization) for the duration! Even if you collaborated with a local drama teacher, you've got your work cut out for you.

Do I say this to discourage you? No, not really. I don't know how many of you will pursue this sort of activity, but there may be those of you who would find this the perfect opportunity to meaningfully connect teens to the classics, and meet other goals as librarians, educators, and members of your community, regardless of the investment in time and resources.

All those things that go into dramatic performances—from auditions to rehearsals, from designing costumes to building sets, from motivating individual commitment to managing teens in groups—are a part of this kind of activity. You've got to collaborate with that drama teacher or you've got to secure a working space for rehearsals and performances on your own, and provide scripts for your cast. If you are seriously considering producing a teen drama performance, look to resources on producing plays with young people or work with those local drama teachers.

All that said, what are the benefits of teen drama performances using classics? Well, on the professional end, collaboration (if you go that route) between school or public librarians and teachers is always a neat thing. You become a part of a larger community working to benefit teens and involve them in a meaningful pursuit—one that will give back to an even larger community. Drama performances of any kind help teens develop speaking and performance skills, and full-scale theatrical productions even more so. Producing a classic play, scene(s), or stage adaptation introduces teens to classic literature in a dynamic way, making its value more real to them. And, to successfully perform a role, teens need to think about the characters they'll be playing and ponder their motivations and actions. Getting inside a character is an excellent way to make a classic work meaningful to a teen. And, if the classic being performed is a play or scenes from a play (rather than a stage adaptation of some other sort of literary work), teens will experience that great work as it was meant to be experienced—acted out on the stage for an audience. Even the teens who aren't acting on the stage but serving in support roles will experience this. Wonderful!

Teen Reader's Theatre and Drama Workshops

Reader's theatre and drama workshops involve a play or a critical scene from a play, a stage adaptation of a short story, a stage adaptation of a novel or other literary work, or a reader's theatre script; a meeting space; a group of teens; and a group leader (that could be you!). No memorization, no costumes, no sets are required.

Here's one way it can work: the group leader you've brought in either asks for volunteers or assigns roles. The teens read through their parts together once or twice with assistance from the group leader to effectively emote (!), then they practice their parts on their own in a personal space in the room, adding in physical gestures or vocal accents (with the group leader wandering around helping out here and there). At a designated time, all teens come together to do a dramatic read-through, bringing all they can as readers and actors to create the scene or story as they feel the author might have intended it to be performed. You can either begin or end the workshop with a few tidbits about the author, the work, or the time period it was set in and other intriguing facts that might make the work even more real to teens. Multiple copies of the original classic work should be made available for teens to check out. That's the short of it!

Drama workshops are good for teens who have a little energy to get out, who like to ham it up but don't want to (or can't) commit to a young life in the theatre, who like group interaction, and who can be drawn to more passive activities like reading through more active activities like, say, a reader's theatre or drama workshop. Interpreting a character both verbally and physically, interacting with other characters as interpreted by their peers, collaborating with fellow actors to further a plot or set a mood, and generally bringing creative juices to a rolling boil can be just the right sort of entry point to classics for some teens—and it can be loads of fun.

If you also have a little energy to get out, you might be able to pull this sort of thing off on your own without an outside group leader—with an engaging classic play (or scene from a classic play) with at least a fair number of parts, a dramatized classic, or a scripted stage adaptation. You're a librarian or educator, so I won't tell you how to find classic plays (although you will find a couple of short starter lists of classic plays in Appendix C), but you might not know that there are books that compile dramatized classics and stage adaptations of classics. *The Big Book of Dramatized Classics: 25 Adaptations of Favorite Novels, Stories, and Plays for Stage and Round-The-Table Reading*, edited in 1993 by Sylvia E. Kamerman, is a good example of this sort of book. So is Joellen Bland's 1987 *Stage Plays from the Classics: One-Act Adaptations from Famous Short Stories, Novels, and Plays*. These aren't the only resources available to you by far (not to mention the abundance of general reader's theatre resources), so check those library shelves for others.

You need time to plan a drama workshop, from finding the right sort of dramatic piece to making multiple copies and creating promotional materials to advertise the program in advance, but other than that all you need is a meeting space. No real costs, lots of fun to be had. If after you've begun, a drama workshop seems too much for you to handle on your own, consider partnering with a library or educational colleague, bring back that group leader, or bring someone else in from your theatrical community to either lead or assist you. Nothing wrong with sharing the preparatory work and the enjoyment of leading a teen group that will act out a classic right before your very eyes! You might adapt a classic currently being or about to be used in the classroom as a drama workshop. Teens might even be offered extra credit for participating.

That reminds me: unless you have a ready-made group of teens of a more or less verifiable number, you might need to prepare a couple of classic scripts—one for a smaller group and one for a larger group of participants—or might advertise the workshop without specifying the drama to be "workshopped" and require registration in advance. When you find out how many teens have signed up by a certain date, you can choose your classic script based on that number (or usually a little less, to account for no-shows). If it turns out that you somehow end up with a load of teens who didn't sign up and have a script with only a few parts, you can divide the group into acting troupes, each to perform the work at the end of the workshop.

Drama workshops can also be longer and more involved, but those are the sorts of workshops it will be more effective to hire someone to conduct. Often local performers enjoy working with young people and for a reasonable fee will come for a full morning or afternoon to help them perfect a scene. If you like think this type of drama workshop would appeal more to your teens, look into the possibilities within your local arts community.

Beyond digging up your own classic plays and exploring the sorts of resources mentioned above on dramatized or adapted classics, there are a few publishers who focus on reader's theatre resources for use with children and teens. Their audience is primarily educators rather than school and public librarians, but the information is readily transferable! These general reader's theatre resources give you both an introduction to the activity and provide a variety of ready-to-use scripts:

Latrobe, Kathy Howard, and Mildred Knight Laughlin. 1989. *Readers Theatre for Young Adults: Scripts and Script Development*. Englewood, CO: Teacher Ideas Press. (For grades 7 to 12.)

Porter, Steven, ed. and comp. 1994. *New Works for Reader's Theatre*. Studio City, CA: Phantom Publications in association with Players Press.

Ratliff, Gerald Lee. 1999. *Introduction to Readers Theatre: A Guide to Classroom Performance*. Colorado Springs, CO: Meriwether Publishing, Limited. (For grades 9 to 12.)

Shepard, Aaron. 2004. *Readers on Stage: A Guide to Reader's Theater (or Readers Theatre), with Scripts, Tips, and Worksheets*. Redondo Beach, CA: Shepard Publications.

Shepard, Aaron, ed. 2004. *Stories on Stage: Scripts for Reader's Theater*. Redondo Beach, CA: Shepard Publications.

Sloyer, Shirlee. 2003. *From the Page to the Stage: The Educator's Complete Guide to Readers Theatre*. Englewood, CO: Teacher Ideas Press. (For grades 4 through 8.)

Walker, Lois. 1997. *Readers Theatre Strategies in the Middle and Junior High Classroom: A Take Part Teacher's Guide: Springboards to Language Development through Readers Theatre, Storytelling, Writing, and Dramatizing*. Colorado Springs, CO: Meriwether Publishing, Limited.

Here are a few reader's theatre resources that treat classic literature:

Barchers, Suzanne I. 2001. *From Atalanta to Zeus: Readers Theatre from Greek Mythology*. Englewood, CO: Teacher Ideas Press. (For grades 4 to 9.)

Barchers, Suzanne I., and Jennifer L. Kroll. 2002. *Classic Readers Theatre for Young Adults*. Englewood, CO: Teacher Ideas Press. (For grades 6 to 12.)

Kroll, Jennifer L., ed. 2003. *Simply Shakespeare: Readers Theatre for Young People*. Englewood, CO: Teacher Ideas Press. (For grades 6 to 12.)

And here are a few reader's theatre resources on special subjects, some of which touch on the classics:

Fredericks, Anthony D. 2001. *Readers Theatre for American History*. Englewood, CO: Teacher Ideas Press. (For grades 4 to 8.)

———. 2002. *Science Fiction Readers Theatre*. Englewood, CO: Teacher Ideas Press. (For grades 4 to 8.)

Latrobe, Kathy Howard. 1991. *Social Studies Readers Theatre for Young Adults: Scripts and Script Development*. Englewood, CO: Teacher Ideas Press.

Shepard, Aaron. 2003. *Folktales on Stage: Children's Plays for Reader's Theater (or Readers Theatre), with 16 Play Scripts from World Folk and Fairy Tales and Legends, Including African, Chinese, Southeast Asian, Indian, Middle Eastern, Russian, Scandinavian, and Native American*. Redondo Beach, CA: Shepard Publications.

White, Melvin Robert. 1993. *Mel White's Readers Theatre Anthology: Twenty-Eight All-Occasion Readings for Storytellers*. Colorado Springs, CO: Meriwether Publishing, Limited.

SUMMING IT UP

There are many ways to integrate classics into your classroom activities and library programming for teens. In addition to those we've discussed in this chapter, you might arrange a field trip to a local movie theater that's playing a film based on a classic with your teen book discussion group (who've already read the book), and talk about the difference between the film and the book in your next meeting. You might develop a writing exercise in which teens write alternative endings to a classic, or a modern version of a classic, or even a fractured fairy tale of their own. You need not be limited to the ideas above—let your imagination run free. Then, design the programs that best fit your budget, teen community, and your own style.

WORKS CITED

Aronson, Marc. 2000. "The Myths of Teenage Readers." *Publishing Research Quarterly* 16 (3): 4–9.

Bland, Joellen. 1987. *Stage Plays from the Classics: One-Act Adaptations from Famous Short Stories, Novels, and Plays*. Boston: Plays, Inc.

Edwards, Kirsten. 2002. *Teen Library Events: A Month-by-Month Guide*. Greenwood Professional Guides for Young Adult Librarians. Series edited by C. Allen Nichols and Mary Anne Nichols. Westport, CT: Greenwood Press.

Green, Ranny. 1995. "For Some Classic Viewing, Don't Miss Wishbone." *Seattle Times* 22 October: final edition, H6.

Kamerman, Sylvia E. ed. 1993. *The Big Book of Dramatized Classics: 25 Adaptations of Favorite Novels, Stories, and Plays for Stage and Round-the-Table Reading.* Boston: Plays, Inc.

Kloberdanz, Kristin. 1999. "So You Don't Think Kids Read Anymore? Think Again. Turns Out They're Booksmart." *Book* July/August: 34–38.

Teenreads.com. New York: Carol Fitzgerald. Available online at: http://www.teen reads.com (accessed 28 August 2003).

Welcome to Living History Lectures. Lakebay, WA: Tames Alan. Available online at: http://www.oz.net/~tamsalan/histmain.html (accessed 1 March 2004).

BOOKS TO HELP YOU FIND CLASSICS ON FILM

Nothing fancy here, just a nice list of books to help you find classics on film, from filmed classic plays to short stories made into film, from women's classics on film to banned film classics that are often based on classic literature. If you're looking for a film to better connect teens to classics, these resources will do the trick.

Baskin, Ellen, and Mandy Hicken, comps. 1993. *Enser's Filmed Books and Plays: A List of Books and Plays from Which Films Have Been Made, 1928–1991.* Brookfield, VT: Ashgate.

Cartmell, Deborah, and Imelda Whelehan, eds. 1999. *Adaptations: From Text to Screen, Screen to Text.* London; New York: Routledge.

Cartmell, Deborah, I. Q. Hunter, and Heidi Kaye, eds. 2000. *Classics in Film and Fiction.* London; Sterling VA: Pluto Press.

Erskine, Thomas, and James M. Welsh, eds. 2000. *Video Versions: Film Adaptations of Plays on Video.* Westport, CT: Greenwood Publishing Group.

Giddings, Robert, and Eric Sheen, eds. 2000. *The Classic Novel: From Page to Screen.* Manchester, UK: Manchester University Press.

Jackson, Russell, ed. 2000. *The Cambridge Companion to Shakespeare on Film.* Cambridge; New York: Cambridge University Press.

Kovacs, Lee. 1999. *The Haunted Screen: Ghosts in Literature and Film.* Jefferson, NC: McFarland and Company.

Lupack, Barbara Tepa, ed. 1999. *Nineteenth-Century Women at the Movies: Adapting Classic Women's Fiction to Film.* Bowling Green, OH: Bowling Green State University.

Moss, Joyce. 1992. *From Page to Screen: Children's and Young Adult Books on Film and Video.* Detroit: Gale Research.

Rosenthal, Daniel M. 2000. *Shakespeare on Screen.* London: Hamlyn.

Sova, Dawn B. 2001. *Forbidden Films: Censorship Histories of 125 Motion Pictures*. New York: Facts on File.

Tibbetts, John C., and James M. Welsh. 1998. *The Encyclopedia of Novels into Film*. New York: Facts on File.

———. 2001. *The Encyclopedia of Stage Plays into Film*. New York: Facts on File.

Wheeler, David, ed. 1989. *No, but I Saw the Movie: The Best Short Stories Ever Made into Film*. New York: Penguin Books.

9

BOOKTALK THE CLASSICS
TO TEENS

Booktalking is a backbone of teen services librarianship, and can be an outstanding addition to any educator's skill set. It is the primary means of introducing the largest number of teens to good reading in traditional and alternative educational environments, in programs in your library, in halfway houses and shelters, in the community. It involves, at the very least, a rudimentary understanding of teenage characteristics, a familiarity with teen literature and other forms of literature that can appeal to and be meaningful for them (like classics!), and some understanding of how to stand up in front of these young people and successfully talk about good stuff to read. I only say *some* understanding, because practice makes proficient, and that just takes time—unless you are among the rare and exalted booktalking prodigies!

We looked at both the developmental and general reading characteristics of teens in Chapter 4, and we've cultivated a relationship with classic literature in Chapters 2, 3, and 5. All are important to the classics booktalker. In Chapter 7, we talked about interacting with teens one on one to connect them with classics. Most of the information found there is readily applicable here. What's left? Some understanding of how to stand up in front of these young people and talk about good books to read, that's what!

Because you may not feel absolutely confident and comfortable as a booktalker—and as a classics booktalker in specific—this chapter takes a brief look at the basics of booktalking to teen audiences and at the particular challenges you may face as a booktalker to teens in group environments. It then explores in detail how you can meaningfully and dynamically booktalk the classics to teens. Once you get your booktalking skills buffed up, you can play a pivotal role in connecting the teens in your schools and community groups to the classics. For public librarians, we'll talk about getting into schools and your community in the next chapter.

A FEW BASICS OF BOOKTALKING

A backbone of teen services it may be, but just what, precisely, is booktalking? Chapple Langemack, in the preface to *The Booktalker's Bible: How to Talk about the Books You Love to Any Audience*, puts it this way:

> Booktalking is, quite simply, talking about books. It requires you, a great book, and an audience. You, clever soul that you are, have read the book and extracted its essence so that you can present it to your audience in a concise, entertaining way. The point is not to tell everything about the book, but the flavor of it, a snapshot if you will, to tantalize your audience into taking their own journey into that book. (2003, xiii)

It's that simple! And once you get the hang of it, it becomes second nature, and is really quite fun. Even better, the elation and deep satisfaction you will experience after a successful booktalking presentation to a group of teens knows no equal. Trust me, you want that feeling. And that's just the selfish all-about-you part! The ultimate result is that you've made meaningful connections between young people and books. We've already talked about how very important that is.

There's loads of information out there about booktalking, but *The Booktalker's Bible*, in my opinion, is the most entertaining, informative, and up-to-date A-to-Z booktalking resource you can lay your hands on, and has a section specific to youth audiences that will be quite useful to you. In this and other basic booktalking resources, you'll find information on preparing and presenting great booktalks—from finding a hook to composing your booktalk, from finding your audience to developing strong presentation skills, to thoughtful evaluation. We'll only touch on a few booktalking basics in this section before moving on to ideas for successfully booktalking the classics in particular, so if you feel you need either an introduction to or refresher in booktalking basics, do yourself a favor and take a look at these sorts of resources. It will well serve both you and teens in making strong reading connections, especially with the classics.

What we will talk about are some of the more daunting challenges in booktalking to teens, discussion you may not find in those other resources. We'll start with a list of booktalking do's and don'ts (something those other resources may actually provide but you can never have too much of!). We'll then take a look at how you might manage the fear factor that's invariably present when you find yourself in front of a group of teens, and we'll look at a few of the possible trouble spots you might encounter in any teen group or classroom environment and how you might handle them. All of which is designed to bolster your confidence in your role as booktalker—a role that puts you in the powerful position to connect a larger number of teens at a single time with great reading choices, namely, the classics!

Booktalking Do's and Don'ts: A List

School librarian, public librarian, or educator, as a booktalker you will be in front of real live teens talking about great books! Here's are some important do's and don'ts to keep in mind when addressing a teen audience:

Do:

- Be yourself
- Be respectful of your audience
- Expect respect from your audience
- Show teens you like them!
- Hold yourself with confidence and keep purposeless movement to a minimum
- Maintain eye contact with your audience
- Speak clearly, at a reasonable pace, and with sufficient but not excessive volume
- Talk about books in a manner that is comfortable for you
- Give the title and author of each book both before and after you talk about it

(continued)

(continued)

- Mention in each booktalk who tells the story (point of view), if someone does
- Relate your booktalks to teen interests, concerns, and experiences when possible
- Include your honest personal response to a book (unless it is truly negative, in which case you should not be booktalking it)
- Keep each booktalk within a five-minute range
- Make it clear you are interested in and value teen responses
- Understand classrooms will have different responses to the same booktalks
- Remain flexible to your teen audience and to impromptu classroom events
- Keep your cool, no matter what
- Leave a list of the books you talked about at the school or educational setting you visited
- Maintain a sense of humor

Don't:

- Condescend to teens
- Disrespect or negate teen responses
- Respond too intensely to teen remarks
- Try too hard to please teens
- Publicly challenge teens or put them on the spot
- Lose your cool (thought this one was worth mentioning in both lists, it's super important for your credibility!)
- Use professional lingo with teens, like "young adult," "readers' advisory," or "collection development"
- Mislead teens regarding the content of a book
- State what you think a book means as an objective truth
- Give away the ending of a book

Over time, you'll add your own custom do's and don'ts to this list and will find that each one you learn makes you a better booktalker, and when you're a better booktalker, you are more successfully connecting teens to wonderful stories that will move and resonate with them.

Preparing Yourself to Booktalk to Teens

If you're new to classroom/group visits in general, as either a public or school librarian or brand new educator, you're at the very least nervous, and probably closer to scared witless. If so, you are in good company. As for you veteran educators, go easy on your quaking peers!

I do not know one single truth-telling teen services librarian or educator in the whole of the world who at the beginning of his or her career did not have serious anxiety about being in front of teens. I know only a handful of veteran librarians and educators who don't still have a nervous reaction to classrooms or teen groups from time to time, and I'm not certain that handful aren't lying through their collective teeth! And I don't know any folks who haven't had a "bad trip" in the classroom on occasion, no matter their comfort level and skill. That's just the way it is, and that's okay. For a moment of saccharine psycho-speak, embrace yourself, and embrace the fact that this type of work can be nerve-wracking. Or, if you prefer the tough love approach, buck up!

On booktalking day, the best way to keep your nerves from crawling into your stomach and causing an upward surge of that morning's breakfast, is not to eat breakfast. Really, although it's not bad advice if you are nervous to stay away from a Cajun sausage, onion, and pepper jack cheese omelet smothered in spicy red sauce with hash browns fried in real butter and five cups of strong coffee with cream and sugar before you booktalk, I'm just joking here! Foodstuffs aside, the best way to keep discomfort to a minimum and to make the best possible classics connections with teens during your booktalks is to prepare thoroughly in advance. Preparation means not only your booktalks, but also yourself. Remain aware of your value as a booktalker and of both the limitations and wonders of teens. Affirm with yourself that you are as "cool" as any teen in your audience. Be prepared to deal with disruptions and work a hard room. And, maximize what is in my opinion the most enjoyable part of the booktalking experience—the time after you've finished speaking when individual teens approach you to ask questions and talk about books.

Revel in Your Value as a Booktalker!

Public presentation is one of the more challenging things the average human being can think to do, even when it's to talk about books and reading, and it touches on all kinds of psychologically intense stuff like, oh, your sense of self! It's especially unnerving when working with a teen audience, one that is less likely to demonstrate appreciation and more likely to challenge you than children or adults. Here are a few thoughts to bolster your courage, and let's start with the mushy stuff:

- You are a miracle of life and this absolute and unarguable fact is no less true when you stand in front of a bunch of teens (miracles of life, themselves!) and talk about books.
- You are a librarian or educator, which are among the most noble of all career pursuits. Hey, stand proud and revel in that.
- You are not just any librarian or educator, you work with *teens*. You decided to play a role in the educational and personal lives of the young of your kind who, being on the road to maturity but not yet arrived at it, are going through an awful lot of change that may not always feel so good to them or to you. You've got to be tough to take that on! If not tough, you are certainly intrepid. One way or the other, you've got what it takes to stand up in front of teens and connect them to extraordinary reading material.

Here are a few thoughts about teens that may help you when standing in front of them:

- Teens need some amount of adult guidance in just about everything, and most of them know it deep down inside. They may not demonstrate it at the time (or ever), but they are usually quite grateful for your interest and involvement in their lives.
- Teens are not brimming over with social grace. They do not have the same understanding of social niceties and acceptable social signals that you do. They won't give you the same responses an adult audience will. They may not give you any response at all, or they may give you a response that does not truly reflect how they feel but reflects what they believe their peers want to see from them. Here comes the good part: this does not mean they don't like you, they think you're stupid, or they are not listening, and it does not mean you and the books you are talking about are not having a strong and positive influence on them.
- Teens are not an alien species. Even if you are incredulous at times, they are indeed the young of your kind! They are human beings living out that experience much as you do, just on the earlier end of the continuum, which only lasts a very short time when you stop to think about it. When standing up in front of teens, remember that you and they are more alike than different. You were their age once, and they will be yours one day. Enjoy who they are as young people with unique young people behaviors. Enjoy the opportunity you have to cross the distances created by age and experience to intersect with their lives, both as yourself and through the books you bring to them.

Being Cool: An Important Aside

If you've followed the professional literature and discussion over the past several years regarding adults, teens, and coolness, you may know that the commonly held belief by both adults and teens is that teens are cool and adults are not. In fact, if you are an adult you shouldn't even think about being cool because it's a completely foolhardy venture with a dismal conclusion. Controversial as it may be, I demand to differ. If you subscribe to this belief that teens are cool and you are not, you allow yourself to be diminished. I implore you never to believe anything in your personal or professional life that makes you a lesser being compared with anyone else!

The *American Heritage Dictionary* defines the slang use of "cool" as "excellent; first-rate" (2000, 403). Are you exempt from that by virtue of your age? No way. There is no doubt in my mind that you are excellent and first rate. *Everyone* is inherently cool, from the cradle to the grave (minus extreme and creepy deviances, of course). Sure, we're all different, but that's got nothing to do with cool.

Teens, especially the younger ones, are at an insular and self-oriented stage of life that separates itself from other stages of life and doesn't know much beyond itself. Teens have strong social systems and networks that define what's in and what's not, and "in" and "out" are, for them, on the same scale with coolness. But you don't have to buy in to that!

First of all, you are not a teen and should not be considering yourself on their coolness scale, nor should you be affected to any great degree when they consider you on their coolness scale. Second, your stage of life is of broader understanding and experience, and part of that broader understanding is that we've *all* got it going on. We're all the children of the stars. We're *all* cool. How could you, a person who has lived much more life, made substantially more choices, witnessed considerably more wonderful and horrifying things, thought wildly more and deeper thoughts, learned much, much more about what it is to be a human being and pursue a personal course, be any less cool than a teen? Don't give that away.

When Good Audiences Go Bad

No matter how well you prepare and present your booktalks, you can have a tough experience with a teen group, and you should be prepared for the possibility. Odd disruptions happen. Deliberate disruptions happen. Some teens are just tough and scary, and so are some teen audiences. There will be times that you have a clue in advance that a bad booktalking trip is possible, and there will be times you'll be blindsided by it.

If you are an educator or school librarian, you are likely to possess at least a few skills to deal with this sort of thing. If you are a public librarian, well, maybe not so much! Here's the good part for you public librarian sorts: there are ways to deal with this when it happens and to minimize its occurrence in the future. You've already read some ways you can avoid or minimize tough audience experiences in the do's and don'ts lists preceding this section, but let's give just a little more time to the topic here.

The Usual Sorts of Disruptions

I'm not so sure you can avoid, minimize or prevent general disruptions during your booktalks. The best advice I can give you is that when they happen, do your best to remain calm, retain your sense of humor, and keep or easily recover your focus. The disruptions I'm talking about here are the usual social and environmental sorts. You know, girls giggling in a clique at the back of the room, a teen who repeatedly swirls a noisy chain around and around on his desk while you're talking, a teen who clowns to your audience as he walks past the window behind you, and rogue school bells or buzzers. You just have to train yourself to keep these sorts of things from bothering you, unless they get out of hand. Think of classroom and group environments as miniature cities, with unique populations, activities, sounds, and so forth. They are dynamic environments and won't shut down for your booktalks.

When they do get out of hand, you'll find that you can fairly easily nip this sort of thing in the bud with little or no fanfare, and without publicly humiliating teens—which you should never, ever, ever do! A good silent action is to walk over and stand right next to the offending teen or teens as you continue to booktalk away. If this doesn't work (it usually does), a hand on the shoulder of the offender will usually do the trick. This does require multitasking, I know, and it can take time to master it, but keep this one in mind. Another silent trick is to focus your eye contact on the offending teen or teens, speak only to them as you booktalk for a bit. Or, at the end of a specific booktalk, you could engage a disruptive teen by asking him or her a question—maybe about a recent book he or she read and totally loved or hated.

Deliberate Disruptions

If the disruption is not just general sort-of-rude teen behavior, but some unkind or challenging action or statement directed specifically at you, you can handle it a few ways. You can make a witty (but not cruel) comeback, you can ask an honest question, or you can make an honest statement. There are probably other ways, but these three seem to work exceptionally well.

The first one is risky, unless you're immensely quick-witted and your humor is good-natured. Don't try it if you aren't and it isn't! The second and third, the honest question and honest statement, are good forms of redirection. If I'd had my wits about me the day a teen asked me why I was wasting his classroom's time, I might have asked with all earnestness, "Why do you ask, are you guys really loaded down with homework and stressed out?" Or, I could have responded to that teen with an honest statement, like, "Hey, that remark really hurts my feelings. I'm sorry you feel this way, but I hope I can change your mind by the end of the class."

What about disruptions that are clearly designed to trip you up? These might include a teen in the back of the room who keeps shooting spitballs at you, or a teen who makes a particular silly or challenging remark over and over again every time you ask for a response from your audience. There's a lot you can do to minimize these sorts of disruptions from happening in the first place, and when they happen anyway, you can handle them with calm directness.

You can start by entering the room with a certain carriage and demeanor and maintaining it throughout your time there. In a nutshell, you need to carry yourself and speak with confidence. This involves holding yourself erect, speaking clearly and with conviction, looking the members of your audience in the eye, and generally sending out the signal that you are in charge of yourself and the room. This is not a bullying, controlling sort of signal. It's a matter-of-fact signal. If you are unsure of yourself, feel undeserving, hunch, speak timidly and without force, look at your feet, fidget, feel hesitant or even fearful, or desperately want to please and be accepted by your audience because you think you're not cool and they are, trust me, you will be eaten alive!

When, in the rare event your commanding presence does not prevent a spitball from sticking to your neck, a calm, direct, and no-nonsense, "Hey, that's incredible aim, but don't shoot any more spitballs at me," should do the trick. What you don't want to do is put too much energy and emotion in the mix. It only demonstrates to teens who are trying to get a rise out of you that they got a rise out of you, which just feeds the behavior.

Working a Hard Room

Many of you may booktalk in urban environments with a tougher, more sophisticated group of teens. Some of you may booktalk to behaviorally challenged teens, or to teens in incarceration. These sorts of teen populations are known for being among the more difficult audiences to woo, but you can find yourself with a difficult audience just about anywhere from time to time. You may find yourself booktalking to a group of teens who were responsive the last time you visited, but just seem closed off this time, or who are agitated, angry, and distracted by something in their environment. What should you do when you find yourself working a hard room?

It may be easier to focus on what you shouldn't do. You shouldn't be discouraged and disheartened! This just happens, it truly does, and to everyone who works with teens. It is a temporary event and is not a harbinger of all your future booktalking interactions. Do your very best to make it through your booktalks, giving as much care to them as you would with an easy audience. Keep in mind that your presence in that tough room may be the salve those teens need, or even only one of those teens needs, whether or not you feel it or are being fed any positive energy as a presenter. That group, or individuals within it, may need the entry you're providing to great stories more than you know.

The After-Chat, or, Save the Best for Last!

The best part of the booktalking experience for you can come at the end, so leave some time for questions or for teens to come to you and chat both about the books you brought, and the books they've read or are reading. This is also the time for teens to browse the lists and the books you've made available, and to make selections before the class period ends. I wouldn't recommend a formal question and answer time as much as an informal chatting time. Teens, especially in the middle grades, are more talkative in smaller, loosely structured groups or one on one than they are in an official classroom or group setting.

What can make this the best part of the booktalking experience for you? It's the time when you see individual teens, seemingly lifeless and vacant during your booktalks, approach you with animation, interest, and enthusiasm, proving they heard most every word you said, and it excited them to read. Righteous! Do they all do this? Nope. But lots do, and it's awesome, worth every unstrung nerve you had before.

Are there times when no one approaches you? Sure. But even the teens who don't approach you to talk about books often flip through lists, stuff them in backpacks to look at later, pick up the books you talked to examine covers or read descriptive text on the jacket. Many quietly take one or two books straight to the checkout desk. Don't be surprised if the first teen you see scoop up his or her bag and head out the door after your booktalks appears in front of you a day or two later asking after those books. This is not an uncommon occurrence. You open up all sorts of doors to teens when you talk to them about books. Regardless of whether you've felt a wreck on the inside, and regardless of whether teens expressed anything directly to you, you are doing a most excellent thing.

BOOKTALKING THE CLASSICS

Which book do you think you're more likely to immediately attract a teen reader with: Andrew Clements's recently written *Things Not Seen*, told in the first person by a boy in high school who wakes up invisible one morning and falls in love with a blind girl, or H. G. Wells's 1897 *The Invisible Man* (this is just such a good example, I have to use it again), about a scientist gone mad when he can't reverse the experiment that made him invisible? They probably both sound pretty good to teens but I'd wager with most of those potential readers, *Things Not Seen* would have more immediate appeal.

Clements's likable protagonist is a contemporary teen who tells his own story in the language of today. He spends most of the story interacting with and falling for a beautiful and clever blind girl. That's a strong connection with teen readers of both genders. (Well, 9th grade and up for the boys. Forget the 7th graders and most of the 8th graders of the male persuasion reading a high school romance. Gross!) And let's not forget, he woke up invisible. Oh, and he runs around naked in pretty cold temperatures because his clothes show up even though his body doesn't. How can you beat that?

Wells's book is OLD, even to you and me, not just in teen terms. 1897? That's, like, forever ago. Didn't people still club their dinner back then? The main character is an adult, and a whacked out, mean one. He doesn't tell his own story, it's told in the third person, which gives the reader a fictional distance from the character and goings-on. The language is really quite accessible for a book written in the Before Time, but comparatively, it's far more challenging than Clements's book. And, it's a lot longer.

So, classics aren't likely to be as immediately appealing and popular with teens as contemporary teen fiction, even with a fascinating theme. Teens might reject a classic out of hand regardless of a fascinating theme, just because it's a classic and, like we discussed in other chapters, they assume it's too long or too old or too boring or not relevant to their lives. That's a challenge for you. Another challenge you may experience as a presenter is how to successfully booktalk the classics in ways that entice potential teen readers and make strong reading connections in the very short time allowed you. Booktalking by its very nature does not provide the time to read and discuss a classic book with teens, section by section, chapter by chapter. You have about five minutes maximum per title to booktalk classics that are not merely narrative but rich with layers—concepts, themes, meanings, historical content, political content, you name it.

I don't press these points to discourage you, but to prepare you! Forewarned is forearmed. You are much more likely to successfully connect teens to classic literature if your eyes are wide open to the challenges you're likely to face when booktalking it. Are these challenges insurmountable? Not by a long shot. The care you put into booktalking will pay back you, and them, tenfold. In a short time you can make the classics come alive for teens, you can show them the classics can be meaningful in their reading lives and beyond. It just takes positive attention to those challenges and some creative techniques to be successful, but successfully booktalk them, you can!

This section will focus on a number of techniques you might use to make more successful classics connections with teens as a booktalker who only has so much time to get the job done.

Ask Teens What They Think about the Classics

Let's assume you're in front of a group of teens to booktalk. You've let them know you are going to share some classics with them. Before doing so, how about asking a question? As the best defense is a good offense, you could dive right in and ask: "What do you think about the classics?" You might get a few positive comments from teens—I usually do—but it's almost a guarantee you'll get at least one "BO—RING." Ah, the Boring Barrier. You will have to break through it many times in your classics booktalking life. You may be so lucky as to receive a wonderfully expressive pantomime, like a doubled-over, barfing gesture! I rather enjoy those.

Whatever the case may be, the best part of asking this question is giving teens the opportunity to tell you what they think, which immediately engages them. It encourage them to participate and invest in the thirty to forty-five minutes you'll be talking about books. The second best part of asking this question is that you get your teen audience to show their cards, and that helps you better play your booktalking hand. Did the whole group sneer and gag, clutch their guts and make rude noises?

You've got your work cut out for you! Challenge accepted. Did the majority of the group express their appreciation for classics, did they all just read a great one chapter by chapter in another class and are feeling magnanimous and perhaps even eager for another? Right on. In that case, you can relax into great booktalks—you don't have to prove the books are worthy, you just have to attract teen readers to the particular works you've brought with you.

Define the Classics with Teens

"Okay," you say, after hearing out your teen audience, "Fair enough. Some classics are great and some are boring. All too true." It's always good to acknowledge the merit of every response, be it similar or not to your own. What now? How about asking another question, like, "So, just what *are* classics, anyway?" You might get a load of learned responses. Not common, but it did happen to me last year. In fact, the group seemed to think I was kind of dumb to ask! You might get a lot of vacant stares. That's a little more common. However your teen audience responds, you've got a great opening here. This is your opportunity to make the concept of classics relevant to them, and to begin the process of breaking through their misconceptions. There are a few ways you can do this. Remember, though, this has to happen in a short time and should lead fairly quickly to your booktalks.

An easy one, although not particularly flashy, is to pull together a few definitions of the classics. You might include some that are serious and some that are humorous. With a number of definitions, some in agreement and some not, you might mention that although many definitions share common elements, ultimately it's all a matter of opinion, and everyone's opinion counts. That's why you asked them. After exploring definitions with teens, you might want to sum up a bit at the end before heading in to your booktalks.

Definitions are straightforward, but they don't necessarily make the concept of classics relevant to teens. To be relevant, you need to tie a definition to current trends or events that are important and real to teens. You might consider a departure from books entirely to take a look at other sorts of "classics." You've got lots of directions to go in. Try to think about the sorts of things that appeal to teens. Let's see. How about food? That's a good one. Even though it's not really food and purportedly rots your stomach, Coke's a classic, it even says so on the can. Why's that? This would be a fun question to explore with teens. This is a good one for imparting interesting factoids, too. Coca-Cola, after all, began as a restorative drink, a "tonic," that contained both cocaine (the "coca" part) and the highly caffeinated kola nut (the "cola" part).

How about sports? You've got local and national sports figures of great renown, and many teens know who they are and care about them. You'll want to be careful that you're not a step or two behind the times on this one, though. You wouldn't want to talk like a retired basketball player is still on the court, or use as an example a football player who's out for the season on a nefarious legal matter. Credibility issue! You might talk about Michael Jordan (after you determine if he's still playing and about to retire, or if he's retired and about to start playing again) as a classic basketball player. Why's that? This would be another interesting question to explore with teens.

There's all kinds of examples of classics that might be relevant to teens. There are classic rock bands, classic cars, and classic sitcoms. You don't have to leave the world of popular literature to find relevant classics to use as examples with your teen audience. You might, were you talking to the upper middle and high school grades, ask your teen audience why Stephen King is a classic horror writer, or ask a teen audience of any age why certain comics, comic book characters, or cartoons are considered classics. Whichever example or examples you choose to explore with your teen audience, be sure to have some answers or summations prepared in advance to help lead the discussion or to use with a less participatory audience.

Explore Why the Classics Should Matter to Teens

What makes classics so blasted important that you are standing there in front of a group of teens talking about them? Discriminating teens want to know! All teens deserve to know. You need to help teens understand not only what define classics, what their characteristics are, but why this matters enough that they should do anything about it. This is most definitely *not* the time, though, to recite the list of classics benefits for teen readers from Chapter 1! That's professional adult-speak, and the worst of all possible things to tell teens.

Instead, what you need to explore with teens is the heart and soul stuff, the fun stuff, the just plain interesting stuff about classics—both the broad, all-applying stuff (we'll talk about this a bit right here) and the stuff particular to a single work (we'll talk about this plenty in the rest of the section). Lots and lots of stuff! Sure, there are all those Chapter 1 benefits of reading classics for teen readers, but they don't need to know that. That's between us. What they do need to know is why classics should matter to them—broadly speaking to start, and in more detail with the specific works you'll be booktalking. Just one or two of the many reasons why classics matter can do the trick. You don't need to plot a persuasive exposition or argument—in fact, you shouldn't—you can just plant a few seeds here and there. You are just the noble messenger, the book itself will do the rest. Following are a couple of examples of seeds you can plant that can be fun with a teen audience.

To Coin a Classic: Phrases and Figures of Speech

For the broad, all-applying stuff, you might start with a phrase or figure of speech you know teens have regularly heard, maybe even used, and ask them what they think it means and where they think it came from. An astonishing number of phrases, adages, axioms, and so forth, come from classic literature. Some incredibly well-spoken (or well-written) author thought up just the right way to word something truly representative of the human condition, and it stuck. Those wily authors have been doing this for a long time, too, and we never stop using their wording.

If you take a common, everyday phrase that teens know and tie it back in an interesting way to its classic source, you're making a connection between their current reality and what came before them. We've already talked about how insular teens can be, how unwilling to accept that they are not the first to feel like, think like, and act like human beings! This is one way of giving them, in a brief by-the-by sort of way, a connection beyond their own time and place.

Most of these teens will hear these phrases in use, see them in newspaper headlines, magazines, editorial cartoons, and more—albeit sometimes corrupted—throughout their lives, and knowing the source and meaning will lend enhanced understanding to what might otherwise be inscrutable. They'll even see classics phrases pop up in cheesy B movies. There's always that rickety plank above the door to a haunted mansion, creepy crypt, or an abandoned (and also haunted) mine shaft that in an anguished text reads, "Abandon hope, all ye who enter here!" That's from Dante's *The Divine Comedy* (1321), and the concept was also used in Kurt Vonnegut's *Player Piano* (1952) and John Cheever's *Falconer* (1977).

Here's a good one: "All hell broke loose!" How many times have you heard that one? You can thank Robert Greene for that. He coined it in his play, *Friar Bacon and Friar Bungay* (1594). No, I don't know who he is, and I have not read the play about the two friars, but still, you and I are using a phrase from a late 1590s dramatic work! That's awesome. It was also used by John Milton in *Paradise Lost* (1667), Robert Penn Warren in *All the King's Men* (1946), Joseph Heller in *Catch-22* (1961), Howard Fast in *The Establishment* (1979), and Robert Ludlum in *The Icarus Agenda* (1988). One good phrase leads to another.

You can give Shakespeare the lion's share of credit for phrases still common in current speech. Did they originate with him? Some did, many didn't. He drew on the phrases conceptualized by his predecessors in many cases, and popularized them. Just to mention a very, very few, you can thank the Bard for immortalizing these: "All that glitters is not gold," "All the world's a stage," "All's well that ends well," "Don't shoot the messenger," "Don't wear your heart on your sleeve," "Every dog has his day," "Fight fire with fire."

A goodly number of the classic works teens will be reading in junior and high school were the original sources of common-use phrases. Here's just a tiny, tiny handful of these for example:

- "All animals are equal, but some animals are more equal than others." From George Orwell's *Animal Farm* (1945)
- "Big brother is watching you." From George Orwell's *1984* (1949)
- "A foolish consistency is the hobgoblin of little minds." From Emerson's essay entitled, "Self-reliance" (1841)
- "It's a Catch-22 situation." From Joseph Heller's *Catch-22* (1961)

Make sure the phrases you use are known to teens. Whether they use them or not, they should have heard them from parents, uncles and aunts, grandparents. Try for the fun ones, and give a fact or two about the phrase's original use and current use. For example, if you were talking about a "Catch-22" situation, you could start with Heller's use in his classic novel. You might describe how Yossarian, the pilot protagonist in this World War II story, wants to get out of flying to avoid being killed. He can only plead insanity to this end, but to get out of combat duty, you can't truly be insane. Huh? There are lots of "Catch-22 situations" you might briefly explore with teens, like you can't go to the high school football away game unless you turn in your late social studies assignment to the teacher in his office at 4 PM, but you have to be on the bus at 3 PM to get to the game.

Do you have to match the phrases to the books you'll be talking? Not necessarily. This is a broad exploration of one of the reasons a relationship with the classics will matter, it doesn't have to tie in to a particular title you've brought to talk. But if it does, all the better, really! Where else might you find these phrases? Check newspapers and magazines for headlines and cartoons. Once you start looking, you'll find these references everywhere. Just about any phrase, saying, or proverb dictionary will do the trick, too. The 1996 *Random House Dictionary of Popular Proverbs and Sayings* is where I dug up the few examples I've shared with you.

Popular Culture: The House the Classics Built

One of the great ways to give teens an understanding of the value of classics is to share their roles as originals, as starting points, in forming popular culture. What carries through from past to the present? Original, time-tested, first-rate, high-impact things. The unforgettable, most meaningful things. Some of the most current, popular, ubiquitous "in" stuff can be traced straight back to an original classic work of some sort. Sharing that with teens will give them a greater sense of the value of the classics.

I've got a great example for you. Dracula. Bram Stoker wrote *Dracula* in 1897, inspired by Eastern European folklore and the real life of a brutal Walachian (Walachia equals present-day Romania) prince/warlord, Vlad Dracul, a.k.a. Vlad the Impaler. Why the Impaler? He had a penchant for impaling people on upright poles, which is a long and torturous way to die. He once managed to have 20,000 (this is not a typo) soldiers from an invading force impaled. Lest you think he only committed this sort of atrocity against peoples other than his own, think again. He was a nasty, nasty man. In any case, although the wretched Vlad was in no way associated with vampirism, Stoker used his imagination to combine local lore with evil prince, and voila! The Count Dracula! You can find these kinds of facts in lots of different resources, some of which we discussed in Chapter 3, but I got these from a neat, single-volume work called *The Monster Factory* written in 1993 by Richard Rainey, which provides lots of interesting behind-the-scenes facts about the authors and the real-life figures who inspired monstrous characters in great literature.

Although stories of vampirism and various local superstitions regarding blood-drinkers had been around for a long time, Stoker's classic brought that folklore and the vile, malevolent, damned Count to a broader audience in an original and highly effective way. More popular cultural trends than you can count (no pun intended) rest on this work's foundation. This character has permeated our culture: he's a Mega Icon, with all that entails. You've got one film on top of another. You can start in the relative here and now with the 2003 *Underworld*, a slick, gritty, film that explores the long-standing enmity between the vampires and the werewolves, the latter of which, to their deep dismay, are enslaved by the former. To go back a mere few years, you've got the 1998 and 2002 *Blade* movies. You've got Gary Oldman as one of the creepiest Counts in recent history in the little more true-to-the-classic film version, *Bram Stoker's Dracula*, from 1992. And, don't forget that Buffy the Vampire Slayer had her start in film, also in 1992, and went on to become a long-running TV series, followed by a book series and a spin-off starring Angel, which also spawned its own book series. And you've got an almost endless list of films in the middle to distant past—almost back to the dawn of the medium.

The written materials—single-issue comics, graphic novels, and books—that have been inspired by this original classic work are legion. We won't do it here, but you could work up a pretty long list of teen fiction titles alone that feature vampires, from Amelia Atwater-Rhodes's vampire novels (she was a teen herself when first published) to Darren Shan's Cirque du Freak series, let alone the books for adults—which even include cross-species human-to-vampire romances!

Film, television programming, and derivative written works aside, Stoker's *Dracula* has had an astonishing impact on modern culture, and a succession of popular cultural identities and behaviors over time. You will run into something or someone vampiric around just about every corner— or in just about every dark alley. How many Draculas do you see at Halloween? Zillions. There's a whole, dynamic subculture of real, live "blood-drinkers" in Amsterdam, comprised mainly of young people who also dress the part. To go a bit younger, teen culture in the not too distant past, and still to some degree now, modeled itself on the vampire tradition. Know any Goths? If you don't know any, you sure can spot them in the hallways at the school you visit. There aren't as many as there were a few years back, but they're still around. Remember Sesame Street's "The Count"? Dracula is even used to teach very young children. Okay, can't resist. I must make mention of the General Mills breakfast cereal, Count Chocula, with eight vitamins and minerals. The Count is everywhere, even in your cereal bowl!

To clear our palates of the dark side, you could use a milder classic with the younger teen set or with sensitive audiences, say, Dickens's *A Christ-*

mas Carol. Many popular culture elements have their roots in this holiday classic, including the still-popular-in-some-circles Donald Duck cartoon and comics. Remember Scrooge McDuck ferociously, almost maniacally, counting his pile of gold coins? And, how about the inimitable Muppets with their 1992 *A Muppet Christmas Carol*? When you see the poverty-stricken fuzzy bunny shivering on Kermit the Scrooge's stoop singing "Good King Wenceslas" in the snow for Christmas alms, just to have the door slammed in his face, you can't help but cry out with the pain and injustice of it!

There's one film and story on top of another that comes from this original classic work of a selfish man turned generous when past, present, and future are revealed in full to him. There are loads of film versions, notable among them starring Albert Finney and George C. Scott as Scrooge. I think Patrick Stewart bah-humbugged his way through a great made-for-TV-movie version just a few years ago. Or, if you wanted to use this example with an older teen audience, you might see if any of them watched Bill Murray in *Scrooged* (1988). That's an irreverent film, but still holds true to the moral message of the story.

All in all, this is the sort of amazing stuff you can share with your teen audience to help them understand that everything had to start somewhere, and that many things they know, do, and love started in the classics. Again, this is the sort of thing you do in a brief, hey-did-you-know sort of way, not in any length. You aren't giving a lesson on the impact a classic has had through time, but you are clueing in teens to its role in current popular culture in a concise, interesting way. And yet again, you can do this in a broad sort of way, or you can tie this in to the classics you are booktalking that particular day.

Reveal Why the Books You're Booktalking Are Classics

You've asked your teen audience what they think about the classics, you've defined the classics with them as best you can, and you've explored one or two of the reasons why a relationship to the classics should matter to teens, which is all general, big-picture stuff. You are about to booktalk a select group of individual classics, though, which are each considered as such for reasons of their own within the broader definition. If you can, take a moment or two to share why each specific work is considered a classic with your teen audience.

Say you are booktalking Daniel Keyes's *Flowers for Algernon*, a classic about a developmentally delayed man who through an experimental form of surgery becomes highly intelligent. You certainly could tell your teen audience that the work won the Hugo Award in 1959 for the short story version, and the Nebula Award in 1966 for the novel version. You might include that when it was first published, reviewers applauded its ability to use the genre of science fiction to meaningfully explore significant moral issues. You might mention that its impact on readers was so great the story was made into a series of plays and films.

If you were booktalking Toni Morrison's *Beloved*, a painful story of a mother's choice during the Reconstruction to keep her baby daughter from a life of slavery, you might mention the incredible reception this work received as an award nominee and award winner. It was nominated for the National Book Award and National Book Critics Circle Award in 1987, and it won the Pulitzer Prize for fiction, the Robert F. Kennedy Award, and the American Book Award (Before Columbus Foundation) in 1988. For her body of work, including *Beloved*, the author was awarded the 1993 Nobel Prize in Literature for "her epic power, unerring ear for dialogue, and her poetically-charged and richly-expressive depictions of Black America" (Nobel e-Museum at http://www.nobel.se/literature/laureates/1993/morrison-bio.html).

It only takes a few brief remarks specific to that classic—awards won, reviewers' comments, especially well-developed themes, unique writing style, originality of work, exceptional expressions of the human condition, and so forth—to give your teen audience more than just your word for it.

Explain the Significance of Classics Titles

Who flew over the cuckoo's nest? I'm back on that bird theme from Chapter 3 when we talked about how useful book notes and study guides can be to hunt down basic information about a classic work. I mentioned then that you might use those resources to make sense of the title of a classic work, like Harper Lee's *To Kill a Mockingbird* or Ken Kesey's *One Flew Over the Cuckoo's Nest*. When booktalking classics to teens, consider clueing them in to the meaning of a book's title. You can pass on this sort of information either as a part of your booktalk or as a hey-did-you-know remark, whichever works best. By providing teens with the significance of a classic's title, you do honor to the intentions of the author, you can cement reader interest, and you might help teens more readily remember a book they'd like to read later, especially if they forgot to take one of your preprepared booklists.

Sometimes there's just no way to link the title of a book to the general goings-on inside it. You might be stumped to build it in to your booktalk. That's okay, just tell your teen audience a bit about the significance of the title in a side remark if you think it's worth sharing. There will be times, though, when it's easy to build the meaning of a title in to your booktalk, or when the title is just too obvious to warrant doing anything extra about it at all. Be certain of the latter; many things that are obvious to you are not obvious to teens! It took me awhile to realize that I had to include a specific remark about Ray Bradbury's *Fahrenheit 451* that explained the title, even when I read from the first chapter as a part of my booktalk:

Fahrenheit 451

Ray Bradbury

(Read first paragraph of Chapter 1):

It was a pleasure to burn.

It was a special pleasure to see things eaten, to see things blackened and changed. With the brass nozzle in his fist, with the great python spitting its venomous kerosene upon the world, the blood pounded in his head, and his hands were the hands of some amazing conductor playing all the symphonies of blazing and burning to bring down the tatters and charcoal ruins of history. With his symbolic helmet numbered 451 on his stolid head, and his eyes all orange flame with the thought of what came next, he flicked the igniter and the house jumped up in a gorging fire that burned the evening sky red and yellow and black. He strode in a swarm of fireflies. He wanted above all, like the old joke, to shove a marshmallow on a stick in the furnace, while the flapping pigeon-winged books died on the porch and lawn of the house. While the books went up in sparkling whirls and blew away on a wind turned dark with burning.

Montag grinned the fierce grin of all men singed and driven back by flame.

Guy Montag is a fireman in a future time. His job is to *start* fires instead of putting them out. Why does he have the number 451 on his helmet? That's the temperature in Fahrenheit at which book paper burns, and Mon-

(continued)

(continued)

tag's job is to burn books. Books aren't allowed in his society. Books are written by people who think about things, and books make their readers think about things, too.

The government doesn't want that. How can it control people who think for themselves? When the government finds out someone has a hidden stash of books, it sends out firemen like Montag to burn them up. That's just how it works.

Montag has always loved his job, at least he thinks he has. But when his 17-year-old neighbor, Clarisse, asks him one day if he's happy, it bothers him that he can't answer her. When he's at a house one day burning up an old lady's hidden library, and his hand snakes out and snatches up a book to hide under his arm, Montag knows his life as a book-burning fireman is about to change.

In addition to book notes and study guides, you can look for the meaning of a title as you're reading a classic. Once you set your mind to it, most will pop right out at you.

Make Classics Real through the Past, the Present, and the People

Why would you dig up historical facts about specific classics, tie the content of a classic to current historical or political events, or impart facts about the authors of those classic works in your booktalks to teens? Plain and simple, you would do so to make those classics more real, interesting, and accessible to teen readers.

The Past

You can make the past come alive in your booktalks, at least alive enough to get teens interested in digging into that work on their own. If, for example, you are going to booktalk Connie Willis's multiple award-winning contemporary science fiction time travel classic, *Doomsday Book*, you are going to make the story far more appealing to teens if you give them a few facts about the location and era her young, female protagonist travels to: England in 1348. It just so happens 1348 was the year the plague—a.k.a. the Black Death—first came to England after decimating other European countries. Millions of souls lost across Europe, all told.

That's likely to be interesting to teens, and that might be enough to draw in readers. You might go further, though, especially with a classic work like this one that relies on the past for its story.

Do you have to do this sort of thing as an introduction to your book-talk, or should you build it into the booktalk proper? Do whatever works best. You can do what I call "the booktalk talk-around," which is nothing more than casual insertions here and there of interesting facts. You could lay a historical foundation built of interesting facts before you start your booktalk. You could build it all into your booktalk. Both the book itself and your creative genius will dictate which way you go with this.

The Booktalk Talk-Around

This is an easy thing to do. You gather up a few great facts about the time or setting, or fascinating facts about the author that relate to the time period, and pass them on, tucking in bits and pieces here and there as you present your booktalk. Since I'm going to revisit *Doomsday Book* in just a moment, let's use a couple of examples from other classic works.

You might, were you booktalking Daniel Defoe's *Robinson Crusoe*, mention that the book was based on the real-life Alexander Selkirk, who was stranded on the island of San Fernandez in the Pacific Ocean off of Chile for five years. He actually asked to be put ashore after an argument with his captain. You might mention that Erich Maria Remarque, author of the antiwar novel, *All Quiet on the Western Front*, fled Germany a day before Hitler got the chancellorship and came into power. Hitler did not tolerate antiwar sentiment, and Remarque would have been, well, made an example of. You could mention that Stephen Crane's *The Red Badge of Courage* was the first war novel that told the story from the point of view of a common soldier instead of an officer or strategist. These just happen to be facts I dug up ages ago and have used in booktalks over time, but I'm sure the information is readily available in just about any resource that includes these authors and titles.

You can always come up with interesting facts. Where do you find them? In addition to all those resources we talked about in Chapter 3 (and those listed at the ends of Chapters 2 and 7), you can get them off the book jacket or opening pages of the classic you're reading, from television shows you stumble across, magazine and newspaper articles, you name it. Once you have your eyes open to them, these kinds of facts are not hard to find. In fact, they start jumping out at you! With them, you can in just a brief moment attract the attention of your teen audience to the book in your hand because you have just made it more real.

Laying a Historical Foundation for Your Booktalk

Let's return to *Doomsday Book* and use it as an example for both laying a historical foundation for your booktalk and for building history into your booktalk. Let's start with the former. Given that this book is built around a time period, you might give your audience an overview of the times, give them a rudimentary understanding of the impact the plague would have on people, give them some of the gory details of the disease and some of the nutso therapies these people used to try to fend it off. Give them a sense of the magnitude and gravity of the situation.

Connie Willis does just this. It's one of the most powerful aspects of this genre classic; the author makes the time period and the people absolutely real. You could just reach out and touch them (not that you should, the plague is there, after all). You can communicate some of that to teens in your booktalk. Keep in mind that when you take the time to do this, you will need to keep your actual booktalk on the shorter side so you don't go on for too long and lose your audience's attention. Here's an example of how you might do this:

Give a brief overview of the era and its people:

> The book I'm about to share with you is set in England in 1348. This was a time when most people lived in small villages, growing crops and raising livestock to feed themselves. They were a highly religious and superstitious people. They had no real science or technology to help them make sense of the physical world, so they relied on their faith and on what you and I would consider some very unusual ideas to get by.

Give a brief overview of the incidence of the Black Death:

> In 1348 the bubonic plague, which became known as the Black Death, made its way for the first time to England from the rest of Europe through fleas that lived on infected rats. When the fleas bit people, the people became infected.

Describe what the Black Death did to people:

> The Black Death was an ugly disease. It all started with a swelling, or lumpy rising in the groin area or in the armpits. These lumps were called "buboes," and that may be where we get the word, "boo-boo," which children still use today when they get a cut or scrape. The victim's body would become covered in purple or black spots, and that person would then develop terrible pain, raging fevers, stinking breath, and would cough up

blood from the lungs. Eventually, the victim went into a sort of coma-like condition and died. From start to finish could be a matter of hours, or a matter of days.

Describe how people tried to treat the Black Death:

Because they had no scientific understanding, the people believed the disease came from all sorts of things: fogs and mists, comets, an angry God, earthquakes, eating too much fruit, not getting enough sunshine, and that sort of thing. They treated the disease with the same ignorance. Here's a few of the treatments they used:

- Dried toads were put on the buboes to suck out the swelling
- Hot irons were applied to the buboes to cauterize them
- Sharp knives were used to slice open the buboes and release the green pus inside
- Victims were "bled" by being cut with a knife to let a large amount of blood drip out of the body
- Victims were "cupped" with hot glasses applied to the skin to suck blood to the surface
- Victims were cut, or burned all over their bodies to form blisters, and the wounds were kept open by rubbing butter or lard on to them so evil vapors from the body could rise out
- Victims were forced to drink concoctions that contained crushed emeralds, liquid gold, powdered stag's horn, and the meat of snakes

Describe the gravity of the Black Death:

Almost no one survived the Black Death. The estimated loss of human life during this incidence of the plague was 24 million in the European countries, including England. It cut the population of London at that time in half. The numbers of dead were so great that huge "plague pits" were dug to contain all the corpses. There were too many bodies for the plague pits, though, and bodies were piled up in public places, where they were eaten by rats, wolves and other wild animals. The stench of sickness, death and decomposition hung constantly in the air.

Where'd I get all these great facts? From an awesome, relatively new history series written for teens called The Way People Live from Lucent Books (2000). One of the volumes is called Life During the Black Death, and is packed full of fascinating information.

Then, follow this up with your booktalk:

Doomsday Book

Connie Willis

Kivrin, a medieval studies student from the year 2054, is "dropped" in England during the Middle Ages. She's worked long and hard to make this time jump, and has picked December of 1320 in a small village outside of London as her destination. Why? 1320 is a more stable year in the tumultuous history of medieval England, and a small village is an easier place for a lone woman to adapt to the culture of the time and study the people without worry.

After the drop, one of Kivrin's first thoughts upon seeing the crisp, medieval English countryside, is how incredibly beautiful England is in 1320. Will it seem so beautiful, though, when Kivrin finds out that even though she *is* in England, she's *not* in the year 1320? How will it look when she finds out she was actually dropped in 1348, the year the Black Death arrived?

Building History into Your Booktalk

Instead of laying a historical foundation before presenting a short booktalk, you can build some of that historical context into your booktalk proper. You aren't likely to get as much detail, or even the same detail, but you can whet appetites to a time period with some interesting content. With *Doomsday Book*, the historical context that seemed to make the most sense for the booktalk was to share what was required of Kivrin to fit in and avoid suspicion in the 1300s, which goes a long way toward defining the way of life at that time. Not much detail about the plague, but it doesn't seem necessary in this booktalk. If teens seemed interested, you could also casually add a remark or two about the plague after your booktalk:

Doomsday Book

Connie Willis

Kivrin is about to drop backward through time to the Middle Ages, and she'll be the first ever to go there. The Middle Ages has always been rated by time travelers as the most dangerous of eras to be in with its political unrest, religious fervor, and host of opportunistic diseases. Until now, the era was off limits.

(continued)

(continued)

Mr. Dunworthy thinks it should still be off limits. He doesn't want his young friend to be subject to the perils of that time. But Kivrin wants to go more than anything, and she's not worried at all. She's going to the year 1320, after all, one of the more stable times in that century. No warfare, no famine, and no major epidemics. And Kivrin's spent a long time learning what a young woman from the year 2054 needs to know to fit in to an English village at that time. So, no matter how hard he tries, Mr. Dunworthy can't stop her from her goal.

Kivrin's had to learn Church Latin, Norman French, Old German, and Middle English. She's had to memorize masses. She's had to learn how to farm, milk cows, gather eggs, and grow vegetables. She's had to develop excellent skills at spinning, weaving, and embroidery. She's had to learn how to live in cold conditions, as she's going back to a time referred to as "The Little Ice Age." She's had to learn how to ride a horse. And she's had to learn medieval medicine, including how to treat wounds and prepare bodies for burial.

Kivrin has also had her own medical treatments: she's had her appendix removed, she's been inoculated against cholera and typhus, and she's had her immune system augmented. Her nurse even wanted to cauterize the lining of Kivrin's nose so she wouldn't be subjected to the vile odors of the time—general filth, bad meat, excrement, and decomposition—but Kivrin turned her down.

And last but not least, Kivrin had to concoct a story of assault and robbery to tell the people of 1320 so no one will question why she's a lone female in a time when that was unheard of. She even has herself deliberately beaten up to look the part.

It's not easy going back in time, especially as the first visitor to such a dangerous era. And when Kivrin finds out she hasn't been sent to 1320, but twenty-eight years later to 1348 when the black plague arrived to decimate England's population . . . not only is it not easy, it's a living nightmare.

The Present

History is not just the past, it's happening now, and if you can find a way to tie a classic to current events, and possibly even current social studies and political studies assignments, you make an even stronger historical connection for teens. If you aren't tying your booktalks to an assignment, think about something that's big in the news that teens might know about or that you can quickly and easily explain to them. Determine if there's some theme or point you can use to make a connection from that to a classic, or, from the classic to the current event.

An obvious example of a significant current event would be the 9/11 terrorist attacks on the World Trade Center in New York City. I'm sure there are other ties to classic literature you could make, but you certainly could tie to classics that explore the racial tensions that are raised by world-scale events such as these. You might start by talking to your teen audience about some of the racial tensions that exist in the post–9/11 United States. You might mention that American citizens of Middle Eastern descent were, for a time following the attack, occasionally detained at airports or kicked off of flights because they were "suspicious." You might mention that visitors to our country from the Middle East are strongly monitored now when they weren't before. You might ask if any teens in your audience are of Middle Eastern descent, and find out if they have experienced any social discomfort since 9/11. Then, you might tie this all in to the only other time when American soil was attacked by a foreign entity, and follow that by booktalking a classic that looks at the racial issues during that time. That would be Pearl Harbor, the starting point for the United States' involvement in World War II, and a time when racial tensions became racial segregation and imprisonment. Jeanne Wakatsuki's *Farewell to Manzanar*, a nonfiction classic that describes the Japanese internment following the bombing of Pearl Harbor, is a perfect tie-in:

Farewell to Manzanar

Jeanne Wakatsuki Houston and James D. Houston

Jeanne was 7 years old in December of 1941 when the Japanese bombed Pearl Harbor. She lived in a fishing community in California, but there wasn't anywhere in America far away from the shock and fear the bombing created in people. People even feared Jeanne and her family. Why? Because Jeanne's mother and father were Issei—Japanese people who'd immigrated to the United States. And wasn't it just possible all Japanese people were in it together, trying to take over the United States?

There was so much fear and confusion that the American government decided it couldn't trust anyone of Japanese ancestry, not even 7-year-old girls. Jeanne's father was taken away from the family by two FBI agents right away, and he wasn't seen by his family until a year later. Shortly after that, President Roosevelt signed an Executive Order that allowed the evacuation of all people of Japanese ancestry from all coastal areas.

Where'd they go? 110,000 people on the West Coast, even if they were American citizens, were moved to internment camps further inland where they couldn't make contact with the Japanese and plot the downfall of the

(continued)

(continued)

United States of America. They had to walk away from their businesses, their homes, their possessions, and everything else in their lives to live imprisoned in poorly constructed barracks out in the middle of nowhere.

Jeanne and her family were sent to Manzanar Camp, in the windy, dust-swept Owens Valley of California, and they lived in those barracks for three years, dependent on the U.S. government for everything. They never left the boundaries of the camp in all that time. Jeanne watched as fear, anger, and depression ripped the close bonds of her family apart, and watched while they drifted away from each other in the harsh conditions in camp. And, when she left the camp those three years later and had to try to fit back into the outside world, she couldn't forget for even an instant that everyone who saw her in school or on the street must distrust and maybe even hate her—just because of her Japanese face.

Jeanne left the internment camp while still a girl, but how long would it take her truly to say farewell to Manzanar?

With current events discussions, make sure that sensitive topics are appropriate for your particular audience, be certain of any facts you impart, and be sure you don't reveal or press any personal political viewpoints.

The People

You can help make classics more real to teens by sharing something about the author or the other people, real and fictional, related to the work you're booktalking. This isn't quite like sharing that Erich Maria Remarque fled Germany the day before Hitler came to power; that's more a way of personalizing an important point in history through the author's actions. This is the more personal sort of detail, the sort of thing that makes the author or other people related to the classic work seem like real people, not just faceless names on the cover of a dusty tome or flat characters within.

For example, were you booktalking S. E. Hinton's *The Outsiders* to a teen audience, you could make a point of telling them the author was only 15 years old when she started writing this truly original and moving classic of teen society and rival gangs. You might tell them she started writing the book because one of her friends was beaten up at school just because of the way he combed his hair. It made her realize her school was strongly divided into groups that all stood against each other, and since this upset and frightened her, she wanted to expose it in writing. You might mention that Charlotte Brontë started writing *Jane Eyre* while in deep pain from a bad tooth and ended up eventually losing all of her teeth. You might let teens know that Aldous Huxley, author of *Brave New World*, took loads of psychedelic drugs to open his mind and to experience, well, more than he was already open to and experiencing. You could share, when booktalking *Childhood's End* or *2001: A Space Odyssey*, that Arthur C. Clarke is also a renowned scientist who invented the space satellite and based his science fiction on a firm understanding of science fact.

When should you share these sorts of details? Whenever they best fit with your booktalk. This is an informal sort of thing, another form of the "booktalk talk-around," so use your best judgment. Some related people facts are so sensational, though, you might wait to impart them until after your booktalk. If you were sharing Yukio Mishima's *The Sound of Waves* about the love between a poor, young Japanese fisherman and the daughter of the wealthiest man on the island, you might wait until after your booktalk to mention that the author, after unsuccessfully trying to overthrow the Japanese government in 1970, committed ritual suicide—seppuku—by disemboweling himself with a sword. A compatriot then beheaded him before also committing suicide. That's something guaranteed to titillate or gross out many members of a teen audience, so don't let it get in the way of the truly lovely story you're there to share.

Here's an example of a booktalk I give on occasion with which I share some basic facts about the author, characters, and other people related to the work:

The Hound of the Baskervilles

Sir Arthur Conan Doyle

They say the Baskerville family is cursed, and that it all started with Hugo Baskerville, who was rejected in love by a young woman. Deeply angered, the evil Hugo and his friends stole her from her family's farm and locked her up in a room in Hugo's manor home.

The woman became so terrified of Hugo and his friends, fast becoming loudly drunk and violent in the rooms below her, that she escaped from a window, crawled down to the ground over ivy, and ran out across the moor.

When Hugo and his friends realized the young woman had fled, they saddled up their horses, unleashed a pack of hounds, and set off across the moor to hunt her down. Hugo swore he would give his body and soul to the Powers of Evil if only he could overtake her.

When his drunken friends, having fallen far behind in the hunt, came upon Hugo, he was lying dead in a clearing with the body of the young

(continued)

(continued)

woman beside him. She had died of fright, but Hugo had his throat ripped out by a huge black hound with blazing eyes and slathering jaws. Ever since, for generation after generation, a curse has lain upon the family and a devil hound has haunted the moors.

When Charles Baskerville dies mysteriously, the locals blame the curse, but Sherlock Holmes has a different idea and sets out to discover how Charles died, and to solve the mystery of the hound of the Baskervilles.

Here are some the general people facts I might share:

- Sir Arthur Conan Doyle was a doctor who served as ship's surgeon on a whaling and sealing ship in the Arctic and on a freighter to Africa.
- After his turns as ship's surgeon, Doyle worked in such a small, slow community in England, he never saw patients. He got bored and started writing stories.
- Sherlock Holmes is actually based on Dr. Joseph Bell, a late 1800s Edinburgh, Scotland, doctor and lecturer who was known to look so closely at the clues around people, he could deduce incredible facts about their lives. Doyle worked as Dr. Bell's assistant for a time and was deeply impressed with his powers of deduction.
- Doyle wrote Sherlock Holmes as a cocaine addict, but that wasn't considered as dangerous in the nineteenth century as it is now.
- Doyle had a strong interest in spiritualism and the supernatural, which he often built into his Sherlock Holmes stories.
- Once Doyle became a famous writer and had the money to pursue his interests, he took up real detective work and solved some difficult crimes.
- The "Sir" in front of Doyle's name comes from being knighted after serving as a doctor in South Africa in 1899 during the Boer War.

Here are some people facts specific to *The Hound of the Baskervilles* I might share:

- Doyle's inspiration to write this story came in part from long-standing legends all over Europe that involved giant black dogs, wolves, or even werewolves that roamed the landscape and wreaked havoc.
- The English moors did at that time have a belief that a howling dog on the moors meant death was coming to someone, somewhere. Some people think this belief came from the Middle Ages, when many people believed the Devil took the form of a dog—the "hellhound."

- The Baskervilles were real people that lived on the moors and were willing to lend their name to Doyle's story because they shared a mutual friend.

Thanks again to Rainey's *The Monster Factory* for all these facts on Doyle and his hound. A couple of other titles you might like to peruse for fascinating facts about classic authors are Elliot Engel's *A Dab of Dickens and a Touch of Twain: Literary Lives from Shakespeare's Old England to Frost's New England* (2002) and Kathleen Krull's *Lives of the Writers: Comedies, Tragedies and What the Neighbors Thought* (1994).

Explore Creative Techniques for Booktalking the Classics

There can be more to booktalking than talking. In addition to all those classics combos we explored in Chapter 5, which can be used in creative booktalking presentations—especially other media formats—there are other techniques you can use to "talk" a book to teens, to get their interest, and whet their appetites to classic works. We talked about reading aloud in Chapter 8, which you can certainly incorporate into your classics booktalks. You can integrate short passages from a book into your booktalk, or you can just out and out read to teens from a book. We'll revisit this with a booktalk example in just a moment. You can also tell stories or use props in your booktalking presentation. You may be more likely to use these techniques with the younger set, but they can find a willing audience in older teens from time to time.

Reading Aloud

If there's a great passage that really says it all or really ties into or sets up your booktalking hook, by all means, read it to your teen audience. Be sure that you can read smoothly (practice makes perfect) and can maintain a good volume. Reading aloud has an additional benefit—it introduces your teen audience directly to the book's descriptive writing style, style of speech in dialogue, overall mood, and so forth, which are significant appeal factors with readers.

I often read brief passages aloud in booktalks. For example, in Alfred Bester's 1956 classic, *The Stars My Destination*, I incorporated some passages that set up the story and demonstrate some of its unusual dialogue. Regarding the dialogue, I made sure I mentioned first that the character speaks in "gutter tongue" to avoid any possible confusion in my audience:

The Stars My Destination

Alfred Bester

(Read the beginning sentences of Chapter 1):

> He was one hundred and seventy days dying and not yet dead. He fought for survival with the passion of a beast in a trap. He was delirious and rotting, but occasionally his primitive mind emerged from the burning nightmare of survival into something resembling sanity.

30-year-old Gulliver Foyle, a gutter tongue–speaking, Mechanic's Mate 3rd Class, is stuck alone on the *Nomad*, a wrecked spaceship drifting halfway between Mars and Jupiter. He lives in the only airtight room left on the wreck—a 4 × 4 × 9-foot locker. Once a week, Gully is forced to pull on a barely-functional spacesuit and plunge through the ship's debris hanging suspended in the vacuum to find more air tanks and rations to keep him alive until the next week.

On one of his weekly trips, Gully spots an approaching spaceship, the *Vorga*. He rushes madly in his patched spacesuit to release the wreck's rescue flares and is filled with ecstatic joy when the ship sees his distress signal and slows. That joy turns to horror when the ship picks up speed again and passes silently by, leaving him alone again in the dark of space.

(Read the passage that ends the scene):

> "You pass me by," he said with slow mounting fury. "You leave me rot like a dog. You leave me die, Vorga . . . Vorga-T:1339. No, I get out of here, me. I follow you, Vorga. I find you, Vorga. I pay you back, me. I rot you. I kill you, Vorga. I kill you filthy."

Gully's rage and desire for revenge, forged in that moment, are so great he vows to rescue himself and dedicate his life to hunting down and destroying the ship that passed him by.

Reading aloud can go beyond just short passages. You might read aloud a longer passage or even the whole first chapter, if short and dynamic, as a part of a booktalking presentation. You're not likely to squeeze in too many unique titles when reading aloud—this takes a lot of time— but it can be a great way to help teens get into a more lengthy or more challenging book. This is something you might consider when your booktalks have a tie-in to an assignment and teens will be required to read one or more of the titles you're sharing. It may work well when a classroom is about to begin a literary section in which they'll be reading a particular title together. Whatever the case may be, don't rule out reading aloud. The pleasure of being read to doesn't stop in childhood, and this can be a highly effective way to draw teens to a book.

You might check out Jim Trelease's *The Read-Aloud Handbook* (there's a new 5th edition from 2001), which discusses the benefits of reading aloud to both children and teens, and provides practical tips for doing so. An educator named William F. Russell has several books out for reading aloud to children and teens which might also be useful to you, including two books on the classics, *Classics to Read Aloud to Your Children* and *More Classics to Read Aloud to Your Children*, and one on classic myths, *Classic Myths to Read Aloud*.

Storytelling

Storytelling can be a great way to "talk" about a book. If you are someone who is a natural-born performer, you might consider creating stories that you tell or perform to promote a classic work. There are lots of resources to help storytellers tell stories, including resources about telling stories specifically to teens. But if you are not comfortable doing this sort of performance, don't!

If storytelling appeals to you, you may find some useful ideas in Gail de Vos's 1991 *Storytelling for Young Adults: Techniques and Treasury*. The book describes the many ways storytelling can benefit teens, provides practical storytelling techniques, discusses how storytelling can be used in a classroom environment, and provides an annotated bibliography of good stories and a section of sample stories. Among many indexes, the index of stories by theme may be especially useful to you.

Using Props

You could bring a bunch of unique, maybe even bizarre objects or props to a classroom. You would then ask members of your audience to select objects, each of which you've connected to a booktalk. A good example of this, although not a classic work, is bringing in a toilet seat ring and booktalking Randy Powell's *Whistling Toilets* when a teen selects the item.

Props can be a way to keep a booktalk a little on the silly side. They can be a way to show off incredibly cool objects, if you have them and they relate well to a book. They can work exceptionally well with the younger set and in special classrooms that have teens with behavioral issues, as long as you can keep a lid on the giddiness! Props can also be great memory triggers for teens who decide at some later date they want to read a book with a title they can't really remember, but it was the one the librarian or educator used a gong to talk about.

Be Honest about Potential Classics Reading Challenges

Because a classic can be a longer, more complex work, you need to find a balance between encouraging teens to read one—because it is either an exceptional book you want to share or has been assigned and it's your job to introduce it—and being honest about the challenges they may face while reading it.

Be straightforward with teens about your experience of a book. Revealing your reading responses like, "I was really challenged by this one," or, "It took a while for me to be interested, but I hung in there and then the story just took off," makes a book more rather than less accessible to teens. It's always a great idea to let your teen audience know that you had to really think about a particular book, had to educate yourself in its meaning, but that once you did, it was an incredible reading experience. This sort of honest response also gives you credibility. If you promote a book without disclosing some of its obvious and likely snags and a teen reader gets hung up on one of them following your booktalks, he or she is not likely to trust your recommendations the next time. You don't want that!

Your honest respond also reinforces the idea that reading isn't always a passive pursuit, and that there can be pleasure in the effort, whatever it may be given the particular classic. Through honesty, you can make it okay for teens to reach—for patience as a reader, for understanding as a reader—and not feel inadequate. Always be sure to include the up side with the down side, though. Remember that you are sharing books that you believe teens will enjoy as readers and will find meaning in, even though it may take more of an investment than they are used to. If you are booktalking Charles Dickens's *Oliver Twist*, for example, you could tell your teen audience that the book was long and packed full of detail, but once you accepted that and relaxed into the story, it was gripping and full of characters to care about along the way.

That said, I do believe there are self-indulgent authors out there who write for themselves and have, with a small group of the literati, received classics status. It is impossible to read their works without assistance, and some of these authors are in the canon. You just shouldn't select these sorts of books to promote to teens.

Captains Courageous, written by Rudyard Kipling in 1897, is a great example of a classic with some potential reading snags that I think requires some honesty when booktalking. Kipling is a huge name in the world of classics, one most teens are familiar with from their childhood years, which makes it easier to "sell" him. This particular book features a teen protagonist, which is always of more appeal than not to a teen audience. The protagonist may be a spoiled brat, but hey, he's still a teen. And, the booktalk I use indicates he may get his comeuppance, which appeals to us all. However, not unlike Shakespeare, it takes some work to get used to the language so you can enjoy the story:

Captains Courageous

Rudyard Kipling

Harvey Cheyne is not a very nice person. He's a rich, babied, self-centered, irritating, disrespectful, 15-year-old with powerful parents who gets what he wants when he wants it.

He's so obnoxious, in fact, that when he goes to the smoking room on the steamship he's traveling on, the men tell him he's not welcome there. When he won't leave, the men play a trick on him. Knowing Harvey thinks he's great and can do anything better than anyone else, one of the men offers him a really strong cigar and tells him how happy he'll be when he smokes it. Having something to prove, Harvey lights it up, and draws in a huge lungful of thick smoke.

His eyes fill with tears and he immediately feels violently sick to his stomach. Embarrassed, he races out onto the steamer's deck to throw up in private.

While Harvey's on deck trying to deal with the painful effects of an incredibly strong cigar on his young body, the steamer tips dangerously low on his side and a huge, gray wave rises over the deck. It picks up the doubled-over Harvey and sucks him into the sea.

When he wakes up, he's onboard a schooner full of rough, no-nonsense fishermen who don't care who he says he is, and don't care how much money he says he has. All they care about is that he pulls his weight until the fishing season is over and they can drop him off on land.

Read *Captains Courageous* to find out how the self-centered, spoiled Harvey copes for an entire season of dangerous sea fishing with a group of men who value hard work and looking out for each other above all things, and who believe it's not who you *are* in the world, but what you *do* in your life that makes you important.

I tell teens after booktalking this one that Kipling used the local dialect of the fishing communities of 1890s New England. He did it deliberately to make these people real to the reader, which is a great thing for an author to do, but if you don't know Upper Eastern Seaboard Fishermanese, you have to take the time to learn as you read along. I may even read a small bit of dialogue to my teen audience, or cull out some of the words into a brief list I read off, so they get the idea.

Here's a passage in which Dan, the teenage son of the fishing schooner's captain, explains to Harvey where the fish go when brought in by the fishermen:

> "That's where the fish goes."
> "Alive?" said Harvey.
> "Well, no. They're so's to be ruther dead—an' flat—an' salt. There's a hundred hogshead o' salt in the bins, an' we hain't more'n covered our dunnage to now." (Kipling 1982, 17)

Or, you might tell them these fisherman say " 'baout" instead of "about," "instid" instead of "instead," "a-holt" instead of "ahold," "kinder" instead of "kind of," "hist" instead of "hoist," and so on.

Share Personal Experiences and Feelings as a Classics Reader

You can share interesting stories from your own life that either build up to or reinforce a classic booktalk. Be careful to keep these sorts of stories short, and allow time for teens to share similar stories of their own if they are so inclined. Chaim Potok's *The Chosen* is a good example. This classic novel opens with a baseball-playing scene that builds up to an unfortunate accident that brings two very different young men together who will in the future become fast friends. Danny Saunders deliberately hits Reuven Malter's pitch low and straight, and Reuven takes the ball right on the forehead, smashing his glasses, knocking him down, and sending him for a stay in the hospital where it's not clear for a time if he'll lose his vision in one eye:

The Chosen

Chaim Potok

It's Brooklyn in the 1940s. All the Jewish schools have been brought to-gether during World War II to play baseball to prove they're not just schol-ars, but as physically fit as the rest of America's young men.

At a ballgame one Sunday afternoon in June, Reuven Malter is on the mound and Danny Saunders is at the plate. Good thing these two are on opposite teams, because they wouldn't be able to play together. Even though both teens have lived only five blocks away from each other for the past fifteen years, they've never had anything to do with one another. Reuven's father is a liberal scholar and Danny's father is a Russian Hasidic rabbi. Reuven's father believes Danny's father is a tyrant who rules over his community, and Danny's father believes Reuven's father is so liberal he's not really even Jewish.

There's definitely no love lost between the two families, and it shows on the diamond. Reuven keeps throwing wicked fastballs at Danny, who's just standing there at the plate with a stiff grin on his face, trying to psyche Reuven out. When Danny finally stops grinning, it's to hit one of Reuven's fastballs straight in to Reuven's face. When all is said and done, Reuven's glasses are smashed, he has a huge lump on his forehead, and every time he blinks he has a sharp pain in his left eye.

It turns out that sharp pain is coming from a piece of shattered eyeglass lens that was driven into his eye. After emergency surgery that still might leave him blind, and during a long stay in the hospital, Reuven has an un-expected visitor. Danny Saunders is there one day when Reuven wakes up from a nap to tell him how sorry he is, and he keeps coming back day after day to sit and talk and ultimately become the closest friend Reuven will ever have—despite their different lives as Jews, despite what their fathers think about each other, and despite what happened at the ballpark that Sunday in June.

When I was in 5th or 6th grade, I was assigned the catcher position in a neighborhood game and knowing not one thing about it, stood too close behind my older brother when he was at bat. I took the wood just to the side of the temple as he swung it around after the hit. I was severely con-cussed and had a literal black eye, a bona fide shiner. My eye stayed com-pletely closed for a couple of weeks, and it took a few more weeks for the shiny black to go purple, green, and yellow. As it healed, some of the skin even came off around my eye, like charcoal flaking off a burnt stick. That was cool! The doctor told my mom that if I'd been hit just an inch over in the temple's soft spot, I would have fallen down dead in the yard. After it stopped hurting, the whole thing was awesome, a great war story for a kid.

Sometimes I tell that that story to teens either before or after I booktalk Potok's classic, if it seems like a good fit for the audience. It makes me more real to those teens, and it makes a book that starts with a similar story more accessible when accompanied by a personal story. If this leads teens to share their own baseball or sports injury stories, it's because you've let them know a little bit about yourself, let them know you are interested in who they are, what their experiences are, and what they have to say. If it gets them thinking about real, everyday lives, and how they are not unlike the stories to be found in classic literature, you've tied a classic to yours and their personal lives.

Sharing your feelings as a reader is close to sharing your honest response to a classic work, but with a slight shift in angle. Being honest about the nature of a classic and your response to it as a reader is a slightly more, shall we say, practical sort of thing. Sharing your feelings as a reader is more the heart and soul stuff. There are lots of good reasons why you would share your personal feelings about a book, but here's a few:

- There's nothing like an enthusiastic personal recommendation. Don't underestimate your powers of persuasion!
- Sharing your personal feelings about a book makes you real to your teen audience. You are not just a presenter, a classroom visitor, a librarian, a teacher. You are a real live person, with rich responses to the books you're sharing.
- Your personal responses as a reader can encourage teens not to grudgingly read classics merely for test-taking, to regurgitate a standard understanding of book, but for their own aesthetic experience.

A warning here: be careful that you don't create an aesthetic response for your teen audience. Different readers find different characteristics of a book meaningful. As teens can be quite suggestible, especially the younger set, how do you avoid prescribing meaning for your teen audience when sharing your personal feelings? You might use qualifying phrases like, "for me, this book was . . ." or "my brother read this and got into a different part, but I really appreciated the way the author described . . . ," or "I really loved . . . but there's so much to love in this book, I bet each one of you would find something completely different you'll feel strongly about."

Also, don't gush or become overly dramatic about your feelings. Doing that can raise reader expectations too high; or conversely, can make you look a bit foolish.

If you are a public or school librarian and find yourself in a situation where you can't set aside a book you didn't particularly care for because you've been asked by an educator to talk about it, or it's one of several on an awards list you've been asked to booktalk, don't reveal this to your teen audience. There's no reason to divulge personal responses in a classroom environment that are not positive, and you do not want to do anything to undermine the educator. The rest of the time, only booktalk books that you love and want to share with teens, and let those positive personal feelings come forth!

Make It Easy for Teens to Get the Classics

Make sure at least a few copies of the classics you booktalk are available in your library. It's a real drag for a teen who has mustered up the energy to come to the library after your booktalk just to find there's only one copy available and someone else already checked it out. Teens are more immediate in their interests, and if they can't get their hands on a book when or soon after the mood strikes them, they are not as likely as you might be to lay in wait for it. They'll move on to something else that catches their interest, and they may not think about reading that book again for a long time to come, if ever.

If you are a school librarian, you may consider pulling your library's multiple copies of booktalking books into a discrete collection that teens can browse and check out after your booktalks. If you are an educator, work with your school librarian (if you have one!) toward the same end. If you're a public librarian visiting a school or working in the community, you can gather multiple copies from your public library and bring them with you.

Provide Classics Booklists and Study Aid Information

For those teens who may not belly up to the book bar right away, but want to pick up some of the books you've talked about at a less public time in a less public place, provide an attractive list of your booktalking titles with brief annotations for them to take for later use. Leave a few stacks of lists around where teens can get to them. Place a stack or two in your library or classroom.

In addition to a list of the books you shared that day, you should consider providing a list of classics study aids. It may not be the most popular list you've ever pulled together, but it can be quite useful, both for teen readers who want to dig into more challenging reads and for other librarians and educators to support them. Keep it short—no need to overwhelm—but include a selection of resources teens can look at to help them through the tough spots in a classic or to give them needed background information. You might include the names of a few book notes and study guide series, the name of a literary resource database if your library subscribes to one or access is available elsewhere in the community, and literary reference resources like we talked about in Chapter 3. Be sure to include those written specifically for students, if you've got them. If the books you talked were particularly challenging, you might include a resource or two that address each specific work. If your booktalks were on a theme, event, or time period, you might include a handful of books and articles that provide good basic information about it.

As well as providing a concise, helpful tool for teen readers, a list of this sort reinforces that it's okay to need to look something up to "get" it, that it's okay to find out more about something to make a reading experience richer, and that reading can often be enhanced through learning. Nothing wrong with that!

SUMMING IT UP

One of the best ways to reach the largest number of teens at a time to help them make outstanding classics connections is through booktalking—attracting an audience to great reading choices through short and dynamic presentations. Whether in a classroom or alternative educational environment, in a library program, or in a community venue or social service agency, there are basic skills you can develop to comfortably and successfully booktalk the classics to teen audiences of all kinds—even the tough ones! In doing so, teens will be introduced and hopefully attracted to exceptional works of literature, presented honestly and meaningfully by you, a librarian or educator playing a pivotal role in the reading successes of the young people in your community.

WORKS CITED

American Heritage Dictionary of the English Language. 2000. 4th ed. Boston: Houghton Mifflin.

Bester, Alfred. 1996. *The Stars My Destination*. New York: Vintage Books. (Orig. pub. 1956.)

Bradbury, Ray. 1991. *Fahrenheit 451*. New York: Ballantine Books. (Orig. pub. 1954.)

Clements, Andrew. 2002. *Things Not Seen*. New York: Philomel Books.

De Vos, Gail. 1991. *Storytelling for Young Adults: Techniques and Treasury*. Englewood, CO: Libraries Unlimited.

Doyle, Arthur Conan, Sir. 2000. *The Hound of the Baskervilles*. New York: Aladdin Classics. (Orig. serialized in *Strand* magazine, 1901–1902.)

Dunn, John M. 2000. *Life during the Black Death*. San Diego: Lucent Books.

Houston, Jeanne Wakatsuki, and James D. Houston. 2002. *Farewell to Manzanar*. Boston: Houghton Mifflin. (Orig. pub. 1973.)

Kipling, Rudyard. 1982. *Captains Courageous*. Bantam Classic Edition. New York: Bantam Books. (Orig. pub. 1897.)

Langemack, Chapple. 2003. *The Booktalker's Bible: How to Talk about the Books You Love to Any Audience*. Westport, CT: Libraries Unlimited.

Potok, Chaim. 1996. *The Chosen*. New York: Fawcett Columbine. (Orig. pub. 1967.)

Rainey, Richard. 1993. *The Monster Factory*. New York: New Discovery Books.

Russell, William F. 1989. *Classic Myths to Read Aloud*. New York: Crown.

———. 1984. *Classics to Read Aloud to Your Children*. New York: Cown.

———. 1986. *More Classics to Read Aloud to Your Children*. New York: Crown.

Titelman, Gregory. 1996. *The Random House Dictionary of Popular Proverbs and Sayings*. New York: Random House.

Toni Morrison—Biography. Stockholm, Sweden: Nobel e-Museum. Available online at: http://www.nobel.se/literature/laureates/1993/morrison-bio.html (accessed 27 September 2003).

Trelease, Jim. 2001. *The Read-Aloud Handbook*. 5th ed. New York: Penguin Books.

Willis, Connie. 1992. *Doomsday Book*. New York: Bantam Books.

10

❖❖ ❖❖ ❖❖

PROMOTE THE CLASSICS IN SCHOOLS AND YOUR TEEN COMMUNITY

Chapters 8 and 9 explored meaningful classics connections you can make with teens in groups—through book discussion and reading programs, creative classics programming and activities, and through booktalking the classics. If you are a school librarian or educator in a traditional or structured alternative educational environment, you've got a ready-made, captive teen audience to work your classics magic on. You're ready to go! You public librarians, however, do not. You serve both a broader and less well-defined teen community. Not only do you serve teens in your community's schools, you serve teens in the community at large—through your own library, clubs, camps, churches, and in unique homeschooling environments. You have to "take your show on the road," so to speak, to reach large numbers of teens at a time.

As you may not already have established relationships with your communities, this chapter will focus on the steps you can take to create those relationships. Although the emphasis here will be on getting into traditional schools and other structured educational environments, the information can be adapted easily to making connections with unique educational groups and other community organizations.

Regardless of the focus on public librarians, I hope you school librarians and educators will read this chapter anyway—there might be some useful information for you here. You may at the very least gain a greater understanding of and appreciation for the unique challenges public librarians face in connecting with educational environments. Knowing this, you may feel motivated to do what you can to help them develop strong working relationships with you, so they have the opportunity to share great books with your teens. Encouraging public librarians to play a strong role in your school library or classroom to promote the classics can be a rewarding experience with far-reaching effects.

To master the understatement, for many public librarians a school or group visit with teens can be intimidating. Unlike your educational colleagues, you aren't in a year-long relationship with the individuals in that group. Nor do you have the same training to be in a relationship with that group as educators do. But there you are anyway, standing in front of a large number of young people, many of whom are wearing what I call the Dead Fish Face. You know the one—that flat, glazed, milky-eyed expressionless stare—reminiscent of the look of just about every dead fish ever seen washed up on a beach! You're there to promote the classics, books that some teens believe they would rather pull out their fingernails one by one than read, and that others have just heard are boring and useless somewhere along the line.

You feel a vein throbbing in your neck, your palms are sweating, you're pretty sure you need to go the bathroom again even though you went only five minutes ago. You might wonder if you're going to throw up, or maybe just choke on your own spit before you even utter one word. You're afraid your sweaty hands are shaking so badly the book you're holding will pop right out of them like a slippery bar of soap and concuss a nearby teen. You believe every teen present—and there are so very many of them—hates you and thinks you're stupid. You imagine they're all formulating truly ungenerous thoughts about your hair and the size of your nose. And that's just for starters!

Why would you put yourself through that?

Educational environments are the all-time best places to connect with the greatest number of teens at a single time, bar none. Plain and simple, there's no other place you are going to get the opportunity to expose so many young people at once to the wonders of reading great books. No doubt, being in an educational environment takes some getting used to, although it's not nearly so bad as you may think it is and can actually be one of the most elating experiences of youth services librarianship! In the end, though, your work there will have rewards that far exceed the challenges—for you, for your educational colleagues, and most importantly, for the teens themselves.

As a public librarian, how do you get into those educational environments, and how do you form successful relationships and meet your goals once you're there? First, you have to sell yourself to the right people. It's up to you—no one else will do it for you! This chapter looks at why and how. Next, you have to understand your audience—the teens, the educators, and maybe a parent or two from time to time. We've talked at length about the teens, and you can hark back to Chapters 4 and 7 for discussions of teens as readers in general, teens as readers of the classics, and the diverse individual and group characteristics of teens. We'll mention the teens again, but briefly. This chapter focuses on understanding your educational colleagues as a significant part of your audience and on their relationships to the classics. It is essential you know them and their attitudes about the classics before you can successfully promote classics to teens in their environment.

IF YOU DON'T SELL YOURSELF, NO ONE ELSE WILL!

If you want to get into classrooms or homeschooled groups to share classics with teens (or for any other reason), you've got to sell yourself. Bottom line. Why? If you don't do it, no one else will!

In my many years as a public librarian working to create strong ties to the educational community so I can make connections with teens in the classroom, I've never been approached out of the clear blue by a school librarian, educator, or homeschool instructor to visit a classroom or meet with a homeschooled group and share my love of classics (or any other sorts of books, for that matter). This may seem odd, especially considering the homeschoolers who rely heavily on the public library for resources and study space, but it's true nonetheless.

I can't imagine there will be many times, if any, when one of your educational colleagues, having heard little or sporadically from you and never having had you or a predecessor present in the classroom or school library, will think, "Wouldn't it be lovely to have that teen services public librarian in to share books with my students this fall? Now, just where is that business card she mailed me at the beginning of the last school year?" If you wait around for that, you'll be, well, waiting around for that. Forever!

Educators have their own thing going on. Lots to do in a day, lots to prepare for the next day. Alas, you most likely do not figure prominently in their thoughts! You should expect this; they are, after all, focused on educating our nation's youth.

It's your job to educate *them* that you are an intelligent, savvy, dedicated professional who also specializes in work with teens, and who can partner with them. You will have to work smartly and diligently to get the attention of your educational community, and to convince those incredibly busy folks that your presence in their world is a good thing that supports a shared goal and that you will not be a distraction or burden to them.

Here's the good news. After a little of the right sort of preparatory and introductory work, it won't take much to convince most of them! Like you, these people are dedicated to working with teens and to providing them with the tools that will help them grow into fully realized, capable, and happy adults. Sure, you'll have trouble storming the citadel with a few, but most will welcome you with open arms, gratitude, and expressions of sheer delight. And they'll connect you to their teen communities. That's certainly worth the effort!

Steering clear of the red-light district connotation, "selling yourself" might sound like a privacy-invading telemarketing sort of deal, or like you've got to make a study of aggressive business people in power suits and just how they trample their equals to become their betters, or that you've got to observe those wretched and cloying salespeople on commission at fancy retailers and imitate them.

Not so! Selling yourself is just a snappy way of saying you've got to let the right people know in the right way who you are and what you can do for them. Although it will require effort, it's not complex and requires no off-putting behaviors! You've simply got to demonstrate that you have the ability to provide the wonderful service(s) you're offering. And you will likely have to do so on a repeat basis. That's the short of it.

For a more in-depth look at this selling-yourself-so-you-can-booktalk stuff, I highly recommend you read Chapple Langemack's book, *The Booktalker's Bible: How to Talk about the Books You Love to Any Audience*, for an entertaining, no-nonsense, step-by-step guide to successfully marketing yourself as a booktalker at large, with specific tips for getting into schools. Even if you aren't trying to get in the door of a particular school to booktalk, this stuff has a broader application that will help you get into a school for any reason at all.

Find the Right People in Your Educational Community

Before you can get the word out to your educational community, you need to know who your educational community is. You might work in a library or library system with clearly defined educational service areas, or you may have access to community studies that identify public, private, religious, and homeschools as well as other sorts of alternative educational programs like, say, an unwed teen mother's halfway home/school or that sort of thing. If so, you're lucky! Just whip up a list from those sources, and there's your target educational community. Dig up any information you might need that's not already included, such as school principals, school librarians, language arts instructors, street addresses, phone numbers, e-mail addresses, Web page addresses, and all that good contact stuff.

If you don't have any internal library resources to begin with, you'll have to do the work to compile a contact list on your own. Use the local phone book, search the Web, ask around, do all the usual sorts of detective work. This may be simple, or it may be painstaking, but it's worth it and will be useful for a long time to come. Once you've developed that core contact list, you can add educational groups as you discover them and as your community grows and new groups come along.

You might consider building a spreadsheet or database to hold this contact information, or use some other computer application that you are familiar with and will easily produce mailing labels for you. This will come in quite handy over time. You should, if your e-mail program is capable of it and if your community is of any size, create online distribution lists so that at a moment's notice you can e-mail all your contacts at once, or just a drop a message off to a specific subset of your contact list. For example, I keep an e-mail distribution list that contains all my educational contacts, and from that I've created additional distribution lists that contain only the middle school educators and school librarians, just the high school educators and school librarians, just the school librarians at all my service area schools, just the "highly capable" and "honors" language arts instructors at all my service area schools, and so on. I even have a distribution list just for school principals, which I don't use but once a year, but when I need it, it's just a click away. Whether you need a series of e-mail addresses once a month or once a year, not having to dig through a file, electronic or otherwise, for them will certainly save you loads of time.

Just Who Are You, Anyway, and What Is It You Do?

Your educational colleagues need to know you're out there. If you do not already enjoy established relationships, these people don't have any idea who you are and what you can do without a whole lot of communicating on your part! There are lots of ways to do this, and there is a good order in which to do it. As you work to get the word out, keep in mind this quote from *The Booktalker's Bible*: "If you're respectful of the time, mission and institutional culture of the folks involved, and if you're able to market yourself as an important addition to the educational process, you're set up for success in school booktalking" (2003, 136). You're also set up for success in just about any other way you might partner with your educational colleagues—booktalking and beyond!

Start at the Top

Start at the top. No, not the State Superintendent of Public Instruction, that's too far up! Go for the principals and other sorts of educational head honchos at the individual school level.

You might first introduce yourself on official letterhead. Some public librarians might advise you to make this level of contact in person, but I'm not convinced. I mean, how much time do you think an educational higher-up, with massive responsibilities, overworked and underpaid union-represented educators, a seething mass of adolescents to control and educate, and no budget to speak of, has to sit down with you just so you might introduce yourself? My opinion is very little time, indeed, and asking for some of it to introduce yourself in person when you might have sent a letter is not as sensitive as it could be. If you've got a school or an alternative educational group that's more casual and relaxed, by all means, make a personal contact. But if you have any suspicions that you're dealing with the other sort, send that letter instead.

Starting at the top is not a means of end-running your educational colleagues, it's simply a common courtesy. Principals and other muckymucks are accountable for all the goings-on in their organization; it never hurts to clue them in, and it might help. If they like the sound of you and believe your goals support theirs (which they do, they do!), you may get faster or even better buy-in down the line from their school librarians and educators, and those school librarians and educators may get the support they need from their leadership to work with you without any hardship.

You might think to start your letter with a bit about yourself, but think twice about that! No one, especially harried leadership types, want to wade through a lot of text to get to the reason why they're reading what you sent them. As important as you are, what you *want* is far more so. To them, that is. Start out with your name, your professional title, the library you work for, and then follow with a clear, concise statement of your reason for making contact.

A statement describing *why* this reason is important should follow. I would advise you to keep the content more professional than effusive. Think "administrator." Stay away from emotionally squishy statements, like "I truly love teenagers and just can't wait to bring tears to their eyes when I open their hearts and souls to the wonders of the books of the ages!" First of all, this is not in the least bit professional and your credibility will be in question, secondly, it doesn't really *say* anything, and thirdly, stay away from those exclamation points. They're just too familiar for this sort of letter. Give these administrators something professionally substantive to chew on for a moment, something that they can then swallow and digest with little disruption to their day.

How you intend to pursue your goal comes next. Again, be brief. You hope to visit school libraries and classrooms to share outstanding classics with teens. You might briefly mention several of the ways in which you can pursue this goal, such as sharing classics with teens in the classroom (yes, this is booktalking, but don't use that library lingo with these folks), brown-bag book discussion groups in the school's cafeteria at lunch periods, book discussions in the public library after school for classroom credit, or any number of reading activities that can connect teens and classics, some of which we talked about in Chapter 8.

You may follow with a *very* brief version of your educational and professional background, if you feel you must, but I don't recommend it. It increases the length of your letter, and it's just too easy to sound like you're a horn-tooting self-aggrandizer! You've already mentioned you're a librarian, after all, and that comes with its own clout in the educational world.

End with a statement indicating that you will be contacting their school librarians and/or educators within a given time frame, and that you are looking forward to establishing these relationships so you might all work together to benefit teens. This part is important, both because it closes the letter nicely and also because most people in leadership positions are trained to solve things, to decide things, to call the shots. You need to make it very clear that this is a courtesy letter, an

"FYI," and that *no action* is required of this person. Rather, you will be doing all the work.

Here's a sample letter to give you an idea of how you might get started:

Hello, Principal [or other administrative title] [name],

My name is [name], and I'm the [position/title] Librarian at the [library].

I write this letter to inform you that I hope to arrange visits through your school librarian and educators this year to introduce teens in the classroom to classics that will appeal to them, provide them with engaging and meaningful reading experiences, and contribute toward creating positive lifelong relationships with great literature.

In addition to providing teens with outstanding reading choices by renowned writers, classics can:

- help them develop an appreciation for quality
- challenge and expand their thinking
- introduce them to life experiences, dilemmas, and choices different from their own
- meaningfully engage them in history at large and in their own cultural identities
- lay a strong educational foundation for future academic or personal life learning

As well as visiting classrooms to talk about classics, other ideas for introducing teens to classics in your school might include:

- holding a regular classics discussion group or read-aloud program during lunchtimes or after school
- starting a teen classics reading incentive program in your school library
- bringing authors or dramatic presenters to your school to introduce teens to specific classic works in creative ways

Over the next two weeks, I will be contacting your [school librarian or appropriate educators] to explore these potential partnership opportunities between the public library and your school.

I thank you most sincerely for your time,
[signature]
[name]
[position/title]
[contact information]

Connect with Your Colleagues

Your next move is to contact those school librarians and/or educators. Do it within the time frame stated in your letter to "the top." This may seem like a small thing, but it's the first proof of your reliability. If the educational organization has a school librarian, contact him or her. This is solid professional protocol. If there is not a school librarian, go for the language arts instructors, or, if a small school of whatever sort, go for the "Renaissance" person or "Master of All Subjects" for each grade (usually 7th through 12th grades, but some schools may include the 6th grade).

You could initiate this contact in any number of ways. You might send a letter on library letterhead. You might consider sending an e-mail message, but the presentation isn't quite so nice. And, if you want to include some goodies, like booklists or public library brochures along with your introductory remarks, you can't do that successfully through e-mail. "Ah," you say, "But I can *attach* them!" Okay, so you've got electronic versions of your booklists and brochures, but you then place the burden of a successful download on your colleagues' shoulders, and you have no idea what level of technical savvy or equipment they possess. You might make phone calls, but getting to either school librarians or educators by phone is not easy. It can also be quite disruptive to them. You might drop by the school's library or central office to try to find your colleagues for an in-person introduction, but keep in mind that some folks think dropping by unannounced is rude. If not rude, it may just prove unfruitful. These folks can be hard to find.

Although it's not the only way to go, I've always liked to send a letter to start things off the very first time. I use professional letterhead, just like with the administrators, for that official look. I'm a bit less formal in my approach, and allow myself a little more room to say a thing or two, but basically the content is similar to what the school administrator received. I often include a small selection of booklists, library brochures, flyers on upcoming programs in the library—anything that might be both interesting for school librarians and educators to pass on to teens and useful for them to use with teens in the educational environment. I think these items show both my library's commitment to teens and my interest in sharing what I've got with my educational colleagues. I usually make a nice packet for them with a pocketed folder (nice and inexpensive and available just about anywhere) to hold all the pieces I'm sending, with introductory letter and business card up in front.

If you choose this method to get the ball rolling, let your contacts know that following this letter, you'll be checking in with them from time to time. This way you don't later seem like a Highly Annoying Person when you send out regular reminder messages through e-mail that you would like to visit classrooms to share classics with teens, that you would like to schedule a time to introduce yourself to faculty at a meeting to get direct educator buy-in, or that you want to offer a classics reader's theater program or classics trivia reading incentive program in their school library. You've let them know from the start that you are committed to the process of forming a mutually successful partnership with them to benefit teens.

How often should you drop a line to jog their memories? After initial contact, I check in about a month later, and thereafter every two to three months. This is likely to vary, dependent on all kinds of variables! Once you've established relationships, though, you'll find it easier to gauge when to connect and when to let well enough alone. You might also hitch a reminder note to multiple-copy packets of booklists, brochures, or a newsletter about something else they may find interesting or important from your public library.

With school librarians and educators in more traditional or structured environments, timing is of the essence with these sorts of communications. It's not a good idea to send a letter in late August or early September when the school year is just beginning. It's not a good idea to send one just before or after a major school break. It's not good to send one near midterms or finals. At these times, your colleagues have what I call Intensive Educational Exhaustion, which means lots of things, some of which should be obvious, but one of which means you aren't getting through to them. Think of this either as a profoundly singular focus that nothing unrelated can penetrate, or as a temporary sort of disassociative condition! Suffice it to say the sender-receiver feedback loop most likely isn't working.

Be careful not to come on too strong or go too far. I say this gently and encouragingly, but do not forget for even a moment that in the educational world, therefore by the grace of your colleagues go you! Use every scrap of social sensitivity and general mannerly behavior you possess to gain entry. Remember that your educational colleagues don't really owe you anything. Some just won't let you in. Others will be delighted to hear from you and will welcome you with open arms, but only once a year. Others will form real professional and personal relationships with you and regularly work in tandem to create great opportunities for you to reach teens with classic literature. Whatever the case may be, you will ever and always be a guest in their world. Be gracious, and don't make them think about filing restraining orders!

Show Them What You've Got

Okay, you've sent out those introductory letters, you've followed up with occasional e-mail messages, notes, or phone calls—whatever was appropriate to each school or educational environment. You haven't had any negative feedback, you may have had some positive feedback, but no concrete date for a classroom visit has been set. You are fidgety. You have yet to meet your destiny. You *could* shoot right down to the next section, where you will read that it can take a long time to create relationships with educational folk and you should never say die! Or, you *could* try to stir up more interest by showing them what you've got.

Now is a good time to get creative. Think about the ways you might more effectively attract positive attention from your educational colleagues. You've introduced yourself. You've followed up, which is a sure-fire way to let people know you are not just sending out letters because your supervisor or job classification required it of you, but because you are dead serious (in a happy-hearted way) about connecting their teens with outstanding classics. You've told them about yourself, and you've probably convinced them you mean business. Now, how about *showing* them what you've got and getting them excited to have you work with their teens?

If you've ever booked presenters or performers in your library, you know that some of the most charismatic, delightful performers have the worst portfolios or publicity sheets, and some of the slickest, glossiest presenters on paper are disjointed bores, muttering and shifting from foot to foot at podium when they advertised themselves as dynamic, stirring speakers.

It's as true today as it was in days of yore when the phrase was coined: the proof is in the pudding. So feed your educational colleagues some pudding! Ask for a personal visit with the school librarian, the "Renaissance" instructor, or "Master of All Subjects." Ask to visit a faculty meeting to introduce yourself to educators. You might even explore if these folks can all come together to your library for coffee and muffins some morning where you can wow them in your own meeting room.

Show these people your dedication to working with teens and your understanding of the value of classic literature in adolescent life; convince them of that value. Give a wonderful (but brief) booktalk of a classic that means a great deal to you and you think will mean a great deal to teens, and show them you know how to draw readers in. Leave them some wonderful annotated booklists.

A lip-smacking pudding doesn't have many ingredients, but they're all necessary and must be in correct measure (if you don't just buy those scary ones that hang in 3-packs without any refrigeration off racks in the grocery store and have a half-life of plus or minus 10,000 years). The same goes for attracting positive attention through presentation. You've got to pull a few, simple elements together in the right balance for a masterful delivery. Lots of media focus on presentation skills, so we won't delve too deeply into the topic here. If you feel you could benefit from this sort of thing, look up a few resources to boost your skills in this area and bolster your confidence. *The Booktalker's Bible* has an excellent section on marketing yourself and mastering presentation skills within a library context. You might want to start there.

When interacting with your peers, you should look good, you should sound good, you should be sensitive to any signals coming from your audience, and you absolutely must keep your presentation to the allotted time. Sounds like a tall order, but it can be done! It's all basic stuff, really. No dirty clothes, no hunching, no shuffling. No speaking so softly it's a strain to hear you, no speaking so loudly it's a pain to hear you, no speaking so rapidly a listener can't follow you. No looking at the floor. No droning on and on! You want to be clear, concise, entertaining, and persuasive. You want to demonstrate your passion for teens and for classic literature. Once you've received positive attention by *showing* them what you can do, you are far more likely to get that date with destiny and find yourself in the classroom environment sharing greats books with teens.

Come On, Make a Commitment!

I had an affirming experience a few years ago when, after much (unsuccessful, I thought) professional selling of myself over what seemed an endless time, and after much grumbling to myself and anyone else who would listen, I got a call to visit an 8th grade history classroom. The educator asked me to talk about outstanding war literature that represented both the reasons for and against violent conflict and the consequences of both aggression and pacifism. After my booktalks (and man, this was a tough one both to prepare for and to present), the educator approached me to thank me. When I responded, "I'd like to thank *you* for allowing me the time with your students," he shrugged and said, "Hey, you can come any time, the door's open. We are *all* teachers when it comes to these young people. They deserve to experience the attentions of as many people as possible who care about them and can show them tools for life."

All my letters to administrators, all my presentations to faculty, all my e-mailing back and forth with school librarians, all my drop-offs of booklists and brochures, all my newsletters about the public library and its services to teens, all my regular reminders of what I can offer educators and teens in the classroom, month in and month out—it was all worth it for that one remark.

This educator (I learned from a later conversation) is a Vietnam War veteran who experienced some rough times both during the Conflict and after, and is dedicated to giving his students any understanding he can about the course of history and the consequences of human conflict, through any means available. I was an available means, a link between great literature and his students, and he only knew I was out there because I'd make it patently clear that I was out there over a very long time! When the time was right for him and his students, he called on me. And, after liking what I did in his classroom, he's invited me back.

So, selling yourself isn't always easy, nor is it usually immediately gratifying. But never say die! Although it may not always seem like it, the commitment to this process *is* worth the time and effort. It will ultimately work in most cases to get you into the schools and other educational environments so you can connect with teens in the classroom. And once you're in, if you do your job well, you'll be called back time and time again and will enjoy a truly satisfying relationship with your educational community and, most importantly, will have opportunities galore to connect teens and great books.

KNOW YOUR AUDIENCE, THE WHOLE LOT OF THEM

Okay, so you're in! You've successfully sold yourself, stayed the course, and you've got a date to visit a classroom full of teens to talk about classics. The best way to make the best possible classics connections with teens once you're there is to prepare thoroughly. A very big part of that, and your starting point, is knowing your audience well—which includes the educators as well as the teens. Thoroughly understanding who's in your audience, their viewpoints, characteristics, expectations, and needs may seem like a lot to keep in mind, but doing so will contribute greatly to the success of your classics visit, and after time will become second nature.

The Teens

We've talked about teens as developing people and as readers in general in Chapter 4, and we've looked in detail at the diverse characteristics and qualities that make up teens as readers in Chapter 7. Those same characteristics that make up individuals can also dominate in classrooms and other group environments and go a long way toward defining your teen audience. With advanced knowledge of which of those characteristics are dominant, you will be far better prepared to bring the sorts of classics with which teens in that particular group or classroom can make meaningful reading connections.

You can, of course, begin to define your teen audience by looking at the type of school or educational program they're in. Will you be talking to teens in a traditional public educational environment or in a private school? Will you be talking to homeschoolers or teens in a parochial school? How about homeless teens in a social services educational program? This seems so rudimentary, and it really is, but it's important to note as your audience is in many ways a representative subset of this larger educational environment.

There are the obvious characteristics that define an educational environment, like age and grade, or if a religious school, shared beliefs. There are the educational systems' sorting of certain kinds of youth into particular groups, like the behaviorally challenged, educationally disadvantaged, or "highly capable" teens. There are characteristics external to the educational environment that can become concentrated in the classroom, including a majority of teens with similar ethnic or socioeconomic backgrounds, a shared rural/suburban/urban living environment, and so forth. When you know which of these characteristics, or combination of them, are present in the group you are visiting, you will have greater success selecting appropriate classics.

Since we're doing some lumping of our own here and probably making some sweeping generalizations, let's balance this out and say it's equally important to keep in mind that a teen audience is comprised of unique individuals. You might, for example, know you are going to share classics with a small group of 7th grade-level homeschoolers, but you may not think to bring books that span a 5th through 9th grade reading level for the wide range of challenged and exceptional readers in the group. Or, you might visit a group of young incarcerated males but don't consider that, against the common stereotype, many of them are bright minds and accomplished readers who crave challenge and intellectual engagement more than just about anything. Not knowing, you brought the thin, quick, high-interest classics when many of these teens are ready for Ayn Rand's *Atlas Shrugged* and Gabriel García Márquez's *One Hundred Years of Solitude*!

The Educators

Now, on to the educators. There are school librarians, educators, home-school instructors. You might even toss in an administrator or two. I've had a number of them (usually from sheer curiosity, although I have wondered on occasion if a plot was afoot) sit in on my classroom visits. You might get parents, too, especially with the homeschoolers. These folks are both your hosts and a part of your audience. Getting on the same page with them regarding your classics visit is essential.

First, you should become familiar with the educational goals of your hosting school or educational organization. You can gain a great deal of understanding from the documents that define and bind an educational environment. These might include local learning standards, literature curriculum, educational charters, and so forth. Second, you should make direct contact with your educational colleagues to find out how literature is taught and thought about in their organization.

Educators' Goals Regarding the Classics

You can and should familiarize yourself with the goals educators have (or not) in connecting teens to classic literature. With an understanding of the educational views on classics instruction, its challenges, and its dissenting voices, you are better prepared to be a successful player among the community of adults who make literary connections with teens.

What value does your local school or alternative educational environment place on the classics? Are your local educators required to teach, or are they being prevented from teaching, the classics? You should understand how (or if) classics fit into the educational curriculum for each grade you work with at each school or alternative educational environment you serve.

How can you discover what you need to know? Ask local school librarians "in the know," ask educators, even ask administrators. Check state and local educational agency Web sites. Check the Web sites of individual schools. Request copies of current literature curricula, local learning standards, charter documents, and read them. Why? So you can be a more informed partner (or inspirational lone wolf, as the case may be!) in connecting teens to classics.

All in all, advanced knowledge of educational goals and issues will prepare you to woo and wow and to avoid tender spots in any educational setting.

Educators' Individual Views on the Classics

By knowing the individual views of your educational colleagues regarding classic literature, you will be able to use greater sensitivity when making classics selections to share with their teens. You will be better able to tie in to proclassics educators' goals for their teens, and will be better armed to promote the cause with ambivalent educators (not uncommon) or defend the cause with anticlassics educators (rare, but out there!), if necessary. You will also be better equipped to head off any possible disaster, like an educator who introduces you to the class with a remark about how little he or she values what you are there to share!

Ask your educators a few tactful questions to find out with whom you'll be interacting and how they feel about classics and your visit to their classroom or group. You might consider designing a survey for your service area school librarians and educators to collect the information you're seeking.

To start, here are some of the things you might like to know.

Are your educators *for* the classics? Do they:

- Value classics and believe they play a critical role in the institutional and personal educational process?
- Encourage teens to pursue their classics reading beyond the classroom?
- Value classics, but feel teens can only have successful experiences with classics in the classroom where they can be guided and the texts can be discussed?

Are your educators *against* the classics? Do they:

- Believe the classics are dry, dusty tomes all teens will instantly reject with a sneer, and therefore do not teach them or encourage their reading?
- Feel the study and reading of classics is an elitist tradition that cannot possibly produce any resonance or meaning with the teens in their school now?
- Think today's teens just don't have the educational capacity or emotional and social maturity to pursue the classics?

Are your educators *ambivalent* to the classics? Do they:

- Feel indifferent to classic literature, not caring one way or the other?
- Allow you into their classroom to talk about classics, but don't offer any real support or encourage their teens to pay close attention to your classics book-talks?

Are your educators *concerned about the content* of the classics? Do they:

- Have a belief system in their alternative educational environment that precludes the promotion of classics containing certain objectionable (to them) content or expressions?
- Want to avoid the promotion of challenged or banned classics, or classics with controversial content in general, in the classroom?

You will probably experience each point of view, each extreme, and the indifferent middle, both in schools and with alternative educational groups during your career as a teen services librarian. It will be of immense value to you to understand what the educators in your community value—or don't—regarding classic literature and its promotion to teens in their educational environments.

Will you be working with an educator who loves classic literature, wants teens to experience the wonders of reading great books, and welcomes you to his or her classroom to connect teens with these books? Excellent. You've got something to look forward to! Will you be working with an educator who has reservations about teens succeeding with classics outside the classroom? Will you be working with an educator who feels classics are dry and unappealing or elitist and of no interest or relevance to the teens in his or her community? In both cases, the books you bring to share with teens for your classroom visit can demonstrate the superb qualities of classic stories, their accessibility to teens, and when selected with care, remove concerns about relevance.

How about that educator who just doesn't give a hoot one way or the other? Well, you might not get a lot of support, but you are unlikely to be sabotaged, either! You can focus on the teens in this educator's classroom and give your all to making meaningful connections between them and the classics you've brought to share with them.

As for those educators who have belief systems not in sync with certain kinds of content, you can (and should) avoid bringing classics to their teens of the sort that concerns them and select and promote classics that they can feel open to and positive about. For those educators who are concerned about controversial classics in general, knowing the titles or particular types of content that pose difficulty will help you make more appropriate selections for their teens. Regarding this issue, revisit the section on banned and challenged classics in Chapter 5.

Popular Young Adult Literature v. Classics in the Classroom

The lines have been drawn and the battle engaged! Although definitely an educator's issue revolving around standard canonical classics titles, it wouldn't hurt you to know about the debate between young adult literature and classics. Forewarned is forearmed, and it could prove useful to have a passing familiarity with this when pursuing school connections with the goal of promoting classic literature.

There are those who say teens should *not* be taught classics—teens just aren't ready for them. Classics:

- Are too difficult and this creates a frustrating reading experience
- Are of no interest or relevance to them whatsoever
- Are elitist
- Don't reflect the myriad cultural realities of the teens in our nation's schools
- Are traditionally taught in a tedious and closed fashion that tortures teens (hey, that's six words that begin with the letter "t")
- Create a disgust of literary works in adolescence that persists for the life of the reader

Instead, teens should be taught current young adult literature—it's great stuff. Young adult literature:

- Has many of the same elements (at least in a skeletal sort of way) as classic literature
- Is sure to engage teens
- Is current, contemporary, hip
- Is about things teens can immediately identify with and grasp
- Will create lifelong readers who can then transition to classic literature at some later date if they so choose (and they will be more inclined in this direction if not put off the classics in youth)

There are those who say teens *should* be taught the classics, for all the reasons we've already explored in Chapter 1 and more. Teens:

- Are being grossly underestimated
- Will never be more ready than in the first stages of adulthood
- Actually do find great meaning in these books
- Can be taught the classics in a fashion that brings their value and meaning home to them

And, there are those who say teens should be taught *both* young adult literature and the classics—educators should take advantage of the immediate interest young adult literature has for teens and make bridges from it to classic literature. In my opinion, the best of both worlds!

Want to know more? Here are a few resources (some go a bit beyond the secondary classroom, but are illuminating nonetheless) to give you the idea:

The Nay Sayers

Bland, Guy. 2001. "Out with the Old, in with the (Not So) New." *English Journal* 90 (3): 20–22.

Bland begins his article with, "I've just finished another article on how to motivate students to read the classics, and I must say I'm bothered by the stubborn assumption that students should be reading the classics in the first place," and proceeds to defend his statement throughout its course.

Bushman, John H. 1997. "Young Adult Literature in the Classroom—Or Is It?" *English Journal* 86 (3): 35–40.

Although his survey of 380 students in grades 6 through 12 does not seem to support his conclusion, Bushman argues that classics turn off teens and young adult literature is more appropriate classroom reading.

Gallo, Donald R. 2001. "How Classics Create an Alliterate Society." *English Journal* 90 (3): 33–39.

Gallo believes classics as taught in the early and teenage years are creating an "alliterate society," a generation of teens who've been forced to read "literary works that most of them dislike so much that they have no desire whatsoever to continue those experiences into adulthood." Rather, educators should encourage popular reading as an act of entertainment, not classic literature as an educational chore.

The Yea Sayers

Grayling, A. C. 2001. "The Age of Ignorance: Benefits of a Classical Education." *New Statesman* 130 (4548): 28ff.

Grayling asserts that without an understanding of our classical origins (Greece and Rome), we cannot truly understand and value a modern world built on and shaped by these ancient civilizations.

Jago, Carol. 2000. *With Rigor for All: Teaching the Classics to Contemporary Students.* Foreword by James Strickland. Portland, ME: Calendar Islands Publishers.

Jago's book is a highly readable, moving look at the educational values of a dedicated and experienced secondary school literature teacher and her methods for meaningfully connecting teens from all walks of life to the classics.

Lefkowitz, Mary. 1999. "2,800 Years Old and Still Relevant (Appreciation of the Classics)." *New York Times*, 21 August: A23(N), A13(L).

This professor of classical studies at Wellesley asserts in this brief article how the literary "old standbys" like Homer's *The Odyssey* are timeless and ever relevant, and worth reading, rereading, and teaching to all generations.

Sommers, Christina Hoff. 1998. "Are We Living in a Moral Stone Age? Teaching the Literary Classics." Transcript. *Vital Speeches* 64 (15): 475–478.

Without being exposed to the ideas found in the great books, Sommers laments that youth "have been thrown back into a moral Stone Age" in which they remain "totally unaffected by thousands of years of moral experience and moral progress."

Thompson, Michael Clay. 1990. *Classics in the Classroom.* Monroe, NY: Trillium Press.

In this short treatise that packs a punch from a highly quotable literature teacher with over twenty years' experience, Thompson persuasively argues that classics should be a focal point of education from childhood onward, and describes the many personal and societal benefits therein. The book includes lengthy suggested reading lists.

The All-Inclusives

Crowe, Chris. 2000. "Using YA Books to Teach Students to Love What We Love." *English Journal* 89 (6): 138–141

This beautifully written article appeals to educators to teach young people a love of reading before teaching great literature and expecting them to appreciate it, and suggests that the love of reading can be fostered through high-appeal young adult literature.

Herz, Sarah K., with Donald R. Gallo. 1996. *From Hinton to Hamlet: Building Bridges between Young Adult Literature and the Classics.* Westport, CT: Greenwood Press.

Herz builds a strong case for using contemporary young adult literature to help students meaningfully engage in the reading and evaluation process, in discussion with peers and adults, and in successfully making the leap to classic literature.

Kaywell, Joan F., ed. 1993–2000. *Adolescent Literature as a Complement to the Classics*. 4 vols. Norwood, MA: Christopher-Gordon Publishers.

Written for middle/high school English educators, this practical book series provides links between young adult literature and commonly-taught classics, pairing texts by themes or issues, including turbulent historical time periods, dogs and their masters, immigration and culture clash, isolation, identity, Celtic mythology, decision making, and more.

SUMMING IT UP

As a public librarian, to successfully promote the classics in schools and community organizations, you first have to successfully promote yourself. By contacting the right people in the right way, building their confidence in you and their enthusiasm for the classics, and by sticking with it, you will make your way into classrooms and other educational environments to share the classics with teens. Your greatest success once there will come from knowing the characteristics of your audience in advance, and that includes your educational colleagues as well as the teens themselves. Learn not only which characteristics dominate in a classroom or group of teens, but learn your educators' goals and attitudes toward the classics so you can be best prepared to positively and effectively share the classics with young people in their environment, that is, "take your show on the road."

WORKS CITED

Langemack, Chapple. 2003. *The Booktalker's Bible: How to Talk about the Books You Love to Any Audience*. Westport, CT: Libraries Unlimited.

APPENDIX A

AN ANNOTATED LIST OF FREE, FULL-TEXT CLASSICS ONLINE

Many full-text classic works, especially those in the public domain, are available on the Internet free of charge. Access may require a download (compressed or PDF files or handheld devices formats), or might be immediately readable on screen in your Internet browser. The visual look of online classics varies from ASCII texts, to graphically slick PDF versions, to facsimile copies of original works or famous editions.

The majority of the free-text Web sites provide information about their organization and its mission, instructions for accessing the text you want, information about copyright restrictions (if any), disclaimers regarding accuracy of text entry if appropriate (many sites rely on volunteers to enter and upload these texts), and information about where the text originally came from (any particular edition of the book or any other site that hosts the full-text copy). As with any Web site, some online book sites are well designed and easy to use, and others are a greater challenge to navigate. Although there are innumerable sites that have one or two full-text classics available, I've only included sites here that offer a larger selection of classic authors and titles, or multiple works by a prolific author.

4Literature

http://www.4literature.net/

In addition to over 2,000 online classics (books, short stories, poetry, dramatic works, historical materials), *4Literature* offers online discussion forums about these full-text works and other writing, including personal writing, if submitted.

Absolute Shakespeare

http://absoluteshakespeare.com

The title says it all. This site offers links to all things Shakespeare—plays, sonnets, pictures, facts, biographical information, a look at the authorship debate, poems, quotes, information about the Globe Theatre, films, a bibliography, and a timeline.

> *Shakespeare's Plays*
>
> http://absoluteshakespeare.com/plays/plays.htm
>
> *Shakespeare's Sonnets*
>
> http://absoluteshakespeare.com/sonnets/sonnets.htm

Access the Great Books

http://www.anova.org/

The Access Foundation and Britannica Online provide access to more than 240 classics authors and their works, with an emphasis on works of philosophy and science and excluding most works of poetry. The site bills itself as the "most extensive site for finding original online texts." The list of works is arranged in chronological order, then by authors' years of birth.

The Alex Catalogue of Electronic Texts

http://www.infomotions.com/alex/

This site contains classics texts from American literature, English literature, and Western philosophy. A unique feature allows word searching for titles and authors, as well as searching the full content of the works themselves by word. Additionally, multiple texts can be searched simultaneously for the incidence of words and themes across literary works.

Bartleby.com: Great Books Online

http://www.bartleby.com

"The preeminent Internet publisher of literature, reference and verse providing students, researchers and the intellectually curious with unlimited access to books and information on the Web, free of charge" (quoted from home page at http://www.bartleby.com/). All classic works are readable by chapter, section or line and are searchable by key word. Bartleby.com offers extensive works of fiction (http://www.bartleby.com/fiction/), nonfiction (http://www.bartleby.com/nonfiction/), and verse (http://www.bartleby.com/verse/).

Bibliomania

http://www.bibliomania.com/bibliomania-static/index.html

This multiple award-winning site features over 2,000 free classic texts, significant nonfiction works, and online resources. Texts are selected by literature professors at Harvard, Princeton, Yale, and Oxford universities. Although most titles are public domain, Bibliomania has copyright on some nonpublic domain titles that are made available for personal use in HTML format.

Bootlegbooks.com
http://www.bootlegbooks.com/
    Twenty-eight authors of classic fiction, eighteen authors of classic nonfiction (with works arranged in five subject categories), a near complete collection of Shakespeare's works, a small handful of the works of classic poets and poetry anthologies, and three reference works, are available at this site.

Classic Bookshelf
http://www.classicbookshelf.com/
    The classic works of over fifty authors can be custom-formatted (text color, font and font size, margins) for reading online. Readers with e-mail accounts can "bookmark" text to pick up at a particular point in a future reading session.

Classic Reader
http://www.classicreader.com/
    This site features 818 classic books and 1,111 classic short stories by 214 authors. Registration is required to use the site, but requires no fees or personal information.

Classics for Young People
http://www.ucalgary.ca/~dkbrown/storclas.html
    The Children's Literature Web site hosted by the Doucette Library of Teaching Resources at the University of Calgary, provides links to numerous well-known classics for children and teens in HTML format.

The Classics in ASCII
http://www.textfiles.com/etext/
    An extensive list of classics, all in ASCII text, are arranged in five broad categories: authors, modern works, fiction, nonfiction, and reference. The site provides links to works at other online classics sites.

The Complete Works of William Shakespeare
http://the-tech.mit.edu/Shakespeare/works.html
    Created by MIT alumnus Jeremy Hylton and hosted by *The Tech*, a well-known and established MIT newspaper, this site provides the near-complete works of William Shakespeare in HTML using the Complete Moby™ Shakespeare server.

The Electronic Literature Foundation
http://elf.chaoscafe.com/elf_by_Author.htm
    Founded and maintained by a husband-and-wife team, the Electronic Literature Foundation (ELF) provides electronic texts from world literature with forums for online discussion. The site currently has over one hundred books available.

Ever the Twain Shall Meet: Mark Twain on the Internet

http://users.telerama.com/~joseph/mtwain.html

Numerous full-text works by the great humorist, Mark Twain, are provided at this site, both in HTML and as downloadable zip files. The site also provides links to general information on the author.

Great Books and Classics: "Your Gateway to the Great Books Online"

http://www.grtbooks.com/

Eastern and Western fiction and nonfiction classics from 200 B.C. forward are accessible chronologically and by author. The site provides links to free online texts in multiple formats and directs the user to the same texts in more traditional, purchasable formats.

Great Books Index: List of Authors and Titles

http://books.mirror.org/gb.titles.html

Although not associated with Encyclopaedia Britannica of the Great Books of the Western World list (GBWW), this site is inspired by the same people who created the GBWW—Robert Hutchins and Mortimer Adler. This site provides links to full-text versions of the major and minor works of well-known classics authors and notes the formats in which the texts are available.

Hypertexts

http://xroads.virginia.edu/~HYPER/hypertex.html

Sixty-three fiction and nonfiction classics representing American history and the American experience are made available in full-text from the American Studies Departments at the University of Virginia.

The Internet Classics Archive

http://classics.mit.edu/index.html

Created at MIT, this site lists 441 works of Greco-Roman classical literature by 59 different authors, as well as a small selection of classical Chinese and Persian works in English translation.

The Literature Page

http://www.literaturepage.com

From the creators of the Quotation Page comes the Literature Page, with 192 works—novels, short stories, poetic works, dramatic works, essays, and speeches—by 78 authors. The site is browsable by type, category or author, and has author, title, and category indexes, as well as a general searching feature.

Litrix Reading Room

http://www.litrix.com/

Book-lover Stan Jones created this site as a labor of love to provide readers with full-text classics in the public domain with the help of a Internet text researcher and encoder, and with special acknowledgment to the Gutenberg Project.

The Modern English Collection

http://etext.lib.virginia.edu/modeng/modeng0.browse.html

Browsable by authors' last names or by area of interest, this collection from the Electronic Text Center at the University of Virginia Library "contains fiction, nonfiction, poetry, drama, letters, newspapers, manuscripts and illustrations from 1500 to the present" (quoted from http://etext.lib.virginia.edu/modeng/modeng0.browse.html). Thousands of texts are coded in SGML and readable online.

The Online Books Page

http://onlinebooks.library.upenn.edu/

Founded and edited by John Mark Ockerbloom, digital library planner and researcher at the University of Pennsylvania, this site provides an extensive list of free online books, accessible by author, title, and subject. The site has a special online exhibit about banned books and censorship attempts at http://digital.library.upenn.edu/books/banned-books.html.

An Online Library of Literature

http://www.literature.org/

Multiple full-text classics by thirty authors are provided at this simply arranged, easy-to-read site.

The Online Medieval and Classical Library

http://sunsite.berkeley.edu/OMACL/

This collection, headed by Douglas B. Killings, contains significant literary works from classical and medieval times and is searchable by keyword or browsable by title, author, genre, or language. Files can be read online or downloaded as zip files.

Oxford Text Archive

http://ota.ahds.ac.uk/

Founded in 1976 by Lou Burnard, the Oxford Text Archive contains thousands of electronic texts in numerous languages, with several searching options and file types.

Page by Page Books

http://www.pagebypagebooks.com/

Page by Page Books provides hundreds of public domain books, especially classic texts, with a unique bookmarking feature to find a place in the text again for a continuing reading session. Some HTML books are included that Page By Page Books has copyright to, and readers may access them for personal use only.

The Perseus Digital Library

http://www.perseus.tufts.edu/

The Perseus Digital Library in the Department of the Classics, Tufts University, is a long-term, massive undertaking resulting in extensive collections of easily accessible online texts and resources from and about the Archaic, Classical Greek, Latin, and Renaissance worlds.

Project Gutenberg
http://gutenberg.net/
   Project Gutenberg was started in 1971 by Michael Hart who "decided that it would be a really good idea if lots of famous and important texts were freely available to everyone in the world." As of 2002, the Project's Web site hosted 6,267 downloadable electronic books of public domain classics.

PSU's Electronic Classics Site
http://www2.hn.psu.edu/faculty/jmanis/jimspdf.htm
   Although an unattractive and cluttered site hosted by faculty member Jim Manis and Penn State University, numerous full-text works by more than 120 authors of English literature are available in an attractive, easy-to-read PDF format.

Publicly Available HTI (Humanities Text Initiative) Modern English Collection
http://www.hti.umich.edu/p/pd-modeng/bibl.html
   The University of Michigan's Humanities Text Initiative is a unit of their Digital Library Production Service and provides this collection of free classics online, arranged by author. The texts are from other Web sites, including the Oxford Text Archive, Project Gutenberg, the Online Book Initiative, and individuals who have volunteered to code books for reading online.

The World eBook Library
http://netlibrary.net/WorldHome.html
   The World eBook Library Foundation provides a slightly different interface for searching the full-text book database created and maintained by the Online Books Page, noted above.

APPENDIX B

AN ANNOTATED LIST OF RESOURCES ABOUT CLASSICS AND THE CANON

We explored in Chapter 1 what classics have to offer to teens, as well as the many definitions of a classic and what those definitions have in common. The selected resources below provide further opportunity for exploring the nature and meaning of classics, and the controversies surrounding the literary canon. Some of these resources are pretty heady stuff but worth at least a dip into sections and chapters that interest you, and some are brief pieces with unique points of view. In addition to the resources listed at the ends of Chapters 2 and 7, the resources here may also include lists of classics to help you make your own reading selections.

Bloom, Harold. 2000. *How to Read and Why*. New York: Scribner.
    Bloom examines multiple works, all considered to be classics, of nine short story authors, fifteen novelists, three dramatists, and fifteen poets.

Bloom, Harold. 1994. *The Western Canon: The Books and School of the Ages*. New York: Riverhead Books.
    An intellectually challenging first chapter, "Elegy for the Canon," is followed by livelier discussions of authors Bloom believes unarguably comprise the literary canon.

Calvino, Italo. 1986. "Why Read the Classics?" *New York Review of Books* 9 October: 19–20.

———. 1999. *Why Read the Classics?* Translated from the Italian by Martin McLaughlin. New York: Pantheon Books.

   The introduction to the book offers a new translation of Calvino's list of fourteen reasons to read the classics as originally translated to English in the 1986 *New York Review of Books* article. The remainder of the book is a posthumous collection of Calvino's critical essays on great authors and works throughout time.

Casement, William. 1996. "Some Myths about the Great Books." *The Midwest Quarterly* 36 (2): 203–218.

   Casement discusses the current trend to discredit the great books or literary canon for elitism, poor ethnic representation, poor gender representation, and more. He matter-of-factly addresses each "myth," or negative view concerning the canon.

Delbanco, Andrew. 1997. *Required Reading: Why Our American Classics Matter Now.* New York: Farrar, Straus and Giroux.

   The author examines a small group of American writers, from the pre–Civil War years to the dawn of WWII, that he feels most represent and celebrate their rights as members a free democracy.

Downs, Robert Bingham. 1983. *Books That Changed the World.* New York: New American Library.

   Focusing on nonfiction works of science and philosophy, Downs discusses the printed works he believes have exerted the greatest influence over humankind throughout history.

Gillespie, Tim. 1994. "Why Literature Matters." *English Journal* 83 (3): 16–21.

   In an eloquent, moving response to pragmatic teachers who don't understand why students need literature to become productive and competitive workers in modern society, Gillespie discusses why literature matters and why its central role in the high school English curriculum is necessary.

The Great Conversation: A Reader's Guide to Great Books of the Western World. 2nd ed. 1991. Philip W. Goetz, Editor in Chief. Chicago: Encyclopaedia Britannica, Inc.

   This title serves as a reader's guide to Britannica's *Great Books of the Western World* set, but also stands alone as an entry point into the world of literature. The book includes visually engaging author and great book timelines, an author-to-author index that shows how authors refer to and use the ideas of preceding authors throughout time, an author-to-idea index, essays on literature, a ten-year reading plan, and more.

Greenbaum, Vicky. 1994. "Expanding the Canon: Shaping Inclusive Reading Lists." *English Journal* 83 (8): 36–39.

   Greenbaum discusses why it is critically important to create a multicultural canon for both public and private school curricula, and asserts that there is no lack of masterful works by "non-male, non-white, non-heterosexual voices" to draw from.

Lefkowitz, Mary. 1999. "2,800 Years Old and Still Relevant (Appreciation of the Classics)." *New York Times* 21 August: A23(N), A13(L).

This professor of classical studies at Wellesley asserts in this brief article how the literary "old standbys" like Homer's *The Odyssey* are timeless and ever relevant, and worth reading, rereading, and teaching to all generations.

Meyer, Bruce. 2000. *The Golden Thread: A Reader's Journey through the Great Books.* Toronto: HarperFlamingo Canada.

Each chapter provides an in-depth examination of a great work that has played or is still playing a part in defining who we are today, including the Bible, Homer's *Odyssey*, Saint Augustine's *Confessions*, Shakespeare's *King Lear*, and Shelley's *Frankenstein*.

Mooney, Bell. 1999. "Tempt the Young to Read the Best of the Old." *Times Educational Supplement*, 30 July.

London columnist Mooney discusses the new curriculum that allows teachers to make their own choices for classroom reading, and promotes the value of the compulsory great books reading lists used in the past.

APPENDIX C

MORE CLASSICS LISTS, FICTION AND NONFICTION

In your ongoing search for classics of all kinds to connect to readers of all kinds, this appendix contains an eclectic mix of short classics lists to meet special interests, divided into fiction and nonfiction categories. The date or dates following each work are original publication dates in the work's original language, or note the era in which older works were written.

For those young women (or young men, but maybe not so many!) who want to read novels written by women and about women's lives and issues, there are two lists of classic novels provided here—one of time-tested works and one of highly lauded contemporary classics. To help you find great classic fiction to share with teens that addresses their and others' ethnic experience, two lists are provided—one that represents the American ethnic experience, and one the world ethnic experience. The first list is arranged by ethnicity, the second by geographical region. For those teens who are either assigned to read about our world's wars (common in secondary education) or prefer to read about our world's wars (common with teen males in both middle and high school), you'll find a list of classics war novels, arranged chronologically by war. For those teens who enjoy learning about the lives and times of real people, the classic biography, autobiography, and memoir classics starter list will come

in handy. As promised in Chapter 5, there are two additional lists of classic poems to be found here for verse-inclined teens—one of narrative or
epic poems from many of the world's cultures, and the other of time-
tested shorter pieces ranging across time from the 700s through the 1900s.
And, for teens who prefer the truth to fiction, which indeed can be
stranger, you'll find a series of nonfiction classics starter lists in major subject areas from the hard sciences to history, from the natural world to the
social sciences.

Of the wide and wonderful world of classic literature—fiction and nonfiction, time-tested and contemporary—these lists only begin to scratch
the surface of what's out there both to enjoy as a reader yourself and to
meaningfully share with teens. Make use of all the resources and lists
noted throughout this book, and dig deeper than what you find here, to
connect just the right classics with just the right teens.

FICTION

Classic Novels By and About Women

Women's Fiction Classics from the 1800s and Early 1900s

The Age of Innocence, Edith Wharton (1920)

The Awakening, Kate Chopin (1899)

Jane Eyre, Charlotte Brontë (1847)

Kristin Lavransdatter trilogy: The Bridal Wreath, The Mistress of Husaby, The Cross,
     Sigrid Undset (1920–1922)

Middlemarch, George Eliot (1871–1872)

O Pioneers!, Willa Cather (1913)

Pride and Prejudice, Jane Austen (1813)

Rebecca, Daphne du Maurier (1938)

Their Eyes Were Watching God, Zora Neale Hurston (1937)

The Yellow Wallpaper, and Other Writings, Charlotte Perkins Gilman (1899)

Contemporary Women's Fiction Classics

The Bean Trees, Barbara Kingsolver (1988)

The Bell Jar, Sylvia Plath (1963)

Beloved, Toni Morrison (1987)

The Dressmaker, Beryl Bainbridge (1973)

The Color Purple, Alice Walker (1982)

The Dollmaker, Harriet Louisa Simpson Arnow (1954)

Fried Green Tomatoes at the Whistle Stop Café, Fannie Flagg (1987)

The Joy Luck Club, Amy Tan (1989)

Like Water for Chocolate, Laura Esquivel (1989)

Wide Sargasso Sea, Jean Rhys (1966)

The American Ethnic Experience in Classic Novels

African America

The Autobiography of Miss Jane Pittman, Ernest J. Gaines (1971)

Beloved, Toni Morrison (1987)

Cane, Jean Toomer (1923)

Go Tell It on the Mountain, James Baldwin (1953)

Invisible Man, Ralph Ellison (1952)

Middle Passage, Charles Johnson (1990)

Native Son, Richard Wright (1940)

Their Eyes Were Watching God, Zora Neale Hurston (1937)

Uncle Tom's Cabin, Harriet Beecher Stowe (1852)

The Women of Brewster Place, Gloria Naylor (1982)

Asian America

The Joy Luck Club, Amy Tan (1989)

The Middleman and Other Stories, Bharati Mukherjee (1988)

Hispanic America

Bless Me, Ultima, Rudolfo Anaya (1972)

The House on Mango Street, Sandra Cisneros (1984)

The Milagro Beanfield War, John Nichols (1974)

Jewish America

The Chosen, Chaim Potok (1967)

Summer of My German Soldier, Bette Greene (1973)

Native America

Ceremony, Leslie Marmon Silko (1977)

Fools Crow, James Welch (1986)

House Made of Dawn, N. Scott Momaday (1968)

Laughing Boy, Oliver La Farge (1929)

Love Medicine, Louise Erdrich (1984)

A Yellow Raft in Blue Water, Michael Dorris (1987)

The World Ethnic Experience in Classic Novels

Africa

Burger's Daughter, Nadine Gordimer (1979)

Cry, the Beloved Country, Alan Paton (1948)

A Bend in the River, V.S. Naipaul (1979)

Things Fall Apart, Chinua Achebe (1958)

Asia

The Good Earth, Pearl S. Buck (1931)

Nectar in a Sieve, Kamala Markandaya (1954)

The Sound of Waves, Yukio Mishima (1954)

The Tale of the Genji, Murasaki Shikibu (11th century)

The Woman in the Dunes, Kobo Abe (1962)

The Caribbean

Annie John, Jamaica Kincaid (1985)

A House for Mr. Biswas, V.S. Naipaul (1961)

Europe

Czechoslovakia (Former)

Closely Watched Trains, Bohumil Hrabal (1965)

The Metamorphosis, Franz Kafka (1915)

The Unbearable Lightness of Being, Milan Kundera (1984)

France

Candide, Voltaire (1759)

The Count of Monte Cristo, Alexandre Dumas (1844)

Germinal, Émile Zola (1885)

The Hunchback of Notre Dame, Victor Hugo (1831)

Madame Bovary, Gustave Flaubert (1857)

Père Goriot, Honoré de Balzac (1835)

The Phantom of the Opera, Gaston Leroux (1910)

The Red and the Black, Stendhal (1830)

A Tale of Two Cities, Charles Dickens (1859)

Germany

All Quiet on the Western Front, Erich Maria Remarque (1929)

Demian, Hermann Hesse (1919)

Divided Heaven, Christa Wolf (1963)

The Magic Mountain, Thomas Mann (1924)

The Sorrows of Young Werther, Johann Wolfgang von Goethe (1774)

The Tin Drum, Günter Grass (1959)

The Train Was on Time, Heinrich Böll (1949)

Greece

Zorba the Greek, Nikos Kazantzakis (1946)

Italy

The Leopard, Giuseppi di Lampedusa (1958)

The Name of the Rose, Umberto Eco (1980)

Bread and Wine, Ignazio Silone (1936)

The Decameron, Giovanni Boccaccio (1353)

The Jewish Experience in Europe

The Collected Stories of Isaac Bashevis Singer, Isaac Bashevis Singer (1983)

Night, Elie Wiesel (1956)

Schindler's List, Thomas Keneally (1982)

Norway

Growth of the Soil, Knut Hamsun (1917)

Hunger, Knut Hamsun (1890)

Kristin Lavransdatter trilogy: The Bridal Wreath, The Mistress of Husaby, The Cross, Sigrid Undset (1920–1922)

Poland

The Painted Bird, Jerzy Kosinski (1965)

Spain

Don Quixote, Miguel de Cervantes (1605–1615)

Mexico, Central America and South America

The House of the Spirits, Isabel Allende (1982)

Like Water for Chocolate, Laura Esquivel (1989)

Men of Maize, Miguel Angel Asturias (1949)

The Old Gringo, Carlos Fuentes (1985)

One Hundred Years of Solitude, Gabriel García Márquez (1967)

The Violent Land, Jorge Amado (1945)

The Middle East

The Arabian Nights, Anonymous (15th century)

The Blind Owl, Sadegh Hedayat (1936)

The Cairo trilogy: Palace Walk, Palace of Desire, Sugar Street, Najib Mahfuz (1956–1957)

The Open Door, Latifa Al-Zayyat (1960)

Russia

Anna Karenina, Leo Tolstoy (1875)

The Brothers Karamazov, Fyodor Dostoyevsky (1880)

Dead Souls, Nikolai Vasilyevich Gogol (1842)

Doctor Zhivago, Boris Pasternak (1958)

Eugene Onegin, Alexander Pushkin (1833)

Fathers and Sons, Ivan Turgenev (1862)

Live and Remember, Valentin Rasputin (1975)

One Day in the Life of Ivan Denisovich, Aleksandr Isaevich Solzhenitsyn (1962)

And Quiet Flows the Don, Mikhail A. Sholokhov (1940)

We The Living, Ayn Rand (1936)

War Fiction Classics

The French-Indian War (1755–1763)

The Last of the Mohicans, James Fenimore Cooper (1826)

The American Revolutionary War (1775–1783)

Johnny Tremain, Esther Forbes (1943)
My Brother Sam Is Dead, James Lincoln Collier (1974)

The French Revolution (1789–1799)

The Scarlet Pimpernel, Baroness Emmuska Orczy (1905)
A Tale of Two Cities, Charles Dickens (1859)

The Napoleonic Wars (1800–1815)

The Horatio Hornblower series, C.S. Forester (1937–1967)
War and Peace, Leo Tolstoy (1865–1869)

The American Civil War (1861–1865)

Across Five Aprils, Irene Hunt (1964)
Andersonville, MacKinlay Kantor (1955)
April Morning, Howard Fast (1961)
Band of Angels, Robert Penn Warren (1955)
The Civil War Short Stories of Ambrose Bierce, Ambrose Bierce (1988 collected)
Gone with the Wind, Margaret Mitchell (1936)
The Killer Angels, Michael Shaara (1974)
Manassas, Upton Sinclair (1904)
Miss Ravenel's Conversion from Secession to Loyalty, John William De Forest (1867)
The Red Badge of Courage, Stephen Crane (1895)
Rifles for Watie, Harold Keith (1957)
The Unvanquished, William Faulkner (1938)

World War I (1914–1918)

The General, C.S. Forester (1936)
Johnny Got His Gun, Dalton Trumbo (1939)
A Son at the Front, Edith Wharton (1923)

All Quiet on the Western Front, Erich Maria Remarque (1929)

A Farewell to Arms, Ernest Hemingway (1929)

The Russian Civil War (1917–1921)

Doctor Zhivago, Boris Pasternak (1958)

And Quiet Flows the Don, Mikhail A. Sholokhov (1940)

The Spanish Civil War (1936–1939)

For Whom the Bell Tolls, Ernest Hemingway (1940)

World War II (1939–1945)

A Bell for Adano, John Hersey (1944)

The Bridge on the River Kwai, Pierre Boulle (1952)

The Caine Mutiny, Herman Wouk (1951)

Catch-22, Joseph Heller (1961)

Ceremony, Leslie Marmon Silko (1977)

Closely Watched Trains, Bohumil Hrabal (1968)

From Here to Eternity, James Jones (1951)

The Good Shepherd, C. S. Forester (1955)

Live and Remember, Valentin Rasputin (1975)

The Naked and the Dead, Norman Mailer (1948)

The Painted Bird, Jerzy Kosinski (1965)

Run Silent, Run Deep, Edward Latimer Beach (1955)

Schindler's List, Thomas Keneally (1982)

Slaughterhouse-Five, or, The Children's Crusade: A Duty-Dance with Death, Kurt Vonnegut (1969)

Summer of My German Soldier, Bette Greene (1973)

The Sword of Honor trilogy: *Men at Arms, Officers and Gentlemen, The End of the Battle*, Evelyn Waugh (1952–1962)

Tales of the South Pacific, James Michener (1947)

The Tenth Man, Graham Greene (1985)

The Thin Red Line, James Jones (1962)

The Train Was on Time, Heinrich Böll (1949)

The Korean War (1950–1953)

The Bridges at Toko-Ri, James Michener (1953)

The Vietnamese Conflict (1961–1975)

Fallen Angels, Walter Dean Myers (1988)

Fields of Fire, James H. Webb (1978)

Going after Cacciato, Tim O'Brien (1978)

The Quiet American, Graham Greene (1955)

The Things They Carried, Tim O'Brien (1990)

The 13th Valley, John Del Vecchio (1982)

NONFICTION
Classic Biography, Autobiography, and Memoir

All Creatures Great and Small, James Herriot (1972)

Anne Frank: Diary of a Young Girl, Anne Frank (1952)

The Autobiography of Malcolm X, Malcolm X (1965)

Farewell to Manzanar, Jeanne Wakatsuki Houston (1973)

Hunger of Memory, Richard Rodriguez (1982)

Incidents in the Life of a Slave Girl, Harriet Jacobs (1861)

Life on the Mississippi, Mark Twain (1883)

Long Walk to Freedom, Nelson Mandela (1994)

Madame Curie, A Biography, Eve Curie (1937)

The Story of My Life, Helen Keller (1903)

Classic Poems

Classic Narrative or Epic Poems

Beowulf, Anonymous (9th century) Anglo-Saxon

The Canterbury Tales, Geoffrey Chaucer (1380–1390) English

The Epic of Gilgamesh, Anonymous (circa 2000 B.C.) Sumerian

The Iliad and *The Odyssey*, Homer (8th century B.C.) Greek

Metamorphoses, Ovid (before 8 A.D.) Roman

The Ramayana, Anonymous (19th century B.C.) Indian

The Saga of the Volsungs, Anonymous (13th century) Icelandic

Sir Gawain and the Green Knight, Anonymous (14th century) English

The Song of Roland, Anonymous (11th century) French

The Sundiata, Anonymous (13th century) African

Classic Poems from Way Back When

"Because I Could Not Stop for Death," Emily Dickinson (1890)

"The Charge of the Light Brigade," Alfred, Lord Tennyson (1854)

"Drinking and Alone under the Moon," Li Po (8th century)

"How Do I Love Thee? Let Me Count the Ways" (Sonnet XLII from *Sonnets from the Portuguese*), Elizabeth Barrett Browning (1856)

"Kubla Khan," Samuel Taylor Coleridge (1797)

"The Raven," Edgar Allan Poe (1845)

"A Reed," Jelaluddin Rumi (13th century)

"The Rime of the Ancient Mariner," Samuel Taylor Coleridge (1798)

"Shall I Compare Thee to a Summer's Day?," (Sonnet XVIII), William Shakespeare (1609)

"She Walks in Beauty," George Gordon, Lord Byron (1814)

Nonfiction Classics

The Hard Sciences

The Ascent of Man, Jacob Bronowski (1973)

A Brief History of Time, Stephen W. Hawking (1988, updated in 1998)

The Double Helix, James D. Watson (1968)

The Immense Journey, Loren Eiseley (1957)

The Lives of a Cell, Lewis Thomas (1974)

The Making of the Atomic Bomb, Richard Rhodes (1986)

Pale Blue Dot: A Vision of the Human Future in Space, Carl Sagan (1994)

Rats, Lice and History, Hans Zinsser (1935)

Relativity, Albert Einstein (circa 1913)

"Surely You're Joking, Mr. Feynman!," Richard Phillips Feynman (1985)

History

Bury My Heart at Wounded Knee, Dee Brown (1970)

"The Good War": An Oral History of World War Two, Studs Terkel (1984)

The Guns of August, Barbara Wertheim Tuchman (1962)

Hiroshima, John Hersey (1946)

Men to Match My Mountains, Irving Stone (1956)

The Oregon Trail, Francis Parkman (1872)

The Right Stuff, Tom Wolfe (1979)

The Rise and Fall of the Third Reich, William L. Shirer (1960)

The Travels of Marco Polo, Marco Polo (1579)

Why We Can't Wait, Martin Luther King Jr. (1964)

The Natural World

Born Free: A Lioness of Two Worlds, Joy Adamson (1960)

Desert Solitaire, Edward Abbey (1968)

Gorillas in the Mist, Dian Fossey (1983)

In the Shadow of Man, Jane Goodall (1971)

My First Summer in the Sierra, John Muir (1911)

Of Wolves and Men, Barry Holstun Lopez (1978)

The Origin of the Species by Means of Natural Selection, Charles Darwin (1859)

The Panda's Thumb: More Reflections in Natural History, Stephen Jay Gould (1980)

A Sand County Almanac, Aldo Leopold (1949)

Silent Spring, Rachel Carson (1962)

Philosophy and Psychology

The Analects, Confucius (5th century B.C.)

The Essays of Ralph Waldo Emerson, Ralph Waldo Emerson (1st series in 1841, 2nd series in 1844)

Meditations, Marcus Aurelius (167 A.D.)

The Republic, Plato (4th century B.C.)

The Snow Leopard, Peter Matthiessen (1978)

Tao Te Ching, Lao-tzu (6th century B.C.)

Toward a Psychology of Being, Abraham Maslow (1962)

Utopia, Sir Thomas More (1516)

Walden, or Life in the Woods, Henry David Thoreau (1854)

Zen and the Art of Motorcycle Maintenance, Robert Pirsig (1974)

Religion and Myth

The Bhagavad Gita (between the 5th century B.C. and the 2nd century A.D.)

The Bible (Old Testament, 1200 B.C. to 100 B.C.; New Testament, 1st century A.D.)

Bulfinch's Mythology, Thomas Bulfinch (1855–1863)

God Is Red: A Native View of Religion, Vine Deloria, Leslie Marmon Silko, and George E. Tinker (1972, updated 1994)

The Golden Bough, Sir James Frazer (1890)

The Hero with A Thousand Faces, Joseph Campbell (1949)

Mythology, Edith Hamilton (1942)

The Qu'ran (circa early 7th century)

The Varieties of Religious Experience, William James (1902)

The Way to God, Mahatma Gandhi (1971)

The Political Sciences

The Art of War, Sun-Tzu (5th century B.C.)

The Communist Manifesto, Karl Marx (1848)

The Declaration of Independence and *The Constitution of the United States*, (1776; 1787–1789)

Democracy in America, Alexis de Tocqueville (Part I in 1835, Part II in 1840)

The Federalist Papers, James Madison, Alexander Hamilton, and John Jay (1788)

On Liberty, John Stuart Mill (1859)

Orientalism, Edward W. Said (1978)

The Prince, Niccolò Machiavelli (1532)

The Universal Declaration of Human Rights, United Nations (1948)

The Wealth of Nations, Adam Smith (1776)

The Social Sciences

The Abolition of Man, C.S. Lewis (1943)

Black Like Me, John Howard Griffin (1961)

The Feminine Mystique, Betty Friedan (1963)

In Cold Blood: A True Account of a Multiple Murder and its Consequences, Truman Capote (1965)

Let Us Now Praise Famous Men: Three Tenant Families, James Agee and photographs by Walker Evans (1941)

On Civil Disobedience, Henry David Thoreau (1849)

Roots: The Saga of an American Family, Alex Haley (1976)

The Souls of Black Folk, W.E.B. DuBois (1903)

Twenty Years at Hull House, Jane Addams (1895)

A Vindication of the Rights of Woman, s Wollstonecraft (1792)

REFERENCE LIST

THE CLASSICS
Drama

Aristophanes. 1970. *Lysistrata*. New York: New American Library. (Orig. pub. 411 B.C.)

Bolt, Robert. 1962. *A Man for All Seasons: A Play in Two Acts*. New York: Random House. (Orig. pub. 1954.)

Chekhov, Anton Pavlovich. 1991. *The Cherry Orchard*. New York: Dover Publications. (Orig. pub. 1904.)

Gibson, William. 2002. *The Miracle Worker*. New York: Pocket Books. (Orig. pub. 1957.)

Greene, Robert. 1972. *Friar Bacon and Friar Bungay*. New York: W. W. Norton and Company. (Orig. pub. 1594.)

Hansberry, Lorraine. 1994. *A Raisin in the Sun*. New York: Vintage Books. (Orig. pub. 1959.)

Ibsen, Henrik. 1972. *A Doll's House*. New York: Samuel French. (Orig. pub. 1879.)

Miller, Arthur. 1995. *The Crucible: A Play in Four Acts*. New York: Penguin Books. (Orig. pub. 1953.)

———. 1984. *Death of a Salesman*. New York: Viking Press. (Orig. pub. 1949.)

Molière. 2000. *The Misanthrope and Other Plays*. New York: Penguin Books. (Title play Orig. pub. 1666.)

Rostand, Edmond. 1981. *Cyrano de Bergerac: An Heroic Comedy in Five Acts*. Translated into English verse by Brian Hooker. New York: Bantam Books. (Orig. pub. 1897.)

Shakespeare, William. 1995. *Henry V*. Oxford: Oxford University Press. (Orig. pub. c.1600.)

———. 2001. *Romeo and Juliet*. New York: Modern Library. (Orig. pub. c.1595.)

Shaw, Bernard. 1959. *Major Barbara*. Baltimore: Penguin Books. (Orig. pub. 1905.)

———. 2001. *Pygmalion*. New York: Washington Square Press. (Orig. pub. 1913.)

Simon, Neil. 1965. *The Odd Couple*. New York: Random House.

Sophocles. 1994. *Oedipus the King*. New York: Washington Square Press. (Orig. 429 B.C.)

Stoppard, Tom. 1967. *Rosencrantz and Guildenstern are Dead: A Play in Three Acts*. New York: Samuel French.

Wilde, Oscar. 1990. *The Importance of Being Earnest*. Washington, D.C.: Orchises. (Orig. pub. 1895.)

Wilder, Thornton. 2003. *Our Town: A Play in Three Acts*. New York: Perennial Classics. (Orig. pub. 1938.)

Williams, Tennessee. 1980. *A Streetcar Named Desire*. New York: New Directions. (Orig. pub. 1947.)

———. 1976. *Three by Tennessee: Sweet Bird of Youth; The Rose Tattoo; The Night of the Iguana*. New York: New American Library.

Wilson, August. 1986. *Fences*. New York: Plume/Penguin.

Genre Novels

Adams, Richard. 1972. *Watership Down*. New York: Macmillan.

Barrie, J. M. 1911. *Peter and Wendy* (adapted from Barrie's 1904 play *Peter Pan; or, The Boy Who Would Not Grow Up*). New York: Scribner.

Baum, L. Frank. 2000. *The Wizard of Oz*. New York: Henry Holt. (Orig. pub. 1900.)

Baxter, Stephen. 1995. *Time Ships*. New York: Eos: HarperPrism.

Beagle, Peter S. 1991. *The Last Unicorn*. New York: Penguin Books. (Orig. pub. 1968.)

Bester, Alfred. 1996. *The Stars My Destination*. New York: Vintage Books. (Orig. pub. 1956.)

Bradbury, Ray. 1991. *Fahrenheit 451*. New York: Ballantine Books. (Orig. pub. 1954.)

———. 1999. *Something Wicked This Way Comes*. New York: Avon Books. (Orig. pub. 1962.)

Bradley, Marion Zimmer. 2000. *The Mists of Avalon*. New York: Ballantine. (Orig. pub. 1982.)

Brand, Christianna. 1989. *Green for Danger*. New York: Carroll and Graf. (Orig. pub. 1945.)

Burroughs, Edgar Rice. 1999. *Tarzan of the Apes*. New York: Tom Doherty Assoc. (Orig. pub. 1914.)

Card, Orson Scott. 2002. *Ender's Game*. New York: Starscape. (Orig. pub. 1985.)

Carroll, Lewis. 2000. *Alice's Adventures in Wonderland*. New York: HarperCollins. (Orig. pub. 1865.)

———. 1994. *Through the Looking Glass*. New York: Penguin Group. (Orig. pub. 1871.)

Chandler, Raymond. 1992. *The Big Sleep*. New York: Vintage Books. (Orig. pub. 1939.)

Chesterton, G. K. 2001. *The Innocence of Father Brown*. Murrieta, CA: Classic Books. (Orig. pub. 1911.)

Christie, Agatha. 2000. *Murder on the Orient Express*. New York: Berkeley Press. (Orig. pub. 1934.)

Clarke, Arthur C. 2001. *Childhood's End*. New York: Del Rey Impact. (Orig. pub. 1952.)

———. 2000. *2001: A Space Odyssey*. New York: ROC. (Orig. pub. 1968.)

Collins, Wilkie. 1984. *The Moonstone*. New York: Penguin Group. (Orig. pub. 1868.)

———. 1985. *The Woman in White*. New York: Bantam Books. (Orig. pub. 1860.)

Crichton, Michael. 1969. *The Andromeda Strain*. New York: Knopf.

Dick, Philip K. 1996. *Do Androids Dream of Electric Sheep?* New York: Ballantine Books. (Orig. pub. 1968.)

———. 1992. *The Man in the High Castle*. New York: Vintage Books. (Orig. pub. 1962.)

Donaldson, Stephen R. 1977. *The Chronicles of Thomas Covenant: The Unbeliever*. 3 vols. New York: Henry Holt.

Doyle, Arthur Conan, Sir. 2000. *The Hound of the Baskervilles*. New York: Aladdin Classics. (Orig. serialized in *Strand* magazine, 1901–1902.)

———. 1993. *The Lost World*. New York: Tor. (Orig. pub. 1912.)

———. 1987. *The Sherlock Holmes Mysteries*. New York: New American Library. (First stories published in 1892.)

Eco, Umberto. 1983. *The Name of the Rose*. San Diego: Harcourt Brace Jovanovich. (Orig. pub. 1980.)

Ellroy, James. 1990. *L. A. Confidential*. New York: Mysterious Press.

Endore, Guy. 1992. *The Werewolf of Paris*. New York: Carol Pub. Group. (Orig. pub. 1933.)

Goldman, William. 2000. *The Princess Bride*. New York: Ballantine Pub. Group. (Orig. pub. 1974.)

Grey, Zane. 2002. *Riders of the Purple Sage*. New York: Modern Library. (Orig. pub. 1912.)

Hammett, Dashiell. 1992. *The Maltese Falcon*. New York: Vintage Books. (Orig. pub. 1930.)

Heinlein, Robert A. 1991. *Stranger in a Strange Land*. New York: Putnam. (Orig. pub. 1961.)

Herbert, Frank. 1999. *Dune*. New York: Ace Books. (Orig. pub. 1965.)

Heyer, Georgette. 1957. *Sylvester, or the Wicked Uncle*. New York: Putnam.

L'Amour, Louis. 1983. *Hondo*. New York: Bantam Books. (Orig. pub. 1953.)

Le Carré, John. 1997. *The Spy Who Came in from the Cold*. New York: Ballantine Books. (Orig. pub. 1963.)

Le Guin, Ursula K. 1968–1990. *The Earthsea Cycle*. 4 vols. Multiple original publishers.

———. 2000. *The Left Hand of Darkness*. New York: Ace Books. (Orig. pub. 1969.)

Leiber, Fritz. 1991. *Conjure Wife and Our Lady of Darkness*. New York: Tor. (First title Orig. pub. 1943.)

L'Engle, Madeleine. 1962–1996. *The Time Quintet*. 5 vols. New York: Farrar, Straus.

Matheson, Richard. 1997. *I Am Legend*. New York: ORB. (Orig. pub. 1954.)

McCaffrey, Anne. 1977. *Dragonsinger*. New York: Atheneum.

McKillip, Patricia A. 1996. *The Forgotten Beasts of Eld*. San Diego: Harcourt Brace. (Orig. pub. 1974.)

Norton, Andre. 2001. *The Gates to Witch World: Comprising Witch World, Web of the Witch World, and Year of the Unicorn*. New York: Tor. (Orig. pub. beginning 1963.)

Peake, Mervyn. 1946–1959. *The Gormenghast Trilogy*. 3 vols. London: Eyre and Spottiswoode.

Portis, Charles. 2003. *True Grit*. Woodstock, NY: Overlook Press. (Orig. pub. 1968.)

Schaefer, Jack. 1975. *Shane*. New York: Bantam Books. (Orig. pub. 1949.)

Seton, Anya. 1944. *Dragonwyck*. Boston: Houghton Mifflin Company.

Stewart, Mary. 2003. *The Arthurian Saga*. New York: HarperCollins Publishers. (Orig. pub. beginning 1970.)

Tevis, Walter. 1999. *The Man Who Fell to Earth*. New York: Ballantine Pub. Group. (Orig. pub. 1963.)

Tolkien, J.R.R. 1997. *The Hobbit, or, There and Back Again*. Boston: Houghton Mifflin Company. (Orig. pub. 1937.)

———. 2001. *The Lord of the Rings*. 1 vol. ed. Includes *The Fellowship of the Ring*, *The Two Towers*, *The Return of the King*. Boston: Houghton Mifflin Company. (Orig. pub. 1954–1955.)

Verne, Jules. 2001. *20,000 Leagues under the Sea*. New York: HarperCollins. (Orig. pub. 1870.)

White, T. H. 1987. *The Once and Future King*. New York: Ace Books. (Orig. pub. 1958.)

Willis, Connie. 1992. *Doomsday Book*. New York: Bantam Books.

Literary Anthologies

The 100 Best Love Poems of All Time. 2003. Edited by Leslie Pockell. New York: Warner Books.

The 100 Best Poems of All Time. 2001. Edited by Leslie Pockell. New York: Warner Books.

101 Classic Love Poems. 2003. Compiled by Sarah Whittier. Chicago: Contemporary Books.

101 Famous Poems. 2003. Compiled by Roy Jay Cook. Chicago: Contemporary Books.

The American Short Story: A Collection of the Best Known and Most Memorable Short Stories by the Great American Authors. 1994. Edited by Thomas K. Parkes. New York: Galahad Books.

The Best American Mystery Stories of the Century. 2000. Edited by Tony Hillerman. Boston: Houghton Mifflin.

The Best American Poetry. 1988–. Annual. New York: Collier Books; Scribner Poetry.

The Best American Short Stories of the Century. 1999. Edited by John Updike and Katrina Kenison. Boston: Houghton Mifflin.

A Century of Great Western Stories. 2000. Edited by John Jakes. New York: Forge.

A Century of Noir: Thirty-Two Classic Crime Stories. 2002. Edited by Mickey Spillane and Max Allan Collins. New York: New American Library.

Children of the Night: The Best Short Stories by Black Writers, 1967 to the Present. 1995. Edited by Gloria Naylor. Boston: Little, Brown and Company.

The Classic Hundred: All-Time Favorite Poems. 1998. Edited by William Harmon. New York: Columbia University Press.

Committed to Memory: 100 Best Poems to Memorize. 1997. Edited and with an introduction by John Hollander. New York: Riverhead Books.

Great American Prose Poems: From Poe to the Present. 2003. Edited by David Lehman. New York: Scribner.

Masterpieces: The Best Science Fiction of the Century. 2001. Edited by Orson Scott Card. New York: Ace Books.

Ornaments of Fire: The World's Best 101 Short Poems and Fragments. 1994. Selected and edited by Edd Wheeler. Santa Barbara, CA: Fithian Press.

The Pushcart Book of Short Stories: The Best Short Stories from a Quarter-Century of The Pushcart Prize. 2002. Edited by Bill Henderson. Wainscott, NY: Pushcart Press; New York: Distributed by W. W. Norton and Company.

The Random House Treasury of Best-Loved Poems. 2003. Edited by Louis Phillips. New York: Random House.

The Science Fiction Hall of Fame, Volume I: The Greatest Science Fiction Stories of All Time, Chosen by the Members of the Science Fiction Writers of America. 2003. Edited by Robert Silverberg. New York: Tor.

We Are the Stories We Tell: The Best Short Stories by North American Women since 1945. 1990. Edited by Wendy Martin. New York: Pantheon Books.

Literary Novels

Abe, Kobo. 1991. *The Woman in the Dunes*. New York: Vintage Books. (Orig. pub. 1962.)

Achebe, Chinua. 1994. *Things Fall Apart*. New York: Anchor Books. (Orig. pub. 1958.)

Alcott, Louisa May. 1999. *Little Women*. New York: Aladdin Paperbacks. (Orig. pub. 1868.)

Allen, Paula Gunn. 1983. *The Woman Who Owned the Shadows*. San Francisco: Spinsters, Ink.

Allende, Isabel. 1986. *The House of the Spirits*. New York: Bantam Books. (Orig. pub. 1982.)

Al-Zayyat, Latifa. 2000. *The Open Door*. New York: American University in Cairo Press. (Orig. pub. 1960.)

Amado, Jorge. 1965. *The Violent Land*. New York: Knopf. (Orig. pub. 1945.)

Anaya, Rudolfo A. 1972. *Bless Me, Ultima*. Berkeley, CA: Tonatiuh International Inc.

Anonymous. 1971. *Go Ask Alice*. Englewood Cliffs, NJ: Prentice-Hall.

Arnow, Harriet Louisa Simpson. 1972. *The Dollmaker*. New York: Avon Books. (Orig. pub. 1954.)

Asturias, Miguel Angel. 1993. *Men of Maize*. Pittsburgh: University of Pittsburgh Press. (Orig. pub. 1949.)

Atwood, Margaret. 1986. *The Handmaid's Tale*. New York: Houghton Mifflin.

Austen, Jane. 1996. *Emma*. New York: Signet Classic, Penguin Putnam. (Orig. pub. 1816.)

———. 1995. *Pride and Prejudice*. Introduction by Anna Quindlen. New York: The Modern Library. (Orig. pub. 1813.)

Bainbridge, Beryl. 1996. *The Dressmaker*. New York: Carroll and Graf Publishers. (Orig. pub. 1973.)

Baldwin, James. 1956. *Giovanni's Room*. New York: Dial Press.

———. 1995. *Go Tell It on the Mountain*. New York: The Modern Library. (Orig. pub. 1953.)

Balzac, Honoré de. 1981. *Père Goriot*. New York: Signet Classic. (Orig. pub. 1835.)

Barnes, Djuna. 1946. *Nightwood*. New York: New Directions. (Orig. pub. 1936.)

Barrett, William. 1982. *The Lilies of the Field*. New York: Warner Books. (Orig. pub. 1962.)

Beach, Edward Latimer. 1955. *Run Silent, Run Deep*. New York: Henry Holt.

Boccaccio, Giovanni. 1982. *The Decameron*. New York: Norton. (Orig. pub. 1353.)

Böll, Heinrich. 1994. *The Train Was on Time*. Evanston, IL: Northwestern University Press. (Orig. pub. 1949.)

Boulle, Pierre. 1954. *The Bridge on the River Kwai*. London: Secker and Warburg. (Orig. pub. 1952.)

Bradford, Richard. 1999. *Red Sky at Morning*. New York: Harper Perennial. (Orig. pub. 1968.)

Brontë, Charlotte. 1997. *Jane Eyre*. New York: Penguin Group. (Orig. pub. 1847.)

Brontë, Emily. 1990. *Wuthering Heights*. London: Puffin, Penguin. (Orig. pub. 1847.)

Brown, Rita Mae. 1988. *Rubyfruit Jungle*. New York: Bantam Books. (Orig. pub. 1973.)

Buck, Pearl S. 1994. *The Good Earth*. New York: Washington Square Press. (Orig. pub. 1931.)

Burgess, Anthony. 1988. *A Clockwork Orange*. New York: Norton. (Orig. pub. 1962.)

Camus, Albert. 1993. *The Stranger*. New York: Knopf. (Orig. pub. 1942.)

Cather, Willa. 1992. *O Pioneers!* New York: Vintage Books. (Orig. pub. 1913.)

Cervantes Saavedra, Miguel de. 2003. *Don Quixote*. New York: Ecco. (Orig. pub. 1605–1615.)

Chopin, Kate. 1996. *The Awakening*. New York: Simon and Schuster. (Orig. pub. 1899.)

Cisneros, Sandra. 1984. *The House on Mango Street*. Houston, TX: Arte Publico Press.

Conrad, Joseph. 1997. *Heart of Darkness and the Secret Sharer*. New York: Signet Classic. (First title Orig. pub. 1902.)

Cooper, James Fenimore. 1981. *The Last of the Mohicans*. New York: Bantam Books. (Orig. pub. 1826.)

Crane, Stephen. 1983. *The Red Badge of Courage*. New York: Bantam Books. (Orig. pub. 1895.)

Defoe, Daniel. 2001. *Robinson Crusoe*. New York: Aladdin Paperbacks. (Orig. pub. 1719.)

De Forest, John William. 2000. *Miss Ravenel's Conversion from Secession to Loyalty*. New York: Penguin Books. (Orig. pub. 1867.)

Del Vecchio, John. 1999. *The 13th Valley*. New York: St. Martin's Griffin. (Orig. pub. 1982.)

Dickens, Charles. 1995. *A Christmas Carol*. New York: Bantam Books. (Orig. pub. 1843.)

———. 1992. *Hard Times*. New York: Knopf. (Orig. pub. 1854.)

———. 1992. *Oliver Twist*. New York: Bantam Books. (Orig. pub. 1838.)

———. 1993. *A Tale of Two Cities*. New York: Knopf. (Orig. pub. 1859.)

Dorris, Michael. 1987. *A Yellow Raft in Blue Water*. New York: Henry Holt.

Dostoyevsky, Fyodor. 1995. *The Brothers Karamazov*. New York: Modern Library. (Orig. pub. 1880.)

Dumas, Alexandre. 1996. *The Count of Monte Cristo*. New York: Modern Library. (Orig. pub. 1844.)

———. 1999. *The Three Musketeers*. New York: Modern Library. (Orig. pub. 1844.)

Du Maurier, Daphne. 1993. *Rebecca*. New York: Doubleday. (Orig. pub. 1938.)

Eliot, George. 1994. *Middlemarch*. New York: Penguin Books. (Orig. pub. 1871–1872.)

Ellison, Ralph. 1994. *Invisible Man*. Preface by Charles Johnson. New York: Modern Library. (Orig. pub. 1952.)

Erdrich, Louise. 1993. *Love Medicine*. New York: Henry Holt. (Orig. pub. 1984.)

Esquivel, Laura. 1992. *Like Water for Chocolate*. New York: Doubleday. (Orig. pub. 1989.)

Fast, Howard. 1962. *April Morning*. New York: Bantam.

Faulkner, William. 1991. *The Unvanquished*. New York: Vintage Books. (Orig. pub. 1938.)

Fitzgerald, F. Scott. 1995. *The Great Gatsby*. New York: Scribner Paperback Fiction. (Orig. pub. 1925.)

———. 1996. *Tender Is the Night*. New York: Scribner. (Orig. pub. 1934.)

Flagg, Fannie. 2000. *Fried Green Tomatoes at the Whistle Stop Café*. New York: Ballantine Books. (Orig. pub. 1987.)

Flaubert, Gustave. 1981. *Madame Bovary*. New York: Bantam Books. (Orig. pub. 1857.)

Forester, C. S. 1947. *The General*. Boston: Little, Brown and Company. (Orig. pub. 1936.)

———. 2001. *The Good Shepherd*. Safety Harbor, FL: Simon. (Orig. pub. 1955.)

———. 1937–1967. The Horatio Hornblower Series. 11 vols. New York: Little, Brown.

Forster, E. M. 1971. *Maurice*. New York: Norton.

Fuentes, Carlos. 1985. *The Old Gringo*. New York: Farrar Straus Giroux.

Gaines, Ernest J. 1972. *The Autobiography of Miss Jane Pittman*. New York: Bantam Books.

García Márquez, Gabriel. 1998. *One Hundred Years of Solitude*. New York: Perennial Classics. (Orig. pub. 1967.)

Gardner, John. 1971. *Grendel*. New York: Knopf.

Gilman, Charlotte Perkins. 1989. *The Yellow Wallpaper, and Other Writings*. Introduction by Lynne Sharon Schwartz. New York: Bantam Books. (Orig. pub. 1899.)

Goethe, Johann Wolfgang von. 1993. *The Sorrows of Young Werther*. New York: Modern Library. (Orig. pub. 1774.)

Gogol, Nikolai Vasilyevich. 1997. *Dead Souls*. New York: Modern Library. (Orig. pub. 1842.)

Golding, William. 1999. *Lord of the Flies*. New York: Penguin Books. (Orig. pub. 1954.)

Gordimer, Nadine. 1979. *Burger's Daughter*. New York: Viking Press.

Grass, Günter. 1993. *The Tin Drum*. New York: Knopf. (Orig. pub. 1959.)

Greene, Graham. 1992. *The Quiet American*. New York: Modern Library. (Orig. pub. 1955.)

———. 1998. *The Tenth Man*. New York: Washington Square Press. (Orig. pub. 1985.)

Hall, Radclyffe. 1981. *The Well of Loneliness*. New York: Avon Books. (Orig. pub. 1928.)

Hamsun, Knut. 1972. *Growth of the Soil*. New York: Vintage Books. (Orig. pub. 1917.)

———. 1998. *Hunger*. New York: Noonday Press. (Orig. pub. 1890.)

Hawthorne, Nathaniel. 1986. *The Scarlet Letter*. New York: Bantam Books. (Orig. pub. 1850.)

Hedayat, Sadegh. 1957. *The Blind Owl*. New York: Grove Press. (Orig. pub. 1936.)

Heller, Joseph. 1996. *Catch-22*. New York: Simon and Schuster. (Orig. pub. 1961.)

Hemingway, Ernest. 1997. *A Farewell to Arms*. New York: Scribner Classics. (Orig. pub. 1929.)

———. 1995. *For Whom the Bell Tolls*. New York: Scribner Paperback Fiction. (Orig. pub. 1940.)

———. 1996. *The Old Man and the Sea*. New York: Scribner. (Orig. pub. 1952.)

Hersey, John. 1988. *A Bell for Adano*. New York: Vintage Books. (Orig. pub. 1944.)

Hesse, Hermann. 1989. *Demian*. New York: Harper and Row. (Orig. pub. 1919.)

———. 2000. *Siddhartha*. Boston: Shambhala. (Orig. pub. 1922.)

Highsmith, Patricia. 1991. *The Price of Salt*. Tallahassee, FL: Naiad Press. (Orig. pub. 1952.)

Hill, Susan. 1993. *Mrs. de Winter*. New York: William Morrow and Company.

Hilton, James. 1960. *Lost Horizon*. New York: Pocket Books. (Orig. pub. 1933.)

Hrabal, Bohumil. 1995. *Closely Watched Trains*. Evanston, IL: Northwestern University Press. (Orig. pub. 1965.)

Hugo, Victor. 2001. *The Hunchback of Notre Dame*. New York: Signet Classic. (Orig. pub. 1831.)

Hurston, Zora Neale. 1998. *Their Eyes Were Watching God*. New York: Perennial Classics. (Orig. pub. 1937.)

Isherwood, Christopher. 1954. *The Berlin Stories*. New York: J. Laughlin.

Jackson, Shirley. 1999. *The Haunting of Hill House*. New York: Penguin Books. (Orig. pub. 1959.)

———. 1991. *The Lottery and Other Stories*. New York: Farrar, Straus and Giroux/Noonday Press. (Orig. pub. 1949.)

James, Henry. 2002. *Daisy Miller*. New York: Modern Library. (Orig. pub. 1878.)

———. 1995. *The Turn of the Screw*. New York: Signet Classic. (Orig. pub. 1898.)

Johnson, Charles. 1990. *Middle Passage*. New York: Macmillan.

Jones, James. 1998. *From Here to Eternity*. New York: Delta. (Orig. pub. 1951.)

———. 1998. *The Thin Red Line*. New York: Delta. (Orig. pub. 1962.)

Joyce, James. 1992. *Ulysses*. With a foreword by Morris L. Ernst, and the 1933 decision of the U.S. District Court rendered by Judge John M. Woolsey lifting the ban on the entry of *Ulysses* into the United States. New York: Modern Library. (Orig. pub. of single-volume work 1922.)

Kafka, Franz. 1981. *The Metamorphosis*. New York: Bantam Books. (Orig. pub. 1915.)

———. 1998. *The Trial*. Translated and with a preface by Breon Mitchell. New York: Schocken Books. (Orig. pub. 1925.)

Kantor, MacKinlay. 1993. *Andersonville*. New York: Plume. (Orig. pub. 1955.)

Kazantzakis, Nikos. 1996. *Zorba the Greek*. New York: Scribner Paperback Fiction. (Orig. pub. 1946.)

Keneally, Thomas. 1993. *Schindler's List*. New York: Simon and Schuster. (Orig. pub. 1982.)

Kesey, Ken. 2002. *One Flew Over the Cuckoo's Nest*. New York: Viking. (Orig. pub. 1962.)

Keyes, Daniel. 1966. *Flowers for Algernon*. New York: Harcourt, Brace and World.

Kincaid, Jamaica. 1985. *Annie John*. New York: Farrar, Straus, Giroux.

Kingsolver, Barbara. 1988. *The Bean Trees*. New York: Harper and Row.

Kipling, Rudyard. 1982. *Captains Courageous*. Bantam Classic Edition. New York: Bantam Books. (Orig. pub. 1897.)

———. 1981. *The Jungle Books*. New York: Signet Classic. (Orig. pub. 1894–1895.)

———. 1988. *Kim*. New York: Bantam. (Orig. pub. 1901.)

Kosinski, Jerzy. 1995. *The Painted Bird*. New York: Grove Press. (Orig. pub. 1965.)

Kundera, Milan. 1991. *The Unbearable Lightness of Being*. New York: HarperPerennial. (Orig. pub. 1984.)

La Farge, Oliver. 1929. *Laughing Boy*. Boston: Houghton Mifflin.

Lampedusa, Giuseppi di. 1991. *The Leopard*. New York: Knopf. (Orig. pub. 1958.)

Lee, Harper. 1995. *To Kill a Mockingbird*. New York: HarperCollins Publishers. (Orig. pub. 1960.)

Leroux, Gaston. 1994. *The Phantom of the Opera*. London: Puffin. (Orig. pub. 1910.)

London, Jack. 2003. *The Call of the Wild*. New York: Aladdin Classics. (Orig. published serially in the *Saturday Evening Post*, June 20–July 18, 1903.)

———. 1994. *White Fang*. London: Puffin. (Orig. published serially in *Outing*, May–October 1906.)

Mahfuz, Najib. 2001. *The Cairo Trilogy: Palace Walk, Palace of Desire, Sugar Street*. New York: Alfred A. Knopf. (Orig. pub. 1956–1957.)

Mailer, Norman. 1998. *The Naked and the Dead*. New York: Henry Holt. (Orig. pub. 1948.)

Mann, Thomas. 1999. *Death in Venice and Other Stories*. New York: Signet Classic. (Orig. pub. 1912.)

———. 1996. *The Magic Mountain*. New York: Vintage International. (Orig. pub. 1924.)

Markandaya, Kamala. 2002. *Nectar in a Sieve*. New York: Signet Classic. (Orig. pub. 1954.)

Marshall, Catherine. 1967. *Christy*. New York: McGraw-Hill.

Maupin, Armistead. 1978. *Tales of the City*. New York: Harper and Row.

McCullers, Carson. 1993. *The Heart Is a Lonely Hunter*. New York: Modern Library. (Orig. pub. 1940.)

———. 1946. *The Member of the Wedding*. New York: Bantam Books.

Melville, Herman. 1998. *Billy Budd and Other Tales*. New York: Signet Classic. (Orig. pub. 1924.)

———. 2001. *Moby-Dick, or, the Whale*. New York: Penguin Books. (Orig. pub. 1851.)

Michener, James. 1973. *The Bridges at Toko-Ri*. New York: Ballantine Books. (Orig. pub. 1953.)

———. 1986. *Tales of the South Pacific*. New York: Macmillan. (Orig. pub. 1947.)

Mishima, Yukio. 1956. *The Sound of Waves*. New York: A. A. Knopf. (Orig. pub. 1954.)

Mitchell, Margaret. 1936. *Gone with the Wind*. New York: Macmillan.

Momaday, N. Scott. 1999. *House Made of Dawn*. New York: Perennial Classics. (Orig. pub. 1968.)

Morrison, Toni. 1987. *Beloved*. New York: Plume Book.

Mukherjee, Bharati. 1988. *The Middleman and Other Stories*. New York: Grove Press.

Murasaki Shikibu. 1992. *The Tale of the Genji*. New York: Knopf. (Orig. 11th century.)

Naipaul, V.S. 1997. *A Bend in the River*. New York: Modern Library. (Orig. pub. 1979.)

———. 2001. *A House for Mr. Biswas*. New York: Vintage International. (Orig. pub. 1961.)

Naylor, Gloria. 1982. *The Women of Brewster Place*. New York: Viking Press.

Nichols, John. 2000. *The Milagro Beanfield War*. New York: Henry Holt. (Orig. pub. 1974.)

O'Brian, Patrick. 1969. *Master and Commander*. Philadelphia: Lippincott.

O'Brien, Tim. 1978. *Going after Cacciato*. New York: Delacorte Press.

———. 1998. *The Things They Carried*. New York: Broadway Books. (Orig. pub. 1990.)

Oke, Janette. 1979–1989. Love Comes Softly Series. 8 vols. Grand Rapids: MI: Bethany House.

Orczy, Baroness. 2000. *The Scarlet Pimpernel*. New York: Signet Classic. (Orig. pub. 1905.)

Orwell, George. 2003. *1984*. New York: Plume. (Orig. pub. 1949.)

———. 2003. *Animal Farm*. New York: Harcourt Brace. (Orig. pub. 1945.)

Pasternak, Boris. 1991. *Doctor Zhivago*. New York: Knopf. (Orig. pub. 1958.)

Paton, Alan. 1995. *Cry the Beloved Country*. New York: Scribner Paperback Fiction: Simon and Schuster. (Orig. pub. 1948.)

Plath, Sylvia. 1999. *The Bell Jar*. New York: Perennial Classics. (Orig. pub. 1963.)

Potok, Chaim. 1996. *The Chosen*. New York: Fawcett Columbine. (Orig. pub. 1967.)

Puig, Manuel. 1979. *The Kiss of the Spider Woman*. New York: Knopf. (Orig. pub. 1976.)

Pushkin, Alexander. 1999. *Eugene Onegin*. New York: Basic Books. (Orig. pub. 1833.)

Pynchon, Thomas. 1986. *The Crying of Lot 49*. New York: Perennial Library. (Orig. pub. 1966.)

———. 1973. *Gravity's Rainbow*. New York: Viking Press.

Rand, Ayn. 1997. *Atlas Shrugged*. New York: Signet. (Orig. pub. 1957.)

———. 1995. *We the Living*. New York: Dutton. (Orig. pub. 1936.)

Rasputin, Valentin. 1978. *Live and Remember*. New York: Macmillan. (Orig. pub. 1975.)

Remarque, Erich Maria. 1996. *All Quiet on the Western Front*. New York: Fawcett Columbine. (Orig. pub. 1929.)

Renault, Mary. 1988. *The Persian Boy*. New York: Vintage Books. (Orig. pub. 1972.)

Rhys, Jean. 1992. *Wide Sargasso Sea*. New York: Norton. (Orig. pub. 1966.)

Richter, Conrad. 1937. *The Sea of Grass*. New York: A. A. Knopf.

Rule, Jane. 1984. *Desert of the Heart*. Salem, NH: Ayer Co. (Orig. pub. 1964.)

Salinger, J. D. 1991. *The Catcher in the Rye*. Boston: Little, Brown. (Orig. pub. 1951.)

Sarton, May. 1965. *Mrs. Stevens Hears the Mermaids Singing*. New York: Norton.

Shaara, Michael. 2003. *Killer Angels*. New York: Ballantine Books. (Orig. pub. 1974.)

Shelley, Mary Wollstonecraft. 1991. *Frankenstein*. New York: Bantam Books. (Orig. pub. 1818.)

Shockley, Ann Allen. 1974. *Loving Her*. Indianapolis: Bobbs-Merrill.

Sholokhov, Mikhail A. 1989. *And Quiet Flows the Don*. New York: Vintage Books. (Orig. pub. 1940.)

Silko, Leslie Marmon. 1986. *Ceremony*. New York: Penguin Books. (Orig. pub. 1977.)

Silone, Ignazio. 1986. *Bread and Wine*. New York: Signet Classic. (Orig. pub. 1936.)

Sinclair, Upton. 2002. *The Jungle*. New York: Modern Library. (Orig. pub. 1906.)

———. 2000. *Manassas*. Tuscaloosa: University of Alabama Press. (Orig. pub. 1904.)

Solzhenitsyn, Aleksandr Isaevich. 1998. *One Day in the Life of Ivan Denisovich*. New York: Signet Classic. (Orig. pub. 1962.)

Stein, Gertrude. 1993. *The Autobiography of Alice B. Toklas*. New York: Modern Library. (Orig. pub. 1933.)

Steinbeck, John. 1992. *The Grapes of Wrath*. New York: Penguin. (Orig. pub. 1939.)

———. 1993. *Of Mice and Men*. New York: Penguin Books. (Orig. pub. 1937.)

———. 1992. *The Pearl*. New York: Penguin Books. (Orig. pub. 1947.)

———. 1994. *The Red Pony*. New York: Penguin Books. (Orig. pub. 1937.)

———. 1997. *Tortilla Flat*. New York: Penguin Books. (Orig. pub. 1935.)

Stendhal. 2003. *The Red and the Black*. New York: Modern Library. (Orig. pub. 1830.)

Stevenson, Robert Louis. 1988. *Dr. Jekyll and Mr. Hyde*. New York: Tom Doherty Associates. (Orig. pub. 1886.)

———. 1994. *Kidnapped*. New York: Knopf. (Orig. pub. 1886.)

———. 2001. *Treasure Island*. New York: Scholastic. (Orig. pub. 1883.)

Stoker, Bram. 1981. *Dracula*. New York: Bantam. (Orig. pub. 1897.)

Stowe, Harriet Beecher. 2002. *Uncle Tom's Cabin*. New York: Oxford University Press. (Orig. pub. 1852.)

Tan, Amy. 1989. *The Joy Luck Club*. New York: Putnam.

Tolstoy, Leo. 2001. *Anna Karenina*. New York: Viking. (Orig. pub. 1875.)

———. 2003. *The Death of Ivan Ilyich*. New York: Signet Classic. (Orig. pub. 1884.)

———. 1994. *War and Peace*. New York: Modern Library. (Orig. pub. 1865–1869.)

Toomer, Jean. 1969. *Cane*. New York: Harper and Row. (Orig. pub. 1923.)

Trumbo, Dalton. 1994. *Johnny Got His Gun*. New York: Carol Pub. Group. (Orig. pub. 1939.)

Turgenev, Ivan. 1981. *Fathers and Sons*. New York: Bantam Books. (Orig. pub. 1862.)

Twain, Mark. 1999. *The Adventures of Huckleberry Finn*. New York: Aladdin Paperbacks. (Orig. pub. 1884.)

———. 2001. *The Adventures of Tom Sawyer*. New York: Aladdin Classics. (Orig. pub. 1876.)

———. 2002. *The Prince and the Pauper*. New York: Signet Classic. (Orig. pub. 1882.)

Undset, Sigrid. 1988. *Kristin Lavransdatter*. New York: Knopf. (Orig. pub. 1920–1922.)

Vidal, Gore. 1948. *The City and the Pillar*. New York: Dutton.

Voltaire. 1992. *Candide*. New York: Modern Library. (Orig. pub. 1759.)

Vonnegut, Kurt. 1999. *Jailbird*. New York: Dell. (Orig. pub. 1979.)

———. 1952. *Player Piano*. New York: Delacorte Press.

———. 1999. *Slaughterhouse-Five, or, The Children's Crusade: A Duty-Dance with Death*. New York: Dell Publishing. (Orig. pub. 1969.)

Walker, Alice. 1982. *The Color Purple*. New York: Harcourt Brace Jovanovich.

Warren, Patricia Nell. 1974. *The Front Runner*. New York: Morrow.

Warren, Robert Penn. 2001. *All the King's Men*. New York: Harcourt. (Orig. pub. 1946.)

———. 1994. *Band of Angels*. Baton Rouge: Louisiana State University Press. (Orig. pub. 1955.)

Waugh, Evelyn. 1993. *Brideshead Revisited*. New York: Knopf. (Orig. pub. 1945.)

———. 1966. *Sword of Honour: Men at Arms, Officers and Gentlemen, The End of the Battle*. Boston: Little, Brown. (Orig. pub. 1952–1962.)

Webb, James H. 2001. *Fields of Fire*. New York: Bantam Books. (Orig. pub. 1978.)

Welch, James. 1986. *Fools Crow*. New York: Penguin Books.

Wells, H. G. 1988. *The Invisible Man*. New York: Tom Doherty Associates. (First published serially in *Pearson's Weekly*, June–July 1897.)

———. 1996. *The Island of Dr. Moreau*. New York: Modern Library. (Orig. pub. 1896.)

———. 1988. *The Time Machine*. New York: Berkley Publishing Group. (Orig. pub. 1895.)

———. 1988. *War of the Worlds*. New York: Tom Doherty Associates. (First published serially in *Pearson's Magazine*, April–December 1897.)

Wharton, Edith. 1998. *The Age of Innocence*. New York: Scribner Paperback Fiction. (Orig. pub. 1920.)

———. 2000. *Ethan Frome*. New York: Signet Classic. (Orig. pub. 1911.)

———. 1995. *A Son at the Front*. DeKalb: Northern Illinois University Press. (Orig. pub. 1923.)

White, Edmund. 1982. *A Boy's Own Story*. New York: Dutton.

Wilde, Oscar. 1992. *The Picture of Dorian Gray*. New York: Modern Library. (Orig. pub. 1890.)

Wilder, Thornton. 1998. *The Bridge of San Luis Rey*. New York: Perennial Classics. (Orig. pub. 1927.)

Wolf, Christa. 1983. *Divided Heaven*. New York: Adler's Foreign Books. (Orig. pub. 1963.)

Woolf, Virginia. 1973. *Orlando: A Biography*. New York: Harcourt Inc. (Orig. pub. 1928.)

Wouk, Herman. 1992. *The Caine Mutiny*. Boston: Little, Brown. (Orig. pub. 1951.)

Wright, Richard. 1998. *Native Son*. New York: HarperCollins. (Orig. pub. 1940.)

Zola, Émile. 1991. *Germinal*. New York: Knopf. (Orig. pub. 1885.)

Nonfiction

Abbey, Edward. 1990. *Desert Solitaire*. New York: Simon and Schuster. (Orig. pub. 1968.)

Adamson, Joy. 2000. *Born Free: A Lioness of Two Worlds*. New York: Pantheon Books. (Orig. pub. 1960.)

Addams, Jane. 1998. *Twenty Years at Hull House*. New York: Penguin Books. (Orig. pub. 1895.)

Agee, James, and photographs by Walker Evans. 1988. *Let Us Now Praise Famous Men: Three Tenant Families*. Boston: Houghton Mifflin Company. (Orig. pub. 1941.)

Angelou, Maya. 1997. *I Know Why the Caged Bird Sings*. New York: Bantam Books. (Orig. pub. 1970.)

The Arabian Nights. 1992. New York: Knopf. (Orig. 15th century.)

Beauvoir, Simone de. 1989. *The Second Sex*. Translated and edited by H. M. Parshley. New York: Vintage Books. (Orig. pub. 1949.)

The Bhagavad Gita. 1994. New York: Oxford University Press. (Orig. between the 5th century B.C. and the 2nd century A.D.)

The Bible. Multiple versions available. (Orig. Old Testament, 1200 B.C. to 100 B.C.; New Testament, 1st century A.D.)

Bronowski, Jacob. 1973. *The Ascent of Man*. Boston: Little, Brown.

Brown, Claude. 1965. *Manchild in the Promised Land*. New York: Signet.

Brown, Dee. 2001. *Bury My Heart at Wounded Knee*. New York: Henry Holt. (Orig. pub. 1970.)

Bstan-dzin-rgya-mtsho, Dalai Lama XIV. 1990. *Freedom in Exile: The Autobiography of the Dalai Lama*. New York: HarperCollins.

Bulfinch, Thomas. 1995. *Bulfinch's Mythology*. New York: Meridian. (Orig. pub. 1855–1863.)

Campbell, Joseph. 1968. *The Hero with a Thousand Faces*. Princeton: Princeton University Press. (Orig. pub. 1949.)

Capote, Truman. 1996. *In Cold Blood: A True Account of a Multiple Murder and Its Consequences*. New York: Random House. (Orig. pub. 1965.)

Carson, Rachel. 2002. *Silent Spring*. Boston: Houghton Mifflin. (Orig. pub. 1962.)

Cicero, Marcus Tullius. 1989. "Orator," Chapter 34, Section 120. From *Cicero: Brutus, Orator*. Translated by H. M. Hubbell (1939). In *Respectfully Quoted: A Dictionary of Quotations Requested from the Congressional Research Service*. Washington DC: Library of Congress. Also available online at: www.bartleby.com/73/ (accessed 3 November 2003).

Confucius. 1997. *The Analects*. New York: W. W. Norton and Company. (Orig. 5th century B.C.)

Curie, Eve. 1986. *Madame Curie, A Biography*. New York: Da Capo Press. (Orig. pub. 1937.)

Darwin, Charles. 1999. *The Origin of the Species by Means of Natural Selection, or, The Preservation of Favored Races in the Struggle for Life*. New York: Bantam Books. (Orig. pub. 1859.)

The Declaration of Independence and *The Constitution of the United States*. 1998. New York: Bantam Books. (Orig. pub. 1776; 1787–1789.)

Deloria, Vine, Leslie Marmon Silko, and George E. Tinker. 1994. *God is Red: A Native View of Religion*. Golden, CO: Fulcrum Publishing. (Orig. pub. 1972.)

Du Bois, W.E.B. 2003. *The Souls of Black Folk*. New York: Modern Library. (Orig. pub. 1903.)

Einstein, Albert. 2001. *Relativity: The Special and the General Theory*. New York: Routledge. (Orig. pub. c. 1913.)

Eiseley, Loren. 1957. *The Immense Journey*. New York: Random House.

Emerson, Ralph Waldo. 1990. *Essays: First and Second Series*. New York: Vintage. (Orig. 1st series pub. in 1841, 2nd series pub. in 1844.)

———. 1983. *Self-Reliance and Other Essays*. Mineola, NY: Dover Publications. (Orig. pub. 1841.)

Feynman, Richard Phillips. 1985. *"Surely You're Joking, Mr. Feynman!"* New York: W. W. Norton and Company.

Fossey, Dian. 1983. *Gorillas in the Mist*. Boston: Houghton Mifflin Company. (Orig. pub. 1983.)

Frank, Anne. 1995. *The Diary of a Young Girl: The Definitive Edition*. New York: Anchor Books/Doubleday. (Orig. pub. 1947.)

Franklin D. Roosevelt's Infamy Speech. Delivered on 8 December 1941. Norman: The University of Oklahoma Law Center. Available online at: http://www.law.ou.edu/hist/infamy.html (accessed 14 October 2003).

Frazer, James, Sir. 1996. *The Golden Bough: A Study in Magic and Religion*. New York: Simon and Schuster. (Orig. pub. 1890.)

Friedan, Betty. 2001. *The Feminine Mystique*. New York: W. W. Norton and Company. (Orig. pub. 1963.)

Gandhi, Mahatma. 1999. *The Way to God*. Berkeley, CA: Berkeley Hills Books. (Orig. pub. 1971.)

Goodall, Jane. 1988. *In the Shadow of Man*. Boston: Houghton Mifflin. (Orig. pub. 1971.)

Gould, Stephen Jay. 1992. *The Panda's Thumb: More Reflections in Natural History*. New York: Norton. (Orig. pub. 1980.)

Griffin, John Howard. 1996. *Black Like Me*. New York: Signet. (Orig. pub. 1961.)

Haley, Alex. 1976. *Roots: The Saga of an American Family*. Garden City, NY: Doubleday. (Orig. pub. 1976.)

Hamilton, Edith. 1999. *Mythology*. New York: Warner Books. (Orig. pub. 1942.)

Hawking, Stephen W. 1988. *A Brief History of Time: From the Big Bang to Black Holes*. Introduction by Carl Sagan. New York: Bantam Books.

Herriot, James. 1972. *All Creatures Great and Small*. New York: St. Martin's Press.

Hersey, John. 1989. *Hiroshima*. New York: Vintage Books. (Orig. pub. 1946.)

Houston, Jeanne Wakatsuki, and James D. Houston. 2002. *Farewell to Manzanar*. Boston: Houghton Mifflin. (Orig. pub. 1973.)

Jacobs, Harriet. 2000. *Incidents in the Life of a Slave Girl*. New York: Signet Classic. (Orig. pub. 1861.)

James, William. 2002. *The Varieties of Religious Experience*. New York: Modern Library. (Orig. pub. 1902.)

Keller, Helen. 2003 *The Story of My Life*. With supplemental accounts by Anne Sullivan and John Albert Macy. Edited with a new foreword and afterword by Roger Shattuck with Dorothy Herrmann. New York: Norton. (Orig. pub. 1903.)

King, Martin Luther, Jr. 1993. *I Have a Dream*. Foreword by Rev. Bernice A. King. San Francisco: HarperSanFrancisco. (Orig. speech at the Lincoln Memorial given on 28 Aug 1963.)

———. 2000. *Why We Can't Wait*. New York: Signet Classic. (Orig. pub. 1964.)

Kingston, Maxine Hong. 1989. *The Woman Warrior: Memoirs of a Girlhood Among Ghosts*. New York: Vintage Books. (Orig. pub. 1976.)

Lamb, Charles, and Mary Lamb. 1995. *Tales from Shakespeare*. Illustrated by Arthur Rackham. London: Everyman. (Orig. pub. 1807.)

Lao-tzu [Laozi]. 1988. *Tao Te Ching: A New English Version*. With foreword and notes by Stephen Mitchell. New York: Harper and Row. (Orig. 6th century B.C.)

Leopold, Aldo. 2001. *A Sand County Almanac*. New York: Oxford University Press. (Orig. pub. 1949.)

Lewis, C. S. 1996. *The Abolition of Man*. New York: Simon and Schuster. (Orig. pub. 1943.)

Lopez, Barry Holstun. 1978. *Of Wolves and Men*. New York: Scribner.

Machiavelli, Niccolò. 1999. *The Prince*. New York: Penguin. (Orig. pub. 1532.)

Madison, James, Alexander Hamilton, and John Jay. 1999. *The Federalist Papers*. New York: Mentor. (Orig. pub. 1788.)

Malory, Thomas, Sir. 1999. *Le Morte d'Arthur*. New York: Modern Library. (Orig. pub. 1469.)

Mandela, Nelson. 1994. *Long Walk to Freedom: The Autobiography of Nelson Mandela*. Boston: Little, Brown.

Marcus Aurelius, Emperor of Rome. 1992. *Meditations*. New York: Knopf. (Orig. 167 A.D.)

Marx, Karl. 1998. *The Communist Manifesto*. New York: Signet Classic, Penguin Putnam. (Orig. pub. 1848.)

Maslow, Abraham. 1999. *Toward a Psychology of Being*. New York: J. Wiley and Sons. (Orig. pub. 1962.)

Matthiessen, Peter. 1996. *The Snow Leopard*. New York: Penguin Books. (Orig. pub. 1978.)

McCall, Nathan. 1994. *Makes Me Wanna Holler: A Young Black Man in America*. New York: Random House.

Mill, John Stuart. 1993. *On Liberty and Utilitarianism*. New York: Bantam Books. (Orig. pub. 1859.)

More, Thomas. 1992. *Utopia*. New York: Knopf. (Orig. pub. 1516.)

Muir, John. 1997. *My First Summer in the Sierra*. New York: Penguin Books. (Orig. pub. 1911.)

Parkman, Francis. 1982. *The Oregon Trail*. New York: Penguin Books. (Orig. pub. 1872.)

Pirsig, Robert. 2000. *Zen and the Art of Motorcycle Maintenance*. New York: Perennial Classics. (Orig. pub. 1974.)

Plato. 1986. *Phaedrus*. Translation and commentary by C.J. Rowe. Warminster, Wiltshire, England: Aris and Phillips. (Circa 380 B.C.–360 B.C.)

———. 2003. *The Republic*. New York: Penguin. (Orig. 4th century B.C.)

———. 1977. *Timaeus and Critias*. Translated with an introduction and an appendix on Atlantis by Desmond Lee. New York: Penguin Books. (A late dialogue, c. 355 B.C.–347 B.C.)

Pliny. 1957. *Pliny's Natural History: An Account by a Roman of What Romans Knew and Did and Valued*. Compacted from the many volumes of *Historia Naturalis* by Loyd Haberly, Fairleigh Dickinson University. New York: Frederick Ungar Publishing Co.

Plutarch. 1985. *Plutarch's Lives: Demosthenes and Cicero, Alexander and Caesar*. Translated by Beradotte Perrin. Loeb Classical Library, no. 99. Cambridge, MA: Harvard University Press. (Orig. pub. c. 46–120 A.D.)

Polo, Marco. 2001. *The Travels of Marco Polo*. New York: Modern Library. (Orig. 1579.)

The Qu'ran. Multiple versions available. (Orig. c. early 7th century.)

Rhodes, Richard. 1986. *The Making of the Atomic Bomb*. New York: Simon and Schuster.

Rodriguez, Richard. 2004. *Hunger of Memory*. New York: Bantam Books. (Orig. pub. 1982.)

Sagan, Carl. 1994. *Pale Blue Dot: A Vision of the Human Future in Space*. New York: Random House.

Said, Edward W. 1978. *Orientalism*. New York: Pantheon Books.

Santayana, George. "Reason in Common Sense," Chapter 12 of *Life of Reason* (1905–1906). In *The Columbia World of Quotations*. New York: Columbia University Press, 1996. Also available online at: http://www.bartleby.com/66/29/48129.html (accessed 3 November 2003).

Shirer, William L. 1990. *The Rise and Fall of the Third Reich*. New York: Simon and Schuster (Orig. pub. 1960.)

Smith, Adam. 2000. *The Wealth of Nations*. New York: Modern Library. (Orig. pub. 1776.)

Stone, Irving. 1956. *Men to Match My Mountains*. Garden City, NY: Doubleday.

Sun-Tzu [Sunzi]. 2002. *The Art of War*. New York: Viking. (Orig. 5th century B.C.)

Terkel, Studs. 1984. *"The Good War": An Oral History of World War Two*. New York: New Press.

Thomas, Lewis. 1974. *The Lives of a Cell: Notes of a Biology Watcher*. New York: Bantam Books.

Thoreau, Henry David. 1987. "Sunday." *A Week on the Concord and Merrimack Rivers*. Orleans, MA: Parnassus Imprints, Inc. (Orig. pub. 1849.)

———. 1999. *Walden and "Civil Disobedience."* Introduction by W. S. Merwin. Revised and updated bibliography. New York: New American Library. (First title orig. pub. 1854.)

Tocqueville, Alexis de. 1994. *Democracy in America*. New York: Alfred A. Knopf. (Part I orig. pub. 1835; Part II 1840.)

Tuchman, Barbara Wertheim. 1994. *The Guns of August*. New York: Ballantine. (Orig. pub. 1962.)

Tutu, Desmond Mpilo. 1999. *No Future without Forgiveness*. New York: Doubleday.

Twain, Mark. 1994. *Life on the Mississippi*. New York: Modern Library. (Orig. pub. 1876.)

United Nations. No date. *The Universal Declaration of Human Rights*. New York: United Nations Publications. (Orig. pub. 1948.)

Watson, James D. 1998. *The Double Helix*. New York: Scribner. (Orig. pub. 1968.)

Wiesel, Eli. 1986. *Night*. New York: Bantam Books. (Orig. pub. 1956.)

Wolfe, Tom. 1983. *The Right Stuff*. New York: Farrar, Straus, Giroux. (Orig. pub. 1979.)

Wollstonecraft, Mary. 2001. *A Vindication of the Rights of Woman*. New York: Modern Library. (Orig. pub. 1792.)

Woolf, Virginia. 1991. *A Room of One's Own*. New York: Harcourt Brace Jovanovich. (Orig. pub. 1929.)

Wright, Richard, 1998. *Black Boy: A Record of Childhood and Youth*. New York: Perennial Classics. (Orig. pub. 1945.)

X, Malcolm. 1999. *The Autobiography of Malcolm X*. As told to Alex Haley. New York: Ballantine Books. (Orig. pub. 1965.)

Zinsser, Hans. 1996. *Rats, Lice and History*. New York: Black Dog and Leventhal Publishers. (Orig. pub. 1935.)

Online Classics—"Bests" Lists and Full-Text

"Bests" Lists

The 50 Best Books of the Century. Wilmington, DE: Intercollegiate Studies Institute. Available online at: http://www.isi.org/publications/ir/50best.html (accessed 30 January 2003).

100 Great 20th Century Works of Fiction by Women. New York: LiteraryCritic.com. Available online at: http://www.literarycritic.com/feminista.htm (accessed 12 April 2003).

The African American Literature Book Club Homepage. Harlem, NY: Troy Johnson. Available online at: http://aalbc.com/ (accessed 30 January 2003).

Best of the Century: The Best Books. Seattle, WA: Amazon.com. Available online at: http://www.amazon.com/exec/obidos/subst/features/c/century/books-best-of-century.html/102-3621410-7398508 (accessed 30 January 2003).

Booklists and Book Awards. Chicago: Young Adult Library Services Association. Available online at: http://www.ala.org/yalsa/booklists/ (accessed 28 February 2004).

Harris, James Wallace. *Classics of Science Fiction*. Available online at: http://classics.jameswallaceharris.com/ (accessed 30 January 2003).

The Hungry Mind Review's 100 Best 20th Century Books. Evanston, IL: Hosted by StartSpot Mediaworks, Inc., BookSpot.com Team. Available online at: http://www.bookspot.com/listhungry100.htm (accessed 30 January 2003).

Kipen, David. "Acute 'Angle' Wins Reader Poll: Wallace Stegner's Novel Earns Top Spot in List of 100 Best Western Works of Fiction" (The Chronicle Western 100). San Francisco: San Francisco Chronicle, 1999. Available online at: http://www.sfgate.com/cgibin/article.cgi?file=/chronicle/archive/1999/11/11/DD16098.DTL&type=books (accessed 30 January 2003).

MegaLit: Fiction. 2002. Staff-generated booklist. King County, WA: King County Library System.

MegaLit: Nonfiction. 2002. Staff-generated booklist. King County, WA: King County Library System.

The Modern Library 100 Best. New York: Modern Library. Available online at: http://www.randomhouse.com/modernlibrary/100best.html (accessed 30 January 2003).

National Review's The 100 Best Non-fiction Books of the Century. New York: National Review. Available online at: http://www.nationalreview.com/100best/100_books.html (accessed 30 January 2003).

The Nobel Prize in Literature. Stockholm, Sweden: Nobel e-Museum. Available online at: http://www.nobel.se/literature/index.html (accessed 30 January 2003).

The Northport, NY Selections for the 60 Best Books of the Century. Northport, NY:

Northport Public Library. Available online at: http://www.georgehart. com/sculpture/bookball-titles.html (accessed 30 January 2003).

Our Readable Century: From Mencken to Mailer, Woolfe to Wolfe: A Compendium of Memorable Books from the Last 100 Years. January Magazine, J. Kingston Pierce, ed. Available online at: http://www.januarymagazine.com/features/ 20thintro.html (accessed 30 January 2003).

Professional Development Center: Knowledge of Books: What Books Should Anyone Working with Teens Know? Chicago: Young Adult Library Services Association. Available online at: http://www.ala.org/ala/yalsa/professsion aldev/whatbooksshould.htm (accessed 28 February 2004).

The Pulitzer Prizes. New York: Columbia University. Available online at: http://www.pulitzer.org/index.html (accessed 30 January 2003).

Ruminator Review's 100 Best 20th Century American Books of Fiction and Nonfiction. St. Paul, MN: Ruminator Review. Available online at: http://www.rumi nator.com/hmr/100.html (accessed 30 January 2003).

The Top 100 Books of All Time. London: Guardian Newspapers, Inc. Available online at: http://books.guardian.co.uk/news/articles/0,6109,711520,00.html (accessed 13 March 2003).

Full-Text

4Literature. Jaret Wilson and Javatar LLC. Available online at: http://www.4liter ature.net/ (accessed 5 September 2003).

Absolute Shakespeare. Available online at: http://absoluteshakespeare.com (accessed 5 September 2003).

Access the Great Books. Kansas City, Missouri: The Access Foundation. Available online at: http://www.anova.org/ (accessed 6 September 2003).

The Alex Catalogue of Electronic Texts. South Bend, IN: Eric Lease Morgan and Infomotions, Inc. Available online at: http://www.infomotions.com/alex/ (accessed 5 September 2003).

Bartleby.com: Great Books Online. Steven H. van Leeuwen Chairman and CEO. Available online at: http://www.bartleby.com/ (accessed 5 September 2003).

Bibliomania. Oxford, England: Bibliomania.com Ltd. Available online at: http:// www.bibliomania.com/bibliomania-static/index.html (accessed 5 September 2003).

Bootlegbooks.com. Available online at: http://www.bootlegbooks.com/Default. htm (accessed 5 September 2003).

Classic Bookshelf. Devon, U.K.: Simon Dempsey and Classic Bookshelf Ltd. Available online at: http://www.classicbookshelf.com/ (accessed 5 September 2003).

Classic Novels in 5 Minutes a Day! Wichita, KS: Classic-Novels.com. Available online at: http://www.classic-novels.com (accessed 9 October 2003).

Classic Reader. Available online at: http://www.classicreader.com/ (accessed 5 September 2003).

Classics for Young People. Calgary, Alberta, Canada: David K. Brown, Doucette Library of Teaching Resources, University of Calgary. Available online at: http://www.ucalgary.ca/~dkbrown/storclas.html (accessed 5 September 2003).

The Classics in ASCII. Available online at: http://www.textfiles.com/etext/ (accessed 9 September 2003).

The Complete Works of William Shakespeare. Cambridge, MA: Jeremy Hylton and MIT's *The Tech.* Available online at: http://the-tech.mit.edu/Shakespeare/works.html (accessed 5 September 2003).

The Electronic Literature Foundation. Scott Gettman and Cindi Barlett Gettman. Available online at: http://elf.chaoscafe.com/elf_by_Author.htm (accessed 6 September 2003).

Ever the Twain Shall Meet: Mark Twain on the Internet. Available online at: http://users.telerama.com/~joseph/mtwain.html (accessed 6 September 2003).

Great Books and Classics: "Your Gateway to the Great Books Online." Available online at: http://www.grtbooks.com/ (accessed 9 September 2003).

Great Books Index: List of Authors and Titles. London, Ontario, Canada: Ken Roberts. Available online at: http://books.mirror.org/gb.titles.html (accessed 6 September 2003).

Hypertexts. Charlottesville, VA: American Studies Program, University of Virginia. Available online at: http://xroads.virginia.edu/~HYPER/hypertex.html (accessed 6 September 2003).

The Internet Classics Archive. Cambridge, MA: MIT. Available online at: http://classics.mit.edu/index.html (accessed 6 September 2003).

The Literature Page. Salt Lake City, UT: The Literature Page.com and Michael Moncur. Available online at: http://www.literaturepage.com (accessed 6 September 2003).

Litrix Reading Room. Anchorage, AK: Stan Jones. Available online at: http://www.litrix.com/ (accessed 9 September 2003).

The Modern English Collection. Charlottesville, VA: Electronic Text Center, Alderman Library, University of Virginia. Available online at: http://etext.lib.virginia.edu/modeng/modeng0.browse.html (accessed 5 September 2003).

The Online Books Page. Philadelphia, PA: John Mark Ockerbloom, University of Pennsylvania. Available online at: http://onlinebooks.library.upenn.edu/ (accessed 6 September 2003).

An Online Library of Literature. Available online at: http://www.literature.org/ (accessed 6 September 2003).

The Online Medieval and Classical Library. Berkeley, CA: University of California Library. Available online at: http://sunsite.berkeley.edu/OMACL/ (accessed 6 September 2003).

Oxford Text Archive. Oxford, UK: Oxford University Computing Services, Oxford

University. Available online at: http://ota.ahds.ac.uk/ (accessed 6 September 2003).

Page by Page Books. Page by Page Books. Available online at: http://www.page bypagebooks.com/ (accessed 6 September 2003).

The Perseus Digital Library. Medford, MA: Department of the Classics, Tufts University. Available online at: http://www.perseus.tufts.edu/ (accessed 6 September 2003).

Project Gutenberg. Oxford, MS: Project Gutenberg Literary Archive Foundation. Available online at: http://gutenberg.net/ (accessed 6 September 2003).

PSU's Electronic Classics Site. Hazelton, PA: Penn State University. Available online at: http://www2.hn.psu.edu/faculty/jmanis/jimspdf.htm (accessed 6 September 2003).

Publicly Available HTI (Humanities Text Initiative) Modern English Collection. Ann Arbor, MI: University of Michigan Library, University of Michigan. Available online at: http://www.hti.umich.edu/p/pd-modeng/bibl.html (accessed 6 September 2003).

The World eBook Library. Honolulu, HI: The World Electronic Text Library Foundation. Available online at: http://netlibrary.net/WorldHome.html (accessed 6 September 2003).

Poetry

Beowulf: A New Verse Translation. 2001. Translated by Seamus Heaney. New York; London: W. W. Norton and Company. (Orig. 9th century.)

Browning, Elizabeth Barrett. 2000. "How Do I Love Thee? Let Me Count the Ways" (Sonnet XLII from *Sonnets from the Portuguese*). In *Americans' Favorite Poems: The Favorite Poem Project Anthology*. Edited by Robert Pinsky and Maggie Dietz. New York: W. W. Norton and Company.

Byron, George Gordon. 2000. "She Walks in Beauty." In *Americans' Favorite Poems: The Favorite Poem Project Anthology*. Edited by Robert Pinsky and Maggie Dietz. New York: W. W. Norton and Company.

Chaucer, Geoffrey. 1994. *The Canterbury Tales*. New York: Modern Library. (Orig. 1380–1390.)

Coleridge, Samuel Taylor. 2001. "Kubla Khan." In *The 100 Best Poems of All Time*. Edited by Leslie Pockell. New York: Warner Books.

———. 2000. "The Rime of the Ancient Mariner." In *Americans' Favorite Poems: The Favorite Poem Project Anthology*. Edited by Robert Pinsky and Maggie Dietz. New York: W. W. Norton and Company.

Dante Alighieri. 1995. *The Divine Comedy*. Translated by Allen Mandelbaum. New York: Knopf: Distributed by Random House. (Orig. 1307–1321.)

Dickinson, Emily. 2001. "Because I Could Not Stop for Death." In *The 100 Best Poems of All Time*. Edited by Leslie Pockell. New York: Warner Books.

Dove, Rita. 2000. "Daystar." In *Americans' Favorite Poems: The Favorite Poem Project Anthology*. Edited by Robert Pinsky and Maggie Dietz. New York: W.W. Norton and Company.

The Epic of Gilgamesh: The Babylonian Epic Poem and Other Texts in Akkadian and Sumerian. 2000. Translated and with an introduction by Andrew George. New York: Penguin Books. (Orig. c. 2000 B.C.)

Frost, Robert. 2000. "The Road Not Taken." In *Americans' Favorite Poems: The Favorite Poem Project Anthology*. Edited by Robert Pinsky and Maggie Dietz. New York: W.W. Norton and Company.

Homer. 1999. *The Iliad*. New York: Signet Classic. (Orig. 8th century B.C.)

———. 1998. *The Odyssey*. Translated by Robert Fitzgerald. New York: Farrar, Straus and Giroux. (Orig. 8th century B.C.)

Hughes, Langston. 2000. "The Negro Speaks of Rivers." In *The Vintage Book of African American Poetry*. Edited and with an introduction by Michael S. Harper and Anthony Walton. New York: Vintage Books.

Jalal al-Din Rumi, Maulana. 1997. "A Reed." In *The Essential Rumi*. Translated by Coleman Barks, with John Moyne, A. A. Arberry, Reynold Nicholson. Edison, NJ: Castle Books.

Kunitz, Stanley. 1988. "The Wellfleet Whale." In *The Norton Anthology of Modern Poetry*. Edited by Richard Ellmann and Robert O'Clair. 2nd ed. New York: W.W. Norton and Company.

Lawrence, D.H. 1977. "Snake." In *The Complete Poems of D. H. Lawrence*. Collected and edited with an introduction and notes by Vivian de Sola Pinto and Warren Roberts. New York: Penguin Books.

Li Po. 2001. "Drinking and Alone Under the Moon." In *The 100 Best Poems of All Time*. Edited by Leslie Pockell. New York: Warner Books.

Milton, John. 2000. *Paradise Lost*. New York: Penguin Books. (Orig. pub. 1667.)

Niane, Djibril Tamsir. 1986. *The Sundiata*. Translated by G.D. Pickett. Harlow, Essex, England: Longman. (Orig. 13th century.)

Ovid. 2004. *Metamorphoses*. New York: W.W. Norton and Company. (Orig. before 8 A.D.)

Poe, Edgar Allan. 2001. "The Raven." In *The 100 Best Poems of All Time*. Edited by Leslie Pockell. New York: Warner Books.

Prime, Ranchor. *Ramayana: A Tale of Gods and Demons*. 2004. Illustrated by B.G. Sharma. San Rafael, CA: Mandala Publishing. (Orig. 19th century B.C.)

The Saga of the Volsungs Together with Excerpts from the Nornageststhattr and Three Chapters from the Prose Edda. 1982. Translated and annotated by George K. Anderson. Newark: University of Delaware Press. (Orig. 13th century.)

Service, Robert W. 2001. "The Cremation of Sam McGee." In *The 100 Best Poems of All Time*. Edited by Leslie Pockell. New York: Warner Books.

Shakespeare, William. 2000. "Shall I Compare Thee to a Summer's Day?" (Sonnet XVIII). In *Americans' Favorite Poems: The Favorite Poem Project Anthology*. Edited by Robert Pinsky and Maggie Dietz. New York: W.W. Norton and Company.

Sir Gawain and the Green Knight, Pearl, and Sir Orfeo. 1975. Translated by J.R.R. Tolkien. Boston: Houghton Mifflin. (Orig. 14th century.)

The Song of Roland. 2002. New York: Signet Classic. (Orig. 11th century.)

Stafford, William. 1995. "Traveling through the Dark." In *The Columbia Anthology of American Poetry*. Edited by Jay Parini. New York: Columbia University Press.

Tennyson, Alfred. 1995. "The Charge of the Light Brigade." In *Alfred Lord Tennyson: Selected Poetry*. Edited by Norman Page. New York: Routledge.

Thomas, Dylan. 2001. "Do Not Go Gentle into That Good Night." In *The 100 Best Poems of All Time*. Edited by Leslie Pockell. New York: Warner Books.

Three Online Poems by Jimmy Santiago Baca: El Gato. Urbana-Champaign, IL: Department of English, University of Illinois at Urbana-Champaign and Cary Nelson, ed. An Online Journal and Multimedia Companion to the *Anthology of Modern American Poetry* (Oxford University Press, 2000). Available online at: http://www.english.uiuc.edu/maps/poets/a_f/baca/online.htm (accessed 18 March 2004).

Virgil. 1992. *The Aeneid*. Translated by Robert Fitzgerald. New York: Knopf: Distributed by Random House. (Orig. between 31–19 B.C.)

Williams, William Carlos. 2001. "The Red Wheel Barrow." In *The 100 Best Poems of All Time*. Edited by Leslie Pockell. New York: Warner Books.

Short Stories and Collections by Classic Authors

Barker, Clive. 1984–1986. The Books of Blood. 6 vols. Multiple original publishers.

Benson, E. F. 1992. *The Collected Ghost Stories of E. F. Benson*. New York: Carroll and Graf Publishers.

Bierce, Ambrose. 1988. *The Civil War Short Stories of Ambrose Bierce*. Lincoln: University of Nebraska Press.

———. 1964. *Ghost and Horror Stories*. Selected and introduced by E. F. Bleiler. New York: Dover Publications.

———. 2002. "An Occurrence at Owl Creek Bridge." In *Shadows of Blue and Gray: The Civil War Writings of Ambrose Bierce*. Edited by Brian M. Thomsen. New York: Forge.

Blackwood, Algernon. 1973. *The Best Ghost Stories of Algernon Blackwood*. Selected with an introduction by E. F. Bleiler. New York: Dover Publications.

Clarke, Arthur C. 2001. "The Nine Billion Names of God." In *The Collected Stories of Arthur C. Clarke*. New York: Tom Doherty Associates.

Gaines, Ernest. 1986. "The Sky is Gray." In *Stories of the Modern South*. Edited by Ben Forkner and Patrick Samway. New York: Penguin Books.

Glaspell, Susan. 2000. "A Jury of Her Peers." In *The Best American Mystery Stories of the Century*. Edited by Tony Hillerman. Boston: Houghton Mifflin.

Godwin, Tom. 2003. "The Cold Equations." In *The Cold Equations and Other Stories*. Riverdale, NY: Baen Books.

Grove, Fred. 2001. "Comanche Woman." In *Red River Stage: Western Stories*. Large type ed. Farmington Hills, MI: Five Star.

Hamilton, Donald. 2000. "The Guns of William Longley." In *A Century of Great Western Stories*. Edited by John Jakes. New York: Forge.

Hawthorne, Nathaniel. 1967. *Twice-Told Tales*. New York: Dutton. (Orig. pub. c. 1839.)

Henry, O. 1989. "The Gift of the Magi." In *Stories by O. Henry*. New York: TOR.

Irving, Washington. 2001. *The Legend of Sleepy Hollow and Other Stories, or, the Sketchbook of Geoffrey Crayon, Gent*. Introduction by Alice Hoffman, notes by William Etter. New York: Modern Library. (Orig. pub. in 1820 in number 6 of *The Sketch Book*.)

———. 1994. *Rip Van Winkle and Other Stories*. New York: Penguin Group. (Orig. pub. 1819–1820.)

Jackson, Shirley. 1991. "The Lottery." In *The Lottery and Other Stories*. New York: Farrar, Straus and Giroux/Noonday Press.

Jacobs, W. W. "The Monkey's Paw." In *The 13 Best Horror Stories of All Time*. 2002. Edited by Leslie Pockell. New York: Warner Books.

King, Stephen. 1998. "Quitters, Inc." In *The 50 Greatest Mysteries of All Time*. Compiled by Otto Penzler. Los Angeles, CA: Dove Books.

Lardner, Ring. 2000. "Haircut." In *The Best American Mystery Stories of the Century*. Edited by Tony Hillerman. Boston: Houghton Mifflin.

Lefanu, J. F. 1964. *The Best Ghost Stories of J. F. Lefanu*. Selected with an introduction by E. F. Bleiler. New York: Dover Publications.

Lovecraft, H. P. 1987. *The Best of H. P. Lovecraft: Bloodcurdling Tales of Horror and the Macabre*. New York: Ballantine Pub. Group.

Martin, George R. R. 1981. "Sandkings." In *Sandkings*. New York: Pocket Books.

Maupassant, Guy de. 1993. "The Necklace." In *Masterpieces of Terror and the Unknown*. Selected by Marvin Kaye. New York: St. Martin's Press.

Oates, Joyce Carol. 1999. "Where Are You Going, Where Have You Been?" In *The Best American Short Stories of the Century*. Edited by John Updike and Katrina Kenison. Boston: Houghton Mifflin.

Ozick, Cynthia. 1998. "The Shawl." In *The Oxford Book of Jewish Stories*. Edited by Ilan Stavans. New York: Oxford University Press.

Poe, Edgar Allan. 1988. *Tales of Mystery and Imagination*. New York: Mysterious Press.

———. 2002. "The Tell-Tale Heart." In *The 13 Best Horror Stories of All Time*. Edited by Leslie Pockell. New York: Warner Books.

Singer, Isaac Bashevis. 1996. *The Collected Stories of Isaac Bashevis Singer*. New York: Noonday Press. (Orig. pub. 1983.)

———. 1971. "Yentl the Yeshiva Boy." In *An Isaac Bashevis Singer Reader*. New York: Farrar, Straus and Giroux.

Twain, Mark. 1981. "The Notorious Jumping Frog of Calaveras County." In *The Complete Short Stories of Mark Twain*. Edited with an introduction by Charles Neider. New York: Bantam Books.

Updike, John. 2003. "A & P." In *The Early Stories, 1953–1975*. New York: A. A. Knopf.

Wharton, Edith. 1997. *The Ghost Stories of Edith Wharton*. New York: Scribner Paperback Fiction. (Comp. 1982.)

Teen and Crossover Novels

Blume, Judy. 1975. *Forever . . .* New York: Simon and Schuster Books for Young Readers.

Childress, Alice. 2000. *A Hero Ain't Nothin' but a Sandwich*. New York: Puffin Books. (Orig. pub. 1973.)

Collier, James Lincoln. 1974. *My Brother Sam Is Dead*. New York: Four Winds Press.

Cooper, Susan. 1965–1977. *The Dark Is Rising*. 5 vols. New York: Harcourt and Atheneum.

Cormier, Robert. 1974. *The Chocolate War*. New York: Knopf.

Craven, Margaret. 1973. *I Heard the Owl Call My Name*. New York: Dell.

Forbes, Esther. 1998. *Johnny Tremain*. Boston: Houghton Mifflin. (Orig. pub. 1943.)

Garden, Nancy. 1982. *Annie on My Mind*. New York: Farrar, Straus, Giroux.

Grahame, Kenneth. 1907. *The Wind in the Willows*. New York: Scribner.

Green, Roger Lancelyn. 1995. *King Arthur and the Knights of the Round Table*. New York: Puffin. (Orig. pub. 1953.)

Greene, Bette. 1999. *Summer of My German Soldier*. New York: Puffin Books. (Orig. pub. 1973.)

Hinton, S. E. 1997. *The Outsiders*. New York: Puffin Books. (Orig. pub. 1967.)

Hunt, Irene. 2002. *Across Five Aprils*. New York: Berkley Jam Books. (Orig. pub. 1964.)

James, Will. 1993. *Smoky, the Cowhorse*. New York: Aladdin Books. (Orig. pub. 1926.)

Keith, Harold. 1957. *Rifles for Watie*. New York: Crowell, HarperCollins.

Knowles, John. 1996. *A Separate Peace*. New York: Scribner Classics. (Orig. pub. 1959.)

Lewis, C. S. 1950–1956. *The Chronicles of Narnia*. 7 vols. New York: Macmillan.

McKinley, Robin. 1993. *Beauty: A Retelling of the Story of Beauty and the Beast*. New York: Harper Trophy.

Montgomery, L. M. 2001. *Anne of Green Gables*. New York: Aladdin Paperbacks. (Orig. pub. 1908.)

Myers, Walter Dean. 1988. *Fallen Angels*. New York: Scholastic Inc.

Paterson, Katherine. 1980. *Jacob Have I Loved*. New York: Harper and Row.

Paulsen, Gary. 1987. *Hatchet*. New York: Macmillan Books for Young Readers.

Rawlings, Marjorie. 2001. *The Yearling*. New York: Aladdin Classics. (Orig. pub. 1938.)

Richter, Conrad. 1991. *The Light in the Forest*. New York: Fawcett Juniper. (Orig. pub. 1953.)

Smith, Betty, 1998. *A Tree Grows in Brooklyn*. New York: Perennial Classics. (Orig. pub. 1943.)

Taylor, Mildred D. 1976. *Roll of Thunder, Hear My Cry*. New York: Dial Press.

White, Robb. 1972. *Deathwatch*. New York: Dell.

Zindel, Paul. 1983. *The Pigman*. New York: Bantam Books. (Orig. pub. 1968.)

THE CLASSICS DEFINED

Brewer, E. Cobham. 1898. *Dictionary of Phrase and Fable*, S.v. "Classics." Philadelphia: Henry Altemus. Also available online at: http://www.bartleby.com/81/3645.html (accessed 28 October 2002).

The *Oxford English Dictionary*. Oxford, UK: Oxford University Press. Available online at: http://dictionary.oed.com (accessed 29 October 2002).

Pound, Ezra. *ABC of Reading*. In *The Columbia World of Quotations*. New York: Columbia University Press, 1996. Also available online at: http://www.bartleby.com/66/18/45218.html (accessed 10 October 2003).

Quiller-Couch, Sir Arthur. "On the Use of Masterpieces." In *On the Art of Reading: Lectures Delivered in the University of Cambridge, 1916–1917*. Cambridge: University Press, 1916. Also available online at: http://www.bartleby.com/191/ (accessed 20 November 2002).

Roget's II: The New Thesaurus. 1995. 3rd ed. Boston: Houghton Mifflin.

Saint-Beuve, Charles Augustin. "What is a Classic?" In *Literary and Philosophical Essays*. Vol. XXXII. The Harvard Classics. New York: P. F. Collier and Son, 1909–1914. Also available online at: http://www.bartleby.com/32/202.html (accessed 20 November 2002).

Twain, Mark. 1989. "Chapter XXV," *Following the Equator: A Journey around the World*. New York: Dover Publications. (Orig. pub. 1897.)

———. 1900. Speech given at the Nineteenth Century Club in New York City on 20 November. In *The Columbia World of Quotations*. New York: Columbia University Press, 1996. Also available online at: http://www.bartleby.com/66/47/62047.html (accessed 10 October 2003).

Van Doren, Carl. Quotation attributed to Van Doren and quoted by James Thurber in the *Bermudian*, November 1950. In *The Columbia World of Quotations*. New York: Columbia University Press, 1996. Also available online at: http://www.bartleby.com/66/11/62711.html (accessed 10 October 2003).

CLASSICS REFERENCE RESOURCES
Book Notes and Study Guides

Barron's Book Notes. 1985–. Woodbury, NY: Barron's Educational Series.

Barron's Classic Novels. 1999. 9 vols. Hauppauge, NY: Barron's Educational Series, Inc.

Barron's Literature Made Easy. 1999–. Hauppauge, NY: Barron's Educational Series, Inc.

Bloom, Harold, ed. 2002–. *Bloom's BioCritiques*. 36 vols. Philadelphia: Chelsea House.

———. 2000–. *Bloom's Major Dramatists*. 26 vols. Broomall, PA: Chelsea House.

———. 1999–. *Bloom's Major Novelists*. 28 vols. Philadelphia, PA: Chelsea House.

———. 1999–. *Bloom's Major Poets*. 34 vols. Broomall, PA: Chelsea House.

———. 1999–. *Bloom's Major Short Story Writers*. 28 vols. Philadelphia, PA: Chelsea House.

———. 1986–. *Bloom's Modern Critical Interpretations*. 96 vols. New York: Chelsea House.

———. 1985–2003. *Bloom's Modern Critical Views*. 141 vols. New York: Chelsea House.

———. 1996–. *Bloom's Notes*. 55 vols. New York: Chelsea House.

———. 1997–. *Bloom's ReViews: Comprehensive Research and Study Guides*. 34? vols. New York: Chelsea House.

———. 1990–1994. *Major Literary Characters*. 11 vols. New York: Chelsea House.

Book Rags. Bookrags, Inc. Available online at: http://www.bookrags.com/ (accessed 25 March 2003).

Cliffs Notes. 1958–. Lincoln, NE: Cliffs Notes, owned by Wiley Publishing, Inc.

Drama for Students. 1997–. 19 vols. Detroit: Gale Research Inc.

Epics for Students. 1997, 2000. 2 vols. Detroit: Gale Research Inc.

Gale Study Guides to Great Literature: Literary Masterpieces. 2000. 5 vols. Detroit: Gale Group.

Gale Study Guides to Great Literature: Literary Masters. 2000. 5 vols. Detroit: Gale Group.

Gale Study Guides to Great Literature: Literary Topics. 2000. 5 vols. Detroit: Gale Group.

The Greenhaven Press Companion to Literary Movements and Genres. 2000–. 19 vols. San Diego: Greenhaven Press.

The Greenhaven Press Literary Companion Series. 1996–. 96 vols. San Diego: Greenhaven Press.

The Greenwood Press "Literature in Context" Series. 1994–. 36? vols. Westport, CT: Greenwood Press.

Literary Movements for Students. 2002. 2 vols. Detroit: Gale Research Inc.

Masterplots: 1,801 Plot Stories and Critical Evaluations of the World's Finest Literature. 1996. 12 vols. Edited by Frank N. Magill; Story Editor, Revised Edition, Dayton Kohler. Pasadena, CA: Salem Press.

Masterplots II: African American Literature Series. 1994. 3 vols. Edited by Frank N. Magill. Pasadena, CA: Salem Press.

Masterplots II: American Fiction Series. 2000. 6 vols. Edited by Steven G. Kellman. Pasadena, CA: Salem Press.

Masterplots II: British and Commonwealth Fiction Series. 1987. 4 vols. Edited by Frank N. Magill. Pasadena, CA: Salem Press.

Masterplots II: Drama Series. 2003. 4 vols. Edited by Christian Hollis Moe. Pasadena, CA: Salem Press.

Masterplots II: European Fiction Series. 1986. 3 vols. Edited by Frank N. Magill. Pasadena, CA: Salem Press.

Masterplots II: Nonfiction Series. 1989. 4 vols. Edited by Frank N. Magill. Pasadena, CA: Salem Press.

Masterplots II: Poetry Series. 2002. 8 vols. Edited Philip K. Jason. Pasadena, CA: Salem Press.

Masterplots II: Short Story Series. 1986–1996. 10 vols. Edited by Frank N. Magill. Pasadena, CA: Salem Press.

Masterplots II: Women's Literature Series. 2004. 6 vols. Edited by Charles E. May. Pasadena, CA: Salem Press.

Masterplots II: World Fiction Series. 1987. 4 vols. Edited by Frank N. Magill. Pasadena, CA: Salem Press.

Nonfiction Classics for Students. 2001–. 5 vols. Detroit: Gale Research Inc.

Norton Critical Editions. 1965–. 169? vols. New York: W. W. Norton.

Novelguide.com. Available online at: http://www.novelguide.com (accessed 9 October 2003).

Novels for Students. 1997–. 18 vols. Detroit: Gale Research Inc.

Pinkmonkey.com. Canyon Lake, TX. Available online at: http://www.pinkmonkey.com/ (accessed 2 September 2003).

Plotbytes. Available online at: http://www.schoolbytes.com/plotbytes/index.html (accessed 26 March 2003).

Poetry for Students. 1997–. 21 vols. Detroit: Gale Research Inc.

Shakespeare for Students. 1992–2000. 3 vols. Detroit: Gale Research Inc.

Short Stories for Students. 1997–. 20 vols. Detroit: Gale Research Inc.

SparkNotes. New York: SparkNotes LLC, part of the Barnes and Noble Learning Network. Available online at: http://www.sparknotes.com (accessed 27 March 2003).

Twayne's Masterwork Studies. 1986–. 174? vols. New York: Twayne.

Umland, Samuel J. 1996. *Fahrenheit 451: Notes*. Lincoln, NE: Cliffs Notes, Inc.

Understanding Great Literature. 2000–. 19 vols. San Diego: Lucent Books.

Viking Critical Library. 1966–. 9 vols. New York: Viking Press.

Classics and the Canon

Bloom, Harold. 2000. *How to Read and Why*. New York: Scribner.

———. 1994. *The Western Canon: The Books and School of the Ages*. New York: Harcourt Brace.

Calvino, Italo. 1986. "Why Read the Classics?" *New York Review of Books* 9 October: 19–20.

———. 1999. *Why Read the Classics?* Translated from the Italian by Martin McLaughlin. New York: Pantheon Books.

Casement, William. 1996. *The Great Canon Controversy: The Battle of the Books in Higher Education*. New Brunswick, NJ: Transaction Publishers.

———. 1995. "Some Myths about the Great Books." *The Midwest Quarterly* 36 (2): 203–218.

Delbanco, Andrew. 1997. *Required Reading: Why Our American Classics Matter Now*. New York: Farrar, Straus and Giroux.

Downs, Robert Bingham. 1983. *Books That Changed the World*. New York: New American Library.

Gillespie, Tim. 1994. "Why Literature Matters." *English Journal* 83 (8): 16–21.

The Great Conversation: A Reader's Guide to Great Books of the Western World, 2nd ed. 1991. Philip W. Goetz, Editor in Chief. Chicago: Encyclopaedia Britannica, Inc.

Greenbaum, Vicky. 1994. "Expanding the Canon: Shaping Inclusive Reading Lists." *English Journal* 83 (8): 36–39.

Kaplan, Carey, and Ellen C. Rose. 1990. *The Canon and the Common Reader*. Knoxville: University of Tennessee Press.

Meyer, Bruce. 2000. *The Golden Thread: A Reader's Journey through the Great Books*. Toronto: HarperFlamingo Canada.

Mooney, Bell. 1999. "Tempt the Young to Read the Best of the Old." *Times Educational Supplement*, 30 July.

Classics on Film

Baskin, Ellen, and Mandy Hicken, comps. 1993. *Enser's Filmed Books and Plays: A List of Books and Plays from Which Films Have Been Made, 1928–1991*. Brookfield, VT: Ashgate.

Books on Film: An Alphabetical Listing. J. M. McElligot. Available online at: http://www.literature-awards.com/books_on_film.htm (accessed 21 October 2003).

Books to Movies. Morton Grove, IL: Morton Grove Public Library. Available online at: http://www.webrary.org/rs/flbklists/Movies.html (accessed 21 October 2003).

Books to Television. Morton Grove, IL: Morton Grove Public Library. Available online at: http://www.webrary.org/rs/flbklists/TV.html (cited 21 October 2003).

Cartmell, Deborah, and Imelda Whelehan, eds. 1999. *Adaptations: From Text to Screen, Screen to Text*. London; New York: Routledge.

Cartmell, Deborah, I. Q. Hunter, and Heidi Kaye, eds. 2000. *Classics in Film and Fiction*. London; Sterling, VA: Pluto Press.

Erskine, Thomas, and James M. Welsh, eds. 2000. *Video Versions: Film Adaptations of Plays on Video*. Westport, CT: Greenwood Publishing Group.

Giddings, Robert, and Eric Sheen, eds. 2000. *The Classic Novel: From Page to Screen*. Manchester, UK: Manchester University Press.

Jackson, Russell, ed. 2000. *The Cambridge Companion to Shakespeare on Film.* Cambridge; New York: Cambridge University Press.

Kovacs, Lee. 1999. *The Haunted Screen: Ghosts in Literature and Film.* Jefferson, NC: McFarland and Company.

Lupack, Barbara Tepa, ed. 1999. *Nineteenth-Century Women at the Movies: Adapting Classic Women's Fiction to Film.* Bowling Green, OH: Bowling Green State University.

Moss, Joyce. 1992. *From Page to Screen: Children's and Young Adult Books on Film and Video.* Detroit: Gale Research.

Rosenthal, Daniel M. 2000. *Shakespeare on Screen.* London: Hamlyn.

Sova, Dawn B. 2001. *Forbidden Films: Censorship Histories of 125 Motion Pictures.* New York: Facts on File.

Tibbetts, John C., and James M. Welsh. 1998. *The Encyclopedia of Novels into Film.* New York: Facts on File.

———. 2001. *The Encyclopedia of Stage Plays into Film.* New York: Facts on File.

Wheeler, David, ed. 1989. *No, but I Saw the Movie: The Best Short Stories Ever Made into Film.* New York: Penguin Books.

Literary Reference

Author Information

American Writers: A Collection of Literary Biographies. 1974–2002. 4 vols., 10 supp. Leonard Unger, Editor in Chief. New York: Scribner.

Dictionary of Literary Biography. 1978–1980. 6 vols. Detroit: Gale Research Company.

Engel, Elliot. 2002. *A Dab of Dickens and a Touch of Twain: Literary Lives from Shakespeare's Old England to Frost's New England.* New York: Pocket Books, Simon and Shuster.

Glossbrenner, Alfred, and Emily Glossbrenner. 2000. *About the Author: The Passionate Reader's Guide to the Authors You Love, Including Things You Never Knew, Juicy Bits You'll Want to Know, and Hundreds of Ideas for What to Read Next.* San Diego: Harcourt.

Krull, Kathleen. 1994. *Lives of the Writers: Comedies, Tragedies (and What the Neighbors Thought).* San Diego: Harcourt Brace.

Toni Morrison—Biography. Stockholm, Sweden: Nobel e-Museum. Available online at: http://www.nobel.se/literature/laureates/1993/morrison-bio.html (accessed 27 September 2003).

Broad Scope

African American Writers. 1991. Valerie Smith, Consulting Editor; Lea Baechler, A. Walton Litz, General Editors. New York: C. Scribner's Sons; Toronto: Collier Macmillan Canada; New York: Maxwell Macmillan International Group.

American Ethnic Writers. 2000. 2 vols. Edited by David R. Peck. Tracy Irons-Georges, Project Editor. Pasadena, CA: Salem Press.

American Women Writers: A Critical Reference Guide from Colonial Times to the Present. 1979–. 4 vols. Edited by Lina Mainiero; Langdon Lynne Faust, Associate Editor. New York: Continuum Publishing Company, a division of Frederick Ungar Publishing Company.

Asian American Literature: Reviews and Criticism of Works by American Writers of Asian Descent. 1999. Edited by Lawrence J. Trudeau. With advisors David Henry Hwang, Ravindra N. Sharma, and Kenneth Yamashita. Detroit: Gale.

Asian American Novelists: A Bio-bibliographical Critical Sourcebook. 2000. Edited by Emmanuel S. Nelson. Westport, CT: Greenwood Press.

Benet's Reader's Encyclopedia of American Literature. 1991. Edited by George Perkins, Barbara Perkins, and Phillip Leininger. New York: HarperCollins Publishers.

British Writers. 1979–1984. 8 vols. Edited under the auspices of the British Council and Ian Scott-Kilvert, General Editor. New York: Scribner.

Contemporary Authors: A Bio-bibliographical Guide to Current Writers in Fiction, General Nonfiction, Poetry, Journalism, Drama, Motion Pictures, Television and Other Fields. 1981–. Detroit: Gale Research Company.

European Writers. 1983–1990. 14 vols. Edited by William T. H. Jackson; George Stade, Editor in Chief. New York: Scribner.

Hart, James David. 1995. *The Oxford Companion to American Literature.* 6th ed. With revisions and additions by Phillip W. Leininger. New York: Oxford University Press.

Latin American Writers. 1989, 2002. 3 vols., 1 supp. Carlos A. Sole, Editor in Chief. New York: Scribner.

Major 20th-Century Writers: A Selection of Sketches from Contemporary Authors. 1999. 4 vols. Edited by Bryan Ryan. Detroit: Gale Research.

Masterpieces of African-American Literature. 1992. Edited by Frank N. Magill. New York: HarperCollins.

Masterpieces of American Literature. 1993. Edited by Frank N. Magill. New York: HarperCollins Publishers.

Masterpieces of Latino Literature. 1994. Edited by Frank N. Magill. New York: HarperCollins.

Masterpieces of Women's Literature. 1996. Edited by Frank N. Magill. New York: HarperCollins.

Modern American Women Writers. 1991. Elaine Showalter, Consulting Editor; Lea Baechler, A. Walton Litz, General Editors. New York: Scribner; Toronto: Collier Macmillan Canada; New York: Maxwell Macmillan International.

The Oxford Companion to Women's Writing in the United States. 1995. Cathy N. Davidson, Linda Wagner-Martin, Editors in Chief; Elizabeth Ammons, et al., Editors. New York: Oxford University Press.

Reference Guide to World Literature. 1995. 2 vols. Edited by Lesley Henderson; Sarah M. Hall, Associate Editor. New York: St. James Press.

Shirey, Lynn. 1997. *Latin American Writers.* New York: Facts on File.

Smith, Verity, ed. 2000. *Concise Encyclopedia of Latin American Literature.* London; Chicago: Fitzroy Dearborn.

Whitson, Kathy J. 1999. *Native American Literatures: An Encyclopedia of Works, Characters, Authors, and Themes.* Santa Barbara, CA: ABC-CLIO.

Literary Criticism

Black Literature Criticism: Excerpts from Criticism of the Most Significant Works of Black Authors over the Past 200 Years. 1992. Edited by James P. Draper. 3 vols., 1 suppl. Detroit: Gale Research Inc.

Classical and Medieval Literature Criticism, 1988–. 66 vols. Detroit: Gale Research.

Contemporary Literary Criticism: Criticism of the Works of Today's Novelists, Poets, Playwrights, Short Story Writers, Scriptwriters, and Other Creative Writers. 1988–. Annual. Janet Witalec, Project Editor. Detroit: Gale Group Inc.

Drama Criticism: Criticism of the Most Significant and Widely Studied Dramatic Works from All the World's Literatures. 1991–. 23 vols. Edited by Rebecca Blanchard and Justin Karr. Detroit: Gale Group Inc.

Hispanic Literature Criticism. 1994. 2 vols., 2 suppl. Detroit: Gale Research.

Internet Public Library: Literary Criticism Collection. Ann Arbor, MI: University of Michigan School of Information. Available online at: http://www.ipl.org/div/litcrit/ (accessed 14 April 2003).

Nineteenth-Century Literature Criticism: Excerpts from Criticism of the Works of Nineteenth-Century Novelists, Poets, Playwrights, Short-Story Writers, and Other Creative Writers. 1981–. 139 vols. Detroit: Gale Research.

Poetry Criticism: Excerpts from Criticism of the Works of the Most Significant and Widely Studied Poets of World Literature. 1991–. David Galens, Project Editor. Detroit: Gale Group Inc.

Shakespearean Criticism: Excerpts from the Criticism of William Shakespeare's Plays and Poetry, from the First Published Appraisals to Current Evaluations. 1984–. 83 vols. Detroit: Gale Research.

Short Story Criticism: Excerpts from the Criticism of the Works of Short Fiction Writers. 1988–. Edited by Laurie Lanzen Harris and Sheila Fitzgerald. Detroit: Gale Research Company.

Twentieth-Century Literary Criticism: Criticism of Various Topics in Twentieth-Century Literature, Including Literary and Critical Movements, Prominent Themes and Genres, Anniversary Celebrations, and Surveys of National Literatures. 1981–. Annual. Janet Witalec, Project Editor. Detroit: Gale Group Inc.

World Literature Criticism: 1500 to the Present: A Selection of Major Authors from Gale's Literary Criticism Series. 1992. 6 vols., 2 suppl. Detroit: Gale Research.

Literary Magazines and Book Reviews

The Atlantic Monthly. 1857–. Boston, MA: Atlantic Monthly Group.

The Book Review Digest. 1905–. Annual cumulation. New York: The H. W. Wilson Company.

The Book Review Index. 1977–. Bimonthly, with annual cumulations. Detroit: Gale Research Company.

Books in Print with Book Reviews. New Providence, NJ: R. R. Bowker. Available through subscription online at: http://www.bowker.com/bowkerweb/catalog2001/prod00001.htm (accessed 26 March 2003).

Harper's. 1913–. Monthly. New York: Harper's Magazine Foundation.

The New Republic. 1914–. Weekly. New York: The Republic Pub. Co.

New York Review of Books. 1963–. Biweekly with intermittent monthly issues. New York: A. W. Ellsworth, et al. Also available online at: http://www.nybooks.com (accessed 14 April 2003).

New York Times Book Review. 1923–. Weekly. New York: The New York Times Company. Also available online at: http://www.nytimes.com/pages/books/review/ (accessed 14 April 2003).

The New Yorker. 1925–. Weekly. New York: F-R Pub. Corp.

Literature in Historical Context

American Decades. 1994–2001. 10 vols. Edited by Vincent Tompkins. Detroit: Gale Research.

American Eras. 1997–1999. 8 vols. Detroit: Gale Research.

American History by Era. 2003. 9 vols. San Diego, CA: Greenhaven Press.

America's Decades. 2000. 10 vols. San Diego, CA: Greenhaven Press.

Dunn, John M. 2000. *Life during the Black Death*. San Diego: Lucent Books.

The Greenwood Press "Daily Life through History" Series. 1995–. 25 vols. Westport, CT: Greenwood Press.

Hopkins, Martha E. 1999. *Language of the Land: The Library of Congress Book of Literary Maps*. Washington, DC: Library of Congress; Pittsburgh, PA: U.S. GPO.

Literature and Its Times. 1997. 5 vols., 1 suppl. Edited by Joyce Moss and George Wilson. Detroit: Gale Research.

Our American Century. 1997–1999. 17 vols. Alexandria, VA: Time Life Books.

Snodgrass, Mary, and Raymond Barrett. 1995. *Literary Maps for Young Adult Literature*. Englewood, CO: Libraries Unlimited.

U.X.L. American Decades. 2002. 10 vols. Edited by Tom Pendergast, Sara Pendergast, and Rob Nagel. Detroit: Gale Group.

World History by Era. 2002. 10 vols. San Diego, CA: Greenhaven Press.

World Literature and Its Times: Profiles of Notable Literary Works and the Historical

Events That Influenced Them. 1999–. 12 vols. (in progress). Edited by Jane Moss. Detroit: Gale Group Inc.

Writer's Guide to Everyday Life. 1993–. Multivolume series with periodic changes to series title. Cincinnati, OH: Writer's Digest Books.

Online Book Discussion Groups

Constant Reader.com: The Website for Discerning Readers. Allen Crocker. Available online at: http://www.constantreader.com (accessed 10 October 2003).

ExxonMobil Masterpiece Theater Book Club. Boston: WGBH Educational Foundation and the Public Broadcasting Service. Available online at: http://www.pbs.org/wgbh/masterpiece/bookclub/index.html (accessed 10 October 2003).

The Great Books Foundation. Chicago: The Great Books Foundation. Available online at: http://www.greatbooks.org/home.shtml (accessed 28 June 2003).

The New York Times Books Forums. New York: The New York Times. Available online at: http://www.nytimes.com/books/forums/index.html (accessed 10 October 2003).

Oprah's Book Club. Chicago: Harpo Productions, Inc. Available online at: http://www.oprah.com/books/classics/books_classics_news.jhtml (accessed 5 March 2003).

The Reader's Place. Available online at: http://www.thereadersplace.com/ (accessed 10 October 2003).

The Washington Post Book Club. Washington, DC: The Washington Post. Available online at: http://www.washingtonpost.com/wp-dyn/style/books/bookclub/ (accessed 10 October 2003).

Online Databases

Bigchalk eLibrary. New York: Bigchalk.com. Available through subscription online at: http://www.bigchalk.com/cgi-bin/WebObjects/WOPortal.woa/wa/BCPageDA/gen%7EPIC%7Epic_elibrary (accessed 26 March 2003).

Essay and General Literature Index. Bronx, NY: H. W. Wilson. Available through subscription online at: http://www.hwwilson.com/sales/ordering.html (accessed 27 March 2003).

Expanded Academic ASAP. Detroit: The Gale Group, Inc. Available through subscription online at: http://www.galegroup.com/servlet/ItemDetailServlet?region=9&imprint=000&titleCode=INFO9&type=4&id=172032 (accessed 26 March 2003).

General Reference Center. Detroit: Gale Group, Inc. Available through subscription online at: http://www.galegroup.com/servlet/ItemDetailServlet?region=9&imprint=000&titleCode=INFO16&type=4id=172039 (accessed 26 March 2003).

Literature Resource Center. Farmington Hills, MI: Gale. Available through subscription online at: http://www.galegroup.com/LitRC/ (accessed 10 October 2003).

ProQuest. Ann Arbor, MI: ProQuest Information and Learning: UMI. Available through subscription online at: http://www.umi.com/division/ (accessed 15 October 2003).

Readers' Guide to Periodical Literature. Bronx, NY: H. W. Wilson. Available through subscription online at: http://www.hwwilson.com/sales/ordering.html (accessed 27 March 2003).

Reading Selection

Award Winners and Notables

Carter, Betty. 2000. *Best Books for Young Adults.* Chicago: American Library Association Editions.

The Europa Directory of Literary Awards and Prizes: A Complete Guide to the Major Awards and Prizes of the Literary World. 2002. London: Taylor and Francis.

The National Book Awards: Winners and Finalists 1950–2001. 2002. New York: National Book Foundation.

The Newbery and Caldecott Awards: A Complete Listing of Medal and Honor Books. 2002. Chicago: Association for Library Service to Children.

The Newbery and Caldecott Medal Books, 1986–2000: A Comprehensive Guide to the Winners. 2001. Chicago: American Library Association.

Smith, Henrietta, ed. 1999. *The Coretta Scott King Awards Book, 1970–1999.* Chicago: American Library Association.

General

Anderson, Stevens W., ed. 1992–. *The Great American Bathroom Book (GABB).* Salt Lake City, UT: Compact Classics.

Bauermeister, Erica, Jesse Larsen, and Holly Smith. 1994. *500 Great Books by Women: A Reader's Guide.* New York: Penguin Books.

Bratman, Fred. 1994. *The Reader's Companion: A Book Lover's Guide to the Most Important Books in Every Field of Knowledge, as Chosen by the Experts.* New York: Hyperion.

Burt, Daniel S. 2001. *The Literary 100: A Ranking of the Most Influential Novelists, Playwrights, and Poets of All Time.* New York: Checkmark Books.

Campbell, John W., ed. 2001. *The Book of Great Books: A Guide to 100 World Classics.* London: Metro Books.

Conway, J. North. 1993. *American Literacy: Fifty Books That Define Our Culture and Ourselves.* New York: W. Morrow.

Dear Author: Students Write about the Books That Changed Their Lives. 1995. Collected by *Weekly Reader's Read*. Introduction by Lois Lowry. Berkeley, CA: Conari Press.

Estell, Doug, Michele L. Satchwell, and Patricia S. Wright. 2000. *Reading Lists for College-bound Students*. 3rd ed. New York: ARCO; Distributed by Prentice Hall Trade Sales.

Givens, Archie, ed. 1997. *Spirited Minds: African American Books for Our Sons and Our Brothers*. New York: W. W. Norton.

Kanigel, Robert. 1998. *Vintage Reading: From Plato to Bradbury; A Personal Tour of Some of the World's Best Books*. Baltimore, MD: Bancroft Press.

Lewis, Marjorie, ed. 1996. *Outstanding Books for the College Bound: Choices for a Generation*. Chicago: American Library Association.

Major, David C., and John S. Major. 2001. *100 One-Night Reads: A Book Lover's Guide*. New York: Ballantine Books.

McGrath, Charles, ed. 1998. *Books of the Century: A Hundred Years of Authors, Ideas and Literature: From the* New York Times. New York: Times Books.

Nagan, Greg. 2000. *The Five-Minute* Iliad *and Other Instant Classics: Great Books for the Short Attention Span*. Illustrated by Tony Millionaire. New York: Simon and Schuster.

New York Public Library. 2001. *The New York Public Library Literature Companion*. Edited by Anne Skillion. New York: Free Press.

Recommended Reading: 500 Classics Reviewed. 1995. Pasadena, CA: The Press.

Rexroth, Kenneth. 1986. *Classics Revisited*. New York: New Directions.

———. 1989. *More Classics Revisited*. New York: New Directions.

Rodriguez, Max, Angeli R. Rasbury, and Carol Taylor, comps. and eds. 1999. *Sacred Fire: The QBR 100 Essential Black Books*. Foreword by Charles Johnson. New York: John Wiley.

Rubel, David, ed. 1998. *The Reading List: Contemporary Fiction; A Critical Guide to the Complete Works of 110 Authors*. New York: Henry Holt.

Seymour-Smith, Martin. 1998. *The 100 Most Influential Books Ever Written: The History of Thought from Ancient Times to Today*. Secaucus, NJ: Carol Publishing Group.

Strouf, Judie L. H. 1997. *The Literature Teacher's Book of Lists*. West Nyack, NY: Center for Applied Research in Education.

Genre

Bloom, Harold, ed. 1994. *Classic Crime and Suspense Writers*. New York: Chelsea House.

———. 1994. *Classic Fantasy Writers*. New York: Chelsea House.

———. 1994. *Classic Horror Writers*. New York: Chelsea House.

———. 1995. *Classic Mystery Writers*. New York: Chelsea House.

———. 1995. *Classic Science Fiction Writers*. New York: Chelsea House.

———. 1995. *Science Fiction Writers of the Golden Age*. New York: Chelsea House.

Dubose, Martha Hailey. 2000. *Women of Mystery: The Lives and Works of Notable Women Crime Novelists*. New York: St. Martin's Minotaur.

Fonseca, Anthony J., and June Michele Pulliam. 1999. *Hooked on Horror: A Guide to Reading Interests in Horror Fiction*. Englewood, CO: Libraries Unlimited.

———. 2003. *Hooked on Horror: A Guide to Reading Interests in Horror Fiction*. 2nd ed. Englewood, CO: Libraries Unlimited.

Herald, Diana Tixier. 1999. *Fluent in Fantasy: A Guide to Reading Interests*. Englewood, CO: Libraries Unlimited.

———. 2000. *Genreflecting: A Guide to Reading Interests in Genre Fiction*. 5th ed. Englewood, CO: Libraries Unlimited.

Herald, Diana Tixier, and Bonnie Kunzel. 2002. *Strictly Science Fiction: A Guide to Reading Interests*. Greenwood Village, CO: Libraries Unlimited.

Jones, Stephen, and Kim Newman, eds. 1998. *Horror: The 100 Best Books*. New York: Carroll and Graf.

Keating, H.R.F. 1987. *Crime and Mystery: The 100 Best Books*. New York: Carroll and Graf.

Kelleghan, Fiona, ed. 2001. *100 Masters of Mystery and Detective Fiction*. 2 vols. Pasadena, CA: Salem Press.

Mort, John. 2002. *Christian Fiction: A Guide to the Genre*. Greenwood Village, CO: Libraries Unlimited.

Niebuhr, Gary Warren. 2003. *Make Mine a Mystery: A Reader's Guide to Mystery and Detective Fiction*. Westport, CT: Libraries Unlimited.

Pringle, David. 1989. *Modern Fantasy: The Hundred Best Novels*. New York: Bedrick Books.

———. 1985. *Science Fiction: The 100 Best Novels: An English Language Selection, 1949–1984*. New York: Carroll and Graf Publishers.

Ramsdell, Kristin. 1999. *Romance Fiction: A Guide to the Genre*. Englewood, CO: Libraries Unlimited.

COMICS—CLASSIC AND CONTEMPORARY

Aquaman. 1962–. Serial comic. New York: DC Comics.

Barr, Mike W., and Brian Bolland. 1997. *Camelot 3000*. New York: DC Comics.

Batman. 1940–. Serial comic. New York: DC Comics.

Captain America. 1941–. Serial comic. New York: Marvel Comics.

The Fantastic Four. 1961–. Serial comic. New York: Marvel Comics.

The Flash. 1940–. Serial comic. New York: DC Comics.

The Green Arrow. 1972–. Serial comic. New York: DC Comics.

The Green Lantern. 1941–. Serial comic. New York: DC Comics.

Hercules, Modern Champion of Justice. 1940–. Serial comic. Norwalk, CT: Blue Ribbon Comics (now Archie Comics).

The Hulk. 1962–. Serial comic. New York: Marvel Comics.

The Justice League of America. 1960–. Serial comic. New York: DC Comics; New York: Marvel Characters, Inc.

Spider-man. 1963–. Serial comic. New York: Marvel Comics.

Spiegelman, Art. 1986. *Maus: A Survivor's Tale.* New York: Pantheon Books.

Superman. 1938–. Serial comic. New York: DC Comics.

Thor. 1966–. Serial comic. New York: Marvel Comics.

Waid, Mark. 2002. *Ruse: Enter the Detective,* vol. 1. Penciled by Butch Guice, inked by Mike Perkins, colored by Laura DePuy. Oldsmar, FL: CrossGeneration Comics.

Wonder Woman. 1942–. Serial comic. New York: DC Comics.

The X-Men. 1963–. Serial comic. New York: Marvel Comics.

CONTEMPORARY FICTION AND NONFICTION
General

Auden, W. H. 1989. *The Dyer's Hand and Other Essays.* New York: Random House: Vintage International. (Orig. pub. 1948.)

Brokaw, Tom. 1998. *The Greatest Generation.* New York: Random House.

Cheever, John. 1977. *Falconer.* New York: Knopf.

Crichton, Michael. 1976. *Eaters of the Dead.* New York: Knopf.

Fast, Howard. 1979. *The Establishment.* Boston: Houghton Mifflin.

Forsyth, Frederick. 1999. *The Phantom of Manhattan.* New York: Thomas Dunne Books/St. Martin's Press.

Fry, Stephen. 2002. *Revenge.* New York: Random House.

Gilstrap, John. 1996. *Nathan's Run.* New York: HarperCollins Publishers.

Haire-Sargeant, Lin. 1993. *Heathcliff: The Return to Wuthering Heights.* New York: Pocket Books.

Judd, Denis. 1978. *Return to Treasure Island.* New York: St. Martin's Press.

King, Laurie R. 1994–. *The Mary Russell Novels.* New York: St. Martin's Press; New York: Bantam Books.

Ludlum, Robert. 1988. *The Icarus Agenda.* New York: Random House.

Martin, Valerie. 1990. *Mary Reilly.* New York: Pocket Books.

Modern Sequels. Hobart, Tasmania: State Library of Tasmania. Available online at: http://www.statelibrary.tas.gov.au/modernsequ/ (accessed 14 October 2003).

Naslund, Sena Jeter. 1999. *Ahab's Wife, or, the Star-gazer.* New York: William Morrow and Company.

Perry, Steve. 2001. *Cybernation.* Tom Clancy's Net Force, no 6. Created by Tom Clancy and Steve R. Pieczenik. New York: Berkley Books.

Preston, Richard. 1994. *The Hot Zone.* New York: Random House.

Ripley, Alexandra. 1991. *Scarlett: The Sequel to Margaret Mitchell's* Gone with the Wind. New York: Warner Books.

Shulman, Irving. 1961. *West Side Story*. Novelization of the original 1958 Broadway musical. New York: Pocket Books.

Tennant, Emma. 1993. *Pemberley, or, Pride and Prejudice Continued*. New York: St. Martin's Press.

———. 1994. *An Unequal Marriage, or, Pride and Prejudice Twenty Years Later*. New York: St. Martin's Press.

Terkel, Studs. 1984. *"The Good War": An Oral History of World War Two*. New York: New Press.

Windling, Terri, and Ellen Datlow, eds. 2000. *Black Heart, Ivory Bones*. New York: Avon Books.

———. 1995. *Ruby Slippers, Golden Tears*. New York: William Morrow and Company.

———. 1993. *Snow White, Blood Red*. New York: William Morrow and Company.

Teen

Angel series. 1999–. 30 vols. New York: Simon Pulse.

Atwater-Rhodes, Amelia. 2000. *Demon in My View*. New York: Delacorte Press.

———. 1999. *In the Forests of the Night*. New York: Dell Laurel-Leaf.

———. 2002. *Midnight Predator*. New York: Delacorte Press.

———. 2001. *Shattered Mirror*. New York: Delacorte Press.

Bennett, Cherie. 2001. *Anne Frank and Me*. New York: Putnam.

Blackwood, Gary L. 1998. *The Shakespeare Stealer*. New York: Dutton Children's Books.

Buffy the Vampire Slayer series. 1997–. 100-plus vols. New York: Simon and Schuster.

Chaucer, Geoffrey. 1988. *Canterbury Tales*. Selected, translated, and adapted by Barbara Cohen; illustrated by Trina Schart Hyman. New York: Lothrop, Lee and Shepard Books.

Clements, Andrew. 2002. *Things Not Seen*. New York: Philomel Books.

Cooper, Susan. 1999. *King of Shadows*. New York: Margaret K. McElderry Books.

Dalkey, Kara. 1998. *The Heavenward Path*. San Diego: Harcourt Brace.

———. 1996. *Little Sister*. San Diego: Harcourt Brace.

Dokey, Cameron. 2002. *Beauty Sleep*. New York: Simon Pulse.

———. 2002. *The Storyteller's Daughter*. New York: Simon Pulse.

Draper, Sharon. 1999. *Romiette and Julio*. New York: Atheneum Books for Young Readers.

Fletcher, Susan. 1998. *Shadow Spinner*. New York: Atheneum Books for Young Readers.

Galloway, Priscilla. 1998. *Snake Dreamer*. New York: Delacorte Press.

Geras, Adele. 2001. *Troy*. San Diego: Harcourt.

Kindl, Patrice. 2002. *Lost in the Labyrinth*. Boston: Houghton Mifflin.

Kositsky, Lynn. 2000. *A Question of Will*. Montreal: Roussan.

Lester, Julius. 1995. *Othello: A Retelling*. New York: Scholastic.

Lynn, Tracy. 2003. *Snow*. New York: Simon Pulse.

McKinley, Robin. 1993. *Beauty: A Retelling of the Story of Beauty and the Beast*. New York: Harper Trophy.

McLaren, Clemence. 1996. *Inside the Walls of Troy: A Novel of the Women Who Lived the Trojan War*. New York: Atheneum Books for Young Readers.

———. 2000. *Waiting for Odysseus*. New York: Atheneum Books for Young Readers.

Naidoo, Beverley. 1989. *Chain of Fire*. Illustrations by Eric Velasquez. New York: J. B. Lippincott.

Napoli, Donna Jo. 2003. *The Great God Pan*. New York: Wendy Lamb Books.

Ogiwara, Noriko. 1993. *Dragon Sword and Wind Child*. New York: Farrar, Straus and Giroux.

Orgel, Doris. 1996. *The Princess and the God*. New York: Orchard Books.

Pascal, Francine. 2000. *Heat. Fearless*, no.8. New York: Simon and Schuster.

Pike, Christopher. 1994–1996. The Last Vampire series. 6 vols. New York: Pocket Books.

Rainey, Richard. 1993. *The Monster Factory*. New York: New Discovery Books.

Shan, Darren. 2001–. Cirque du Freak: The Saga of Darren Shan series. Boston: Little, Brown.

Spinner, Stephanie. 2002. *Quiver*. New York: Alfred A. Knopf.

Stein, R. L. 1992–. Goosebumps series. New York: Scholastic Inc.

Straubing, Harold Elk. 1993. *In Hospital and Camp: The Civil War through the Eyes of Its Doctors and Nurses*. Harrisburg, PA: Stackpole Books.

Teenreads.com. New York: Carol Fitzgerald. Available online at: http://www.teen reads.com (accessed 28 August 2003).

Viguie, Debbie. 2003. *Midnight Pearls*. New York: Simon Pulse.

Windling, Terri, and Ellen Datlow, eds. 2003. *Swan Sister: Fairy Tales Retold*. New York: Simon and Schuster Children's Publishing.

———. 2000. *A Wolf at the Door: And Other Retold Fairy Tales*. New York: Simon and Schuster Books for Young Readers.

Wisler, Clifton G. 2001. *When Johnny Went Marching: Young Americans Fight the Civil War*. New York: HarperCollins.

CONVERSATIONS, CORRESPONDENCE, AND QUESTIONNAIRES

Bothell High School Seniors. 2002. Written responses to questionnaires. Bothell, WA: 2 October.

Brown, Max. 2002. Conversation with the author. Kenmore, WA: 29 November.

———. 2003. E-mail exchange with the author. Bothell, WA: 2 October.

Coons, Rochelle. 2003. Written response to questionnaire. Bothell, WA: 10 January.

Doherty, Kathleen. 2003. E-mail correspondence with the author. New York: 24 February.

Driscoll, Scott. 2002. Written response to questionnaire. Seattle, WA: 22 October.

Lockerby, Jackie. 2002. Written response to questionnaire. Faribault, MN: 22 October.

O'Boyle, Elizabeth. 2002. Written response to questionnaire. Bothell, WA: 18 June.

Rosolowsky, Diane. 2002. Conversation with the author. Kenmore, WA: 28 August.

Vanderkooi, JoAnn. 2002. Written response to questionnaire. Issaquah, WA: 29 October.

EDUCATIONAL AND PROFESSIONAL RESOURCES
Censorship

Challenged and Banned Books. Chicago: American Library Association. Available online at: http://www.ala.org/Content/NavigationMenu/Our_Associa tion/Offices/Intellectual_Freedom3/Banned_Books_Week/Challenged_ and_Banned_Books/Challenged_and_Banned_Books.htm#wdcb (accessed 29 June 2003).

Foerstel, Herbert N. 2002. *Banned in the U.S.A.: A Reference Guide to Book Censorship in Schools and Public Libraries*. 2nd ed. Westport, CT: Greenwood Press.

Hull, Mary. 1999. *Censorship in America: A Reference Handbook*. Santa Barbara, CA: ABC-CLIO.

Karolides, Nicholas J., Margaret Bald, and Dawn B. Sova. 1999. *100 Banned Books: Censorship Histories of World Literature*. New York: Checkmark Books.

Office for Intellectual Freedom. Chicago: American Library Association. Available online at: http://www.ala.org/Content/NavigationMenu/Our_Associa tion/Offices/Intellectual_Freedom3/Intellectual_Freedom.htm (accessed 29 June 2003).

Scales, Pat. 2001. *Teaching Banned Books: 12 Guides for Young Readers*. Chicago: American Library Association.

Classics in the Classroom

Bland, Guy. 2001. "Out with the Old, in with the (Not So) New." *English Journal* 90 (3): 20–22.

Bushman, John H. 1997. "Young Adult Literature in the Classroom—Or Is It?" *English Journal* 86 (3): 35–40.

Crowe, Chris. 2000. "Using YA Books to Teach Students to Love What We Love." *English Journal* 89 (6): 138–141.

Gallo, Donald R. 2001. "How Classics Create an Aliterate Society." *English Journal* 90 (3): 33–39.

Grayling, A. C. 2001. "The Age of Ignorance: Benefits of a Classical Education." *New Statesman* 130 (4548): 28ff.

Herz, Sarah K., with Donald R. Gallo. 1996. *From Hinton to Hamlet: Building Bridges between Young Adult Literature and the Classics.* Westport, CT: Greenwood Press.

Jago, Carol. 2000. *With Rigor for All: Teaching the Classics to Contemporary Students.* Foreword by James Strickland. Portland, ME: Calendar Islands Publishers.

Kaywell, Joan F., ed. 1993–2000. *Adolescent Literature as a Complement to the Classics.* 4 vols. Norwood, MA: Christopher-Gordon Publishers.

Lefkowitz, Mary. 1999. "2,800 Years Old and Still Relevant (Appreciation of the Classics)." *New York Times,* 21 August: A23(N), A13(L).

Sommers, Christina Hoff. 1998. "Are We Living in a Moral Stone Age? Teaching the Literary Classics." Transcript. *Vital Speeches* 64 (15): 475–478.

Thompson, Michael Clay. 1990. *Classics in the Classroom.* Monroe, NY: Trillium Press.

Libraries and Librarianship

Edwards, Kirsten. 2002. *Teen Library Events: A Month-by-Month Guide.* Greenwood Professional Guides for Young Adult Librarians. Series edited by C. Allen Nichols and Mary Anne Nichols. Westport, CT: Greenwood Press.

"If All of Seattle Read the Same Book." Seattle, WA: The Seattle Public Library, Washington Center for the Book. Available online at: http://www.spl.org/wacentbook/seattleread/samebook.html (accessed 14 February 2003).

Jones, Patrick, ed. 2002. *New Directions for Library Services to Young Adults.* Chicago: American Library Association.

FICTION_L. Morton Grove, IL: Morton Grove Public Library. Available online at: http://www.webrary.org/rs/flmenu.html (accessed 1 March 2003).

Nichols, Mary Anne, and C. Allen Nichols, eds. 1998. *Young Adults and Public Libraries: A Handbook of Materials and Services.* Westport, CT: Greenwood Press.

PUBYAC. Pittsburgh: School of Library and Information Science. Available online at: http://www.pallasinc.com/pubyac/ (accessed 28 June 2003).

YALSA—Electronic Resources—Websites and Mailing Lists. Chicago: Young Adult Library Services Association. Available online at: http://www.ala.org/Content/NavigationMenu/YALSA/Electronic_Resources/Websites_and_Mailing_Lists.htm (accessed 28 June 2003).

Readers' Advisory and Literature Promotion

Benedetti, Angelina. 2001. "Leading the Horse to Water: Keeping Young People Reading in the Information Age." In *The Readers' Advisor's Companion.*

Edited by Kenneth D. Shearer and Robert Burgin. Englewood, CO: Libraries Unlimited.

Herald, Diana Tixier. 2003. *Teen Genreflecting: A Guide to Reading Interests.* 2nd ed. Westport, CT: Libraries Unlimited.

Langemack, Chapple. 2003. *The Booktalker's Bible: How to Talk about the Books You Love to Any Audience.* Westport, CT: Libraries Unlimited.

Rochman, Hazel. 1987. *Tales of Love and Terror: Booktalking the Classics, Old and New.* Chicago: American Library Association.

Saricks, Joyce G. 2001. *The Readers' Advisory Guide to Genre Fiction.* Chicago: American Library Association.

Saricks, Joyce G., and Nancy Brown. 1997. *Readers' Advisory Service in the Public Library.* 2nd ed. Chicago: American Library Association.

Reading Programs and Activities

Altmann, Anna E., and Gail De Vos. 2001. *Tales, Then and Now: More Folktales as Young Adult Literary Fictions.* Englewood, CO: Libraries Unlimited.

Barchers, Suzanne I. 2001. *From Atalanta to Zeus: Readers Theatre from Greek Mythology.* Englewood, CO: Teacher Ideas Press.

Barchers, Suzanne I., and Jennifer L. Kroll. 2002. *Classic Readers Theatre for Young Adults.* Englewood, CO: Teacher Ideas Press.

Bland, Joellen. 1987. *Stage Plays from the Classics: One-Act Adaptations from Famous Short Stories, Novels, and Plays.* Boston: Plays, Inc.

De Vos, Gail. 1991. *Storytelling for Young Adults: Techniques and Treasury.* Englewood, CO: Libraries Unlimited.

De Vos, Gail, and Anna Altmann. 1999. *New Tales for Old: Folktales as Literary Fictions for Young Adults.* Englewood, CO: Libraries Unlimited.

Fredericks, Anthony D. 2001. *Readers Theatre for American History.* Englewood, CO: Teacher Ideas Press.

———. 2002. *Science Fiction Readers Theatre.* Englewood, CO: Teacher Ideas Press.

Kamerman, Sylvia E., ed. 1993. *The Big Book of Dramatized Classics: 25 Adaptations of Favorite Novels, Stories, and Plays for Stage and Round-the-Table Reading.* Boston: Plays, Inc.

Kroll, Jennifer L., ed. 2003. *Simply Shakespeare: Readers Theatre for Young People.* Englewood, CO: Teacher Ideas Press.

Latrobe, Kathy Howard. 1991. *Social Studies Readers Theatre for Young Adults: Scripts and Script Development.* Englewood, CO: Teacher Ideas Press.

Latrobe, Kathy Howard, and Mildred Knight Laughlin. 1989. *Readers Theatre for Young Adults: Scripts and Script Development.* Englewood, CO: Teacher Ideas Press.

Porter, Steven, ed. and comp. 1994. *New Works for Reader's Theatre.* Studio City, CA: Phantom Publications in association with Players Press.

Ratliff, Gerald Lee. 1999. *Introduction to Readers Theatre: A Guide to Classroom Performance.* Colorado Springs, CO: Meriwether Publishing, Limited.

Read 3, Get 1 Free! 2003. Staff-generated teen reading incentive brochure. King County, WA: King County Library System and the Library Foundation.

Russell, William F. 1989. *Classic Myths to Read Aloud.* New York: Crown.

Russell, William F., ed. 1984. *Classics to Read Aloud to Your Children.* New York: Crown.

———. 1986. *More Classics to Read Aloud to Your Children.* New York: Crown.

Shepard, Aaron. 2003. *Folktales on Stage: Children's Plays for Reader's Theater (or Readers Theatre), with 16 Play Scripts from World Folk and Fairy Tales and Legends, Including African, Chinese, Southeast Asian, Indian, Middle Eastern, Russian, Scandinavian, and Native American.* Redondo Beach, CA: Shepard Publications.

———. 2004. *Readers on Stage: A Guide to Reader's Theater (or Readers Theatre), with Scripts, Tips, and Worksheets.* Redondo Beach, CA: Shepard Publications.

Shepard, Aaron, ed. 2004. *Stories on Stage: Scripts for Reader's Theater.* Redondo Beach, CA: Shepard Publications.

Signet Classic Essay Contest. New York: Penguin Group (USA), Academic Marketing Department, Signet Classic Student Scholarship Essay Contest. Available online at: http://www.penguinputnam.com/static/html/us/academic/essayhome.html (accessed 2 November 2003).

Sloyer, Shirlee. 2003. *From the Page to the Stage: The Educator's Complete Guide to Readers Theatre.* Englewood, CO: Teacher Ideas Press.

Trelease, Jim. 1995. *The Read-Aloud Handbook.* 3rd rev. ed. New York: Penguin Books.

———. 2001. *The Read-Aloud Handbook.* 5th ed. New York: Penguin Books.

Walker, Lois. 1997. *Readers Theatre Strategies in the Middle and Junior High Classroom: A Take Part Teacher's Guide: Springboards to Language Development through Readers Theatre, Storytelling, Writing, and Dramatizing.* Colorado Springs, CO: Meriwether Publishing, Limited.

Welcome to Living History Lectures. Lakebay, WA: Tames Alan. Available online at: http://www.oz.net/~tamsalan/histmain.html (accessed 1 March 2004).

White, Melvin Robert. 1993. *Mel White's Readers Theatre Anthology: Twenty-Eight All-Occasion Readings for Storytellers.* Colorado Springs, CO: Meriwether Publishing, Limited.

Research and Statistics
Adolescent Development

The Adolescent Years. New York: The Columbia University College of Physicians and Surgeons. Available online at: http://cpmcnet.columbia.edu/texts/guide/toc/toc08.html (accessed 4 January 2003).

CNNfyi.com: Your Brain. Atlanta, GA: Cable News Network. Available online at: http://www.cnn.com/fyi/interactive/news/brain/newsroom.html (accessed 12 April 2003).

FRONTLINE: Inside the Teenage Brain. 2002. Written, produced, and directed by Sarah Spinks. Alexandria, VA: PBS and WGBH Boston/FRONTLINE. Originally aired 31 January 2002 on PBS WGBH. Videocassette. Also available online at: http://www.pbs.org/wgbh/pages/frontline/shows/teen brain/ (accessed 4 April 2003).

Havighurst, Robert. *Developmental Tasks of Normal Adolescence*. Bloomington, IN: School of Education, Center for Adolescent and Family Studies, adapted from Gary M. Ingersoll's book, *Normal Adolescence*, forthcoming. Available online at: http://education.indiana.edu/cas/devtask.html (accessed 4 January 2003).

Normal Adolescent Development: Late High School Years and Beyond. Washington, DC: American Academy of Child and Adolescent Psychiatry. Available online at: http://www.aacap.org/publications/factsfam/develop2.htm (accessed 4 January 2003).

Normal Adolescent Development: Middle School and Early High School Years. Washington, DC: American Academy of Child and Adolescent Psychiatry. Available online at: http://www.aacap.org/publications/factsfam/develop. htm (accessed 4 January 2003).

The Parent Soup Development Tracker. New York: iVillage.com: The Women's Network. Available online at: http://www.parentsoup.com/tracker (accessed 4 January 2003).

Spinks, Sarah. 2002. "Adolescent Brains are Works in Progress." Alexandria, VA: PBS and WGBH Boston/FRONTLINE. Article published in association with *Inside the Teenage Brain* television program 31 January 2002. Available online at: http://www.pbs.org/wgbh/pages/frontline/shows/teenbrain/ work/adolescent.html (accessed 3 April 2003).

Stages of Intellectual Development in Children and Teenagers. Villa Park, CA: Child Development Institute, Robert F. Myers, Ph.D. Available online at: http:// www.childdevelopmentinfo.com/development/piaget.shtml (accessed 4 January 2003).

Stages of Social-Emotional Development in Children and Teenagers. Villa Park, CA: Child Development Institute, Robert F. Myers, Ph.D. Available online at: http://www.childdevelopmentinfo.com/development/erickson.shtml (accessed 4 January 2003).

Literacy and Reading

2002 Trial Urban District Assessment. Washington, DC: United States Department of Education, Institute of Education Sciences, National Center for Education Statistics, National Assessment of Educational Progress. Available online at: http://nces.ed.gov/nationsreportcard/reading/results2002/dis trictresults.asp (accessed 29 August 2003).

Abrahamson, Maria. 2001. "Why Boys Don't Read." *Book* January/February: 86–88.

Aronson, Marc. 2001. *Exploding the Myths: The Truth about Teenagers and Reading*. Lanham, MD: Scarecrow Press.

———. 2000. "The Myths of Teenage Readers." *Publishing Research Quarterly* 16 (3): 4–9.

Baker, Marianne I. 2002. "Reading Resistance in Middle School: What Can Be Done?" *Journal of Adolescent and Adult Literacy* 45 (5): 364–366.

Cardman, Michael. 2002. "SAT Math Gains, Verbal Drops Reflect High School Curricula." *Education Daily* 28 August. Available online from: Infotrac Onefile, a Gale Group Database, Farmington Hills (MI) (accessed 9 March 2003).

Clinton, Patrick. 2002. "Literacy in America: The Crisis You Don't Know about, and What We Can Do about It." *Book* September/October: Available online at: http://www.bookmagazine.com/issue24/literacy.shtml (accessed 29 August 2003).

Education Week. 1981–. Irregular weekly. Bethesda, MD: Editorial Projects in Education, Inc.

English Journal. 1998–. Bimonthly. Urbana, IL: National Council of Teachers of English.

The International Reading Association. Newark, DE: The International Reading Association. Available online at: http://www.reading.org/ (accessed 29 August 2003).

Journal of Adolescent and Adult Literacy. 1995–. Monthly. Newark, DE: The International Reading Association.

Kloberdanz, Kristin. 1999. "So You Don't Think Kids Read Anymore? Think Again. Turns Out They're Booksmart." *Book* July/August: 34–38.

Latest Survey Results: Teen Read Week 2002. Ann Arbor, MI: Smartgirl.org. Available online at: http://www.smartgirl.org/reports/1493716.html (accessed 16 March 2003).

Moore, David W., et al. 1999. *Adolescent Literacy: A Position Statement*. Newark, DE: The International Reading Association.

The National Reading Conference Online. Rochester, MI: The National Reading Conference, Department of Reading and Language Arts, Oakland University. Available online at: http://nrconline.org (accessed 6 September 2002).

The Nation's Report Card. Washington, DC: United States Department of Education, Institute of Education Sciences, National Center for Education Statistics, National Assessment of Educational Progress. Available online at: http://nces.ed.gov/nationsreportcard/ (accessed 29 August 2003).

RAND Reading Study Group. Santa Monica, CA: RAND Corporation. Available online at: http://www.rand.org/multi/achievementforall/reading/ (accessed 29 August 2003).

Reading 2002 Major Results. Washington, DC: United States Department of Education, Institute of Education Sciences, National Center for Education Statistics, National Assessment of Educational Progress. Available online at: http://nces.ed.gov/nationsreoprtcard/reading/results2002/ (accessed 29 August 2003).

Reading Today. 1985–. Bimonthly. Newark, DE: The International Reading Association.

Reed, Arthea J. S. 1988. *Comics to Classics: A Parent's Guide to Books for Teens and Preteens.* Newark, DE: International Reading Association.

The Shell Poll: Teens Talk to America. Houston, TX: Shell Oil Company, Volume 1, Issue 4, Summer 1999. Peter D. Hart Research Associates. Available online at: http://www.countonshell.com/products/poll/poll_teens_fs.html (accessed 16 February 2003).

Snow, Catherine E. 2002. *Reading for Understanding: Toward a R&D Program in Reading Comprehension.* Santa Monica, CA: The RAND Corporation.

"Supporting Young Adolescents' Literacy Learning: A Joint Position Paper of the International Reading Association and National Middle School Association." 2001. Newark, DE: The International Reading Association. Available online at: http://www.reading.org/positions/supporting_young_adolesc.html (accessed 29 August 2003).

Teen Reading: Data and Resources. Chicago: The American Library Association, Young Adult Library Services Association. Available online at: http://www.ala.org/teenread/resources_main.html (accessed 16 March 2002).

Teen Reading: Teen Read Week. Chicago: American Library Association, Young Adult Library Services Association. Available online at: http://www.ala.org/ala/yalsa/teenreading/teenreading.htm (accessed 29 August 2003).

TRU: Teen Research Unlimited. Northbrook, IL: Teen Research Unlimited. Available online at: http://www.teenresearch.com (accessed 16 March 2003).

MEDIA
Film and Television

The 13th Warrior. 2002. Videodisc. Burbank, CA: Touchstone Home Video: distributed by Buena Vista. (Originally produced in 1999 as a motion picture.)

Angel. 1999–2003. Television series. Created by Joss Whedon and David Greenwalt. Burbank, CA: The WB Television Network.

Blade. 1999. Videocassette. Los Angeles: New Line Home Video. (Originally produced in 1998 as a motion picture.)

Blade II. 2002. Videodisc. Los Angeles: New Line Home Entertainment: distributed by Warner Home Video. (Originally produced in 2002 as a motion picture.)

Blade Runner. 1993. Videocassette. Burbank, CA: Warner Home Video. (Originally produced in 1982 as a motion picture.)

Bram Stoker's Dracula. 1997. Videodisc. Culver City, CA: Columbia TriStar Home Video. (Originally produced in 1992 as a motion picture.)

Brideshead Revisited. 2002. Videodiscs. Produced by Derek Granger, directed by Michael Lindsay-Hogg and Charles Sturridge. Silver Spring, MD: Acorn Media. (Originally broadcast in 1981 for British Television by Granada Television.)

Buffy the Vampire Slayer. 1996. Videocassette. Beverly Hills, CA: Fox Video. (Originally produced in 1992 as a motion picture.)

Buffy the Vampire Slayer. 1996–2002. Television series. Created and produced by Joss Whedon. Los Angeles, CA: UPN.

Carmen: A Hip Hopera. 2003. Videodisc. Burbank, CA: Warner Home Video. (Originally produced in 2001 for the MTV Network.)

A Christmas Carol. 1995. Videocassette. Beverly Hills, CA: Fox Video. (Originally produced in 1984 for television.)

A Christmas Carol. 2003. Videodisc. Burbank, CA: Distributed by Warner Home Video. (Originally produced in 1999 for television.)

Clueless. 1995. Videocassette. Hollywood, CA: Paramount. (Originally produced in 1995 as a motion picture.)

C-SPAN American Writers: A Journey through History. Washington, DC: C-SPAN, National Cable Satellite Corporation. Available online at: http://www.americanwriters.org/index_short_list.asp (accessed 27 March 2003).

C-SPAN American Writers II: The 20th Century. Washington, DC: C-SPAN, National Cable Satellite Corporation. Available online at: http://www.americanwriters.org/ (accessed 27 March 2003).

Dr. Jekyll and Mr. Hyde. 2003. Burbank, CA: Bravo. Original Bravo movie broadcast on 18 October.

Frasier. 1992–2004. Television series. Hollywood, CA: Grub Street Production; Paramount Television Production Division; Viacom Entertainment Group.

Great Books. 1993–1996. Videocassettes. 10 vols. Produced by Dale Minor. A presentation of Discovery Productions in association with Cronkite Ward. Narrated by Donald Sutherland. Bethesda, MD: Discovery Communications. (Originally televised on the Discovery Channel.)

Great Expectations. 1999. Videocassette. A co-production of BBC America and WGBH/Boston. Troy, MI: Anchor Bay Entertainment. (Originally broadcast on television on Mobil Masterpiece Theatre.)

Green, Ranny. 1995. "For Some Classic Viewing, Don't Miss Wishbone." *Seattle Times,* 22 October: final edition, H6.

Hercules: The Legendary Journeys. 1993–1999. Syndicated television series. Created by Christian Williams.

Jane Austen's Pride and Prejudice. 1996. Videocassette. 6 vols. Screenplay by Andrew Davies, directed by Simon Langton, produced by Sue Birtwistle, a

BBC/A&E Network co-production. New York: A&E Home Video. (Originally produced in 1995 for television.)

Kate and Leopold. 2002. Videodisc. Burbank, CA: Mirimax Home Entertainment. (Originally produced in 2001 as a motion picture.)

L. A. Confidential. 1998. Videodisc. Directed by Curtis Hanson. Burbank, CA: Warner Home Video. (Originally produced in 1997 as a motion picture.)

The Lord of the Rings: The Fellowship of the Ring. 2002. Videodisc. Directed by Peter Jackson. Los Angeles: New Line Home Entertainment. (Originally produced in 2001 as a motion picture.)

The Lord of the Rings: The Two Towers. 2003. Videodisc. Directed by Peter Jackson. Los Angeles: New Line Home Entertainment. (Originally produced in 2002 as a motion picture.)

Master and Commander: The Far Side of the World. 2003. Motion picture. Directed by Peter Weir. Los Angeles, CA: Twentieth Century Fox Film Corporation, Universal Studios, and Miramax Film Corp.

A Muppet Christmas Carol. 1995. Videocassette. Burbank, CA: Jim Henson Video: distributed by Buena Vista Home Video. (Originally produced in 1992 as a motion picture.)

Roxanne. 1987. Videocassette. Screenplay by Steven Martin. Burbank, CA: RCA/Columbia Pictures Home Video. (Originally produced in 1987 as a motion picture.)

Saving Private Ryan. 1999. Videodisc. Produced and directed by Steven Spielberg, et al. Written by Robert Rodat. Universal City, CA: DreamWorks Home Entertainment. (Original production in 1998 by DreamWorks Pictures and Paramount Pictures as an Amblin Entertainment production in association with Mutual Film Company.)

Scrooge. 1991. Videocassette. Beverly Hills, CA: Fox Video. (Originally produced in 1970 as a motion picture.)

Scrooged. 1989. Videocassette. Hollywood, CA: Paramount. (Originally produced in 1988 as a motion picture.)

The Search for Atlantis. 2000. Videocassette. Narrated and hosted by Ted Danson. (Originally aired on A&E Television Network, 10 September 2000.)

Simon, Richard Keller. 2000. "Much Ado about 'Friends': What Pop Culture Offers to Literature." *The Chronicle of Higher Education* 46 (41): B4–B6.

Two Mules for Sister Sarah. 2003. Videodisc. Universal City, CA: Universal. (Originally produced in 1969 as a motion picture.)

Underworld. 2004. Videodisc. 16mm. Culver City, CA: Columbia Tristar Home Entertainment. (Originally produced in 2003 as a motion picture.)

West Side Story. 2003. Videodisc. Santa Monica, CA: MGM Home Entertainment. (Originally produced in 1961 as a motion picture based on the 1958 Broadway musical.)

X-2: X-Men United. 2003. Videodisc. Twentieth Century Fox Home Entertainment. (Originally produced as a motion picture.)

The X-Men. 2000. Videodisc. Beverly Hills, CA: Twentieth Century Fox Home Entertainment. (Originally produced in 2000 as a motion picture.)

Music and Imagery

Associated Press. 1972. "Vietnam Napalm." Photographed by Nick Ut, AP staff photographer on July 8 in Trang Bang, Vietnam. Image number 6268036 (3QCG4). In *AccuNet/AP Multimedia Archive*. Bensalem, PA: AccuWeather Inc. and The Associated Press. Available by subscription online at: http://ap.accuweather.com/apphoto/index.htm (accessed 21 October 2003).

Islam, Yusuf (Cat Stevens). 1970. *Tea for the Tillerman*. A&M audiocassette CS-4280 and compact discs SP-4280 and 314 546 884-2.

Lloyd Webber, Andrew. 1987. *The Phantom of the Opera: Original Cast Recording*. Really Useful Group Ltd. and Universal Classics Group compact disc 314 543 928-2.

Welles, Orson. 1980. *The War of the Worlds*. Audiocassette recording of original broadcast on 31 October 1938. Old time radio series. San Francisco: Jabberwocky.

MISCELLANEOUS REFERENCES

Adler, Mortimer Jerome, and Charles van Doren. 1972. *How to Read a Book*. Revised and updated ed. New York: Simon and Schuster.

American Heritage Dictionary. 1982. Second college edition. Boston: Houghton Mifflin.

American Heritage Dictionary of the English Language. 2000. 4th ed. Boston: Houghton Mifflin.

Baldick, Chris. 1990. *The Concise Oxford Dictionary of Literary Terms*. Oxford: Oxford University Press.

Titelman, Gregory. 1996. *The Random House Dictionary of Popular Proverbs and Sayings*. New York: Random House.

"Vandals Sentenced to History Lesson." 2000. *Seattle Times*, 30 August, final edition.

INDEX

About the Author

HOLLY KOELLING is Young Adult/Reference Librarian, Bothell Regional Library, King County Library System, Washington, and a reviewer for *Booklist*, among other professional journals.

CLASSIC CONNECTIONS
TURNING TEENS ON TO GREAT LITERATURE

Holly Koelling

IN THE SERIES:

LIBRARY MATERIALS AND SERVICES FOR TEEN GIRLS
Katie O'Dell

MERCHANDISING LIBRARY MATERIALS TO YOUNG ADULTS
Mary Anne Nichols

SERVING OLDER TEENS
Edited by Sheila B. Anderson

THINKING OUTSIDE THE BOOK
Alternatives for Today's Teen Library Collections
Edited by C. Allen Nichols

ISBN: 1-59158-072-2

Libraries Unlimited
88 Post Road West
Westport, CT 06881
www.lu.com

Cover design by Joseph DePinho
Cover image: Punchstock

ISBN 1-59158-072-2

90000

9 781591 580720